DIVINE HONOURS FOR THE CAESARS

Divine Honours for the Caesars

The First Christians' Responses

Bruce W. Winter

WILLIAM B. EERDMANS PUBLISHING COMPANY
GRAND RAPIDS, MICHIGAN / CAMBRIDGE, U.K.

Published 2015 by

Wm. B. Eerdmans Publishing Co.

2140 Oak Industrial Drive N.E., Grand Rapids, Michigan 49505 /

P.O. Box 163, Cambridge CB3 9PU U.K.

Printed in the United States of America

21 20 19 18 17 16 15   7 6 5 4 3 2 1

Library of Congress Cataloging-in-Publication Data

Winter, Bruce W.

Divine honours for the Caesars: the first Christians' responses / Bruce W. Winter.

pages   cm

Includes bibliographical references and index.

ISBN 978-0-8028-7257-9 (pbk.: alk. paper)

1. Church and state — Rome.

2. Christianity and politics — History — Early church, ca. 30-600.

3. Christians — Political activity — Rome.

4. Church history — Primitive and early church, ca. 30-600.

I. Title.

BR170.W56   2015

270.1 — dc23

2015018067

www.eerdmans.com

Contents

CONTENTS

Preface

'Why were imperial cultic activities not a problem for the first Christians?' is a question posed by ancient historians. They have demonstrated that imperial cultic activities grew rapidly and exercised a far more dominant rôle in the lives of citizens in the Latin West and the Greek East in the Roman Empire, regularly affecting them much more than had been previously thought. Its effect on their psyche is not to be underestimated nor is the enormous challenge it had to have posed for the first Christians. Thus their question is an appropriate one.

The intention here is first to harvest some of the riches of the primary evidence of imperial cultic veneration recorded in official inscriptions, coins and statues and archaeological evidence of imperial cult temples in those major cities or provinces where early Christian communities were established.

Against this background it is then proposed to examine the New Testament *corpus* to see if there is evidence of the first Christians facing the challenge of divine honours needed to be given to the Caesars and the ways in which they coped, in view of the undivided loyalty they were required to give to their divine king, Jesus.

This method of focusing firstly on ancient primary sources was originally acquired in the 'school' (σχολή) of Emeritus Professor E. A. Judge.[1]

1. He would disclaim any notion of founding 'a school' as is popularly assumed by the term σχολή. However, this Greek word aptly describes what he has done, creating space where scholars can helpfully engage in learned discussions and interactive disputations with others. It is also the context that benefits the rising generation of students. In such a setting his intellectual gifts and Christian graces have been shared with generations of students from the 1960s to the present day. Hence 'school' (σχολή) is felt to be an appropriate term.

His 1957 Tyndale New Testament Lecture mapped out critical aspects of early Christianity in relation to the Graeco-Roman world that would earn him the prestigious Hulsean Prize in Classics at the University of Cambridge in 1959. When published, it initiated a major paradigm shift in studies on the intersection of the New Testament within its first-century social, political and religious settings.[2] He did the same for those who heard his Annual Tyndale Lectures in the Divinity Faculty of the University of Cambridge delivered on a return visit to his *alma mater* in Lent Term, 2001.

His approach has rightly been seen as a highly significant example for subsequent studies, greatly influencing generations of doctoral students at Macquarie University, Sydney, and elsewhere. Like many students beginning their dissertation, I recall him taking me down to the university library to be shown a largely unexplored but a neglected primary source that was a crucial starting point for my own doctoral thesis.

His scholarly example, personal kindness, warm on-going encouragement and wisdom have long supported many researchers, and not least of all myself. By first-century Roman social conventions the term 'friend' would not be an adequate description, given its overtone of 'the politics of friendship'. In New Testament terminology, as a Christian he has long been a 'brother'. Rather, using first-century terminology that Paul surprisingly but appropriately plundered from the Graeco-Roman social world to aptly describe the contribution of Phoebe to Paul's ministry in Romans 16:1-2, he 'became a patron of many' (προστάτις πολλῶν ἐγενήθη) 'and mine' (καὶ ἐμοῦ αὐτοῦ). Hence this monograph has been dedicated to him.

It is only right that I record my thanks to Professor Alanna Nobbs, the Deputy Director Ancient Cultures Research Centre, Macquarie University, for kindly agreeing to read a draft of this book and for her corrections and helpful suggestions and also to my wife for her patience as I researched this project in the Tyndale House Library and the Classics Library, University of Cambridge, and for her commitment to editing the draft of this monograph.

---

2. It was published as E. A. Judge, *The Social Pattern of Christian Groups in the First Century* (London: Tyndale Press, 1960) and republished as the foundational chapter in D. M. Scholer, ed., "The Social Pattern of the Christian Groups in the First Century," in *Social Distinctives of the Christians in the First Century: Pivotal Essays by E. A. Judge* (Peabody, MA: Hendrickson, 2008), ch. 1.

CHAPTER 1

The All-Pervasive and Inescapable Imperial Cultic Phenomena

There is a perception that the most striking feature of the first century A.D. was the speedy rise and expansion of Christianity. However, ancient historians have shown that in the same century an even stronger cultic movement spread far more rapidly both in the East and West of the vast Roman Empire.

In his two-volume work, *Anatolia: Land, Men, and Gods in Asia Minor,* Mitchell concluded, 'The diffusion of the cult of Augustus and of other members of his family in Asia Minor and throughout the Greek East from the beginning of the empire was rapid, indeed almost instantaneous.'[1] Wardle also observed, 'To a Roman of the first century A.D. who chose to reflect on the changes the state had witnessed over the previous century perhaps one of the most striking would be the introduction of imperial cult.'[2] Garnsey and Saller likewise commented, 'Rome's main export to the empire was the cult of the emperors . . . it appealed to Augustus, as it did to later emperors, as a way of focusing the loyalty of provincials on the imperial *persona.*'[3] Emperors were known as 'the god of the Romans' *(Romanorum deus)* in the days of the second-century Christian apologist Tertullian.[4]

---

1. S. Mitchell, *Anatolia: Land, Men and Gods in Asia Minor: The Celts and the Impact of Roman Rule* (Oxford: Clarendon Press, 1993), I, p. 100.

2. D. Wardle, "*Deus* or *Divus:* The Genesis of Roman Terminology for Deified Emperors and a Philosopher's Contribution," in *Philosophy and Power in the Graeco-Roman World: Essays in Honour of Miriam Griffin,* ed. G. Clark and T. Rajak (Oxford: Oxford University Press, 2002), p. 181.

3. P. Garnsey and R. Saller, *The Roman Empire: Economy, Society and Culture* (London: Duckworth, 1987), pp. 164, 165.

4. Tertullian, *Apology* 24.9.

Mitchell further noted that in all three of the Roman cities in central Anatolia, namely Ancyra, Pessinus and Pisidian Antioch, 'the central feature of these excavations has been a temple dedicated to the imperial cult built in the time of Augustus and Tiberius. Emperor worship was from the first an institution of great importance to provincial communities'.[5] Other cities where Christians resided in the East were no different in terms of the central location of these temples.

How had it come about that the Greek East, 'incorporated' as it was by Rome into its vast empire, saw divine imperial veneration spread so spectacularly at both the local and provincial levels? There were intense social pressures brought to bear on all provincials and Roman citizens residing in the East to reciprocate with appropriate divine honours to and for emperors in their temples because of the enormous benefits and other blessings brought by the *pax romana* socially, economically and politically. Performing cultic acts before statues of living emperors, and at times members of their family, on the numerous official high and holy days in the city's annual calendar was considered the only appropriate expression of loyalty. Rome's great achievements were attributed to the divine imperial peace and prosperity, long anticipated but only now being enjoyed throughout its empire by its loyal subjects.[6] All this is well attested in official and literary sources.

How then would the first Christians cope with the requirement to give divine honours to the Julio-Claudian Caesars? Would they remain steadfast, observing the clear parameters laid by the founder of their faith by obeying his command regardless of enormous societal pressures — 'the things that are Caesar's you must render to Caesar and the things of God to God' (τὰ Καίσαρος ἀπόδοτε Καίσαρι καὶ τὰ τοῦ θεοῦ τῷ θεῷ) (Mark 12:17)? This book sets out to explore the first Christians' different responses to requirements at both local and provincial levels to render divine honours to the Caesars as the conventional public expression of loyalty to Rome and its rulers.

In this opening chapter it is proposed (I) to record the reasons for the enigma felt by leading ancient historians as to why imperial cultic activities were not a problem for the first Christians; (II) to map recent, changing

---

5. Mitchell, *Anatolia: Land, Men and Gods in Asia Minor: The Rise of the Church*, II, p. 100.

6. On the centrality of the emperors in the Roman Empire, see J. E. Lendon, "The Emperor," in *Empire of Honour: The Art of Government in the Roman World* (Oxford: Clarendon Press, 1997), ch. 3.

perceptions of such activities by the former whose predecessors had until recently underestimated the intrusive nature of the imperial cult in the lives of all citizens in the Roman empire, not least of all in the East; and (III) to explain the rationale for, and outline of, the chapters in *Divine Honours for the Caesars: The First Christians' Responses.*

I. The Enigma for Ancient Historians Concerning the First Christians

Over forty years ago in 1972 Millar posed this important question with its inescapable implication — 'But when gentiles began to convert to Christianity, might we not expect that the pagan communities in which they lived would begin to use against them the accusation of not observing the Imperial cult?'[7]

A decade later in a landmark monograph for ancient historians on the imperial cult, Price noted of Asia Minor —

> non-participation by Christians, whose communities were already very widespread in Asia Minor before Constantine, were deeply worrying to the rest of the population. Indeed the problem was already pressing to the assembly of the province of Asia under Hadrian [A.D. 117-38].[8]

Mitchell writing on cults in Anatolia in 1993 has perceptively and succinctly described the enormous societal pressures that existed for the early Christian converts to apostatize because of the requirement on everyone to give divine honours publicly to statues of the Caesars. He comments —

> One cannot avoid the impression that the obstacle which stood in the way of the progress of Christianity, and the force which would have

7. F. Millar, "The Imperial Cult and the Persecutions," in W. den Boer, *Le Culte des Souverains dans l'empire romain* (Geneva: Vandoeuvres, 1972), p. 163. Millar was then Camden Professor of Ancient History, Oxford University.

8. S. R. F. Price, *Rituals and Power: The Imperial Cult and Asia Minor* (Cambridge: Cambridge University Press, 1984), pp. 123-24 citing Eusebius, *Ecclesiastical History*, iv, 8-9. See also his "Rituals and Power," in *Paul and Empire: Religion and Power in Roman Imperial Society,* ed. R. A. Horsley (Harrisburg, PA: Trinity Press International, 1997), ch. 3, where the first generation of Christians' responses was not his focus.

drawn new adherents back to conformity with the prevailing paganism, was the public worship of the emperors ... where Christians could not (if they wanted to) conceal their beliefs and activities from their fellows, it was not a change of heart that might win a Christian convert back to paganism, but the overwhelming pressure to conform imposed by the institutions of his city and the activities of his neighbours.[9]

Certainly in the early years of the second century A.D. Pliny the Younger interrogated a later generation of those who were named 'Christians'. Enormous pressure was put on them to perform cultic honours before the emperor's statue. Among those he interrogated were lapsed Christians, some of whom had been apostate for 'two or more years previously, and some up to twenty years ago'. Others compromised when this distinguished governor of Bithynia and Pontus pressured them to burn incense to the statue of the living emperor, Trajan. Those provincials 'who refused three times to do this were led away to their execution', while Roman citizens among them were put on 'the list of persons to be sent to Rome for trial'.[10] The important question is, if imperial veneration were alive and thriving in the era of the Julio-Claudian emperors of the first century, why would not the first Christians be likewise 'dragooned' into imperial veneration or even executed if they refused?

In 2000 Clifford Ando, in his work *Imperial Ideology and Provincial Loyalty in the Roman Empire*, went to the heart of the issue for Christians, concluding with this comparison.

In the end, Rome gave to the empire as a whole two very different gods, who shared one essential quality. So long as his power endured, the emperor's immanence in his ubiquitous portraits made him ἐφανέστατος, 'the most manifest', of the numinous powers of this world. His chief rival, who became his chief patron [from the time of Constantine onwards when the empire became Christian], was likewise present everywhere in potentiality and promise.... 'Wherever

---

9. Mitchell, *Anatolia: The Rise of the Church,* II, p. 10. In section IV, "Christians," ch. 16, "Pagans, Jews, and Christians from the First to the Third Century," p. 36, devotes two paragraphs to the New Testament era. His second volume focuses on the later Christian period.

10. Pliny, *Ep.* 10.96,6. For a discussion see D. Fishwick, "Pliny and the Christians: The Rites *ad imaginem principis,*" *AJAH* 9 (1984): 123-30.

two or three of you are gathered in my name, there I am in their midst'
(Matt. 18:20).[11]

'Christians invited persecution by their denial of the gods of Rome'
is the conclusion of Garnsey and Saller in their 1987 edition of *The Roman
Empire: Economy, Society and Culture,* and repeated in the second edition
of 2015.[12]

This book seeks to explore the inescapable challenge for the first
Christians of the rendering of divine cultic honours to Rome's imperial
rulers. It commences by examining evidence from the first century that
shows the earliest Christians in the Graeco-Roman East simply could not
have ignored imperial cultic celebrations that had such a high profile. They
faced a powerful, all-pervasive and competing messianic-like ideology
propagated and publicly endorsed empire-wide ever since Augustus, in
all the cities where the Christian message took root.

Cultic activities would also create a not inconsiderable challenge for
them on the many public high and holy days. These days were set aside
so that all citizens could perform cultic acts of worship in their local or
provincial imperial cult temples and shrines. The imperial veneration was
also combined with other public activities, including spectacles such as
gladiatorial and wild beast shows, athletics, chariot races and public feasts,
such was its assimilation into the life of cities in the Roman Empire. The
Jews did not participate because they had negotiated with the Romans
to offer up a daily sacrifice for the safety of the emperor as an acceptable
expression of their loyalty to the empire in their sole temple located in
Jerusalem. However, the first Christians had no temple or sacrificial system. It will be argued that New Testament documents record a variety of
responses to these unavoidable and widespread imperial cultic activities.

II. New Insights into Imperial Cultic Veneration

It was Momigliano who traced the recent history of interpretation of the
imperial cult by ancient historians in an illuminating discussion in 1987.

11. C. Ando, "A Religion for the Empire," in *Imperial Ideology and Provincial Loyalty
in the Roman Empire* (Berkeley: University of California Press, 2000), ch. 10, p. 239.

12. P. Garnsey and R. Saller, "Religion," in *The Roman Empire: Economy, Society and
Culture* (London: Duckworth, 1987) and (Oakland: University of California Press, 2015²),
p. 197.

His review went back as far as 1929 following the signing of the bi-lateral agreement between the Vatican and Italy when Mussolini was immediately cast in the divine rôle of 'the man of providence'. He noted that studies diverged, with some seeking to show how the cult was 'grafted into the traditional patterns of Greco-Roman religion' and others saw the necessity to keep the cult outside 'the zone of true religion', noting Nock's memorable but clearly incorrect aphorism that 'the emperor's cult was homage, not worship'.[13] Momigliano's deconstruction of Nock's conclusion certainly demanded a reassessment of the issue.

A sea change, if not something of a tsunami, occurred in understanding imperial cultic activities in the East when Price published *Rituals and Power: The Imperial Cult and Asia Minor* in 1984. His primary sources were inscriptions from 104 archaeological sites in Asia Minor where imperial temples and shrines had been located. This groundbreaking work concluded with a significant and succinct summary concerning the nexus between cultic activities and political and diplomatic issues that were germane to life in the East. His view was that '[t]he imperial cult, along with politics and diplomacy, constructed the reality of the Roman empire'.[14]

Price also presented a very different picture of the veneration of emperors from the received one. He also argued that the long-standing misunderstanding of its rôle had arisen from a false dichotomy in studies by ancient historians in the 1930s between politics and religion in Roman society.[15] The reality of what Augustus promoted was epitomized in an official statue type of himself that was replicated throughout the empire. As the *pontifex maximus* of the entire empire, literally 'the greatest bridge builder', he was portrayed offering up a sacrifice to the gods for his empire, dressed in the manner of a Roman magistrate. An excellent example of this standard statue type is to be found in the museum in Corinth as well as in other cities.[16]

The anachronistic dichotomy of discrete spheres of 'cult' and 'politics' was traced to the much later Christianizing of the Roman Empire.

---

13. A. Momigliano, "How Roman Emperors Became Gods," in *On Pagans, Jews and Christians* (Middletown, CT: Wesleyan University Press, 1987), ch. 6, esp. 92-99; cf. A. D. Nock, "Notes on Ruler Cult, I-V," *JHS* 48 (1928): 21-43; "Religious Development from Vespasian to Trajan," *Theology* 16 (1928): 152-60; and "Σύνναος Θεός," *HSCP* 41 (1930): 1-62.

14. Price, *Rituals and Power*, p. 248.

15. Price, *Rituals and Power*, pp. 234ff.

16. For other examples of this statue type see D. Gill, "The Importance of Roman Portraiture for Head Coverings in 1 Corinthians 11:2-16," *TynB* 41, no. 2 (1990): 247-50.

Price blamed the third-century Christian theologian Origen for this.[17] Even today some still speak of 'church and state' as autonomous spheres. As will be seen, no such divisions existed in the ancient world. This is well attested in the mind of the first-century author of the Book of Revelation when writing to churches in the same geographical locations where some of Price's archaeological evidence was based, and where Paul and others founded the first Christian churches.

There occurred a significant link between imperial cultic activity and daily commerce because the buying and selling of all commodities could only be legally undertaken in the official market in any city. This emerges in the specific stipulations laid out in Revelation 13:16-17, where one could neither buy nor sell unless he had the mark or the name of the beast or even the number of his name on the right hand or forehead. So politics, commerce and cultic activities functioned comfortably side by side not only in the same public space but also with all three located in the same agora or forum. Furthermore they were ideologically and legally intertwined. (See chapter 12.)

The most comprehensive work on imperial cultic activities ever undertaken is the eight volumes published to date by Fishwick — *The Imperial Cult in the Latin West: Studies in the Ruler Cult of the Western Provinces of the Roman Empire*.[18] In the preface to his first volume he acknowledges his indebtedness to Price 'in straightening out my ideas on the emperor's divinity'.[19] His next series deals with provincial imperial cultic centres and their high priests while volume III.1 deals specifically with the institution and evolution of the provincial cult from the reign of Augustus to the mid-third century A.D. Volume III.2 traces the extent and principal features of the provincial priesthood in the Latin West, and III.3 focuses on provincial imperial cult centres, their principal features and the worship that was offered there on behalf of particular provinces. Volume III.4 contains some important addenda.[20]

17. Price, *Rituals and Power,* p. 15. For his important catalogue of the sites see pp. 249-74 confirming what is known elsewhere — that it operated in all the cities in the empire.

18. D. Fishwick, *The Imperial Cult in the Latin West: Studies in the Ruler Cult of the Western Provinces of the Roman Empire* (Leiden: E. J. Brill, 1993-2004), I.1, p. x. His project represented some twenty-five years of research and published papers.

19. Fishwick, *The Imperial Cult in the Latin West,* I.1 and I.2 (1987), II.1 (1991), II.2 (1992). The first volumes he called 'the preliminary set of studies' and they went to second editions in 1993.

20. D. Fishwick, *Provincial Cult: Institution and Evolution, Provincial Cult: The Pro-*

In the history of scholarship these volumes are the first to provide such an exhaustive treatment of the origins and historical development of local and province-wide cultic activities in the Latin West. As Fishwick's general title indicates, his primary concern is with the West but he has also rendered invaluable service by making brief and sometimes incisive comments on, and comparisons with, aspects of the same cult in the East by drawing attention to similar and distinctive features.[21] To date there is no similar project for the East, but if such were undertaken on the same scale, the enormous amount of extant archaeological evidence may well produce as many comparable lengthy tomes.

For the Greek East, Mitchell's two significant volumes on Anatolia are based on his exhaustive archaeological knowledge of the region of Asia Minor.[22] It was supplemented in the same year by Friesen's *Twice Neokoros: Ephesus, Asia and the Cult of the Flavian Imperial Family* that focused on the state of the cult in the province of Asia and Ephesus in the latter half of the first century.[23] These publications are essential for our understanding because of their focus on the East.

Standing between studies on the imperial cult in the Greek East and Latin West of the Roman Empire is the monograph of Gradel, *Emperor Worship and Roman Religion,* published in 2002. His contribution to the discussion focuses on the nature of the imperial cult in Rome and Italy, providing contrasts with the peculiar characteristics of cultic activities in the Greek East.[24]

---

vincial Priesthood, *The Provincial Cult: The Provincial Centre, The Imperial Cult in the Latin West: Studies in the Ruler Cult of the Western Provinces of the Roman Empire, Provincial Cult: Bibliography, Indices, Addenda,* III.1,2,3,4. He also predicts that the completion of all the projected volumes will not occur in his lifetime; see *Provincial Cult: Institution and Evolution,* III.1, pp. xi-xii.

21. Fishwick, *The Imperial Cult in the Latin West.* His Festschrift was a tribute to his marathon work on the cult that is unprecedented in ancient history research. See A. Small, ed., *Subject and Ruler: The Cult of the Ruling Power in Classical Antiquity,* Papers Honouring D. Fishwick, *JRA* Supplementary Series 17 (Ann Arbor, MI: Journal of Roman Archaeology, 1996).

22. Mitchell, "The Celts and the Impact of Roman Rule," and "The Rise of the Church," in *Anatolia: Land, Men and Gods in Asia Minor.*

23. S. J. Friesen, *Twice Neokoros: Ephesus, Asia and the Cult of the Flavian Imperial Family* (Leiden: E. J. Brill, 1993).

24. I. Gradel, *Emperor Worship and Roman Religion,* Oxford Classical Monographs (Oxford: Clarendon Press, 2002), pp. vii and x, where he himself indicates the monograph has not taken cognizance of much scholarly discussion before and after 1998. On his focus on Roman Italy, see p. 13. Fishwick saw Gradel as not having taken careful enough cognizance of his own magisterial work and has made substantial criticisms and important corrections

These volumes have brought about significant advances in our understanding of the impact of these all-intrusive imperial cultic activities. They have shown the nature of both local and provincial imperial divine honours in the East that in general terms did not differ substantially from those in the Latin West at the grassroots level. There were, however, important precedents for imperial cultic functions in the Greek East that help explain in part its spontaneous acceptance in contrast to what may have been a more gradual embracing in the Latin West and in Rome itself. This is the concept of giving 'equal divine honours' (ἰσόθεοι τιμαί) to a ruler and the gods, embedded in Greek thinking from the time of Homer onwards.[25]

Fishwick himself acknowledged the need to investigate fully what he calls the 'theological problems' in a projected volume VII in his series on the cult in the Latin West. In this same preface he writes, 'Plainly the scope of this project is beyond the capacity of one author — or one lifetime — and I can only hope that other hands will one day bring the whole undertaking to a successful conclusion.'[26]

III. The Approach and Outline of *Divine Honours for the Caesars*

This book seeks to adopt something of a comparable approach to that of Fishwick by focusing on individual cities or provinces in the Greek East where Christians resided and are mentioned in the New Testament, and also the challenge posed for the first Christians. The aim then will be to explore certain major locations in the provinces of Macedonia, Achaea, Asia and Bithynia for official primary sources including imperial edicts and coins and archaeological evidence where Christianity first took root.

(i) The Methodological Approach and Aim of This Book

Readers may be surprised by the substantial number of official inscriptions relating to imperial cultic activities that are in block quotations in this work. They have been cited separately to help readers see for themselves,

---

to some of Gradel's conclusions in his "Addenda," *The Imperial Cult in the Latin West,* III.4 (Leiden: E. J. Brill, 2005), pp. 211, 214-15, 230-31, and especially his critique of Gradel's treatment of *numen* and *genius,* pp. 237-50.

25. D. Fishwick, "ISOTHEOI TIMAI," in *The Imperial Cult in the Latin West,* I.1, ch. 3.
26. Fishwick, *Provincial Cult: Institution and Evolution,* pp. xi-xii.

reflect on this hard evidence and explore what was encoded in these official imperial, provincial and local decrees. There is an important reason for doing this. 'Throughout antiquity, inscribed monuments and texts form a fecund relationship. Inscriptions are ideological artefacts that populate public space textually and symbolically'.[27] Scheid in his chapter "Epigraphy and Roman Religion" also made an important observation.

> [T]he study of Roman religion cannot do without epigraphy any more than it can do without archaeology. No one neglects the literary sources, obviously, but it is essential to recognize that without direct documentation . . . [it is] very fragmentary, imprecise and burdened with the lumber of the scholars of Antiquity.[28]

He cites in support of his argument Pliny the Younger (A.D. 61-c.112), who wrote to his correspondent Romanus — 'You will also find food for study in the numerous inscriptions, by many hands all over the pillars and the walls, in praise for the spring and its titular deity,' *Letter* 8:8. While it has as its reference the sanctuary of Clitumnus it was true for all the inscriptions involving Roman Religion[29] and, it must be added, not least of all on imperial cultic activities. This is generally an omission in New Testament studies, with notable exceptions.[30]

27. A. V. Zadorojnyi, "Shuffling Surfaces: Epigraphy, Power, and Integrity in the Greco-Roman Narratives," in *Inscriptions and Their Uses in Greek and Latin Literature,* ed. P. Liddel and P. Low (Oxford: Oxford University Press, 2013), p. 336.

28. J. Scheid, "Epigraphy and Roman Religion," in *Epigraphy and the Historical Sciences,* ed. J. Davies and J. Wilkers, Proceedings of the British Academy no. 177 (Oxford and New York: Oxford University Press, 2012), p. 37. He later notes a major omission among Latin scholars in this area, *viz.,* Greek inscriptions as 'Romans were bilingual, and their empire included Greek-speaking provinces within which were Roman colonies', p. 43. See also A. Chaniotis' comment, 'Ancient inscriptions offer us material which has never been fully exploited.' He argues this with respect to the 'emotional dimensions of oral communication' but his point has wider application in this sub-discipline of ancient history, "Listening to the Stones: Orality and Emotions in Ancient Inscriptions," in *Epigraphy and the Historical Sciences,* ed. J. Davies and J. Wilkers, Proceedings of the British Academy no. 177, p. 303. On the chasm felt by some mainstream ancient historians with the research and specialist publications of professional archaeologists, epigraphists and specialists in numismatics, see the introductory comments by R. Laurence and J. Berry, eds., *Cultural Identity in the Roman Empire* (London: Routledge, 1998), p. 1.

29. Pliny the Younger, *Letter* 8:8 cited by Scheid, "Epigraphy and Roman Religion," p. 31.

30. See for example the effective use of epigraphic evidence in J. R. Harrison, *Paul and the Imperial Authorities at Thessalonica and Rome,* WUNT 273 (Tübingen: Mohr Siebeck, 2011).

The original placement of these official documents engraved on stone in conspicuous, public places in the city's forum by the civic authorities was intentional. They were meant to be educative, informing the original readers of their purpose and objectives, and, at times, specified the particular cultic honours that were to be rendered to the imperial gods on allocated days in the annual calendar. It is hoped that contemporary readers can likewise benefit from exploring these primary inscriptions as part of the process of understanding the impact of imperial cultic activities on citizens in the empire, along with literary sources, and especially those relevant to New Testament passages. Any discussion following these original sources is intended to be a further reflection on their significance for imperial cultic venerations.

Imperial cult temples and their precincts were strategically located in the public domain in or near the agora, the place where inhabitants engaged not only in commercial, cultural, judicial, administrative activities, but in cultic ones as well. Their actual location in the *polis* stressed their importance, as they were usually the highest building intentionally overlooking the city, reminding everyone of Rome's rule. Hence temple inscriptions as well as statues not only spelt out the divine honours to be given to the Caesars but also had an ideological and political message to be absorbed by the city's inhabitants. This, together with feasts, cultural and sporting activities, was rapidly integrated into civic life.

Coins were also important as propaganda tools because they conveyed a deliberate message to those who used them in the marketplace where all commercial transactions occurred, including the purchase of daily needs. Hoster has shown this with respect to those bearing imperial images —

[C]oinage was a specific and deliberate way to demonstrate the self-definition and self-representation of the minting city. Coins were a means of propagating not only a city's status, wealth and prominence, but also its good relations with Rome. . . . [B]y choosing to place representations of members of the imperial family on their coins, the minting city (or, better, their élite) may have demonstrated their alleged close relationship and a more personalized expression of that relationship, to the ruling Romans.[31]

31. M. Horster, "Coinage and Images of the Imperial Family, Local Identity and Roman Rule," *Journal of Roman Archaeology* 26 (2013): 258.

The ancient historians cited in this chapter have shown the value of focusing their efforts primarily on official inscriptions and coins relating to imperial cultic activities and the extant material evidence of temples on the archaeological sites, including statues that promoted the divine propaganda concerning the reigning emperor and his family.[32] They have thus provided the most composite picture we possess to date of the cult in the Latin West and in the Greek East.

The value of such archaeological and literary evidence is that it can also help illuminate the setting of New Testament texts relevant to this subject and indeed in other areas. This can be a more effective method as the productive work of Judge has amply demonstrated, rather than engaging in generalizations or reading the text with contemporary approaches borrowed from other disciplines.[33]

The reading of primary sources with apposite comments has also been the way forward in guiding and stimulating discussions of ancient literary sources. Galinsky, writing in "In the Shadow (or Not) of the Imperial Cult," commends as progress these approaches that gather extant evidence from a specific region. He also notes that cognizance needs to be taken of ideological issues, which is the approach in this book.[34]

This topic has long captured my research interests. In the last two decades some of the papers and public lectures on the imperial cultic phenomena in relation to the New Testament were subsequently published as articles or chapters.[35] However, given the wisdom of adopting a focus

32. See P. Zanker, "The Roman Empire of Augustus: Imperial Myth and Cult in the East and West," in *The Power of Images in the Age of Augustus* (Ann Arbor: University of Michigan Press, 1990), ch. 8, for an exploration of this propaganda tool.

33. E. A. Judge, *The First Christians in the Roman World: Augustan and New Testament Essays,* WUNT 229 (Tübingen: Mohr Siebeck, 2008).

34. K. Galinsky, "In the Shadow (or Not) of the Imperial Cult: A Cooperative Agenda," in *Rome and Religion: A Cross-Disciplinary Dialogue on the Imperial Cult,* ed. J. Brood and J. L. Reed (Atlanta: Society of Biblical Literature, 2011), pp. 218-20. See also his opening chapter in this composite volume, "The Cult of the Roman Emperor: Uniter or Divider?" ch. 1.

35. "The Imperial Cult in Acts and Roman Religion," in *The Book of Acts in Its Graeco-Roman Setting. The Book of Acts in Its First-Century Setting,* vol. 2 (Grand Rapids: Eerdmans, 1994), ch. 4, Part II; ch. 7; "The Achaean Federal Imperial Cult II: The Corinthian Church," *TynB* 46, no. 1 (May 1995): 169-78; "On Introducing Gods to Athens: An Alternative Reading of Acts 17:18-20," *TynB* 47, no. 1 (May 1996): 71-90; "Gallio's Ruling on the Legal Status of Early Christianity (Acts 18:14-15)," *TynB* 50, no. 2 (Nov. 1999): 213-24. "The Imperial Cult and the Early Christians in Pisidian Antioch (Acts 13 and Galatians 6)," presented at the First International Conference on Pisidian Antioch 1997 and published in T. Drew-Bear,

primarily on epigraphic, numismatic and archaeological evidence to which must be given the highest credence because of the official status of the first two, my own perceptions of aspects of imperial cult veneration have been modified or, in some areas, have undergone something of a metamorphosis. This monograph is a major rethink of the nexus between the imperial cult and the first Christians. Focusing primarily on first-century non-literary evidence has been highly informative, as I trust it will also be for the reader.

The recent publication of Fantin's doctoral dissertation subsequently published as *Lord of the Entire World: Lord Jesus, a Challenge to Lord Caesar?* explores the use of the term 'Lord' from the LXX, Jewish and epigraphic sources, drawing attention to the fact that while it was used occasionally of previous emperors, extant sources show it became the one most used of Nero.[36] He went on to spell out the implications of this in his penultimate chapter, "*Kyrios Christos* and *Kyrios Kaisar:* Christ's Challenge to the Living Caesar." In his conclusion Fantin acknowledges his study of this term 'was a tree in the midst of the forest'.[37] This monograph seeks to explore the other 'trees in the forest', i.e., other official divine titles also used of the Caesars in the Julio-Claudian era. Hopefully it will provide a comprehensive picture of the enormous challenge posed for the first Christians when comparable imperial divine titles are used of Jesus and the Caesars.

Apart from reaping the benefits of learned publications by ancient

---

M. Tashalan and C. M. Thomas, eds., *Actes du 1er Congrès International sur Antioche de Pisidie* (Lyon: Université Lumière-Lyon, 2002), pp. 67-75, and at the conference in New Corinth, "Identify the Offering, the Cup and the Table of the 'Demons' in 1 Corinthians 10:20-21," in *Saint Paul and Corinth: International Scholarly Conference Proceedings Corinth, 23-25 September 2007,* ed. C. J. Belezos (Athens: Psichogios Publications, 2010), II, pp. 815-36; "Suffering with the Saviour: The Reality, the Reasons and the Reward," in *The Perfect Saviour: Key Themes in Hebrews,* ed. J. Griffith (Leicester: Apollos/Wheaton, IL: Crossway, 2012), ch. 8, and finally a contribution to a volume celebrating the centenary of the Pontifical Biblical Institute in 2009, "The Enigma of Imperial Cultic Activities and Paul in Corinth," in *Greco-Roman Culture and the New Testament: Studies Commemorating the Centennial of the Pontifical Biblical Institute,* ed. D. Aune and F. Brenk (Leiden: E. J. Brill, 2012), pp. 49-72.

36. J. D. Fantin, "*Kyrios Christos* and *Kyrios Kaisar:* Christ's Challenge to the Living Caesar," in *Lord of the Entire World: Lord Jesus, a Challenge to Lord Caesar?* New Testament Monograph 31 (Sheffield: Sheffield Phoenix Press, 2011).

37. Fantin, "Conclusion and Perspective," in *Lord of the Entire World: Lord Jesus, a Challenge to Lord Caesar?* ch. 6, p. 267.

historians, many visits over almost two decades with doctoral students to major archaeological sites in Greece and Turkey have not only helped them to read the extant material evidence but have also been highly informative in furthering my own understanding of just how dominant imperial cultic activities were in life in the cities in the East.

Secondly, to assist the reader, the remainder of this chapter explains the rationale for, and the layout of this book. It is divided into two sections. The approach adopted in Section I acts as an ancient lens through which New Testament evidence from specific cities or provinces in Section II may be better understood.

These early chapters record some of the significant, extant primary evidence of divine titles endorsed in imperial decrees, official communications from Rome, the imperial diplomatic convention of 'refusing' divine honours, while allowing a temple to be erected for the reigning emperor, and also propaganda promoting the concept of the imperial golden ages of Augustus and Nero. These ideological issues washed over and influenced the psyche of citizens in the Greek East and the Latin West as they were intended to do, shaping their perception of the divine rôle and stimulating loyalty to the Caesars.

The second section explores different responses by the first Christians when faced with pressure to fulfill their obligation as citizens to participate in imperial cultic celebrations on designated festive days as a visible expression of loyalty to the Roman Empire. It seeks to do so in the light of the findings of Section I.

The reader will notice substantial cross-referencing in the body of the text. The reason for doing this is the hope that it will further facilitate the reader's grasp of the background issues laid out in Section I relevant to the discussion of the New Testament *corpus* in Section II and *vice versa* for ancient historians.

There has been a long-standing interest in the problem that imperial veneration created for Christians in the Book of Revelation with the preoccupation of sorting out the enigma of the six hundred and sixty and six mark of the beast. Price discussed the cult, but his focus was primarily on Christians of a later era and not those of the era addressed in this book.

Conflicts that arose within the competitive system of the imperial cult are also found in the clash between the imperial cult and Christianity. Though I would not wish to return to the old picture between Christ and the Caesars, the imperial cult was clearly one of the features of the contemporary world that troubled the Christians. Their responses during the first three centuries of the empire consisted essentially of passive resistance.[38]

The aim in this work then is to further the discussion of imperial cultic activities and the complexity they created for the first Christians with different reactions to this all-pervasive, high-profile first-century reality. It will be argued there was not one but a variety of responses to the diverse celebrations at the time the early Christian movement was founded by Jesus in the reign of Tiberius and recorded in the New Testament primarily throughout the time of the remainder of Julio-Claudian emperors.

(ii) The Outline of This Book

Part I, Divine Honours for the Caesars and the Roman East, commences with "Festivities, Holidays, New Honours and Golden Ages" (chapter 2) and explores the diverse nature of these festivities connected to imperial cultic celebrations, which were incorporated into major public events such as horse races, bull fights, gladiatorial shows, public feasts and choral performances. This explains why it spread so rapidly and became part of the fabric of everyday life in cities in the East. In addition, 'no work' days in the official civic calendars were set aside specifically for the veneration of the Caesars.

Propaganda during the time of Augustus and later in Nero's reign attributed to both of them the inauguration of Rome's two 'Golden Ages', with many material and other benefits said to flow to all the empire. For Christians in between these two reigns and beyond, another messianic age had been inaugurated. It was to this kingdom of God that Christians were required to be loyal citizens, as Paul reminded the Philippian Christians — 'our citizenship is in heaven' (Phil. 3:20).

"Honours to, for and by the Caesars and Reciprocal Benefits" (chapter 3) records the diverse nature of what is commonly but imprecisely known as 'emperor worship'. It consisted of praying and sacrificing to the Caesar, as well as praying to the gods for his safety. It was also the rôle of each emperor as 'the high priest' to pray and sacrifice to the gods for the well-being of the Roman Empire. On the accession of a new emperor,

---

38. Price, *Rituals and Power*, p. 123, n. 44.

delegations from cities in the empire descended on Rome to declare their loyalty and devotion to him. Some also hoped to secure benefits or concessions for their citizens in their audience with him.

"Imperial Endorsement of Divine Titles and 'Declining' New Temples" (chapter 4) explores how the Caesars in official imperial decrees issued to provinces and cities used titles acknowledging their divine status. Delegations from all over the empire came to Rome customarily offering to build a temple for the new Caesar which he traditionally 'declined' as a diplomatic convention, although archaeological evidence shows some cities went ahead and built altars and temples to him.

"Adopt, Adapt, Abstain: Jewish Responses to Divine Honours" (chapter 5) examines these three Jewish responses. First, Herod the Great during his lifetime built a temple in the capital of his Jewish kingdom, Caesarea Maritima, to *Roma* and Augustus for provincials to give imperial cultic honours at the same time he began construction on the Jewish temple in Jerusalem.

Second, the Jews later skilfully adapted by showing imperial honours as expression of loyalty within the parameters of their own sacrificial system. They offered up a daily sacrifice in their temple in Jerusalem *for* the safety of the emperor but never *to* the emperor, within the acceptable boundaries of their own temple rituals. A comparable course of action was not open to the first Christians, who did not build temples or perform cultic sacrifices, given the primacy of the once-for-all sacrifice of their Messiah on the cross. The Diaspora Jews were permitted to pay the temple tax to their one shrine that was in Jerusalem, yet, as archaeological evidence shows, they did express their loyalty to the emperor in their synagogues with an imperial portrait but never statues.

Third, in A.D. 66 the Jewish priests in Jerusalem abstained from offering up their regular sacrifices for the safety of the emperor, thus signaling their revolt against Roman rule. These were the different responses of the Jews from which the Christian movement arose.

Part II examines on a city-by-city or provincial basis Christians' responses to imperial cultic activities. While Price suggested that '[t]heir [Christians'] responses during the first three centuries consisted essentially of passive resistance',[39] it will be argued that the reactions of the first generation of Christians in the East were far from uniform, as they struggled with the unavoidable reality of cultic honours to the divine Caesars as a

---

39. Price, *Rituals and Power*, p. 123.

conventional expression of loyalty to the Roman Empire. There was compromise, evasion, the temptation to commit apostasy, imprisonment and the possible punishment of exile and even summary executions. The remaining six chapters explore these different reactions of the first Christians in different places and under different circumstances.

This section commences with "The Admission of New Gods to Athens: Rome's and Paul's" (chapter 6). Acts 17:15-34 provides a bridge to Christianity beginning with the Areopagus Council's ancient judicial rôle of officially admitting new gods to Athens. It focuses on evidence of imperial cult temples and shrines in this Roman 'freed and allied city' *(civitas libera et foederata)* and the response to Rome's new rulers as well as Paul's formal *apologia* to its council of his 'unknown' god and the resurrected Jesus. It also explores compromises by Stoic and Epicurean philosophers who, like Christians, were confronted with the same inescapable phenomena that were also contrary to aspects of their beliefs.

"Promoting Cultic Honours in Achaea and Exemption for Christians" (chapter 7) explores how imperial cultic activities had been assiduously promoted in Messene and in other leading cities of the province of Achaea including Corinth. This was initiated *c.* A.D. 1-2 by a senior Roman official. It also argues that, as a result of the legal ruling by Gallio at the preliminary court hearing of the case of the Corinthian Jews *versus* Paul, Christians, like the Jews residing there, were given *de facto* exemption from having to participate in local divine honours to the Caesars in the imperial cult temple and shrines in the province.

"New Imperial Honours: Some Corinthian Christians Compromise" (chapter 8) examines important epigraphic evidence from Corinth and also Athens of a new provincial-wide imperial cult established by Rome and centred in Corinth. It was initiated soon after Paul left there to work in Ephesus. Some Christians sought to rationalize theologically their decision to recline to dine in the imperial cult temple precincts at the annual provincial feasts as a legitimate exercise of their civic 'right'. Paul's lengthy response refutes their arguments (1 Cor. 8:1–11:1). Further evidence is found of an innovation in imperial cultic activities with the venerating of the *genius* of the emperor with designated sacrifices, cups and the tables to the *daimonion* (δαιμονίον) of Nero (1 Cor. 10:20-22).

"Avoiding Divine Honours for Caesars: Some Galatian Christians' Strategy" (chapter 9) argues that Gentile Christians in Galatia were pressured by fellow believers to take evasive action to avoid the persecution for all Christians that non-participation in imperial cultic veneration could invoke. Gentile converts were being cajoled by arguments to undergo the rite of circumcision, the Jewish identification mark, and observe Jewish customs. The whole Christian community could thereby safely shelter under the wings of Diaspora Judaism by all of them being Jews either by birth or as proselytes. All Christians would thus evade persecution for the cross of Christ (Galatians 4–6).

"Confrontation for Thessalonian Christians and the Most Divine Caesar" (chapter 10) explores the allegations made against new Christians immediately upon conversion before the ruling officials of the city. They were accused of acting contrary to the decrees of Caesar by affirming their loyalty to another king (Acts 17:1-10). On conversion a widely known characteristic of their new faith was that they had turned from all idolatry, which would have included the veneration of any statues of the Caesars in the imperial cult temple, in order to serve the Lord (1 Thess. 1:9-10). Subsequently, there would be a potential confrontation with the imperial self-promotion as 'the most divine' of Rome's imperial gods (2 Thess. 2:4).

"Impending Exile for Christians in Hebrews" (chapter 11) explores the immediate bleak future facing Christians who had already experienced multiple punishments such as public physical afflictions and confiscation of personal property as well as imprisonment. These were administered through what had to have been the due process of Roman law. Pending was the threat of exile — a punishment so dreaded in the first century that it was regarded as being exceeded only by the death penalty.

The final chapter (chapter 12), "Conformity and Commerce or Capital Punishment: New Honours for Caesar," traces an official move by a provincial governor to outdo any of his predecessors by introducing a unique, highly visible ritual honour to be given by all inhabitants of his province as a prerequisite to buying and selling in the official market — the only place where all commercial transactions could occur in the cities of the empire. As a result, Christians would be faced with an inescapable choice — compromise by engaging in this imperial cultic innovation, worshipping in the imperial cult temple on a regular basis, fleeing the cities in which they lived or undergoing the death penalty.

It will become apparent how helpful ancient historians have been by raising the issue that the first Christians had to confront the reality of divine imperial cultic honours. In addition they have provided invaluable insights into the all-pervasive phenomenon in the Roman Empire. It is recognised that all Christians were required to give appropriate imperial honours but only within the parameters of their faith, as Paul outlined in

Romans 13:1-7.[40] Paul defines the Caesar as God's servant (διάκανος) and his minister (λειτουργός) (13:4, 6) but certainly not as a man who, upon becoming Caesar, was 'a god', 'a son of a god', 'god manifest', 'saviour of the world', and 'the great high priest' of all his empire and to be thus venerated. His instructions to render to each their obligation was to pay taxes, honours that resonated with Jesus' edict to give appropriate honours to Caesar but never to compromise in any way by giving them divine honours that alone were due to God (Mark 12:17).

40. See my "Civic Honours for Christian Benefactors, Romans 13:3-4 and 1 Peter 2:14-15," in *Seek the Welfare of the City: Early Christians as Benefactors and Citizens* (Grand Rapids: Eerdmans/Carlisle: Paternoster, 1994), ch. 2.

PART I

Divine Honours for the Caesars and the Roman East

CHAPTER 2

Festivities, Holidays, New Honours and Golden Ages

This chapter records evidence that reveals how imperial cultic veneration was well integrated into the regular life of citizens in the Roman Empire in the East. It is generally assumed that imperial cultic activities were only of a liturgical nature and conducted in the appropriate temple or shrine. They were in fact also woven into the very fabric of the life of the city, being integrated into a number of cultural and sporting activities as well as liturgical events. This explains why they were so attractive for its inhabitants throughout the Roman Empire.

On occasion imperial cult processions paraded through the streets of cities where citizens paid homage to the divine Caesars at altars outside their homes. Celebrations were spread through the year as official calendars record, as imperial cultic honours were given on public holidays, also known as 'no work' days.

Intriguing evidence in the form of copies of an inscription located in five leading cities of the Province of Asia bears witness to the fact that a governor, who had married into the Augustan family and had been declared a 'friend of Caesar', diligently promoted new divine honours among the inhabitants of his provinces. Furthermore, poets wrote lyrically of the reigns of Augustus and Nero as 'golden ages'.

It is therefore proposed to explore (I) the variety of festivities held for entertainment as an integral part of imperial cultic celebrations; (II) the intensity of local celebrations throughout the year on high and holy days, called 'no work' days in official calendars; (III) the changing of New Year's day in the official annual calendar in the Province of Asia to the anniversary of the birth of 'of the most divine Caesar' Augustus; and (IV) the poetic lauding of Augustus for giving the empire its first 'Golden Age' and Nero its second.

I. Entertaining Festive Imperial Cultic Celebrations

'The veneration of the emperors, living and dead, through games held for imperial festivals and through the procession and presence of their images at games is well attested in the provinces by inscriptions, texts and archaeology'.[1] Price wrote of celebrations in Ancyra, a provincial imperial cult centre in the province of Galatia in the Augustan era — 'the festival at Ancyra is explicitly stated to have been held at the imperial temple; horse races were run there and the other spectacles, gladiatorial and animal fights, competitions, sacrifices and feasts, may also have taken place nearby'.[2]

An inscription from the same province records the variety and intensity of such festivities and helps us understand how quickly divine honours were incorporated into the regular festivals of cities in the East. Feasts may have been restricted to certain classes of citizens, but that would not be the case with spectacles and others public events.

The Galatians who sacrificed to the divine Augustus and divine Roma . . . son of King Brigatus, gave a public feast and provided olive oil for four months; he presented spectacles and 30 pairs of gladiators and gave a beast-hunt with bulls and wild beasts. Rufus gave a public feast and presented spectacles and a beast-hunt.

In the governorship of Metilius. Pylaemenes, son of King Amyntas, twice gave a public feast and twice presented spectacles and presented games with athletes, chariots and race-horses. Likewise a bull-fight and a beast-hunt. He gave oil to the city. He offered up young animals where the temple of Augustus is situated and the festival and horse racing takes place. Albiorix, son of Ateporix, gave a public feast and dedicated two statues, of Caesar and of Julia Augusta. Amyntas, son of Gaezatodiastes, twice gave a public feast and sacrificed a hecatomb and presented public spectacles and gave corn rations at the rate of 5 modii . . . of Diognetus. Albiorix, son of Ateporix, for the second time gave a public feast.

In the governorship of Fronto. Metrodorus, son of Menemachus

1. N. T. Elkins, "Placement of Imperial Images in the Colosseum," *Papers of the British School at Rome* 82 (2014): 74.

2. S. R. F. Price, *Rituals and Power: The Imperial Cult and Asia Minor* (Cambridge: Cambridge University Press, 1984), p. 109.

and the natural son of Dorylaus, gave a public feast and provided olive oil for four months. Musaeus, son of Articnus, gave a public feast . . . son of Seleucus, gave a public feast and provided oil for four months. Pylaemenes, son of King Amyntas, gave a public feast for the three tribes[3] and at Ancyra sacrificed a hecatcomb and presented spectacles and a procession; likewise, a bull-fight and bull-fighters and 50 pairs of gladiators. He provided oil for the three tribes for the whole year and presented a wild beast-fight.[4]

Fishwick concludes of the impact of the celebrations on those in the Latin West — 'The end result was that sacrifices became more and more a pretext for a good meal, religious anniversaries simply an occasion for a free dinner when one might indulge oneself in over-eating and over-drinking' and 'inscriptions and papyri confirm that games and banquets were a staple appurtenance of major festivals of the imperial cult throughout the empire.'[5]

Mitchell notes, 'It is clear that gladiatorial games reached the East. . . . The vast majority of gladiatorial inscriptions are linked with the imperial cult, and in most cases the responsibility for mounting gladiatorial fights lay with the high priests.'[6] Price also observed, 'The gladiatorial games and animal fights, which spread from Rome and became very popular in the Greek world under the empire, were put on almost exclusively in connection with the imperial cult.'[7] As a result, 'when a high priest organized gladiatorial games, he was acclaimed by the crowd and responded by further munificence; "the spectacle, especially of the gladiators, caused the greatest astonishment and even incredulity as roses and gifts were thrown into the amphitheater where the variety of the gladiators' arms was wondered at"' and 'at the provincial level, imperial choirs are only known . . . in the provincial cult of Asia'.[8]

As a united sign of loyalty to Roman rule, 'The city also expected participation in festivals by its members and made prescription for their

3. The three tribes made up the Galatians: the Tolistobogii, Tectosages and Trocmi.

4. *OGIS* 533.

5. D. Fishwick, *Imperial Cult in the Latin West* (Leiden: E. J. Brill, 1991), II.1, pp. 585, 587-88.

6. S. Mitchell, *Anatolia: Land, Men and Gods in Asia Minor: The Celts and the Impact of Roman Rule* (Oxford: Clarendon Press, 1993²), I, p. 110.

7. Price, *Rituals and Power,* p. 89.

8. Price, *Rituals and Power,* pp. 116, 88.

attendance.'[9] Therefore any withdrawal by Christians could not go unnoticed. It must have been further complicated when divine honours were given to Caesars in imperial cult temples. There was yet a further complication: '[T]he home was brought into this public activity by prescriptions for sacrifices at imperial altars outside the houses as the [the imperial cultic] procession passed'[10] as a further declaration of loyalty to Rome. If they no longer did this, then it would have been obvious to their neighbours.

As already noted, 'The diffusion of the cult of Augustus and of other members of his family in Asia Minor and throughout the Greek East from the beginning of the empire was rapid, indeed almost instantaneous.'[11] It is certainly explicable how this happened when imperial cultic celebrations, including dining and other civic functions, were officially incorporated into the cultural life of citizens in the East.

II. The Annual Calendar for Imperial Cult Public Holidays

Celebrations on many official high and holy days record the significant events in the emergence of the Roman Empire, its 'founder' and the present ruler. The Calendar of Cumae (A.D. 4-14) reveals the illustrious high points in the Principate of Augustus that were celebrated on what were designated as 'no work' days throughout the year.[12]

19 August	On this day Caesar entered his first consulship. [*supplicatio* . . .]
4-22 September	On this day Lepidus' army went over to Caesar. [*supplicatio* . . .]
23 September	Birthday of Caesar. Sacrifice of animal to Caesar and *supplicatio* to Vesta
7 October	Birthday of Drusus Caesar. *Supplicatio* to Vesta
18 October	On this day Caesar put on the *toga virilis*. *Supplicatio* to Spes (Hope) and Iuventas (Youth)
16 November	Birthday of Tiberius Caesar. *Supplicatio* to Vesta

---

9. Price, *Rituals and Power*, p. 121.
10. Price, *Rituals and Power*, p. 121.
11. Mitchell, *Anatolia: Land, Men and Gods in Asia Minor*, I, p. 100.
12. *CIL* 10, 8375 cited in Fishwick, *Imperial Cult in the Latin West*, II.1, p. 490.

15 December	*Fortuna Redux* brought back Caesar from overseas provinces.
7 January	On this day Caesar first took the *fasces.*
16 January	On this day Caesar was named *Augustus. Supplicatio* to Augustus.
30 January	On this day the altar of Peace was dedicated. *Supplicatio* to the *imperium* of Caesar Augustus Guardian of the Roman Empire
6 March	On this day Caesar was appointed *pontifex maximus. Supplicatio* to Vesta, to the *Penates* the public gods of the Roman people, the Auirites.
15 April	On this day Caesar won his first victory. *Supplicatio* to Victoria Augusta
16 April	On this day Caesar was first saluted *Imperator. Supplicatio* to *Felicitas* of the empire
12 May	On this day the temple of Mars was dedicated. *Supplicatio* to Vesta to the Might of Mars
24 May	Birthday of Germanicus Caesar. *Supplicatio* to Vesta

The structuring of the calendar was significant, as it reflects one of the principles for calculating the chronology of Augustus and hence the commencement of the calendar. This one records the preference of Augustus, who wished to have the date he was appointed consul for the first time as its beginning and the month named after him. The choice reflects his *imperium,* not in its republican sense, but in its imperial one, and is promoted in terms of Augustus as the one who is in 'first place' *(principatus).*

On 23 September and 16 January the sacrifice was offered not 'on his behalf' or even 'for his well-being' but 'to' Augustus, the emperor *(immolatio Caesari hostia).*[13] It shows that this was an acceptable cultic practice.[14] (See p. 174.) Furthermore, in the Roman legal code, *Lex Irnitana,* provision was made for the magistrates to revisit the official calendar of a city, and the city constitution assumes that this was done for other cities as well on holy days 'for the veneration of the imperial family'.[15]

---

13. Fishwick, *Imperial Cult in the Latin West,* II.1, p. 509. M. Beard, J. North and S. Price, *Religions of Rome: A Sourcebook* (Cambridge: Cambridge University Press, 1996), II, p. 71.

14. Fishwick, *Imperial Cult in the Latin West,* II.1, p. 517.

15. *Lex Irnitana,* ch. 31, cf. chs. 79, 90 and 92. C. Ando, "A Religion for the Empire,"

III. Augustus' Birthday 'Equal to the Beginning of All Things'

The lengthy inscription from five cities in Asia — Priene, Apamea, Eumensei, and Maeonia in Greek and Dorylaion — and comprising three separate official documents provides important evidence as to how the reign of Augustus was promoted.[16] Of their significance, Sherk comments that 'these documents are of great importance, not only for the light they shed on Roman chronology and the Asian calendar, but also for the history of the provincial *koinon* and the early imperial cult'.[17]

In the case of imperial cultic veneration, the proconsul's intention was specifically stated — 'in order that our plan for the honouring of Augustus may abide forever' (*ll.* 27-28). This plan provided for a province-wide, everlasting veneration of the one who is described as 'the most divine Caesar' (τοῦ θεοτάτου Καίσαρος) (*l.* 22). The superlative of θεῖος was chosen to describe Augustus and also records that there were 'many great benefactions' (*l.* 17). They were such that it was said it had been exceedingly difficult to think of sufficient appropriate honours, given that he had brought into being the lasting and wonderful golden age of the *pax romana*.

An official letter received from the proconsul of the province of Asia at that time, Paullus Fabius Maximus, had prompted this decree. As the Roman governor, he attributed the reason for his participation to a 'competition' because it had been announced some two decades before in 29 B.C. by the Secretary of the League of 'Asia [the League] decreed in Smyrna' when 'the proconsul was Lucius Volcacius Tullus and the secretary was Papion from Dios Hieron' (*ll.* 41-42). It had laid down a challenge for someone to think of honours for Augustus commensurate with the enormous 'messianic' blessings he had brought to this province.[18] This

---

in *Imperial Ideology and Provincial Loyalty in the Roman Empire* (Berkeley: University of California Press, 2000), ch. 10.

16. This is a composite document that integrated what survived from inscriptions of the one provincial decree in Greek in the four cities and the other in Latin from Dorylaion and incorporated the governor's letter. V. Ehrenberg and A. H. M. Jones, *Documents Illustrating the Reigns of Augustus & Tiberius* (Oxford: Clarendon Press, 1976²), no. 98. The first three lines of the eighty-eight are lost, but otherwise the text can be restored from its extant portions, allowing a composite text to be established.

17. R. K. Sherk, *Roman Documents from the Greek East: Senatus Consulta and Epistulae to the Age of Augustus* (Baltimore: Johns Hopkins University Press, 1969), p. 336, for his comments on these decrees.

18. Sherk, *Roman Documents from the Greek East,* pp. 334-35, n. 1, contends in an extended footnote that 'although the [Roman] consul of 33 B.C. became governor of Asia

would not be successfully done until 9 B.C., and then it was initiated not by a provincial but by Rome's present proconsul of Asia himself. This would have indicated to all in the province that Maximus was not simply acting on his own initiative but on that of his predecessor, and his participation was a move the League had officially endorsed.

A 'crown' of gold that had been promised in the 29 B.C. competition was actually awarded to Maximus (*l.* 43) as the prize for the one 'who found the greatest honours for Caesar' (*ll.* 56-57).[19] A further honour was that 'he [Maximus] shall always be publicly acclaimed at the gymnasium festival in Pergamum [held in honour] of *Roma* and Augustus', i.e., the Roman imperial gods worshipped by provincials (*ll.* 57-59).

The date of Augustus' birthday was providentially seen to have coincided with that for the annual election of magistrates to their public office, so it was perceived as even more propitious. It was Apollonius, the high priest of the imperial provincial cult of Asia, who moved that the decree be officially implemented.

This evidence puts to rest any concept that only provincials initiated further imperial cult honours and not the emperor's consul from Rome. In seeking to understand why a senior Roman provincial official would promote such extravagant and appropriate divine honours for Augustus, it is important firstly to explore his profile and his motivation for doing so.

(i) Caesar's Friend, Relative, Proconsul and an Imperial Cult Promoter

Paullus Fabius Maximus was 'a friend *(amicus)* of Augustus'.[20] Official coins were struck in the city of Hierapolis with the head of Maximus imprinted

---

in *c.* 26/25 B.C., he need not necessarily have been the same man mentioned as governor in our decree of the *Koinon*'. He is concerned about the awarding of the prize some fifteen years later unless there was the annual award. For this there is no evidence. Regardless of Sherk's decision to suspend judgement on this, the incorporation of the name of Tollius in the official decree, *l.* 42 and the actual name of Papion, son of Diosierites the secretary of the *Koinon,* suggests there is some historic nexus in spite of the substantial time lapse. The decree indicates that the crown was promised, *l.* 57.

19. For the importance of the benefaction crown, see my *Seek the Welfare of the City: Early Christians as Benefactors and Citizens* (Grand Rapids and Cambridge: Eerdmans, 1994), pp. 30-31.

20. J. A. Crook, *'Amici Principis',* in *Consilium Principis: Imperial Councils and Counsellors from Augustus to Diocletian* (Cambridge: Cambridge University Press, 1955), 10-9 B.C. no. 143.

on them.[21] This confirms that he exercised the right given to proconsuls from that decade onwards whereby 'a friend of the emperor' *(amicus principis)* who was a proconsul was alone given the privilege of having his portraiture on official coins.[22] Crook has shown this was no purely honorific title in his discussion of *'Amici Principis'*. Maximus is included in the list of names in his 'Prosopographical Index'. He wrote, 'It served to indicate to the inhabitants of the Empire the importance of those sent to govern them; they are representatives of the *auctoritas* [power] of the emperor.'[23] As officially 'Caesar's friend' he had an obligation to promote the honour and interests of the emperor, and this inscription bears eloquent evidence as to how he assiduously did this.

Maximus had married Marcia, the first cousin of Augustus and the daughter of Augustus' half-brother, L. Marcius Philippus. Syme has demonstrated how Augustus sought to extend his imperial power and influence through strategic marriages into his wider family. He notes that 'the schemes devised by Augustus in the ramification of family alliances were formidable'.[24]

Syme specifically refers to Maximus by name as an example of one of the successful fruits of Augustus' policy to nurture 'the young generation of *nobiles* [who] grew up and passed through the avenue of political honours to the consulate'. 'Of his [Augustus'] allies among the young *nobiles* . . . [was] the accomplished Paullus Fabius Maximus.'[25] His brother was also a proconsul of Africa *c.* 6-5 B.C. in the same decade as Maximus exercised the *imperium* in the Province of Asia in 10-9 B.C.[26]

In the preceding year Maximus had been appointed one of Rome's two consuls for the year, holding this prestigious post along with Quintus Aelius Tubero. It is recorded that they had recommended to the Senate

21. *RPC* nos. 2929-30, 2932, 2934, 2936, 2939 and 2941-42. Coins were also minted for C. Asinius Gallus, another proconsul of Asia in 6-5 B.C. who was 'Caesar's Friend'. See Crook, *'Amici Principis'*, "Prosopographical Index," no. 38.

22. M. Grant, *From* Imperium *to* Auctoritas*: A Historical Study of* Aes *Coinage in the Roman Empire* (Cambridge: Cambridge University Press, 1946), pp. 139, 387. See pp. 379-400 for his discussion of the policy of having the heads of officials on coins. One name he cites as an example is that of Maximus.

23. Crook, *'Amici Principis'*, p. 24. For his "Prosopographical Index," see pp. 148-90 where he has numbered with short biographical details each one of Caesar's friends.

24. R. Syme, *The Roman Revolution* (Oxford: Clarendon Press, 1939), pp. 378-79.

25. Syme, *The Roman Revolution,* p. 379. See also his extended discussion 'Fabius Maximus', in *The Augustine Aristocracy* (Oxford: Clarendon Press, 1986), ch. 28.

26. See Crook, "Prosopographical Index," no. 142.

how the conservation of the public water supply, so critical for the capital, might be better utilised and preserved by the water commissioners. This resulted in a decree being passed by the Senate of Rome to enact the law governing Rome's water supply in which their forethought and wisdom were lauded.[27] Furthermore, Augustus in outlining his significant achievements in *Res Gestae Divi Augusti* recorded additional powers that Maximus sought to secure for him on two previous occasions but which Augustus had consistently refused.

> In the consulship of Marcus Vinicius and Quintus Lucertius [B.C. 19], and afterward in that of Publius and Gnaeus Lentulus [B.C. 18], and thirdly that of Paullus Fabius Maximus and Quintus Tubero [B.C. 11], the Senate and the People of Rome agreed that I should be appointed sole guardian of the laws and morals with supreme power, but I would not accept any office inconsistent with the custom of our ancestors.[28]

So Maximus came to the province of Asia with a good track record of recommending further imperial honours for Augustus that he would seek to replicate in his provincial post.

Horace in his *Odes* provides further light on Maximus' creativity, clearly from first-hand knowledge. The main body of the poem is concerned with this young aristocrat, Paullus Fabius Maximus, who was shortly to marry Augustus' cousin. This acts as a prelude to the praises of the new generation of public men and was written around 8 B.C.[29] It emphasizes further the importance of this player at the centre of Augustan politics. Of him Horace writes —

> It will be more seemly for you to revel in the house of Paullus Maximus . . . for he is aristocratic and good-looking, and as a young fellow of a hundred accomplishments he will carry far and wide the banner of your army. When he has prevailed over the gifts of his big-spending rivals, he will laugh and set you up in marble under a citron roof beside

27. See H. B. Evans, *Water Distribution in Ancient Rome: The Evidence of Frontinus* (Ann Arbor: University of Michigan Press, 1994), pp. 41, 43-45, 49.

28. Augustus, *Res Gestae Divi Augusti,* Col. 1.6.1. See E. A. Judge, "Real Basis of Augustan Power," in *The First Christians in the Roman World* (Tübingen: Mohr Siebeck, 2008), p. 118.

29. Horace, *Odes* 4.1. N. Rudd, *Horace Odes and Epodes,* Loeb Classics Library no. 33 (Cambridge, MA: Harvard University Press, 2004), p. 8.

the Alban Lake. There you will inhale incense in profusion and enjoy the mingled strains of the lyre and the Berecyntian pipe, not forgetting the pipes of Pan.[30]

Later Maximus became a confidant of the ageing Augustus, apparently seeking some form of reconciliation with his estranged son. Tacitus described him as his 'companion' *(comes)* and records that

> a rumour had gone abroad that a few months before he had sailed to Planasia on a visit to Agrippa, with the knowledge of some chosen friends, and with one companion, Fabius Maximus; that many tears were shed on both sides, with expressions of affection, and that thus there was a hope of the young man being restored to the home of his grandfather.[31]

Plutarch also notes that Augustus confided in Maximus who was his 'companion' on his secret journey to Planasia and that he was thinking of recalling his discredited son, Agrippa, from exile. Maximus told his wife who then foolishly repeated this to Livia, the wife of Augustus, whose son by another marriage, Tiberius, was the possible successor of the emperor. Because of this indiscretion on his part, Maximus fell out of favour with the emperor. He either died soon after or, according to Plutarch, committed suicide after the emperor rejected him because of this betrayal of a confidence.[32]

Thus the profile of Maximus was that of a long-standing, well-connected and loyal imperial official who was also highly entrepreneurial in promoting the reign and prestige of Augustus. This had already been borne out with his proposal to the Senate amending regulations for rationalizing the water supply of Rome. He had broken a new frontier for the province by recommending a major change in the calendar that officially recognized Augustus' divine rule.

Maximus was a good example of the strategy of Augustus to create a generation of unswervingly loyal officials. The former clearly understood that part of his rôle was to see the province of Asia fully appreciated and thus appropriately express thanks with on-going remembrances for the

---

30. Horace, *Odes* 4.1, *ll.* 10-27.
31. Tacitus, *Annals* 1.5.
32. Plutarch, "Concerning Talkativeness," 508A-B.

enormous blessings that Augustus had achieved within such a short period of time. The *pax romana* and the one who achieved it was later reflected in the famous *Res Gestae* whereby the 'divine Augustus' would himself list all the benefits of his rule.[33]

This background helps throw light on Maximus' motive in seeking to promote provincial loyalty to the emperor by emphasising the blessings of Augustus' golden age. As proconsul of a leading province in the East, he was 'recommending' appropriate cultic expressions of lasting gratitude to Augustus. This also corrects any notion that it was only the leading residents in cities in the East who were at the forefront of encouraging divine imperial honours and that no official appointed from Rome was party to this, not least of all one close to Augustus.

(ii) The Proconsul's Proposal for Divine Imperial Honours for Augustus

Maximus' letter 'suggests' a 'proposal' to the League of Asia, but as Sherk notes, it 'is worded in such a way as to constitute virtually a directive'.[34] The League would be endorsing what was said to have been initiated long ago during the former proconsulship of Tullus with the promise to confer honours on the one who met the challenge to propose the most appropriate honours for Augustus.

This proconsul's letter states that a 'decree' by the League of Asia 'shall be drafted encompassing all his [Augustus'] excellent virtues' (δεήσει γραφῆαι πάσας ἐνπεριειληγὸς τὰς ἀρετας αὐτοῦ) (*l.* 27), indicating the procedures the League would normally take when propagating such. So Maximus was laying out the future procedures for fulfilling the League's intention initiated some two decades before.

The proconsul's stated purpose was to create an everlasting memorial to Augustus 'so that the plan formulated by us for the honour of Augustus may remain forever' (*ll.* 27-28). He then promised, 'I shall order (προστάξω) the decree to be inscribed and erected in the temple,' i.e., the imperial cult temple to *Roma* and Augustus. He also gave instructions for

---

33. In the introduction before Augustus lays out his achievements, he is referred to as *divus Augustus,* which in the Greek text is rendered as Σεβαστὸς θεός. For the text, see P. A. Brunt and J. M. Moore, eds., *Res Gestae Divi Augusti: The Achievement of the Divine Augustus* (Oxford: Oxford University Press, 1967), pp. 19-36.

34. Sherk, *Roman Documents from the Greek East,* p. 336.

'the ordinance to be inscribed in both languages', i.e., Greek and Latin. The latter language was used in official decrees emanating from Rome and exclusively in Roman colonies in this era while the former was in Greek for the majority in the East.

In addition he made it clear that his suggestion was merely 'the starting point' (ἀφορμή) of honours for Augustus. This was because 'it is difficult to return for his great many benefactions thanks in equal measure, unless for each of them we think of some manner of repayment' (ll. 16-17). He made a personal 'proposal' to the League that 'it seems good to me that one and the same New Year's day for all states should be the birthday of "the most divine Caesar"' (l. 22). This was the same title he used to introduce Augustus at the beginning of his official letter (l. 4).

How does Maximus describe the golden age of Augustus? He begins his arguments in favour of his proposal by asking the League concerning 'the birthday of the most divine Caesar [Augustus]' (ἡ τοῦ θειοτάτου Καίσαρος γενέθλιος) as to which alternative is the 'more pleasant or more beneficial' (l. 4).[35] The reason he asks this is because 'we might justly consider [it] equal to the beginning of all things' (ἢν τῇ τῶν πάντων ἀρχῇ ἴσην δικαίως). He qualifies what he means — 'If not exactly from the point of view of the natural order of things, at least from the point of view of the useful' (l. 5).

Maximus further explicated how beneficial the coming of Augustus had been. '[I]f there is nothing that has fallen to pieces and to an unfortunate condition has been changed' that Augustus 'has not restored', so much so that 'he has given to the whole world a different appearance, a world which would have met its ruin with the greatest of pleasure, if as the common good fortune for everyone (τὸ κοινὸν πάντων εὐτύχημα) Caesar had not been born' (ll. 6-9).[36]

So the coming of Augustus was said not only to have rescued the Roman world from disaster by the bringing of peace but also to have seen its restoration and transformation. Although not stated explicitly here, the *pax romana* was being heralded because it served 'the interests of the emperor in safeguarding his position and enhancing his glory',[37] quite apart from bringing unprecedented prosperity.

---

35. The neuter πότερον is used as the beginning of an interrogative sentence that contains two alternatives and asks 'which' of the audience.

36. *OGIS* 458.

37. See B. H. Isaac, *The Limits of Empire: The Roman Army in the East* (Oxford: Clarendon Press, 1990), p. 416.

The Governor of the Province of Asia called on all its inhabitants to 'justly consider' the personal implications of this new age. 'The time of the birth' (γενέθλιος ἡμέρα) of Augustus for each inhabitant in the province 'has become the beginning of life and of living' (ἀρχὴν τοῦ βίου καὶ τῆς ζωῆς γεγονέναι) (*l.* 10). In diplomatic language the proconsul further affirms its importance for each inhabitant 'and since from no day for both the League and each person (εἴς τε τὸ κοινὸν καὶ εἰς τὸ ἴδιον ἕκαστος) could one day be more fortunate than the day that has been fortune (εὐτυχοῦς) for everyone' (*ll.* 11-13). Furthermore, his birthday providentially coincided in the cities of Asia with the official day for 'the entrance of magistrates into public office' (*l.* 14).

He could only conclude from this that it was by 'some divine will in order that it should be a beginning of honour for Augustus' (*l.* 4), whom the proconsul again declared to be the 'most divine Caesar' (ὁ θειότατος καῖσαρ), using the superlative 'most divine' (*l.* 22). Is this meant to be a Greek equivalent for the Latin *divis* that was used of 'perpetual divinity'?[38] The fragment of Latin inscription of this decree from Dorylation actually has *divina merita,* the former being the neuter plural of *divinus,* which is a cognate of *divus,* and *meritus* is the past passive participle of *mereor,* 'to deserve', so that the cognate of *divus* was used by Maximus to indicate that Augustus was deserving of perpetual divine honours.[39]

In light of all the attributes of Augustus, Maximus concluded, 'It seems good to me that all the communities should have one and the same New Year's day, for all should be the birthday of the most divine Caesar and on that day all men should enter into public office' (*ll.* 20-21).

The final clause 'in order that' (ὅπως) traditionally indicated benefits and in this case to the whole province.

38. Contra Sherk, *Roman Documents from the Greek East,* no. 65, p. 337, n. 7, who argued that Maximus 'may have been unwilling to call Augustus "most divine" in either Latin or Greek, even when addressing Greeks. . . . But it cannot be denied that the use of the word χειοταϛτο in Greek and the absence of a corresponding word in the Latin are striking facts, not noticed by previous editors'. However, see the following note.

39. *CIL* 3, 13651, *l.* 7, an inscription Sherk cites in *Roman Documents from the Greek East,* p. 329. On the importance of the use of term *divis* for 'perpetual divinity', see pp. 63-66 based on a perceptive discussion by D. Wardle, "*Deus* or *Divus:* The Genesis of Roman Terminology for Deified Emperors and a Philosopher's Contribution," in *Philosophy and Power in the Graeco-Roman World: Essays in Honour of Miriam Griffin,* ed. G. Clark and T. Rajak (Oxford: Oxford University Press, 2002), pp. 181-209. Sherk suggests in the light of his argument that '[i]t could mean that the composer was a Greek'.

[I]n an even more extraordinary manner the day may be honoured by acquiring in addition from without a certain cultic observance and this may become better known for everyone. I think that this observance will render the greatest advantage (πλείστην εὐχρηστίαν) to the province. (*ll.* 23-26)

The last phrase, 'the greatest advantage', more than hints that by so doing the province will secure maximum reciprocal benefits from Augustus. This was how this 'Empire of Honour' worked, to borrow the title of Lendon's excellent monograph that encapsulates this important reality as to how things operated politically and materially for cities and provinces in the empire.[40]

(iii) The Decree: New Year's Day Changed to the Birthday of Augustus

As a result, the members of the *Koinon* of the province of Asia passed this lengthy resolution, expressing their reasons for the honours to be conferred.

Since the Providence (ἡ πρόνοια) that divinely ordered our existence having employed zeal and ardour, has arranged the most perfect good in Augustus, bestowing upon us and our descendants whom for the benefit (εὐεργεσία) of mankind she has filled with virtue, and she has sent him as a saviour for us and, a saviour (σωτῆρα) who has brought war to an end and set all things in order. (*ll.* 31-36)

'Providence' is important because it is attributed here to the divine blessing that has been brought to the empire by 'the most perfect good' located in Augustus, who 'is filled with virtue for the benefit of mankind'. 'Providence', a Roman deity, gives 'care' or 'foresight' to the emperor and is one of five imperial virtues. This one is defined by Norena as a 'benevolent force that shaped the universe; a quality associated with the gods; and an attribute that helped define a political leader'.[41] It is of interest that from

40. J. E. Lendon, *Empire of Honour: The Art of Government in the Roman World* (Oxford: Clarendon Press, 1997).

41. C. F. Norena, "Values and Virtues: The Ethical Profile of the Emperor," in *Impe-*

the time of Tiberius to that of Trajan, coins make reference to this with Augustus portrayed as *Providentia Augusta* with the sceptre and the orb, the insignias of absolute power.[42] The decreed then proceeds —

> and with his appearance Caesar exceeded hopes of all those who antic-ipated good tidings (εὐαγγέλια) before us, not only surpassing those who had been benefactors before him, but (ἀλλά) not even leaving those to come any hope of surpassing him in the future. (*ll.* 36-39)

This is indeed a most extravagant accolade and an incredible claim made for Augustus over against any of his successors. It goes some way to ex-plain in part why his Principate was promoted as 'the Golden Age'. (See pp. 44-47.)

The inscription proceeded to declare that 'the birthday of our god (γενέθλιος ἡμέρα τοῦ θεοῦ) marked for the world the beginning of good news (εὐαγγελίων) through his coming' (*ll.* 40-41). The parallel for the first Christians would be an angelic announcement to the shepherds of Jesus' birth. 'Fear not, behold I bring you good news (εὐαγγελίζομαι) of great joy that will be for all the people, for to you this day in the city of David is a saviour who is Christ [Messiah] the Lord' (Luke 2:10-12). There was already an ideological clash with the saviour of the Christians and that of the citizens of Rome.

For such an innovative recommendation for honouring Augustus, the golden crown promised to the 'winner' had to go to Maximus, their provincial benefactor.

> [A]nd since Asia decreed in Smyrna, when the proconsul was Lucius Volcacius Tullus and the secretary was Papion from Dios Hieron, that the person who found the greatest honours for the god should have a crown, and Paulus Fabius Maximus the proconsul, as bene-factor (εὐεργετής) of the province having been sent from that god's right hand and mind [Augustus' appointee] together with other men through whom he bestowed benefits on the province, the size of which benefit no speech would be adequate to relate, has found something unknown until now to the Greeks for the honour of Augustus, that the

---

rial Ideals in the Roman West: Representation, Circulation, Power (Cambridge: Cambridge University Press, 2011), ch. 2, esp. pp. 92-99 on *providentia* and the definition, p. 93.

42. Norena, "Values and Virtues: The Ethical Profile of the Emperor," p. 96, nn. 212-13.

birthday of Augustus should begin the time for life (ἄρχειν τῷ βίῳ τὸν χρόνον). (*ll.* 41-49)

Then followed the decree's traditional stipulation —

for this reason, with good fortune (τύχῃ ἀγαθῇ) and for our salvation (σωτηρίᾳ) it has been decreed (δεδόχθαι) by the Greeks of Asia that the New Year's first month shall begin for all the cities on the ninth day before the Kalends of October (23 September) that is the birthday of Augustus. (*ll.* 49-52)

The implications of this were far reaching in Asia, where the commencement of each New Year was altered for the reasons outlined in the decree.[43] However, the first Christians would see their Messiah's birthday as the beginning of all things given the benefits that his reign inaugurated (John 1:1-14).

Lastly, in any decree the obligations or consequences of such honouring were spelt out for all to see.

[I]n order that (ὅπως) always the day might correspond in each city, the Greeks shall use the Greek day along with the Roman; they shall make the first month — called 'Caesar', as previously decreed — begin with the ninth day before the Calends of October, the birthday of Caesar; and that the crown voted for (τὸν ἐψηφισμένον στέφανον) the one who found the greatest honours for Caesar shall be given to Maximus the proconsul. (*ll.* 52-57)

Given the imperial blessing brought to the empire, it was only right that each city in the province would change the name of the first month of the calendar year from 'Dios' to 'Caesareius', and the New Year would appropriately begin on the birthday of Augustus, recorded as the 'most propitious' day.

Apart from the traditional gold crown for benefactors that would be publicly conferred, there was a long-term reward because of what Maximus did. It 'should also forever be proclaimed of him at the athletic festival of the Roman *Augusti* held at Pergamum' (*ll.* 57-59).

---

43. G. Forsythe, *Time in Roman Religion: 1,000 years of Religious History* (New York and London: Routledge, 2012), p. 128.

Maximus was also declared to have been sent by 'that right hand and mind of the god', i.e., Augustus (*l.* 45) — his was an imperial appointment. The many imperial benefits that came to the province were described as being of such 'a size as to beggar description'. Furthermore, he devised an ingenious way 'to honour Augustus, something hitherto unknown to the Asian Greeks: to begin time from his birthday' (*ll.* 48-49). Syme, therefore, rightly describes Maximus as a Roman official whose 'loyalties concentrated on devotion to the ruler'[44] and were recorded in this provincial-wide, invaluable and highly visible inscription.

Later another senior Roman official would also take it upon himself to promote directly additional imperial cult activities in the province of Achaea. Publius Cornelius Scipio, a proconsul of Asia soon after Maximus, assiduously did the same in Messene and also encouraged leading cities of Achaea to act similarly. (See pp. 55-59.) While some see the Messene inscription of Scipio as the best example of a proconsul directly promoting imperial cultic veneration, that of Maximus certainly parallels, if not surpasses it.

The proconsul in an official letter to the League of Asia had ruled —

A decree must be drafted by the League of Asia encompassing all his virtues so that our plan for the honouring of Augustus may abide forever. I shall order the decree to be inscribed on a pillar and erected in the temple, having instructed that the ordinance be inscribed in both languages [Greek and Latin].[45]

The League of Asia responded, noting Apollonius, the provincial high priest, had indicated where the decree should be appropriately placed.

Decreed by the Greeks of Asia, on the proposal of the high-priest [of the imperial cult] . . . that the letter of the proconsul and the decree of Asia should be placed in the sacred precinct of Roma and Augustus . . . inscribed on pillars of white marble in the leading cities of the assize-districts and that these pillars are placed in the temples of Caesar.[46]

44. Syme, *The Augustan Aristocracy*, p. 408.

45. *OGIS* 458 and *SEG* 4, 490. Ehrenberg and Jones, *Documents Illustrating the Reigns of Augustus & Tiberius*, no. 98. See *ll.* 26-30 for the citation.

46. Ehrenberg and Jones, *Documents Illustrating the Reigns of Augustus & Tiberius*, no. 98, *ll.* 3-85 and the Latin decree, *ll.* 31-32, 62-67.

The intention was that all citizens in the province would be able to read it in the imperial cult temples of *Roma* and Augustus when engaged in imperial cultic veneration as a constant reminder of the blessings of this imperial golden age.

(iv) Augustus, the 'Saviour of the Common Race of Men'

It would seem that the city of Halicarnassus in the neighbouring province of Caria was not to be outdone by the League of Asia's resolution. Their inscription reflects the same theme of the blessings of the 'messianic' age of Augustus.

It begins by laying out the reasons for the one being honoured with the traditional epigraphic introductory reason for the official action: 'since' (ἐπεί).

> [S]ince the eternal and immortal nature (φύσις) of everything has bestowed upon mankind the greatest good with extraordinary bene-factions by bringing Caesar Augustus in our blessed time, the father of his own country, divine Roma and ancestral Zeus, saviour of the common race of men (σωτῆρα τοῦ κοινοῦ τῶν ἀνθρώπων γένους), whose providence has not only fulfilled all the prayers but also ex-ceeded them (οὗ ἡ πρόνοια τὰς πάντων εὐχὰς οὐκ ἐπλήρωσε μόνον ἀλλὰ καὶ ὑπερῆσεν).[47]

The origins of the benefits are attributed to the 'gods', i.e., 'the god-dess *Roma* and the ancestral Zeus', who are lauded for sending Augustus. These blessings had been given to everyone through him, hence the ac-colade that Augustus is 'saviour of the common race of men' (σωτῆρα τοῦ κοινοῦ τῶν ἀνθρώπων γένους). The term 'saviour' was an ambiguous one in the ancient world and refers not only to the one who rescues from danger or death, but could also be used of the one who brings 'health' and 'blessings'. The benefits of this 'saviour' were said to be given not only to the upper class but, as the inscription stresses, to all who were described as 'the common race of men' regardless of ethnicity or social status — a competitor for Jesus as the saviour and benefactor of all humanity.

The blessings of this imperial saviour far exceeded the ideals or

---

47. *IBM* 4, 1, no. 894.

prayers that were offered with thankfulness to 'the providence' (ἡ πρόνοια). This 'was a quality associated with the gods; an attribute that helped define a political leader . . . in principle any action on the part of the emperor could be attributed to it'. As one of the five virtues attributed to the emperor,[48] it is used here too of Augustus. The results of this quality were further explained.

> For on the one hand (μὲν γάρ) land and sea are at peace (εἰρήνευουσι μὲν γὰρ γῆ καὶ θάλαττα) and also cities flourish with good or-der (εὐνομία), and both concord and prosperity (ὁμονοίᾳ τε καὶ εὐετηρίᾳ) — and both the highest and productive of all good, as mankind is filled with high hopes for the future (ἐλπίδων μὲν τὸ μέλλον) and high spirits for the present (εὐθυμία[ς] δὲ εἰς τ[ὸ] παρὸν ἀνθρώπων ἐνπεπλησμέννων), with festivals, dedications, sacrifices and hymns.[49]

It records that theirs was not only a peace that had followed decades of war fought on land and sea[50] but was also something that cities longed for and its citizens were now said to be experiencing, i.e., 'good order' (εὐνομίαι) as well as 'concord' (ὁμονοία). Epstein's book whose title epitomises the problem of the Roman Republic, *Personal Enmity in Roman Politics 218-43 B.C.*, documents the strife and jealousy that were also endemic in public life in the Roman Republic.[51] The need for a god called 'Harmony' (*Concordia* or Ὁμονοία) among individuals was no less so in the imperial era, but the reference here is to one that was both city- and provincial-wide in the empire.[52]

48. For divine providence as one of the virtues of emperors, see Norena, "Values and Virtues: The Ethical Profile of the Emperor," pp. 92-99, with the citations on p. 93. An altar to *Ara Providentiae Auguestae* was erected in Rome. From the time of Tiberius coins were struck with that image and inscription; see pp. 93, 97.

49. *IBM* 4, 1, no. 894.

50. While this may have been so in the province, the reality was that 'this period, in spirit and in fact, was one of aggressive expansion', but poetic licence and imperial, provin-cial and civic propaganda argued that it was not the case that 'the Roman peace of the prin-cipate (of Augustus) [was] an object of admiration' on its Eastern borders; see B. H. Isaac, *The Limits of Empire: The Roman Army in the East* (Oxford: Clarendon Press, 1990), p. 1.

51. D. Epstein, *Personal Enmity in Roman Politics 218-43 B.C.* (London and New York: Routledge, 1987).

52. Hence the number of orations with the title of 'concord' in Dio Chrysostom (*Ors.* 39-41) and others addressing the same issue on the need but inability of cities in the East to

The accolades continue. What Augustus provided 'is both the highest and productive of all good' (ἀκμή τε καὶ φορὰ παντός ἐστιν ἀγαθοῦ). It is significant that 'the office of the *aediles cerealis* also functioned with few practical responsibilities, as the emperor in effect took over the oversight of grain distribution in the city', i.e., Rome.[53] There is then a reference to provincial imperial cultic celebrations 'as mankind was filled with high hopes for the future and high spirits for the present, with festivals, dedications, sacrifices and hymns.'

Regrettably the next twenty-five lines of this long inscription have been lost, as it would have been highly informative to discover yet further details of cultic veneration. The next surviving section indicates that not only was this resolution to be inscribed but also to be placed in the precincts of the imperial cult temple of *Roma* and Augustus in Halicarnassus and in other cities in order to be seen by its inhabitants.

> ... and that a copy of this decree be inscribed and placed in the precincts of Rome and Augustus by the high-priest, Gaius Julius M[..t]o[u] ... friend of Caesar, and in the other cities by the magistrates, and that the altars be dedicated on 25ᵗ November by the priests and magistrates ... while people keep festival (ἑορταζόντων τῶν ἀνθρώπων).[54]

This was to be done 'by the high-priest' (ὑπο τοῦ ἀρχιερέως), who is also cited as 'Caesar's friend' (φιλοκαίσαρος). The first office was for the provincial imperial cult, and it required the approval of the emperor and the Senate in Rome. The person had to be a distinguished provincial, as this appointment was 'the summit of a man's career' in the East.[55] Syme aptly comments, 'When religion is the care of the State in an oligarchical society, it is evident that sacerdotal preferment will be conferred, not upon the pious and learned, but for social distinction and for political success.'[56] Clearly there was no dichotomy between political and cultic issues in the Roman Empire.

---

achieve this because of the nature of political life. Many coins were issued throughout the empire bearing the term 'Harmony'.

53. *IBM* 4, 1, no. 894.

54. Sadly *ll.* 14-39 have not survived, nor have the concluding *ll.* 48-55, but given the extravagant language used one can rightly speculate that it continued in that similar effusive vein, praising the golden rule of Augustus.

55. Fishwick, *Imperial Cult in the Latin West,* III.2, p. 306.

56. Syme, *The Roman Revolution,* p. 382.

The other title, 'Caesar's friend', 'served to indicate to the inhabitants of the Empire the importance of those sent to govern or acting as supporters'.[57] Any attempted reconstruction of the *cognomen* of 'Gaius Julius M[..t]o[u]' to date fails to identify him, as there is none cited in the Prosopographical Index of 'Friends of Caesar'.[58] The closest is 'Julius Montanus', who from the time of Tiberius was a poet whom Seneca the Younger described as 'a middling good poet, noted for his friendship with Tiberius. . . . He always filled his poems with a generous sprinkling of sunrises and sunsets'.[59] Certainly the poetic nature of the lauding of Augustus suggests someone of a poetic bent, but there is no secure evidence that the high priest was the framer of this official resolution. His identity remains unresolved.

Altars were dedicated in Halicarnassus by 'Gaius Julius M[..]t]o[u]'. The layout of the acropolis of Halicarnassus lent itself to a provincial imperial cult centre.[60] The record adds, 'and in the other cities (ἐν δὲ ἄλλαις πόλεσι) by the magistrates while the people celebrated the festival'.[61]

A further inscription from Halicarnassus from the same period has divine honours being given 'to the Emperor Caesar [Augustus], god' (αὐτοκράτορι Καίσαρι θεῷ) and one of his two adopted sons of Augustus and an heir, the young' (Καίσαρι νεότητος), presumably Gaius. 'Augustus allowed the imperial princes to receive divine honours', to which this inscription bears witness.[62] These official decrees spelt out how, in the time of Augustus, great blessings were said to have been given to all inhabitants of this province by this 'son of the divine Julius', who was also declared to be 'the most divine Caesar'.

---

57. Crook, *'Amici Principis'*, in *Consilium Principis*, ch. 3, cit. p. 24. He notes further on p. 23 that the term *'Amicus* was used in official documents of provincial governors, procurators, equestrian secretaries and in one notable case of two distinguished residents of Alexandria with no official status at all'.

58. For extant evidence of 353 individuals designated 'friends of Caesar' that cover the whole period of the Roman Empire see Crook, *Consilium Principis*, pp. 148-89.

59. Seneca the Younger, *Epistle* 122.11.

60. D. Fishwick, *Imperial Cult in the Latin West: Provincial Centre; Provincial Cult* (Leiden: E. J. Brill, 2004), III.3, pp. 1-2.

61. *IBM* 4, 1, no. 894.

62. G. Hirschfeld, *The Inscriptions of the Greek East in the British Museum* (Oxford: Clarendon Press, 1893), IV.1, no. 892, *ll.* 29-31, p. 59.

IV. The Golden 'Messianic' Ages of Augustus and Nero[63]

First-century poets reflecting on imperial propaganda coined the phrase "The Golden Age" to describe the divine, empire-wide benefits initiated by Augustus and "The Second Golden Age" of Nero. There were also claims that what today would be termed 'utopia' had arrived. Wistrand in his book *Felicitas Imperatoria* chose the term 'messianic' to aptly and succinctly describe the nature of the peace and benefits Rome's imperial gods were said to have bestowed on 'the whole world', i.e., the Roman Empire. He observes —

> Towards the end of the republic another idea of *felicitas* came to Rome from the Hellenistic East. There people had long lived in expectation of a Saviour of the world, chosen by gods from his birth to introduce a Golden Age of peace, justice and general prosperity. This 'Messianic' idea of *felicitas* was attached to the Roman Emperor. Intensely propagated, the ruler-cult became the religious force that united and sustained the Empire.[64]

Wistrand also notes the peace that Augustus brought to the world —

> When the Hellenistic conception of a World Saviour and a new Golden Age first came to Rome and took the form of grateful confidence in Augustus and the *Pax Augusta,* men seem to have felt a new wonderful hope, a new faith in Rome's future. It is now that the phrase *Roma Aeterna* is coined.[65]

While Wistrand makes no comparison with Jesus' divine Messianic blessings of an 'eternal' kingdom with the heavenly Jerusalem as its everlasting capital, and the prophecy of the destruction of the Roman Empire's 'eternal' city in Revelation 18, his choice of the descriptive term 'messianic' is an apposite ideological one. How could the first generation of Christians in any way endorse such a concept of Caesar's messianic kingdom while acknowledging that of the Kingdom of God?

---

63. J. D. Crossan and J. L. Reed use the evocative chapter heading, "The Golden Age or as Golden as It Gets," in *In Search of Paul: How Jesus' Apostle Opposed Rome's Empire with God's Kingdom* (London: SPCK, 2005), ch. 3.

64. E. Wistrand, *Felicitas Imperatoria,* Studia Graeca et Latina Gothoburgensia (Göteborg: Berlings, 1987), p. 6.

65. Wistrand, *Felicitas Imperatoria,* p. 64.

Following the assassination of Julius Caesar 'it is said that a comet appeared on seven nights during the games staged by Octavian in Caesar's name, as if giving approval to the senatorial decision to deify him. The comet was interpreted as Caesar's soul rising to heaven, and as the inauguration of a new Golden Age *(saeculum aureum)* under the rule of a new god.'[66]

Of this first golden age the poet Virgil (70-19 B.C.) declared of Augustus —

> And in your consulship, Pollio, yes, yours, shall this glorious age begin, and the mighty months commence their march; under your sway any lingering traces of our guilt shall become void and release the earth form its continual dread. He shall have the gift of divine life, shall see heroes mingled with gods, and shall himself be seen by them, and shall rule the world to which his father's prowess brought peace.[67]

Evidence exists that Julio-Claudian emperors sought to promote their Principate as a golden 'messianic' age. There is also evidence that in the time of Nero some sought to present his Principate as a second Golden Age in messianic terms in the same way that was done for Augustus. The dating of the works of the poet Calpurnius Siculus have been determined from his first, fourth and seventh Eclogues; the first was written soon after Nero became emperor in October, A.D. 54 or early in 55, and the fourth in 55 while the seventh was composed in 57.[68]

> Amid the untroubled peace, the Golden Age springs to a second birth; at last kindly Themis, throwing off the gathered dust of her mourning,

---

66. J. Bardill, *Constantine, Divine Emperor of the Christian Golden Age* (Cambridge: Cambridge University Press, 2011), p. 44, citing Pliny, *Natural History* 2.23, Dio Cassius, *Roman History* 45.7.1, Virgil, *Aeneid* 8.681. This ideology was so implanted in the minds of those in the Roman Empire that Constantine thought it appropriate to plunder the concept as a propaganda theme when he 'Christianized' its vast domain. See chapter 7, "Constantine and Christianity," and chapter 9, "Constantine as Christ".

67. Virgil, *Eclogue* 4, *ll.* 11-17.

68. G. B. Townend, "Calpurnius Siculus and the Munus Neronis," *JRS* 70 (1980): 166-76, who refers to his evidence which mentioned the appearance of a comet, 1.77-83, a fact verified by Chinese astronomical records. See also R. Mayer, "Calpurnius Siculus: Technique and Date," *JRS* 70 (1980): 175-76, for the additional arguments supporting the Neronean dating and refuting the discussion of E. J. Champlin, "The Life and Times of Calpurnius Siculus," *JRS* 68 (1978): 95-110.

returns to earth; blissful ages attend the youthful prince who pleaded a successful case for the *Iuli* of the mother town.[69]

For long, Meliboeus, have I been pondering verses, verses of no woodland ring but fit to celebrate the golden age, to praise even that very god who is sovereign over the nations and cities and toga-clad peace.[70]

Do you see how the green woods are hushed at the sound of Caesar's name? ... Yes, all the earth and every nation adores him. He is beloved of the gods; as you see, the arbutus-tree pays him silent homage; at the sound of his name the sluggish earth has warmed to life and yielded flowers; invoke him, and in his honour the wood spreads its thick, perfumed foliage, and the spellbound tree breaks into bud again. As soon as the earth felt his divine influence, crops began to come in rich abundance, where furrows previously disappointed hope; at length the beans scarce rattle in their well-filled pods: no harvest is choked with the spread of barren tare, or whitens with unproductive oats.

O you gods, I pray recall only after a long span of life this youth, whom you, I know it well, have sent us from heaven itself: ... let him be a god and yet loath to exchange his palace for the sky.[71]

His Eclogue concludes with a request that this poem be taken to 'the Emperor-God'. He stood in the shoes of Virgil, but glorified the reign of Nero as a new golden age modeled on Virgil's *Eclogue*.[72]

Nero's tutor before he became emperor at age sixteen years and nine months was Seneca the Younger, who from then on was known as the 'first citizen', *amicus principus*. He clearly was the most influential person in Nero's life. In his *Apocolocyntosis* he refers to 'The Ages of Gold spun out in a lovely line' and 'As age by age the pretty thread runs down the golden days'.[73] 'The theme of the Golden Age inaugurated by the new emperor

---

69. Calpurnius Siculus, *Eclogue* 1, *ll.* 42-45. Themis was the Greek goddess of justice. See also Suetonius, *Nero* 7 and Tacitus, *Annals* xii.58 for confirmation of a speech young Nero delivered on behalf of the inhabitants of Illium, and Townend, "Calpurnius Siculus and the Munus Neronis," pp. 108-9.

70. Calpurnius Siculus, *Eclogue* 4, *ll.* 5-8.

71. Calpurnius Siculus, *Eclogue* 4, *ll.* 96-97, 107-16, 137. The reference is to the divine emperor, Nero, residing in his palace in the Palatine Hill and not undergoing an apotheosis at this time.

72. Calpurnius Siculus, *Eclogue* 4, *l.* 158.

73. Seneca the Younger, *Apocolocyntosis* 3.4.

is not infrequent in Neronian propaganda, being used also by Calpurnius Siculus and perhaps reflected in Nero's Golden House'.[74]

It is significant just how long the concept of the 'golden age' remained embedded in the Roman psyche. It would later be replicated in the widespread propaganda of Constantine the Great, who was portrayed as having inaugurated a brilliant golden age, this time a Christian one. The very title of Bardill's book *Constantine, Divine Emperor of the Christian Golden Age* indicates the longevity of this concept. Hence Constantine exploited this by promising its Christianizing would result in another age to which the accolade 'golden' would be an appropriate term.[75]

In conclusion, the initiative and arguments used by Rome's proconsul in Asia in promoting province-wide divine honours for Augustus contradicts any notion that the veneration of emperors was exclusively a local or provincial idea used to curry favour with, and secure benefits from, the emperor. Its promotion by an emperor's provincial vice-gerent was not simply a peculiarity of the province of Asia. Another proconsul of Asia would subsequently move to the province of Achaea and take initiatives that, after his departure, would continue to see the giving of further divine honours to the imperial family in its major cities including its capital, Corinth. (See chapter 7.)

It cannot be said that during the eras of the Julio-Claudian emperors, imperial cultic activities in any way lay dormant. Multiple cultic activities were not only alive but thrived in the era of the first Christians, as divine honours were skilfully woven into the cultic and festive activities of inhabitants in the East of the empire. All this helps explain how divine honours for the Caesars spread so rapidly and only furthered the quandary of ancient historians — this had to be a major issue for the first Christians.

---

74. H. Hine in his essay explores the presentation of Nero, "Rome, the Cosmos, and the Emperor in Seneca's *Natural Questions*," *JRS* 96 (2006): 63-67.

75. J. Bardill, *Constantine, Divine Emperor of the Christian Golden Age* (Cambridge: Cambridge University Press, 2012), pp. 30-33. It is interesting that just as statues of Roman emperors as gods traditionally were unclothed, Bardill reproduces a bronze statue of Constantine also naked.

CHAPTER 3

Honours to, for and by the Caesars and Reciprocal Benefits

New Testament and some related studies on the Roman world have traditionally assumed that there was 'the imperial cult'. This chapter commences by exploring whether this sufficiently and adequately describes the reality of giving divine honours to the Caesars that the first Christians faced. Primary evidence shows that such cultic honours involved sacrifices and prayers to the gods for the safety of the emperor, and also sacrifices and prayers to the emperor as a divinely venerated 'god' and 'son of a god'. The emperor also had a strategic cultic rôle. He himself offered up sacrifices and prayers to the gods for the Roman Empire's well-being in his priestly office as *pontifex maximus* — literally the 'greatest bridge builder' between the gods and his empire, a title rendered in Greek in imperial inscriptions as 'high priest' (ἀρχιερεύς), and one also used of Jesus.

Here then were imperial cultic activities or rôles 'for', 'to' and 'by' the reigning emperor. All are encapsulated in one official inscription from the city of Sardis in the province of Asia. This is not an isolated piece of evidence. There is another example of a senior Roman official in the province of Achaea, a former proconsul of Asia, vigorously promoting the three-fold cultic activities in all its leading cities before Paul's era. (See chapter 7.)

This chapter will examine an inscription from Sardis, again from the Province of Asia, that encapsulates (I) the trilogy of activities epitomising imperial cultic veneration; and (II) Augustus' response to citizens, showing the official connection between cultic activities and imperial reciprocal benefits sought for their devotion to him and later emperors.

I. Imperial Cultic Rites and Roles 'to', 'for' and 'by' the Emperor

How have ancient historians defined Roman cultic phenomena? Hillard rightly argued we should not speak of *the* imperial cult but imperial *cults*.

> Absolute consistency probably ought not be sought. . . . Contradictions were inherent in the cult(s) (which excited various responses). Superstition, political manipulation, opposition and criticism, acquiescence, the desire for material advancement and imperial assertions all had their part. Contradictions, rather than bedevilling the study of the imperial cult, help to explain its force.[1]

Given the vast empire that was 'embraced' by the conquest of diverse kingdoms and cultures in the East and West, he suggested, 'The controversy that is likely to occur is when any attempt is made to define exactly what was going on in the imperial cult.' This he sees as 'the truly sticky question' in what he prefers to call 'the imperial cults'.[2]

One particular event prompted the city of Sardis to promulgate an official resolution. The occasion was the transition of Gaius, the grandson of Augustus, to manhood in a ceremony celebrated with the official putting on the traditional *toga virilis* in Rome. It was an important milestone, as Augustus had already adopted Gaius along with his brother, Lucius, as his sons for the purpose of making them his successors. This resolution recorded all three of the imperial cultic activities, namely prayers 'to' Augustus, sacrifices to the gods 'for' Augustus and his family, and his cultic response as the *pontifex maximus* involving his intercession to the gods for the welfare of the empire.

(i) Prayers to Augustus

> Since Gaius Iulius Caesar, the eldest of the sons of Augustus, has put on the *toga* most earnestly prayed for (and) radiant with every decoration, in place of the one with purple border, and there is joy among all men

1. T. W. Hillard, "Vespasian's Death-Bed Attitude to His Impending Deification," in *Religion in the Ancient World: New Themes and Approaches,* ed. M. Dillon (Amsterdam: Hakkert, 1996), pp. 197-98.

2. Hillard, "Vespasian's Death-Bed Attitude to His Impending Deification," pp. 197-98, n. 33.

to see the prayers that have been awakened everywhere (by this event) to Augustus (τῷ Σεβαστῷ) on behalf of his sons.[3]

Firstly, the decree specifically states there had been 'prayers to Augustus for his sons' (τῷ Σεβαστῳ τὰς ὑπὲρ τῶν παίδων εὐχάς) (*l.* 9), and in future, there would be 'prayers offered through the sacred heralds for his [Gaius'] safety' (ὑπὲρ τῆς σωτηρίας) (*ll.* 11-12). The Sardinians had also officially resolved that the statue of Gaius would be 'jointly consecrated and set up in his father's temple' (τῷ τοῦ πατρὸς ἐνιδρύοντας ναῷ), i.e., the temple of Augustus (*ll.* 13-14).

The day on which Gaius assumed the toga in 5 B.C. was also incorporated into cities' imperial calendars to be celebrated annually, just as it had been for Augustus when he assumed the *toga virilis*. According to the Calendar of Cumae in Italy (A.D. 4-14) it would be celebrated on 18 October.[4] This milestone in the life of an heir of Augustus was now a fixed high and holy day in that city. Elsewhere in Italy in Puteoli 'Lucius Calpurnius, son of Lucius, at his own expense built a temple for Augustus *(templum Augusto)* with its adornment', where it can be assumed prayers and other cultic activities were offered to the statue of Augustus.[5] Many inscriptions attest to prayers and sacrifices offered for the safety of the emperor. After the Sejanus conspiracy against the emperor Tiberius failed in A.D. 31, it was seen as an act of loyalty to pray for the emperor's preservation of the empire.[6]

(ii) Sacrificing to the Gods for the Divine Augustus and His Family

Secondly, in Sardis the *strategies,* i.e., officials, of the year were to offer up sacrifices to the gods, but this celebration would not involve just a few cultic officials.

---

3. *IGRR* 4, 1756, *ll.* 7-10.

4. *CIL* 10, 8375. See Duncan Fishwick, *The Imperial Cult in the Latin West: Studies in the Ruler Cult in the Western Provinces* (Leiden: E. J. Brill, 1993), II.1, p. 490.

5. *CIL* 10, 1613.

6. For the Sejanus conspiracy and its legal implications see B. Levick, "Tiberius and the Law: The Development of *Maiestas,*" in *Tiberius the Politician* (London: Thames & Hudson, 1976), ch. 11. For example, inscriptions in Corinth record the sacrifices for 'the protection of the emperor' (Providentia Aug.) and for public safety *(Salus Publica)*. A. B. West, *Corinth: Latin Inscriptions 1896-1926* (Cambridge: Cambridge University Press), 8.2, nos. 15, 110.

[O]ur city on the occasion of such a great good fortune has ruled that the day which completed his transition from boy to manhood to be a holy day, on which each year all our people in their brightest clothing shall wear wreaths, and [on which] sacrifices shall be performed by the *strategoi* of the year to the gods (τοῖς θεοῖς), and prayers shall be offered through the sacred heralds for his (i.e. Gaius') safety (ὑπὲρ τῆς σωτηρίας), and (on which) his image shall be jointly consecrated and set up in his father's temple, and on that (day) on which our city received the glad tidings (εὐανγελίσθη) and this decree was passed, on that day too wreaths shall be worn and most splendid sacrifices performed to the gods (θυσίας τοῖς θεοῖς). (*ll.*10-15)

The city authorities 'ruled all were to wear wreaths' (ἔκρινεν . . . στεφανηφορεῖν ἅπαντας) (*l.* 11). This was to be done not only when his statue was to be consecrated in the temple dedicated to his father, but also on the anniversary of Gaius' rite of passage to manhood. The resolution clause of the inscription stipulated 'this decree was passed, on that day too wreaths shall be worn' (*ll.* 14-15).

There were also to be annual sacrifices, i.e., 'most splendid sacrifices performed to the gods' (θυσίας τοῖς θεοῖς ἐκπρεπεστάτας ἐπιτελέσαι) (*l.* 15) and when the statue of Gaius was consecrated in the temple of Augustus (*ll.* 13-14). As well, coins of Sardis recording the divinity of the imperial family were later minted in the time of Nero with the inscription 'Nero Caesar' and also the 'goddess Octavia' (ΘΕΑΝ ΟΚΤΑΟΥΙΑΝ) portraying a bust of her with a wreath made out of ears of corn.[7] Gaius was also fêted in 'the Games of the Imperial Family in Sardis' with 'Gaius Caesar (victor) in the Isthmian boys stadion-race' *c.* A.D. 5.[8]

Fishwick has suggested that making a dichotomy between the human and divine in relation to first-century thinking is anachronistic.

> To a modern mind, accustomed to the Judaeo-Christian concept of God as a single, all-powerful, good and eternal being, the notion of paying cult to a man as though he were a god seems a very strange one indeed. But once the nature of divine honours is properly grasped it becomes much easier to understand that for a man to be

---

7. *RPC* nos. 2997-3001.
8. *SIG*³ 1065.

given *isotheoi timai* [honours equal to the gods] in no way implies any recognition.[9]

He further observes, 'The boundary between gods and man was narrower in Graeco-Roman belief than in ours and more fluid. . . . So if a man performed meritorious and extraordinary deeds, if he was endowed with great beauty or strength, that was recognized as manifestations of a godlike quality and a title to "divinity" with its appropriate recognition.'[10]

Friesen makes the same observation when it came to first-century sacrifices.

[T]he ancient imperial sacrifices should not be understood as a way of indicating who was divine and who was human. Particular kinds of sacrifice were appropriate in the context of particular relationships. It was appropriate for the inhabitants to sacrifice to the emperors because the emperors functioned like gods in relation to them. It was also correct for the inhabitants of the empire to sacrifice to the gods on behalf of the emperors because the emperors were not independent of the gods. . . . The [sacrifices] were two complementary aspects of the larger sacrificial system.[11]

He further explains another seeming contradiction when it came 'to prayers to the emperor and to the gods *on behalf of* the emperor'. He concludes, 'the twofold prayer accurately reflected imperial theology: the gods looked after the emperors, who in turn looked after the concerns of the gods on earth for the benefit of humanity. Imperial authority ordered human society, and divine authority protected the emperors'.[12] It was therefore appropriate to pray to the emperor as one would to other gods. Much later than our era, Aelius Aristides (A.D. *c.* 117–*c.* 189) delivered a speech to the imperial court in Rome indicating that a person 'stands up, praises and reverences him, and offers a double

---

9. Fishwick, *The Imperial Cult in the Latin West*, I.1, p. 33.

10. Fishwick, *The Imperial Cult in the Latin West*, I.1, p. 33.

11. S. J. Friesen, *Twice Neokoros: Ephesus, Asia and the Cult of the Flavian Imperial Family* (Leiden: E. J. Brill, 1993), p. 150; cf. Fishwick, *The Imperial Cult in the Latin West*, I.1, p. 233, who argues that in the West the relationship of the emperors to the gods was undefined.

12. Friesen, *Twice Neokoros: Ephesus, Asia and the Cult of the Flavian Imperial Family*, p. 152.

prayer (διπλῆν εὐχὴν), one to the gods on the emperor's behalf (τὴν μὲν ὑπὲρ αὐτοῦ τοῖς θεοῖς) and the other concerning his personal affairs to the emperor himself (τὴν δὲ αὐτῷ ἐκείνῳ περὶ τῶν ἑαυτοῦ)'.[13] He saw no difficulty calling this 'a double prayer', indicating it was a normal cultic practice in Rome itself.

It was decreed by 'the Council and the People' of Sardis who resolved that a copy of the decree sealed with the public seal would be personally conveyed to Augustus in Rome by their named envoys (*ll.* 17-19). This official endorsement was one done as part of diplomatic protocol, presumably to assure him of its authenticity.

The cultic celebrations in Sardis were not isolated events by a few citizens or an idiosyncratic occurrence in one city in the province of Asia seeking imperial favours. The *Koinon* of Asia honoured the Sardinian envoys 'for what was written below' (*l.* 5), i.e., the Sardinian decree that was preceded by an official commendation by the *Koinon* of Asia:

> The *Koinon* of the Greeks of Asia and the people of the Sardinians and the Elder Citizens honoured Menagones (son) Isidoros (grandson) of Menogenes by which is written below.[14]

This Sardinian inscription only highlights what Millar and Mitchell observed (see pp. 3-4). Christians would have to deal with the high-profile imperial cult celebrations with all citizens wearing wreaths and taking part in sacrifices performed to the gods on the imperial high and holy days. This would be no less true for those whose presence in Sardis was later recorded in Revelation 3:1-6. Some had 'not soiled their garments' and thus will 'walk with me in white'. Others were called upon to repent for 'soiling' their garments that were part of the dress code when participating in imperial cult processions (Rev. 3:4).

(iii) Augustus as the High Priest (Pontifex Maximus) for the Roman Empire

Augustus' response to the Sardinian embassy is recorded in the same inscription.

13. Aelius Aristides, *Or.* 16.32.
14. *IGRR* 4, 1756, ll. 4-6.

Imperator Caesar, son of god (θεοῦ υἱός), Augustus, *pontifex maximus* (ἀρχιερεύς), holder of the tribunician power for the nineteenth time (5 B.C.) to the Sardinian magistrates, Council and People, greetings. Your envoys, Iollas (son) of Metrodores and Menogenes (son) of Isidoros, (grandson) of Menogenes, met with me in Rome and gave me the decree from you by means of which you disclosed what had been decreed by you concerning yourselves and rejoiced with me at the translation to manhood of the elder of my sons. (*ll.* 23-27)

He uses his traditional titles, 'Imperator Caesar, son of god, Augustus', to which 'high priest' was added. In 17 B.C. his sacrifice and prayers were recorded —

in the Campus, by the Tiber, Imperator Caesar Augustus sacrificed to the divine Moerae nine she-lambs, offered whole, in the Greek manner, and in the same manner, nine she-goats and he prayed as follows: Moerae, as it is written in your regard in those books, that each and everything may prosper for the Roman people I beseech you and pray that you increase the empire and majesty of the Roman people . . . at war and at home . . . that you would bestow upon the Roman people . . . and the legions of the Roman people eternal safety, victory and health; and that you favour the Roman people . . . keep safe the state of the Roman people . . . be well disposed and propitious to the Roman people . . . myself, my family, my household.[15]

In Rome he was supported by a number of cultic officials,[16] so his rôle was neither just ceremonial nor titular, and not, as Rutgers concluded 'perhaps to a very limited extent, religiously'.[17] Beard-North-Price agree with Hillard: 'There was no such thing as "*the* imperial cult".'[18] They further

---

15. *ILS* 5050.

16. These included *pontifices, vestals, flamines, arvales,* as well as those connected to the 'cult of the divine family' *(cultus domus divinae).* For the lists of names of the holders of these offices in the Julio-Claudian era, see J. Rüpke and A. Glock, *Fasti Sacerdotum: A Prosopography of Pagan, Jewish, and Christian Religious Officials in the City of Rome, 300 BC to AD 499* (Oxford: Oxford University Press, 2008), pp. 123-96.

17. L. Rutgers, *The Hidden Heritage of Diaspora Judaism* (Leuven: Peeters, 1998), p. 227.

18. M. Beard, J. North and S. Price, *Religions of Rome: A History* (Cambridge: Cambridge University Press, 1998), I, p. 348.

describe it as '[c]ult offered to, or on behalf of the emperor, his family or dead ancestors' and 'temples dedicated to the emperor had cult statues which depicted the emperor in the act of performing a sacrifice' in his rôle as the *pontifex maximus* of the whole empire.[19] They agreed with Fishwick's succinct summary following his work on relevant inscriptions in the Latin West.

> Rites *for, by* and *to* the emperor would then all be part of imperial re-
> ligion, the prevalent form of which was the direct cult of the emperor,
> modelled on the cult of the gods because the emperor functioned like
> a god in ordering human society. . . . [T]his seems to be roughly the
> position of Beard-North-Price taking cult offered to or for the emperor
> as part of a wider set of associations, which would include the image
> of the emperor offering sacrifice.[20]

An inscription from Messene in the province of Achaia in the same era as that from Sardis records the imperial cultic activities of an import-ant Roman official, Publius Cornelius Scipio, a stepson of Augustus and 'a friend of Caesar'. These were officially described actually using the same trilogy of terms. (See pp. 172-75.) An apposite summary of imperial cultic venerations then is 'cultic activities' — not a cult and certainly not a 'reli-gion' *(religio)*.[21]

II. Seeking Reciprocal Imperial Benefits by Cities and Provinces

What is not always appreciated in discussions of imperial cultic activities is that 'the imperial cult was often associated with diplomatic approaches to the emperor. Offers of cult were sometimes made in association with requests for civic privileges and other benefits. Ambassadors to the em-

---

19. Beard, North and Price, *Religions of Rome*, I, p. 350.

20. D. Fishwick, *The Imperial Cult in the Latin West*, III.3, p. 360; Beard, North and Price, *Religions of Rome*, I, p. 348.

21. *Religio* was not a first-century term but a later one, and therefore the descriptor preferred in this book is that of imperial cultic activities or rites. See E. A. Judge, "Did the Churches Compete with Cult Groups?" in *Early Christianity and Classical Culture: Compar-ative Studies in Honor of Abraham J. Malherbe,* ed. J. T. Fitzgerald, T. H. Olbricht and L. M. White (Leiden and Boston: E. J. Brill, 2003), pp. 502-3.

peror were frequently also imperial priests, as Price noted.[22] He further commented, 'The Greek diplomatic advances to Rome with offers of cult are seen as elaborate ploys intended to gain Roman favour; the fact that the emperor might decline the honours did not discourage the Greeks and shows that there were no Roman pressures on the cults.'[23]

In the highly informative Sardinian inscription discussed in the previous section the nexus between imperial cultic celebrations and political or economic civic advantages seems somewhat blatant, being openly declared in the official resolution presented to the emperor.

> And since our city has decided to send an embassy to Rome on these matters to congratulate both him [Gaius] and Augustus, the Council and the People have resolved to send envoys chosen from the best of men to give him the city's greetings and to deliver a copy of this decree, sealed with the public seal, and to discuss with Augustus both the welfare of Asia and of the city (διαλεξομένους τε τῷ Σεβαστῷ περὶ τῶν κοινῇ συμφερόντων τῇ τε Ἀσίαι καὶ τῇ πόλει). (*ll.* 17-21)

It was not merely the intention of the carefully selected members in this delegation to deliver the officially sealed copy of the resolution concerning Gaius, but they came also 'to discuss with Augustus the welfare of [the province of] Asia (i.e., the *koinon*) and our city' (*ll.* 19-20).

Augustus' response was clear, even if encoded in diplomatic language.

> Therefore I praise your zeal in showing gratitude to both me and to all my family for the benefactions you have received from me (ἐπαινῶ οὖν ὑμᾶς φιλοτειμουμένος ἀνθ' ὧν εἴς τε ἐμὲ καὶ ἐμοὺς πάντας ἐνδείκνυσθαι). (*ll.* 28-29)

He first commended them for honouring him and his appointed heir: 'I praise your zeal' (*l.* 26), along with the cultic celebrations proposed for Gaius of which he officially approved. Secondly, he fully endorsed the proposal in their official decree — 'what had been decreed by you concerning yourselves' (τά τε δόξαντα ὑμεῖν περὶ ὑμῶν δηλοῦντες) (*l.* 25), i.e., their promised prayers, future sacrifices, annual celebrations with stipulated

---

22. S. R. F. Price, *Rituals and Power: The Imperial Cult and Asia Minor* (Cambridge: Cambridge University Press, 1984), p. 243.

23. Price, *Rituals and Power,* p. 65.

festive dress codes, together with the setting up of a statue of Gaius in the temple of *Roma* and Augustus, a shrine meant for imperial veneration by provincials.

His official communication concluded by drawing their attention to the fact that he had been the originator of their existing benefits. The implication was clear that no further benefits were forthcoming. Sherk observes, 'One expects the clause ["the benefaction bestowed by me [Augustus]" *ll.* 26-27] to be followed by the usual statement that the writer, in this case Augustus, will be the author of some good for the city in the future. Its omission is noteworthy.'[24] The embassy must have returned back to Asia somewhat disappointed considering that their offer of bestowing imperial cultic honours for Gaius was accepted.

How emperors would respond to delegations could not be predicted. Embracing, modifying or declining the honours that were proposed were not unknown. There is an example of Tiberius who responded to people of Gytheum, the port for the city of Sparta in Achaea, by setting out measures as to how they would 'show piety towards my father and honours towards us', i.e., he and his mother. In commending them while declining cult to himself he stated —

> it is fitting that all mankind in general and your city in particular should observe special honours, commensurate with the size of my father's benefactions to all the world, honours fit for the gods (τῷ μεγέθει τῶν τοῦ ἐμοῦ πατρὸς εἰς ἄπαντα τὸν κόσμον εὐεργεσιῶν τὰς θεοῖς πρέπουσσας τιμάς).[25]

The citizens there had wanted 'all mankind' to know that they wished to show their 'everlasting gratitude towards the *principes*' (*ll.* 39-40).

Price notes of the delegation in the Augustan era, 'ambassadors from Mytilene showed no embarrassment in presenting more divine honours to Augustus. . . . [T]hey were to address Augustus as one who had attained the eminence and power of the gods, and promised further divine honours which would "deify him [θεοποιεῖν] even more".'[26]

---

24. R. K. Sherk, *Rome and the Greek East to the Death of Augustus* (Cambridge: Cambridge University Press, 1984), p. 135, n. 4.

25. *SEG* 11, 923(b), *ll.* 18-19.

26. Price, *Rituals and Power*, p. 243.

That he should ponder upon his own self-esteem because it is never possible to match those honours which are insignificant both in accidence and in essence with those who have attained heavenly glory and possess the eminence and power of gods. But it is more glorious than these provisions found hereafter the enthusiasm and piety of the city will not fail in anything that can deify him even more (πρὸς μηδὲν τῶν θεοποιεῖν αὐτὸν ἐπὶ πλέον δυνησομένων ἐλλείψειν τὴν τῆς πόλεως προθυμίαν καὶ εὐσέβειαν).[27]

The use of divine honours to fulfill the requirements of due deference to the emperor was 'so that our city might appear to have employed every possible honour and act of piety towards the house of the Lord Nero Augustus' (εἰ δέ τι ἵνα τούτων πᾶσαν τειμὴν καὶ εὐσέβειαν ἐκπεπληρωκυῖα εἰς τὸν τοῦ κυρίου Σεβαστοῦ Νέρωνος οἶκον).[28]

Information in inscriptions similar to the one in Sardis is like the tip of an iceberg. Local or provincial imperial cultic honours are recorded along with benefactions sought but not always given. The Roman Empire was an 'empire of honour' to cite Lendon's evocative title. His thesis is the centrality of imperial cultic honours and Rome's *modus operandi* of giving reciprocal benefits as part of its philosophy of ruling and securing further devotion to his vast empire.[29]

Augustus had created an empire with minimal provincial bureaucracy. The *imperium* was exercised through the emperor's vice-gerent, namely the governor, when operated with a small number of legal advisors for the purpose of administering criminal law, and fixing tax rates in provinces. Provincial 'tax farmers', as they were called, were private local individuals and tax-gathering was put out to private tender. Armies were not located permanently in one province but could be moved to trouble spots and, when not engaged in battles, undertook the building of their famous roads.[30]

Under the blessings of the *pax romana* cities saw themselves largely as *de facto* self-governing, apart from criminal jurisdiction. The administration of civil and commercial law continued to be the responsibility of

---

27. *IGR* 4, 39 = *OGIS* 456.

28. *IG* 7, 2713.

29. J. E. Lendon, "The Emperor," in *Empire of Honour: The Art of Government in the Roman World* (Oxford: Clarendon Press, 1997), ch. 3.

30. J. Rogan, *Roman Provincial Administration* (Stroud, UK: Amberley Publishing, 2011).

local magistrates and the *aedile,* as had been the case prior to the Roman conquest. Those who administered civic affairs were elected to honorary public office annually by the local citizen body. Rome operated a 'carrot and stick' policy, and those cities that secured imperial favours were rewarded with additional privileges. Where there was civil strife they could be punished with the loss of privileges, as is hinted in Acts 19:40.

Participation in these cultic activities in the Greek East and the Latin West in the first century provided the opportunity for everyone to express publicly undivided loyalty to those who brought them the divine blessing of the *pax romana.* These included not only peace and security, but also technological, commercial and cultural benefits. The promise of imperial cultic honours was the officially acceptable route whereby envoys might secure further benefits for their cities by sometimes innovative expressions of veneration of the emperor.[31]

Thus there was no dichotomy between politics and cults in the minds of first-century citizens. This is important to understand, as it explains just how intrusive the cult really was in the cities and lives of the inhabitants of the Roman Empire. It is little wonder that this cult was so enthusiastically embraced and promoted in the East.

Furthermore, there was no better way of showing loyalty to the emperor on his accession than by sending a delegation offering to build a new temple in his honour. This demonstrated how zealous they were apart from observing the numerous imperial high and holy days for deceased emperors who had undergone an apotheosis and also for their new 'son of a god'.[32] (See pp. 26-28.) This was certainly borne out in the East of the empire. In Asia Minor archaeologists have located to date ten temples or sanctuaries erected between A.D. 1 and 50, a further seven for the remainder of that century and fifteen for the first half of the next.[33] Fishwick concludes, 'Despite Julio-Claudian "refusals" of divine honours for the emperor himself, this was a welcome extension of the ruler cult which official policy could afford to leave unchecked.'[34]

31. For a discussion of the specific character of Romanization in the East, see R. MacMullen, "The East," in *Romanization in the Time of Augustus* (New Haven: Yale University Press, 2000), ch. 1.

32. C. Ando, *Imperial Ideology and Provincial Loyalty in the Roman empire* (Berkeley: University of California Press, 2000), p. 59.

33. Price, *Rituals and Power,* p. 59.

34. D. Fishwick, *Imperial Cult in the Latin West,* I.2, p. 198, and citation p. 330. On the declining honours, see E. Mary Smallwood, *Documents Illustrating the Principates Gaius,*

The seeking of tangible provincial and local benefits was made known through embassies to Rome. This particular inscription was couched in the diplomatic language of 'the welfare' of the *koinon* of Asia and the city of Sardis. They sought an official audience with Augustus, clearly signalling to him the envoys' agenda in a document that would have been presented in advance. In this case it was 'Greeks bearing gifts'.[35] However, as the official response records, there were no more tangible imperial concessions or favours forthcoming to Sardis at the time of this delegation.

In conclusion, the trilogy of imperial cultic acts 'to', 'for' and 'by' the emperor was followed by imperial reciprocity to those delegations. This reveals how skilfully the Roman Empire held together despite its vastness and cultural differences. The official resolution of Sardis reveals the overt local agenda that Hillard aptly described as 'the desire for material advancement'.[36] It exposes something of the local and provincial motivation and expectation for promoting this phenomenon.

Claudius and Nero (Cambridge: Cambridge University Press, 1967), no. 371; L. R. Taylor, "Tiberius' Refusal of Divine Honors," *TAPA* 60 (1929): 87-101; and M. P. Charlesworth, "The Refusal of Divine Honours: An Augustan Formula," *BSR* 15 (1939): 1-10.

35. For the importance of this in the Greek classical period, see L. G. Mitchell, *Greeks Bearing Gifts: The Public Use of Private Relationships in the Greek World, 435-323 B.C.* (Cambridge: Cambridge University Press, 1997). The social convention would subsequently fit well into the relationship between Greek cities and Roman emperors.

36. Hillard, "Vespasian's Death-Bed Attitude to His Impending Deification," p. 198.

CHAPTER 4

Imperial Endorsement of Divine Titles and 'Declining' New Temples

'Rome's main export to the empire was the cult of the emperors', which 'appealed to Augustus, as it did to later emperors, as a way of focusing the loyalty of provincials on the imperial *persona*'.[1] What terms were used to express the emperor's divinity? How did they themselves respond to their divine status, knowing it was the way their citizens conventionally expressed loyalty to the Roman Empire? Following the accession of the new emperor, delegations were sent to Rome offering to build a temple for his veneration in their city or province. While this was diplomatically 'declined', in some instances extant archaeological evidence confirms that construction still went ahead. Such embassies often had another agenda, seeking at the same time other benefits and concessions for their own cities.

To understand these central issues, it is proposed to examine (I) honouring 'the god of the Romans' with divine titles, some of which emperors also used in their official decrees and many of which were also used of Jesus Christ, i.e., 'god', 'son of a god', 'lord', 'saviour', 'god manifest' and 'high priest'; and (II) how citizens and provincial officials affirmed loyalty to the new emperor by sending delegations to Rome following his accession, traditionally offering to build a temple for his veneration in their city or province but also with an agenda seeking imperial privileges and concessions.

---

1. P. Garnsey and R. Saller, *The Roman Empire: Economy, Society and Culture* (London: Duckworth, 1987), pp. 164, 165.

I. Imperial Divine Titles Also Used of Jesus Christ

In the Julio-Claudian dynasty, emperors actually used divine titles of them-selves in their official decrees to individual cities and provinces. It has been rightly noted, 'There has been no shortage of inscriptions attesting divine honours for emperors.'[2] These are not the only source, as there is a mass of extant numismatic evidence as these same authors have recorded. Imperial provincial coinage did not generally portray living emperors as gods with the divine radiate crown in the Julio-Claudian era, with two notable excep-tions, *viz.,* 'Caligula and especially, Nero'.[3] They were used in the time of Augustus' successor, Tiberius, of the deceased *Divus Augustus,*[4] and also in the representation of empresses as various goddesses as a 'constant theme of the provincial coinage'.[5]

After an extensive survey of numismatic evidence in provinces and cities where coins were minted, Hoster notes that 'by choosing to place representations of members of the imperial family on their coins, the mint-ing city (or better, their élite) may have demonstrated their alleged close relationship and a more personalized expression of that relationship to the ruling Romans'.[6] Cuss also concludes coins were 'the indirect way of promulgating the imperial cult'.[7]

Evidence assembled in this section records divine titles used of the reigning emperors, some of whom were given the title of perpetual divinity by the Senate after their death but all of whom were declared to be 'a god, a son of a god', 'the saviour', 'god manifest' as well as 'the great high priest' in their lifetime. The first Christians affirmed that Jesus Christ possessed

2. A. Burnett, M. Amandry and P. P. Ripollès, *Roman Provincial Coinage: From the Death of Caesar to the Death of Vitellius (44 B.C.-A.D. 69)* (London and Paris: British Museum Press and Bibliothèque nationale de France, 1998), p. 47.

3. Burnett, Amandry and Ripollès, *Roman Provincial Coinage,* p. 47. Also C. How-gego, "Chronological Development of Roman Provincial Coin Iconography," in *Coinage and Identity in the Roman Provinces,* ed. C. Howgego, Christopher V. Heuchert and A. Burnett (Oxford: Oxford University Press, 2005), p. 45.

4. Howgego, "Chronological Development of Roman Provincial Coin Iconography," p. 45.

5. Burnett, Amandry and Ripollès, *Roman Provincial Coinage,* p. 47. Hereafter it is cited as *RPC* when referring to an individual coin or coins by number.

6. M. Horster, "Coinage and Images of the Imperial Family, Local Identity and Roman Rule," *Journal of Roman Archaeology* 26 (2013): 258.

7. D. Cuss, *Imperial Cult and Honorary Terms in the New Testament* (Fribourg: Fri-bourg University Press, 1974), p. 37.

perpetual divinity and was 'the Son of the God', 'the saviour of the world', 'God manifest' and 'the great high priest'.

Whatever the spectrum of the understanding of each of these titles in the Roman Empire, it is clear that Christians in the first century could not at the same time and in all good conscience use divine titles both of Jesus and of any emperor, reigning or deceased, and in some instances, members of his family.

(i) The Divinity (Divus) *of the Caesars*

When it came to choosing the appropriate Latin term for imperial gods, what terminology best expressed their divinity and bestowed the greatest honour? Wardle has conducted a detailed examination of the Latin terms *divus* and *deus* and noted the distinction that Varro (116-27 B.C.) drew between *divus,* 'a perpetual divinity', and *deus,* a 'deified human being', but Wardle makes the important observation that this was 'the very opposite of the distinction that came to dominate'.[8] What Rome needed for the deification of Julius Caesar was a term to indicate his change in status, and 'to provide a form of address for this new divinity and to distinguish Caesar from the plurality of *Julii Caesares* in the late Republic'.[9]

Following his historic and linguistic survey, Wardle concludes —

> The chosen form *Divus Iulius* required relegating his *cognomen* in favour of a *nomen* and juxtaposing a term specifying 'god': C. *Iulius Caesares* become *divus Iulius. . . . Divus,* then, was applied first to the deified Julius Caesar because it was perceived as the more archaic of the two nouns for god and the one more appropriate to laws (and thus to a legally conferred status); it was chosen for political rather than philological reasons.[10]

This indicates a new day in Rome, with divinity officially being attributed to Julius Caesar.

---

8. D. Wardle, "*Deus* or *Divus:* The Genesis of Roman Terminology for Deified Emperors and a Philosopher's Contribution," in *Philosophy and Power in the Graeco-Roman World: Essays in Honour of Miriam Griffin,* ed. G. Clark and T. Rajak (Oxford: Oxford University Press, 2002), p. 183.

9. Wardle, "*Deus* or *Divus,*" p. 191.

10. Wardle, "*Deus* or *Divus,*" p. 191.

How did this change come about? Soon after his death early in 44 B.C. unofficial worship was paid to Julius Caesar, and 'long afterwards they continued to make sacrifices there, undertake vows, and to sort out certain disputes by an oath made in Caesar's name'.[11] Divine significance had been read into the appearance of a comet seen for seven days after his ascension into heaven. The term 'apotheosis' (ἀποθέωσις) was used of this and that of his successors.[12]

Julius Caesar was officially deified in 42 B.C., and in the same year Cicero began applying the term *divus* to him.[13] An official Latin inscription from Aesernia in southern Italy was dedicated 'To the *genius* of Divine Julius *(Genio Divi Iuli)*, father of the fatherland, whom the Senate and People of Rome placed among the number of the gods.'[14] During the siege of Perusia in 41-40 B.C. slingshots inscribed with the title *divom Iulium* were fired by the troops of Augustus.[15]

The first Roman coins struck by Augustus were *denarii* in 38 B.C. and were used to pay the troops after a great victory. On them, Julius Caesar and Augustus were depicted facing each other and the legends read 'god Julius' *(Divus Iulius)* and 'son of a god' *(Divi f.)*.[16] The title was extended to the wife of Augustus. A tomb of a freedman of Livia situated in the Palatine in Rome read '. . . freedman of Augusta *(Aug. lib.)*, sacristan of the temple of the divine Augustus and divine Augusta' *(templi divi Aug. [e]t divae Augustae)*.[17]

Beyond Rome, in the Latin West in Lugdunum, a coin was minted in *c.* 38 B.C. with the laureate head of Julius Caesar and the bare head of Augustus with the inscription 'son of a god, god Julius' *(divi f. divi Iuli.)*.[18] A milestone inscription in Latin on the road from the Cottian Alps to Arles in 3 B.C. also uses *divus*. It read, 'Father of the fatherland *(pater patriae)*, the emperor Caesar, son of the deified, *pontifex maximus*.'[19]

In the East in the Roman colony of Apamea in Bithynia and Pontus, another coin struck in 27 B.C. recorded, 'Julius, god' *(Julius Divus)* and on

---

11. Suetonius, *The Deified Julius Caesar* 85.
12. Wardle, "*Deus* or *Divus*," pp. 182-83, 189-90.
13. Cicero, *Phil.* 2.110.
14. *CIL* 10, 2668.
15. *CIL* 11, 6721, 21.
16. Wardle, "*Deus* or *Divus*," pp. 189-90, for a detailed discussion.
17. *ILS* 4995.
18. *RPC* no. 516.
19. *ILS* 100.

the reverse 'Augustus, son of a god' *(div. f.)*.[20] According to Suetonius, a column almost twenty feet high of Numidian marble in the forum in Rome was inscribed 'to the Father of the Fatherland and for a long time they [the citizens of Rome] continued to sacrifice, make vows, and settle some of their disputes by an oath in the name of Caesar *(per Caesarem)*'.[21]

The Roman Senate would also confer the title *divus* on Augustus. An inscription in Rome dedicated to his successor read: 'To the *genius* of Tiberius Caesar Augustus, son of the divine Augustus *(divi Augusti)*'.[22]

Official inscriptions in Corinth were all in Latin from the founding of the colony in 44 B.C. through the first century A.D., hence the title *divus* was applied to Julius Caesar, Augustus, Claudius and Livia, the grandmother of Claudius.[23] They read '[Sacred] to the deified Caesar' *(divo Iulio Caesari sacrum)* and '[Sacred to] the deified Augustus' *(divo Augusto sacrum)*.[24] The same term was also located in an inscription on a building dedicated to Livia, the grandmother of the emperor Claudius, whom, according to Suetonius, he had deified. It read 'to the deified Augusta *(divae Augustae)*, the grandmother of [Tiberius] Claudius Caesar Augustus Germanius'.[25] The choice of the term *divus* and not *deus* in the first-century Latin inscriptions meant that the claim of perpetual divinity was not only officially declared but also widely recorded.[26]

Price notes, 'It is important that there was no readily available translation of *divus* into Greek and bases [of statues] have employed the term *theos*. It was only in heavily Romanized contexts, such as direct translations from Latin, or other official contexts, that various periphrases were invented' in the Greek East.[27]

As an example, Paulus Fabius Maximus, the proconsul of Asia from 10 to 8 B.C., wrote to the League of Asia and chose the superlative 'most

---

20. *RPC* no. 2007.

21. Suetonius, *The Deified Julius* 85.

22. *ILS* 6080.

23. Suetonius in his *Lives of the Caesars* rightly only uses the term *divus* with reference to the following Julio-Claudian emperors: Julius Caesar, Augustus and Claudius.

24. J. H. Kent, *Corinth: Inscriptions 1926-1950* (Athens: American School of Classical Studies, 1966), VIII.2, nos. 50-53, 72, 81.

25. J. H. Kent, *Corinth,* VIII.3, no. 55, Suetonius, *Divine Claudius* 11.2. A. B. West, *Corinth: Latin Inscriptions 1896-1926,* VIII.2, Augustus, no. 50, Julius Caesar and Claudius, no. 68.

26. S. R. F. Price, *Rituals and Power: The Imperial Cult and Asia Minor* (Cambridge: Cambridge University Press, 1984), p. 75.

27. Price, *Rituals and Power,* p. 75.

divine' (θειότατος) when referring to Augustus in his lifetime as the 'most divine Caesar' (τοῦ θειοτάτου Καίσαρος).[28] Sherk commented on this, 'But it cannot be denied that the use of the word in Greek and the absence of a corresponding word in the Latin are striking, facts not noticed by previous editors'.[29]

Later in Nero's era another Greek synonym was chosen when he was declared to be 'the son of the greatest of gods, Tiberius Claudius' (τὸν υἱὸν τοῦ μεγίστου θεῶν Τιβερίου Κλαυδίου).[30] While the use of the Greek term by Maximus may have reflected this, we are on more solid ground with this inscription. The superlative 'the greatest' (ὁ μέγιστος) seems to have gone some way to encapsulate the Latin concept of 'perpetual'.

Furthermore, a bilingual inscription related to the imperial provincial cult from Amastra in the province of Paphlagonia in the East provides the clearest evidence of equivalence. After beginning the inscription with the 'peace of Augustus', it names Gaius Julius Aquila as its 'high priest', and then introduces Claudius as Tiberius Claudius Germanicus Augustus. There follows the phrase 'the highest god, Augustus' (τοῦ ἐπουρανίου θεοῦ Σεβαστοῦ), which was rendered into Latin as *divi Aug. perpetui*. The framers of this inscription appear to have chosen the term 'highest' (ἐπουρανίος) as an apposite rendering of the Latin *divus* to which they added *perpetuus,* possibly to explicate even further for those in Amastra in the Greek East the meaning of the title of *divus* that the Roman Senate awarded Claudius.[31] The superlative 'the highest' (ἐπουρανίος) was also the cult title of the great god Zeus.[32]

The official attribution of divinity to the emperors had to have posed an enormous challenge for the first Christians because of the New Testament's affirmation of the perpetual divinity of Jesus and his edict that his disciples had to observe a strict dichotomy between Caesar and God (Mark 12:17). Both the Gospel of John (John 1:1-4) and the Epistle to the Hebrews (Heb. 1:2-3) commence by declaring the perpetual divinity of Jesus, emphasising that he was not a man who became God.

28. *OGIS* 458.

29. R. K. Sherk, *Roman Documents from the East: Senatus Consulta and Epistulae to the Age of Augustus* (Baltimore: Johns Hopkins University Press, 1969), p. 337, n. 9. He goes on to speculate, 'It could mean that the composer was a Greek.'

30. *Die Inschriften von Magnesia am Mäander,* no. 156b.

31. *IGRR* 3, 83.

32. For the reference to Zeus see *SEG* 31, no. 1080, cited in the entry for ἐπουρανίος, *L&S Supplement.*

(ii) A Son of a God and the Son of the God

Augustus and Claudius, all the remaining Julio-Claudian emperors, Tiberius, Gaius, Claudius and Nero, were also addressed, or designated themselves in official decrees, as 'a son of a god'. This section cites the uses of the term 'son' (υἱός) used both of emperors and Jesus. Only of Nero, the adopted son of Claudius, has evidence been located of the use of the article 'the' (ὁ) with reference to himself as 'the son of a god'. This exception can be explained because the only birth son of Claudius, Britannicus, Nero's stepbrother, was poisoned a few months after Nero was declared Caesar. From then on Nero was technically 'the' son. This was in stark contrast to that of Jesus, who was always recorded in the Gospels as 'the Son of the God' or 'the only begotten Son of the God'.[33]

In late 39 or early 38 B.C. in the Roman East, Augustus himself wrote to the Magistrates, the Council and the People of Ephesus describing himself as 'Imperator Caesar, son of god Julius' (Αὐτοκράτωρ Καῖσαρ θεοῦ Ἰουλίου υἱός).[34] He also addressed the Mylasan magistrates in 31 B.C. as 'Imperator Caesar, son of the god Julius'.[35]

The oath of loyalty sworn by the inhabitants and the Roman businessmen of Gangra in the twelfth consulship to 'Imperator Caesar Augustus, a son of a god' was identical to the one sworn by the inhabitants at Neapolis 'in the temple of Augustus by the altar of Augustus'.[36] In Egypt an official inscription recorded the dedication of a porch that began with a reference to 'Imperator Caesar Zeus the Liberator, god, son of a god, Augustus' in A.D. 1.[37] Coins in Thessalonica were struck showing the crowned head of Julius Caesar with the inscription θεός, and on the reverse the bare head of Augustus and the word 'Thessalonica'.[38]

It was officially recorded that Augustus himself addressed the Samarians as 'Imperator Caesar Augustus, son of the divine Julius' (θεοῦ Ἰουδίου

---

33. An exception was the Roman centurion ἀληθῶς θεοῦ υἱὸς (Matt. 27:54), which is entirely explicable for a polytheist to speak of Jesus as 'truly a son of a god'.

34. J. Reynolds, *Aphrodisias and Rome,* The Society for the Promotion of Roman Studies (Hertford: Stephen Austin, 1982), no. 12, *l.* 1. See also the letter from Augustus describing himself as 'Imperator Caesar, son of the god Julius' to the city of Mylasa in 31 B.C. *SIG*³ 768. αὐτοκράτωρ=*imperator* and *dictator.*

35. R. K. Sherk, *Roman Documents from the Greek East,* p. 310.

36. *ILS* 8781 (Paphlogonia and Neapolis).

37. *OGIS* 659.

38. *RPC* nos. 1554-55.

υἱός).[39] Reference is also made to 'a letter of Augustus Germanicus Caesar, god' in relation to a legate of Nero Claudius Caesar Augustus Germanicus redrawing boundaries in Pisidia.[40]

The people of Mytilene dedicated a statue to Julia, 'daughter of Imperator Caesar god Augustus'.[41] In Thasos somewhere between 19 and 2 B.C. they honoured 'Livia Drusilla, the wife of Augustus Caesar, divine benefactress' (θεὰν εὐεργέτιν).[42]

It was not only Augustus and his contemporaries who used the term but also his successors who were not all natural-born sons of their predecessor. Latin inscriptions recording the names of emperors indicate that they were either a son, or a grandson or great-grandson of a god. One begins with Augustus as 'son of a god', Julius Caesar. Gaius Caesar and Lucius Caesar are both called 'grandson of a god' i.e., Julius Caesar, and Tiberius likewise as 'grandson of a god'. Germanicus was a 'great-grandson of a god'.[43]

The designation would become hereditary for the successor of the imperial office, as a single inscription in Cyprus aptly testifies. Between 9 B.C. and A.D. 2 it was dedicated 'To Imperator Caesar Augustus, god, son of god . . . and his two sons, Gaius and Lucius Caesar', both of whom would pre-decease him, and subsequent to his death somewhere between A.D. 19 and 23 there was added to the same inscription, 'To Tiberius Caesar Augustus, god, son of a god' (θεῷ υἱῷ θεῷ).[44] A bilingual inscription from

39. J. H. Oliver, *Greek Constitutions of Early Roman Emperors from Inscriptions and Papyri,* Memoirs of the American Philosophical Society (Philadelphia: American Philosophical Society, 1989), no. 1, "Augustus to the Samarians," p. 26. Oliver notes that the actual phrase 'son of divine Julius' also occurs elsewhere in an inscription in Eleusis and in Latin in Nicopolis as *divi Iuli f. Contra* Reynolds, *Aphrodisias and Rome*, no. 13, *l.* 1, who rejects this title, arguing it was rarely used, although he concedes it was in Egypt in the time of Augustus, but suggesting it was added in the third century (p. 103).

40. *SEG* 19, 765.

41. *IG* 12, 2.204.

42. *ILS* 8784 (Thasos) and in the same inscription it honoured 'Julia, daughter of Caesar Augustus', as a benefactress by descent.

43. *ILS* 107, cited in R. Seager, *Tiberius* (London: Methuen, 1972), pp. 46-47.

44. V. Ehrenberg and A. H. M. Jones, *Documents Illustrating the Reigns of Augustus and Tiberius* (Oxford: Clarendon Press, 1976²), no. 115 a and b, Θεοῦ, υἱῷ θεῷ. P. Steward, *Statues in Roman Society: Representation and Response* (Oxford: Oxford University Press, 2003), p. 167, has made suggestions that in 'Latin inscriptions the recipient of the statue is in the dative case. Greek dedications are more varied. They routinely identify the subject in the accusative. . . . The dative is also used, but rarely for mortal recipients of statues. So when the dative is used for imperial subjects it is possible that it carries divine connotations, elevating, perhaps almost "consecrating" the emperor with words'. However, this inscription reads

Cyrene in the time of Nero clearly traces his 'ancestry' back to Augustus and provides evidence of the terms considered equivalent in the first century.

> Nero Claudius Caesar Augustus Germanicus, son of the divine Claudius (*divi Claudi f.,* θεοῦ Κλαυδίου υἱός) grandson of Germanicus Caesar, great-grandson of Tiberius Caesar Augustus great-great-grandson of the divine Augustus (*divi Augusti,* θεοῦ Σεβαστοῦ), *pontifex maximus* (ἀρχιερεύς), with tribunician power, imperator, consul, through Lucius Acilius Strabo, his legate, restored land occupied by private persons to the Roman people.[45]

The phrases 'a son of a god', 'son of the divine' or 'the son of greatest of the gods', i.e., a deceased emperor, would be heard and understood differently in the first century, as would the term 'god'. Extant evidence shows that these official designations of the imperial rulers enjoyed wide currency in the Roman East. Price suggests that the linguistic development of the terms may well have been lost on the rank and file in the Greek-speaking context because both Latin terms were rendered as 'god' (θεός).[46] The official bilingual inscription in Cyrene and those elsewhere drew attention to the linguistic equivalents.

Was Jesus accused of claiming to be equal with, or a competitor of, the reigning emperor Tiberius as 'a son of a god'? During his trial as recorded in John 19:1-16 and after ordering his scourging, Pilate declared before the crowd, 'See, I am bringing him out to you that you may know that I find no fault in him.' The chief priests and the officers immediately responded, calling for his crucifixion on the grounds 'that He made himself a son of a god' (ὅτι υἱὸν θεοῦ ἑαυτὸν ἐποίησεν) (John 19:7).

After further interrogation of Jesus away from the crowd, Pilate sought to release him and it was then that the Jews confronted the Roman governor. They retaliated. 'If you release this man, you are not Caesar's friend' (οὐκ εἶ φίλος τοῦ Καίσαρος) (19:12). While there is no extant epigraphic or other literary evidence that Pilate had this important honorary

---

'to Imperator Caesar Augustus, to god, to son of god', where one would expect the dative if addressed to both Caesar and 'his son'.

45. For this bilingual inscription of Nero see M. P. Charlesworth, "Nero," in *Documents Illustrating the Reigns of Claudius and Nero* (Cambridge: Cambridge University Press, 1939), no. 4.

46. Price, *Rituals and Power,* pp. 83-85, for examples of *divus* and *deus* both being rendered in Greek as Θεός.

title of a 'friend of Caesar', he was a close associate and loyal official of Tiberius, and substantial extant evidence exists of leading Roman officials bearing this title. (See p. 30.)

The accusers reminded Pilate who was on his annual assize in Jerusalem of his judicial rôle as governor to punish breaches of Roman law, that 'everyone who makes himself a king opposes Caesar' (πᾶς ὁ βασιλέα ἑαυτὸν ποιῶν ἀντιλέγει τῷ Καίσαρι). Later when the governor said, 'Behold your king', they again asserted their total loyalty to Rome by declaring, 'we have no king but Caesar' (19:15).

It is significant that the chief priests' and Jewish officials' case rested on their assertion not that Jesus called himself 'the Son of the God' as attested in John's Gospel, but that he was said to have made himself a rival of Tiberius — hence their claim of the present divine emperor as 'a son of a god' (υἱον θεοῦ), both of which were recorded without the article before either of the nouns. The Jewish officials would be aware of the claims of Tiberius and his title 'a son of a god'. Theirs was the appropriate charge of sedition or treason to bring against Jesus in that he was a self-made rival of Tiberius. The implication was that Pilate could be guilty of 'treason' (maiestas) by reason of guilt by association if he set him free.[47]

At the crucifixion of Jesus, the Jews who had heard of his comment about the destruction of the temple taunted him and are recorded repeating his claim, 'If you are a son of the God (εἰ υἱὸς εἶ τοῦ θεοῦ), come down from the cross' (Matt. 27:40). At the same time others report the claim of Jesus, 'He trusts in God who should deliver him, for He said, "I am a son of a god"' (εἶπεν γὰρ ὅτι θεοῦ εἰμι υἱός) (Matt. 27:43). In the New Testament surprisingly, but not out of character in terms of cultural usage, immediately after the death of Jesus, a Roman centurion is recorded as declaring literally, 'Truly this man was a son of a god' (οὗτος ὁ ἄνθρωπος υἱὸς θεοῦ ἦν) (Matt. 27:54; Mark 15:39). He was reading into the superscription not only his Roman understanding of divinity from the headpiece 'King of the Jews' that was placed at the insistence of Pilate, but also the nature of the way he died. It is interesting to see the absence of the definite article with respect to 'son' recorded here verbatim.

There was a critical linguistic subtlety, the implications of which would not be lost on the nascent Christian movement. Compared with

---

47. Treason 'was the political crime par excellence,' according to J. A. Crook, Law and Life in Rome, 90 B.C.–A.D. 212, Aspects of Greek and Roman Life (Ithaca, NY: Cornell University Press, 1967), p. 269.

the Greek-speaking Roman East, Christians inserted the article when using certain terms, so that Jesus was 'the' son of 'the' God. At the same time the New Testament records non-Christians, including Jews, using the terms 'a son' and 'a god' as shown above.

John writes his Gospel with the specific intention 'that you might believe that Jesus is the Messiah, "the Son of the God" (ὁ υἱὸς τοῦ θεοῦ), and believing you might have life through His name' (John 20:31). John the Baptist had already declared emphatically, 'I have seen and have borne witness that this is "the" Son of God' (ὁ υἱὸς τοῦ θεοῦ) (1:34). In John's Gospel the phrase 'the only begotten (μονογενής) God in the bosom of the Father' (1:14) distances the title even further from 'a son of a god' that was officially used of emperors. The New International Version translates the phrase 'the one and only Son of God' (1:14, 18; 3:16, 18).

When coupled with the definite article, one can appreciate the conflict for the first Christians over the rival claims of the emperor and Jesus. The Jewish high priest is recorded as questioning Jesus, 'Tell us if you are the Messiah, the Son of the God' (εἰ σὺ εἶ ὁ χριστὸς ὁ υἱὸς τοῦ θεοῦ) (Matt. 26:63). 'God' and 'the Son of the God' were terms used specifically of Jesus by Christians; they could not call a reigning emperor 'a son of a god'. They did not use the official phrase 'son of god' of Jesus but rather added the definite article 'the' (ὁ), so that he was declared '*the* Son of *the* God', i.e., the only God. However, this claim put the early Christians on an inevitable ideological clash with their compatriots whose polytheistic view of the divinity could readily incorporate the concept of the reigning emperor as 'a god, a son of a god', with men who became gods and some of whom were posthumously awarded perpetual divinity.

(iii) The Saviour and God Manifest

The use of divine imperial terminology by the first Christians was only further aggravated when Jesus was recorded as the one 'who is saviour of all mankind' (ὅς ἐστιν σωτὴρ πάντων ἀνθρώπων) (1 Tim. 4:10). This very title, 'the saviour of all mankind' (τὸν πάντων ἀνθρώπων σωτῆρα), was also inscribed on the plinth of a statue of Claudius.[48]

Towards the end of his Principate it was written of Claudius that

---

48. E. Mary Smallwood, *Documents Illustrating the Principates Gaius, Claudius and Nero* (Cambridge: Cambridge University Press, 1967), no. 135, *ll.* 21-22 (A.D. 52-53).

he was 'the most divine Caesar and truly our saviour' (τοῦ θειοτάτου Καίσαρος καὶ ὡς ἀληθῶς σωτῆρος ἡμῶν).[49] An even earlier official inscription from Halicarnassus involving surrounding cities had declared Augustus to be 'saviour of the common race of man' (σωτῆρα τοῦ κοινοῦ ἀνθρώπων γένος).[50] An Alexandrian coin A.D. 62-63 with Nero's head on the obverse side declared on the other side he was 'the saviour of the world' (ὁ σωτὴρ τῆς οἰκουμένης).[51] This was an equivalent title used of Jesus (ὁ σωτὴρ τοῦ κόσμου) in John 4:42.

An A.D. 37 inscription refers to Gaius now ruling with the 'great gods' (τηλικούτων θεῶν).[52] In the next century the citizens of Delphi, on whose famous shrine and city Hadrian had bestowed many benefactions, addressed him a 'great god' (θεός τηλικοῦτος).[53] The 'appearing of the great God and Saviour of ours, Jesus Christ' (τοῦ μεγάλου θεοῦ καὶ σωτῆρος ἡμῶν) was seen as the foundation for every Christian's future hope (Titus 2:13).

In Arneae, Lycia and Aezani, Phrygia, references were made to Claudius as 'god manifest, and saviour of our people' (θεὸν ἐπιφανῆ σωτῆρα καὶ τοῦ ἡμετέρου δήμου) and 'divine saviour and benefactor . . . god manifest' (θεοῦ σωτῆρος καὶ εὐεργέτου . . . θεοῦ ἐπιγανοῦς.[54] In a papyrus from Oxyrhynchus announcing the death of Claudius and Nero's succession, the former was officially declared to be 'god manifest' (ἐνφανὴς θεός).[55] In what some have suggested was a formal Christian creed, Jesus was confessed to be 'God manifest in the flesh' (θεός ὃς ἐφανερώθη σαρκί) (1 Tim. 3:16).

The papyrus continues, 'and the expectation and hope of the world (ὁ δὲ τῆς οἰκουμένης καὶ προσδοκηθεὶς καὶ ἐλπισθείς) has been declared emperor (αὐτοκράτωρ), the good *genius* of the world (ἀγαθὸς δαίμων δὲ τῆς οἰκουμέης) and the source of all good things (ἀρχὴ ὤν μεγιστε πάτων), Nero has been declared Caesar (Νέρων Καῖσαρ ἀποδέδεικται)'.[56] The con-

49. *IGRR* 1, 1118, *ll.* 34-35 (5 April, A.D. 54).
50. *IBM* 4, 1, 894.
51. *RPC* no. 5271E.
52. *IGRR* 4, 145, 9.
53. *Fouilles de Delphes* 3.4.3.
54. *Tituli Asiae Minoris* 2.760 and *IGRR* 4, 584. In the former inscription the full titles of Britannicus is spelt out, 'Tiberius Claudius Caesar Britannicus, son of Imperator Tiberius Claudius Caesar Augustus', and is followed by the titles of Claudius including 'god manifest'. In the case of the latter the formal construction used throughout the inscription of the sponsor of the imperial games of Augustus Claudius and the temple officer (νεωκόρος) of Zeus and of Claudius, the phrase 'god manifest' refers to Claudius and not Britannicus.
55. *P.Oxy.* 1021, *ll.* 2-3.
56. *P.Oxy.* 1021, *ll.* 5-13.

fidence of the early community of believers was 'Christ in you, the hope of glory' (Col. 1:17), and that 'all things were made through him [Christ] and without him nothing was made that was created' (John 1:3). Genesis declares this to be only good (Gen. 1:4, 10, 12, 18, 21, 25, 31), and Colossians 1:27 states that in Christ 'all things hold together'. Again these affirmations conflicted with the claims of the Caesars in the first century.

An official civic inscription records Nero's presence in Corinth at the Isthmian Games on 29 November, A.D. 67, where Epaminondas, the high priest of the Achaean provincial imperial cult, declared him to be 'the Lord of all the world' (ὁ τοῦ παντὸς κόσμου κύριος).[57] He was to be worshipped at the existing altar dedicated to Zeus the Saviour by the citizens of the Greek city of Acraephia. Statues were to be erected in the ancestral temple of Ptoian Apollo, where he was specifically declared 'Nero Zeus, Liberator' and his wife 'goddess Augusta Messallina'.[58] Christians confessed another as the Lord of the world and believed that all humanity would one day bow and acknowledge that this title rightly belonged to Jesus, whom they alone confessed was God incarnate (Phil. 2:10-11).

In Rome after the deification of the first Flavian emperor, Vespasian, Titus his son could claim to be a son of a god and his brother Domitian also to be a god, according to the late first-century writer Tacitus.[59] It was Domitian who insisted that he be addressed in person as both 'Lord and God'.[60] Much earlier the apostle Thomas is recorded as addressing Jesus in a post-resurrection experience as 'my Lord and my God' (ὁ κύριος μου καὶ ὁ θεός μου) (John 20:28). On the other hand Corinthian Christians could not endorse imperial titles because of their 'creed' — 'But for us (ἀλλ᾽ ἡμῖν) there is one God, the Father . . . and one Lord, Jesus Christ' (1 Cor. 8:6).

A combination of titles could be used of the emperor as in the case of an inscription to Augustus in Eleusis, a city located between Athens and Corinth. He was called 'Imperator Caesar, son of god, Julius, his saviour and benefactor' (Αὐτοκράτορα Καίσαρα θεοῦ Ἰουλίου υἱόν τὸν α(ὐ)τοῦ σωτῆρα καὶ εὐεργέτην).[61]

---

57. *SIG* 3, 814, *l.* 26.

58. *SIG* 3, 814, *ll.* 51-52.

59. Pliny, *Paneg.* 11.1. D. Fishwick, *Imperial Cult in the Latin West* (Leiden: E. J. Brill, 1993[2]), I.2, p. 297.

60. Suetonius, *Domitian* 13.

61. Oliver, *Greek Constitutions of Early Roman Emperors from Inscriptions and Papyri,* p. 26, citing E. Vanderpool, *Deltion* 23 (1968): 7.

The convention associated with ancient rulers of the Greek and Hellenistic eras had been to give 'appropriate' titles and veneration that were of 'equal honours to the gods' (ἰσόθεοι τιμαί). Imperial gods and goddesses could be assimilated into the existing local pantheon for provincials in the Roman East especially when they prayed to their gods for the emperor as part of the imperial cultic activities.[62] The precedent for this is said to have stretched back to Philip and Alexander the Great.[63]

In Ephesus 'the initiates' (οἱ μύσται) of Dionysus described the placing of a statue of the second-century emperor Hadrian alongside a divinity as 'sharing the throne of Dionysus' (σύνφρονον τῷ Διονύσῳ).[64] Such a *rapprochement* would not have been possible for the Christian movement with its roots in Judaism. For them the initial commandment in the Mosaic Law was binding and against the worship of one god without denying the existence of other gods, i.e., monolatry — 'You shall have no other gods alongside me' (Exod. 20:2). They could never entertain the concept, as these Ephesians did, of any imperial gods 'sharing' the throne of God because of their firm belief that there was only one God and Father; any others were not divine (1 Cor. 8:6; Eph. 4:6).

At the end of the New Testament *corpus* in the Book of Revelation the term 'throne' (θρόνος) occurs forty-seven times and its rightful occupancy by God and the Lamb is a central concern of its author. There is one reference to the throne of the beast and a kingdom (16:10). Again, for the first Christians the concept of a throne that could be shared by divine reigning and deceased emperors with God and Jesus, the Lamb of God, was impossible.

(iv) 'The Greatest Bridge Builder' and the Great High Priest

In addition, emperors held the title of *pontifex maximus.* The title chosen was not that of 'greater' *(maior)* but the superlative of 'great' *(magnus).* Its holder was the chief priest who supervised public and private sacrifices and was the head of the college of priests *(pontifices)* in Rome.

---

62. For helpful discussion see D. Fishwick, "Isotheoi Timai," in *Imperial Cult in the Latin West*, I.1, ch. 3.

63. E. A. Fredricksmeyer, "On the Background of the Ruler Cult," in *Ancient Macedonian Studies in Honor of Charles F. Edson* (Thessaloniki: Institute for Balkan Studies, 1981), no. 158, pp. 145-56.

64. *SEG* 26, 1272 = *I Ephesos* 275.

In Rome itself his person [Julius Caesar] was already sacralised by the pontificate he had held since 73 B.C. and by the life-long position of *pontifex maximus* which he received in 63 B.C., thus making him the mediator between his fellow-citizens and the state-gods; the office conferred great prestige and paved the way for divine honours.[65]

Augustus assumed this designation in 12 B.C., as did all subsequent emperors.[66]

Furthermore the life appointment of high priests to conduct imperial cultic activities at the provincial level throughout the empire required senatorial approval.[67] The Halicarnassus inscription uses the term 'the high priest' (ὁ ἀρχιερεύς),[68] and a bilingual inscription in the East also renders *pontifex maximus* as ἀρχιερεύς.[69] This indicates the Latin phrase was not used exclusively of the emperor, even through his rôle was unique. The task of provincial imperial high priests was to preside over what was normally an annual week of major imperial cult celebrations involving leading citizens from cities within the province. (For the provincial imperial cult of Achaea celebrated in Corinth, see ch. 8.) In the Jewish context Caiaphas was also 'the high priest' who was cited as 'the chief priest' in Jerusalem (Matt. 26:3). He was a very significant person in the Jewish sacrificial system, especially in his unique function on the Day of Atonement. Rome had to sanction this appointment, as it did all such appointments for provincial imperial cults.[70]

Christians also had a great high priest. He held the title not just for life, as did the reigning emperor, those involved with imperial sacrifices at the provincial cult level,[71] and Jewish ones as well. His high priesthood is eternal, hence he is called 'the high priest' forever (Heb. 6:20). He is empathetic and accessible to Christians in all their needs, having been made man and 'tempted in all points as we are' (Heb. 4:15). He is presented as a superior *pontifex maximus* presiding over an eternal kingdom, compared

---

65. Fishwick, *Imperial Cult in the Latin West,* I.1, p. 56.

66. Fishwick, *Imperial Cult in the Latin West,* I.1, pp. 99, 161.

67. For discussion see p. 42.

68. *IBM* 4, 1, no. 894.

69. *SEG* 9, 352.

70. See Josephus, *Jewish Antiquities* 14.143 for Hyrcanus' appointment and his sons, 194.

71. See p. 138 for Spartiaticus in Corinth, who is recorded as having been given the post of High Priest 'for life' of the Federal imperial cult of Achaea.

with the office held by the Roman emperor that lasted until the time of his apotheosis.[72]

(v) The Lord

Epaminondas identified Nero as 'the lord of all the world' (ὁ τοῦ παντὸς κόσμου κύριος Νέρων) in the giving of thanks for the exemption of Greece from the Roman tax. Other accolades identified him as Zeus Liberator, the Saviour, 'Nero forever' (Νέρωνι εἰς αἰῶνα) and refers to 'the house of the Lord Augustus Nero' (τὸν τοῦ κύριου Σεβαστοῦ Νέρωνος οἶκον).[73] This also had implications for Corinthian Christians.

In his important monograph *Lord of the Entire World: Lord Jesus, a Challenge to Lord Caesar?* Fantin has carefully explored the extant evidence on the use of the term 'the Lord' in inscriptions, arguing that, while used occasionally of previous emperors, it seems to have been used mostly of Nero.[74]

A stark comparison was inevitable between the Christian claim of the God who became man and after his death ascended to exercise his cosmic rule, and comparable titles and rôles of men who became gods ruling over the Roman Empire in their lifetime, with some becoming perpetual divinities after their demise. To the latter were attributed such titles as 'son of a god', 'the saviour of the world' or 'the saviour of mankind', 'god manifest', *pontifex maximus* and lastly 'perpetual divinity' — a term officially used of Julius Caesar, Augustus and Claudius after their demise. This is the reason why ancient historians have commented there were competing claims of loyalty and consequential conflict for the first Christians.

Did Christians borrow these imperial titles to use of Jesus, thus portraying him as a rival of the Roman emperors? Was Jesus a superior divinity whose perpetual divinity was not awarded by his followers, as he claimed to have possessed it before he became man? The first disciples in Judea would be well aware of imperial claims and imperial veneration undertaken in Caesarea Maritima, capital of the Roman province of Judea,

---

72. Hebrews 5:10.

73. *SIG*³ 814, *ll.* 31, 49, 55.

74. J. D. Fantin, '*Kyrios Christos* and *Kyrios Kaisar*: Christ's Challenge to the Living Caesar', in *Lord of the Entire World: Lord Jesus, a Challenge to Lord Caesar?* New Testament Monograph 31 (Sheffield: Sheffield Phoenix Press, 2011), ch. 5.

with its own temple dedicated to '*Roma* and Augustus'.[75] However, there could be no advantage whatsoever in doing so, but only a deliberate and inevitable confrontation with Roman authorities.[76]

II. Honouring Emperors Who 'Declined' New Temples

Price notes that 'the imperial cult was often associated with diplomatic approaches to the emperor. Offers of cult were sometimes made in association with requests concerning privileges and other matters. Ambassadors to the emperor were also imperial priests.'[77] In support of this he states as an example —

> ambassadors from Mytilene showed no embarrassment in presenting divine honours to Augustus. The instructions given to them by the city for their speech survive in part; they were to address Augustus as one who had attained the eminence and power of the gods, and were to promise further divine honours to 'deify him' [θεοποιεῖν] even more.[78]

Furthermore, the inhabitants of Halicarnassus and neighbouring cities were exhorted by the proconsul 'so that they will not fail in anything that can deify him even more (πρὸς μηδὲν τῶν αὐτὸν ἐπὶ πλέον δυνησομένων ἐλείψειν τὴν τῆς πόλεως προθυμίαν καὶ εὐσέβειαν).[79]

The emperor Gaius (A.D. 37-41) bestowed client kingdoms on the three sons of Cotys, the king of Thrace. Their jurisdiction exceeded the boundaries of the kingdom of their father, who had been murdered some eighteen years previously.[80] In a lengthy inscription it was acknowledged that these client kingdoms were given 'by the grace of Gaius Caesar' (ἐκ

---

75. Fishwick, *Imperial Cult in the Latin West*, I.1, p. 126, notes that Augustus 'provided the point of departure for the worship of the emperor by the provinces of the Roman empire. . . . Octavian gave permission for sacred precincts to be dedicated to *Roma* and *Divus Iulius* in the East at Ephesus and Nicaea, where he commanded Roman citizens to participate in the cult'.

76. *Contra* M. David Litwa, *Iesus Deus: The Early Christian Depiction of Jesus as a Mediterranean God* (Minneapolis: Fortress Press, 2014).

77. Price, *Rituals and Power*, p. 243.

78. Price, *Rituals and Power*, p. 43.

79. *IGR* 4.

80. See A. A. Barrett, *Caligula: The Corruption of Power* (London: Batsford, 1989), p. 223.

τῆς Γαιου καίσαρος χάριτος) and the kings were 'incapable of equally re-
ciprocating (ἴσας ἀμοιβάς) the favour of such a god for the benefactions
they have received' but at a special festival occasion the citizens 'should
pray for the eternal endurance of Gaius Caesar'. He was described as 'the
new Sun' and wanted to rule in such a way that 'the greatness of his immortality might be all the more hallowed'. The inscription ends with the statement 'that the decree is a matter of piety towards Augustus (i.e., Gaius) and
honour towards the kings (i.e., the three kings)'.[81] Reciprocity was entirely
appropriate, but the problem for the three kings was that Gaius' gift was
diplomatically declared to be so magnanimous that there was no way they
could reciprocate appropriately.

'The use of divine honours to fulfill the requirements of deference to
the emperor' was the essence of imperial veneration, as Lendon astutely
observed.[82] He cites in support the inscription recording the reciprocal
response for the exemption of Achaea from taxes by Nero — 'in order
that our city might appear to have employed every possible honour and
act of piety towards the house of the lord Nero Augustus' (ἵνα τούτων
πᾶσαν τειμὴν καὶ εὐσέβειαν ἐκπεπληρωκυῖα εἰς τὸν τοῦ κυρίου Σεβαστοῦ
Νέρωνος οἶκον).[83]

It shows how politically important it was that on significant imperial
festivals and holy days, all citizens reciprocate by publicly participating in
appropriate divine venerations as expressions of their thankfulness for all
the imperial blessings they enjoyed and their undying loyalty to Rome.

Tiberius is recorded as refusing what was known as 'equal honours
to the gods' (ἰσόθεοι τιμαί).[84] On the basis of that evidence alone, the conclusion could not be drawn that the imperial cult only came into being
much later in the century and therefore posed no problem for the first
generation of Christians.

When embassies came from cities all over the empire offering to
build a temple and acknowledging the divine right of the new emperor to
rule, that offer was refused as a matter of diplomatic protocol. The emperor
told them that 'temples were only for gods'.

According to Suetonius, Tiberius refused divine titles.[85] Significant

81. *IGRR* 4, 145.

82. J. E. Lendon, *Empire of Honour: The Art of Government in the Roman World* (Oxford: Clarendon Press, 1997), p. 16, *ll.* 52-54.

83. *ILS* 8794, *ll.* 52-54.

84. Suetonius, *Tiberius* 26.

85. Suetonius, *Tiberius* 26.

evidence survives from Tacitus in which Tiberius stated emphatically during a debate in the Senate that it would be inappropriate for him to be worshipped as a god in the provinces. Tacitus recorded this *verbatim*.

> 'Gentlemen, I call you to witness that I am a mortal, and I behave as a man, and am content to take a leading place among men; and I wish future generations to recall this. They will do ample justice to my memory if they believe me to have been worthy of my ancestors, to have shown foresight in managing your interests, to have been steadfast in dangers and unafraid of causing offence for the sake of the public good. These are my temples, in your minds, these are the most beautiful and lasting of images.' Subsequently he [Tiberius] persisted, even in private talks, in rejecting such worship of himself. Some explained this as modesty, many as diffidence, some thought it indicated an ignoble spirit — for, they said, the best of men have always deserved the highest honours, i.e., honours equal to the gods.[86]

However, the above protestations to the Senate and in imperial audiences had been precipitated by his previous action whereby he had granted permission for a temple to be built to him. Tacitus relates that 'the province of Further Spain sent an embassy to the Senate and petitioned to be allowed to follow the example of Asia and erect a temple in honour of Tiberius and his mother. Caesar was in general steadfast in rejecting honours'.[87]

Then follows a defense that Tiberius felt compelled to make to the Senate to cover his duplicity. His inconsistent actions on this matter had caused serious doubts as to his sincerity and would be indicative as to how he would operate in his new rôle as Principate. He reminded the members of the Senate of the combined cult that venerated this august body and then assured them that his one exception was not a precedent for all the empire.

> I know, Senators, many think me inconsistent because recently, when the cities of Asia made the same request, I did not oppose it. Therefore I shall at one and the same time present the justification of my previous silence and also my decision regarding the future. Since the deified

---

86. Tacitus, *Annals* 4.38.

87. Tacitus, *Annals* 4.37. See D. Fishwick, *Imperial Cult in the Latin West: Provincial Cult*, III.1, pp. 107, 169.

Augustus, all of whose deeds and pronouncements I regard as having the force of law, did not forbid the establishment of a temple to himself and the city of Rome at Pergamum, I followed the example he set, more readily because my own cult was conjoined with veneration of the Senate. However, although a single acceptance might be excusable, to allow oneself to be worshipped in all the provinces through statues with divine attributes would be vainglorious and arrogant.[88]

This policy statement to the Senate would seem to be confirmed in a letter that 'Tiberius Caesar, son of the deified Augustus' sent to Gytheum near Sparta in the province of Achaea in response to their official embassy. This was reproduced in an inscription.

> Decree and letter of Tiberius. Tiberius Caesar, son of the deified Augustus (θεοῦ Σεβαστοῦ υἱός), *pontifex maximus,* of the tribunician power for the eighteenth time, sends greetings to the ephors and the city of Gytheum. Your envoy sent to myself and to my mother, Decimus Turrnaius Nicanor, has conveyed to me your letter to which was attached the legislation passed by you in veneration (εὐσέβειαν) of my father and honours towards us (τιμήν δὲ ἡμετέραν). I praise you for this and consider it fitting both for all men in general and for your city in particular to reserve special honours befitting the gods (τὰς θεοῖς πρέπουσας τιμὰς), for the greatness of the benefits conferred by my father upon the whole world: but I myself am satisfied with more moderate ones proper for men.[89]

There may or may not be anything significant in the distinction between the use of the terms εὐσέβεια and τιμή, for the term was used by Tiberius of 'us' and then of the deified Augustus for special honours appropriate for the gods. Given that their delegation was to himself and his mother, he added in his official response, 'My mother, however, will reply to you when she learns from you your decision about honours for her.'[90] Was it up to his mother, Livia, to decide whether to accept divine hon-

---

88. Tacitus, *Annals* 4.37.

89. *SEG* 11, 922, *ll.* 11-21. At the end of the century Domitian was declared by the poet Martial to be 'Sovereign ruler of the earth and Father of the World' *(summe munid rector et Parens Orbis)* 7.7 verse 4, but no earlier evidence of this title can be located in either literary or non-literary or numismatic evidence.

90. *SEG* 11, 922, *ll.* 21-22.

ours, for his use of ἡμετέραν would include honours not only for Tiberius? His mother bore him by Tiberius Claudius Nero. She was divorced from him and then married Augustus, who was deified by the Senate after his apotheosis.

However, what happened in that city after the delegation returned home from Rome is revealing. Tiberius went on to give these directions.

> Let him place . . . on the first pedestal [the statue] of the deified Augustus, the father [i.e., of Tiberius or 'Father of the Fatherland'], and on the second on the right that of Julia Augusta, and on the third that of the emperor Tiberius Caesar, son of Augustus, the statues being provided to him by the city. A table is to be set by him in the middle of the theatre and an incense burned on it, and the councillors and all their fellow magistrates are to offer sacrifice on it before the performers enter for the safety of the principes.[91]

It would seem that in the minds of the city fathers 'three carved images, of the deified Augustus, Julia Augusta and Tiberius Caesar, son of Augustus' and the incense burnt on the table were to all of them as part of a public ritual.

Sherk records that another official record shows 'there is already a cult of the future emperor, Tiberius, in the Greek East'. This was long before he succeeded Augustus in A.D. 14.[92] In 1 B.C. another inscription states — 'Helidoros (son) of Maiandrios (son) of Theodotos, who was priest of Tiberius Claudius Nero for life'.[93] This occurred before the heirs appointed by Augustus, Lucius and Gaius, had died in A.D. 2 and 4.

On an Augustan inscription from the island of Cyprus dated between 9 B.C. and A.D. 2, later city fathers had no difficulty adding to the same inscription on 16 November A.D. 29 identical honours they had previously given to Augustus — 'To Tiberius Caesar Augustus, god, son of divine Augustus'.[94]

---

91. *SEG* 11, 923, *ll.* 1-6.

92. R. K. Sherk, *Rome and Greek East to the Death of Augustus* (Cambridge: Cambridge University Press, 1984), no. 105, n. 1.

93. *SIG*³ 781 I.

94. *BSA* 42 (1947), p. 222, no. 9. Ehrenberg and Jones, *Documents Illustrating the Reigns of Augustus and Tiberius*, no. 115 a and b, θεοῦ υἱῷ θεῷ Σεβαστῷ, and also no. 226, where in the temple of Asclepius in Cos a statue was erected to Gnaeus Capito who was the procurator of Tiberius Caesar Augustus, 'god' (θεοῦ).

In the town of Lapethus, also on Cyprus, Adrastus set up an inscription in the same year, on 16 November, on the base of a statue of Tiberius in the gymnasium dedicated to him.

> To Tiberius Caesar Augustus, god, son of the deified Augustus (θεῷ θεοῦ Σεβαστοῦ υἱῷ), saluted as victorious commander, high priest, of the tribunal power for the 31st time, when Lucius Axius Naso was proconsul and Marcus Etrilius Lupercus was his legate and Gaius Flavius Figulus, his quaestor, Adrastus, son of Adrastus, Friend of Caesar (Φιλοκαῖσαρ), the hereditary priest of the temple and cult statue of Tiberius Caesar Augustus was set up in the gymnasium by him [i.e., Adrastus] at his own expense, the patriotic and most excellent and unpaid and voluntary gymnasiarch and priest of the gods in the gymnasium, built the temple and statue at his own expense to his god (κατεσκευνασεν τὸν καὶ τὸ ἄγαλμα ἰδίοις αἰαλώμασιν τῷ α(ὐ)τοῦ θεῷ) [i.e., Tiberius], when Dionysius, son of Dionysius and Apollodotus, Friend of Caesar (Φιλοκαῖσαρ), was ephebarch. Adrastus, Friend of Caesar, dedicated (them), being assisted by the dedication of his son, Adrastus, Friend of Caesar (Φιλοκαῖσαρ), who is also unpaid and voluntary gymnasiarch of the boys, on the birthday of Tiberius on the 24th day of Apogonicus (i.e., 16th November).[95]

There are a number of significant features in this inscription. Adrastus claimed the reigning emperor, Tiberius, was 'his god' (τῷ α(ὐ)τοῦ θεῷ). The dedication is to the divine Tiberius, 'god, son of god' but was not combined with *Roma*.[96] He dedicated this presumably with the approval of the proconsul, legate and the *questor* of the province whom he named in this official inscription.

That Apollodotus was called a 'friend of Caesar' (Φιλοκαῖσαρ) (*l. 5*) is significant, for this title was not a self-designated one or an accolade given by others but by the emperor himself. According to Crook it was 'an active and arduous honour, which may well have taken a man's whole time and attention'.[97] It was also recorded in the same inscription of Adrastus (*ll.* 11, 12).

---

95. *OGIS* 583.

96. *OGIS* 583, *l.* 6.

97. For an important discussion see J. A. Crook, *'Amici Principis'*, in *Consilium Principis: Imperial Councils and Counsellors from Augustus to Diocletian* (Cambridge: Cambridge University Press, 1955), ch. 3, cit. p. 26. See also his discussion of Vitellius in the time of Tiberius who also distinguished himself as the friend of Claudius, pp. 38-39 and 41.

An oath of loyalty and worship was sworn to Tiberius by the inhabitants of Palaepaphos, again on Cyprus, where the traditional imperial goddess is linked to his name.[98] It was prefaced with addresses to other deities, and proposed to vote divine honours to Rome and Tiberius.

> Our own Aphrodite of the Headland, our own Maiden, our own Apollo of Hyle, our own Apollo of Keryneia, our own Saving Dioskouroi, the Common Hearth of Cyprus within the Council House, the gods and goddesses of our Fathers that are common to this island, the offspring of Aphrodite [the Roman Venus, the mother of the imperial family] who is the god Caesar Augustus (ἔκγονον τῆς Ἀφροδίτης Σεβαστὸν Θεὸν Καίσαρα), Roma the Everlasting (τὴν ἀέναον Ῥώμην) together with all the other gods and goddesses (ἄλλους θεοὺς θεάς). We, ourselves and our children [swear] to harken and obey alike by land and sea, to regard with loyalty and to worship Tiberius Caesar Augustus, son of Augustus, with all his house, to have the same friends and foes as they, to propose the voting of divine honours to Rome and Tiberius Caesar Augustus . . . and to the sons of his blood to these only, together with the other gods, and to no other at all (καὶ οὐδενὶ ἄλλῳ τῶν πάντων).[99]

Three years earlier, in A.D. 26, Tiberius granted permission to have a second provincial imperial cult sited in the province of Asia. This was finally located in Smyrna with senatorial approval, the previous site being in Pergamum and established in 29 B.C. to *Roma* and Augustus. Surprisingly the former was dedicated to Tiberius, Livia his mother and the Senate.[100]

Suetonius noted of Augustus, 'Although well aware that it was usual to vote temples even to proconsuls, he would not accept one even in a province, save jointly in his own name and that of Rome. In the city itself (Rome) he refused this honour most emphatically, even melting down the silver statues set up in his honour.'[101] Another provincial cult

---

98. T. B. Mitford, "A Cypriot Oath of Allegiance to Tiberius," *JRS* 50 (1960): 75-79.

99. Mitford, "A Cypriot Oath of Allegiance to Tiberius," pp. 75-76. *SEG* 18:578.

100. Tactius, *Ann.* 4.55-56. See P. Trebilco, *The Early Christians in Ephesus from Paul to Ignatius* (Grand Rapids and Cambridge: Eerdmans, 2007), pp. 30-31.

101. Suetonius, "The Divine Augustus," in *Lives of the Caesars* 52; S. J. Friesen, *Twice Neokoros: Ephesus, Asia and the Cult of the Flavian Imperial Family* (Leiden: E. J. Brill, 1993), pp. 15-21; and S. J. Friesen, *Imperial Cults and the Apocalypse of John: Reading Revelation in the Ruins* (Oxford: Oxford University Press, 2001), p. 36.

was established in Hither Spain as well as in Lusitania in the reign of Tiberius.[102]

In this Principate of Tiberius, Roman freedmen operated as 'the priests of Tiberius' not only in Roman colonies in the East but also close to Rome itself.[103] They succeeded those who had held the title under his predecessor as 'the priests of Augustus'.[104]

It was not only distinguished provincials in the East who built temples for Tiberius and freedmen who became his priests. Herod the Great, Rome's client king, had already built an imperial cult temple to *Roma* and Augustus, placing it in the traditional location — the highest visible place in the city of Caesarea Maritima in Samaria, which he founded and laid out in the Roman centuriation pattern.[105] It was part of his kingdom of Judea and became the seat of Roman government in the province of Judea soon after his death.

Tiberius' own appointee to the governorship of Judea did the same, as the well-known inscription in the shrine there affirms. 'Tiberius Pontius Pilate, governor of Judea gave and dedicated it ([————]s *Tiberieum* [*.Po*]*ntius Pilatus* [*praef*]*ectus Iud*[*ae*]*e* [*dedit dedicavit*]).[106] Pilate did not dedicate a shrine to *Roma* and Tiberius or Augustus but to the reigning emperor. Combined with the temple Herod the Great erected in Caesarea, it clearly indicated that the temple was meant for the veneration of the Caesars by provincials and not just by Roman citizens.

Not only were the Roman governor, Pontius Pilate and provincials in the East keen to acknowledge his 'divinity', in Rome itself towards the end of the Principate of Tiberius *c.* A.D. 30, Valerius Maximus wrote in the opening of the preface to his *Memorable Doings and Sayings* —

> You, therefore, I invoke for this enterprise, into whose hands the common consent of mankind and gods has desired to place the rule of

---

102. Fishwick, *Imperial Cult in the Latin West*, III.1, pp. 43, 52-53, 168.

103. Price, *Rituals and Power*, p. 58, notes there were priests of Augustus recorded in thirty-four cities in Asia Minor and priests of Tiberius in eleven cities in Asia Minor.

104. S. Mitchell, *Anatolia: Land, Men, and Gods in Asia Minor* (Oxford: Clarendon Press, 1993), I, p. 107. In fact there is a third-century 'priest of Tiberius' in the Lycian assembly, *IGR* III.474.

105. D. W. Roller, *The Building Program of Herod the Great* (Berkeley: University of California Press, 1998), pp. 136, 138-39. For a coin minted by King Agrippa I showing himself clasping hands with Claudius in front of the imperial cult temple, see *RPC* no. 4982.

106. *Approximate Date:* 26-37 CE Caesarea, Israel 1961 Israel Museum (Jerusalem) *Inventory number: AE* 1963 no. 104.

sea and land, Caesar [Tiberius], the surest salvation of our fatherland *(certissima salus patriae)*, by whose heavenly forethought the virtues of which I am about to speak most generously encouraged and vices most severely punished. For if the orators of old began rightly with Jupiter the Best and Greatest, if the finest poets have taken their beginning from some divine power, my humble person would have recourse to your favour all the more appropriately in that while the divinity *(divinitas)* of others is deduced from belief, yours is seen by tangible proof to be equal to the star of your father and grandfather, by whose exceptional splendour much illustrious brilliance has been added to our ceremonies: for we have inherited the other gods, but we have bequeathed the Caesars.[107]

He dedicated this to the reigning emperor, Tiberius, and used the term 'divinity' *(divinitas)* of him in the preface, explicating it by stating, 'yours is seen by present certainty as equal to the star of your father and grandfather', i.e., Julius Caesar and Augustus [*numen*].[108] This was comparable with the designation of *Divus Augustus*.[109]

Wardle makes some important observations in his careful examination of this preface. 'Valerius' choice of an invocation to Tiberius and his deliberate confounding of *deus* and *divus* show as indisputable his knowledge of the formal restriction against calling the emperor *deus* and his determination to circumvent the restriction.' He concludes that 'Valerius understands well the language and images that the first emperors promoted and himself assiduously supports them. Among our extant sources Valerius' particular contribution, as has been shown here, is to highlight the persuasiveness and importance of the imperial cult in the emperors' [Augustus and Tiberius] self-presentation'.[110]

107. Valerius Maximus, *Memorable Doings and Sayings* I. Preface.

108. The reference is to coins issued with a star above the head of Augustus and Julius Caesar with a comet that was said to have appeared after his death. H.-F. Mueller, *Roman Religion in Valerius Maximus* (London and New York: Routledge, 2002), p. 180: '[I]n Valerius' day state and religion were personified in one man, a temporal ruler and god'.

109. Valerius Maximus, *Memorable Doings and Sayings* 1.7.1, 3.8.8, 7.7.3-4, 7.8.6 and 9.15.2. For an illuminating discussion see D. Wardle, "Valerius Maximus on the *Domus Augusta*, Augustus, and Tiberius," *C.Q.* 50, no. 2 (2000): 479-93.

110. Wardle, "Valerius Maximus on the *Domus Augusta*, Augustus, and Tiberius," pp. 492-93, and for a detailed discussion see his "The Preface to Valerius Maximus," *Athenaeum* 87 (1999): 523-25. See pp. 63-65 for a discussion of *deus* and *divus*.

Muller in his discussion of Roman religion in *Valerius Maximus* summarizes his findings. 'Gods are also in close connection to the imperial family, whose *pater familias,* Tiberius, also happens to be *pontifex maximus* of the state religion, *princeps* of the restored republic, and a participant in the divinity of his ancestors.'[111] He further notes the benefits that have flowed to the empire.

> Valerius' own *princeps,* Tiberius, is himself a god on earth who promotes virtue and punishes vice *(praef.).* He holds the reins of power, and Jupiter accompanies him as a personal attendant. . . . He is the prime mover and warden of our safety. . . . He cares for us according to the divine place. The results of such divine intervention: Peace prevails, law rules, the course of private and public duties is kept pure.[112]

The conclusion is that the nexus between ethics and cultic honours is important for Valerius Maximus, and the divine rôle that Tiberius plays in all this is critical.

Germanicus, the nephew and now adopted son of Tiberius, in an official proclamation issued to the Alexandrians when he visited their city in A.D. 19, makes an important declaration for one who is now part of the imperial family. He was in Alexandria 'to regulate overseas provinces . . . [and that] has torn me from the embrace of my father [in Rome]'.[113] He gave an explicit affirmation of the appropriate acclaim of divinity for his adopted father, mother and grandmother and verified that his own position was merely a reflection of that. Divine acclamation was to be given to his father, Tiberius, who was still alive.

> Proclamation of Germanicus Caesar, son of Augustus [Tiberius] and grandson of the deified Augustus (θεοῦ Σεβαστοῦ), proconsul: your goodwill, that you always display when you see me, I acknowledge but your acclamations that are odious to me and such as are accorded to the gods; for your acclamations [of divinity] I completely deprecate. For they are appropriate only to him who is actually the saviour and benefactor of the whole human race (τῷ σωτῆρι οὕτως καί εὐεργέτῃ

---

111. H.-F. Muller, *Roman Religion in Valerius Maximus* (London and New York: Routledge, 2002), p. 20.

112. Muller, *Roman Religion in Valerius Maximus,* p. 180.

113. *P.Oxy.* 2435.

τοῦ σύνπαντος τῶν ἀνθρωπων γένους), my father and to his mother, my grandmother. My position is a reflection of their divinity (ἐκείνων θειότητος), so that unless you comply with my request, you will force me to appear in public but seldom.[114]

In discussing Tiberius' speech to the Senate at the commencement of his Principate, Tacitus concluded that he 'involved himself more than ever in indefiniteness and ambiguity', a characteristic patently obvious to the Senate, but one they went along with.[115]

The vital pieces of official evidence concerning cult paid to Tiberius can be easily overlooked and sole credence given to his official protestation rejecting 'honours equal to the gods' taken at face value. That latter disclaimer has long been invoked by New Testament scholars of previous generations in support of their view that the imperial cult was not operative until the reign of Domitian.[116]

Tacitus' observation made in retrospect at the end of the first century of Tiberius' characteristics of 'indefiniteness and ambiguity' does not sufficiently account for his policies on 'honours equal to the gods' in his Principate.[117] One can only conclude of Tiberius that at times he 'protests too much' and there was what might charitably be called something of an inconsistency concerning such venerations. The idea of Tiberius' staunch opposition to imperial cultic veneration has gained wide currency but is firmly contradicted by official evidence and supported by a credible literary source.

What can be said of the cult for the remainder of the Julio-Claudian emperors on this issue that would be relevant to the early Christian move-

---

114. "Two Edicts of Germanicus," *Select Papyri* 211, *ll.* 31-45.

115. Tacitus, *Annals* 1.11.

116. See for example D. Cuss, *Imperial Cult and Honorary Terms in the New Testament* (Fribourg: Fribourg University Press, 1974). His comprehensive use of sources on the imperial cult and the New Testament implications towards the empire and emperor moves on to explore the Book of Revelation and concludes that persecutions were only in the later period.

117. R. Seager, *Tiberius* (Oxford: Blackwell, 2005²) challenges the traditional view of Tiberius as a consummate hypocrite, and portrays him instead as a man whose virtues and beliefs were corrupted by power, losing his grasp on reality as his fears of conspiracy and assassination spiralled out of control and finally resorted to ruling by terror. The second edition of this biography contains a substantial 'Afterword', pp. 213-42, reconsidering various questions and discussing new evidence that has come to light since the first edition of 1972.

ment? Tiberius would not be the last emperor formally to reject divine honours. When Gaius succeeded him as emperor on 16 March A.D. 37 he also adopted the convention of declining honours. His official response to the important Leagues of the Achaeans, Boeotians, Locrians, Phocians and Euboeans was —

> I have read the decree given to me by your ambassadors and have recognized that you have spared no extravagance in your zeal and devotion to me, in that you have both each personally offered a sacrifice for my security and have joined in a common festival (ἰδίᾳ τε ἕκαστος θυσάμενοι ὑπὲρ τῆς ἐμῆς σωτηρίας καὶ κοινῇ ἑορτάσαντες) [*ll.* 26-27] and decreed the greatest honours you could; for all this I both praise you all (ἐφ' οἷς ἅπασι ἐπαινῶ ὑμᾶς) and give my approval. And remembering the distinction from ancient times of each of the Greek republics, I permit you to meet as a league. But as for the statues you voted me, if you please, reduce the great number and be content with those that will be placed at Olympus and Nemea and at the Pythian sanctuary and at the Isthmus. By doing this you will [venerate me] and burden yourself less with expense.[118]

On the return of this embassy from Rome, reference was made to the beginning of his Principate as the 'time when for all the most blessed reign of the new divine emperor has dawned' (καιρὸν ἡ πᾶσιν μακαριωτάτη ἐπέλαμψεν ἡγεμονία τοῦ νέου θεοῦ Σεβαστοῦ).[119] Again, how Gaius formally responded to their acknowledgement of his heavenly mandate and their regional affirmation of the new divine emperor was different. What is put down to his period of mental instability when he planned to set up a statue of himself in the temple in Jerusalem may not have been as an extreme disorientation as has been thought.[120] In his time another provincial imperial cult in Asia was established for Gaius Caligula in Miletus but was discontinued after his assassination.[121]

---

118. Oliver, *Greek Constitutions of Early Roman Emperors from Inscriptions and Papyri*, no. 18, ll. 24-33, *IG* 7, 2711, ll. 21.

119. Oliver, *Greek Constitutions of Early Roman Emperors from Inscriptions and Papyri*, no. 18, ll. 59-60.

120. On Gaius' madness and assassination, see A. A. Barrett, *Caligula: The Corruption of Power* (London: Batsford, 1989), pp. 214-15.

121. Friesen, *Twice Neokoros: Ephesus, Asia and the Cult of the Flavian Imperial Family*, pp. 21-26.

In a letter to the Thasians, Claudius likewise refused honours on his accession in a convention established by his predecessors.

> What I replied to [all the embassies sent to me] I say to you too, namely that I approve the [verbal expressions] of [your] zeal and piety in their entirety, but that I decline the temple because I judge that to be the privilege for the gods alone, though I accept other honours, which befit the best *Principes*. And I confirm to you, in accordance with the decrees of the divine Augustus, everything that was an honour from him in reference to what you previously had and especially to the export of grain. [The] immunity [shall remain and I shall] write to [the] prefect so that if there is nothing [on record?] in the prefecture [as to] these (privileges) having been given to you he may let me know. Rest assured that I am considerate of the city in all other ways.[122]

Those in Thasos were clearly seeking confirmation of economic and other privileges and Claudius was careful to declare his response as consistent with his own policy.

Claudius also wrote in the same vein to the Alexandrians. 'I decline my high priest and temple establishments, for I do not wish to seem vulgar to my contemporaries. I judge that temples and the like have been defined and set apart by all ages for the gods alone. I decline a temple, which, I judge, is for the gods alone'.[123]

This did not prevent Lucius Aemilius Rectus, the Prefect of Egypt, prefacing the letter of Claudius to the Alexandrians with a notice to be read by the inhabitants of that city.

> Seeing that all the populace, owing to numbers, was unable to be present for the reading of the most sacred and most beneficial letter to the city, I have deemed it necessary to display this letter publicly in order that reading it one by one you may both wonder at the greatness of our god Caesar (τὴν τε μεγαλιότητα τοῦ θεοῦ ἡμῶν Καίσαρος θαυμάσητε) and be grateful for his goodwill towards the city (καὶ τῇ πρὸς τὴν πόλειν ὁμοίᾳ εὐνοίᾳ χάριν ἔχητε).[124]

---

122. C. Dun and and J. Pouilloux, *Recherches sur l'Histoire et les Cultes de Thasos,* II (1958), pp. 66-69, no. 179, cited in Smallwood, *Documents of Gaius, Claudius and Nero,* no. 371, *ll.* 3-13. On Claudius see Fishwick, *Imperial Cult in the Latin West,* I.1, p. 200ff.

123. *P. Lond.* 1912, *ll.* 48-51.

124. *P. Lond.* 1912, *ll.* 6-8.

Not just in the East but also in the Latin West there is evidence of a personal temple cult to the living Claudius.[125] Seneca the Younger who operated at the seat of imperial power at the end of the Principate of Claudius, and certainly in the early years of Nero, noted that at Camulodunum (Colchester), Claudius 'has a temple in Britain, that the Barbarians worship him and beseech him, as a god'.[126]

Nero on his accession was no different. The diplomatic language used concerning the refusal of divine honours could possibly be the work of Seneca the Younger, Nero's tutor turned *amicus principis* on his accession. The emperor had not yet reached his seventeenth birthday. Nero refers to Menecles and Metrodorus who came on the embassy on behalf of Aezani in Phrygia.

> Menecles and Metrodorus, your sons came to me and explained to me in full how you yourself have striven in my regard and the innovations you have made in the city concerning my honours. On account of this, it was in no ordinary fashion that I heard firm news of your goodwill towards me and your perpetual eagerness to devise something extra in my honour . . . [three fragmentary lines] . . . may your energy on my account be without cost to you, who have already shown so much that you do not choose to spare your energy for the sake of your own resources. Menecles, your son, was also prepared to stay with me as long as I might wish . . . [fifteen fragmentary lines follow].[127]

It is interesting to note the stated aim of their city was to be innovative in seeking to honour the new emperor. His response, that it should be without cost to them, was his diplomatic way of saying 'no' to building a temple to him. He continued —

> I decline that of a temple because this honour is rightly assigned by men to the gods alone; and as for the gold crown you sent, I shall gratefully remit it, for at the beginning of my Principate I do not wish to burden you.[128]

---

125. On Claudius see Fishwick, *Imperial Cult in the Latin West*, I.1, p. 200ff.

126. Seneca the Younger, *Apocolocyntosis* 8. For a discussion Fishwick, *Imperial Cult in the Latin West*, I.1, pp. 201-3, of the debate surrounding the date and the event.

127. *OGIS* 475.

128. *OGIS* 475. See also Oliver, *Greek Constitutions of Early Roman Emperors*, no. 40.

The distinction in worship of the Divine Julius and *Roma* by Roman citizens and Augustus or the reigning emperor and *Roma* by provincials continued in the Principate of Augustus in the East — sometimes, but not always, linked to the goddess *Roma*. By the time of Tiberius a provincial imperial temple was dedicated, no longer following the dichotomy between Roman citizens and provincials or links with the goddess *Roma* but, as has been noted, including his mother and the Senate as well as himself. (See p. 79.)

New emperors customarily declined divine honours for two different audiences, i.e., that of Rome and those from the cities in the East who made this offer.[129] With the Julio-Claudians there is sufficient extant evidence to conclude that there was an unwritten convention whereby a new emperor formally refused the offer by embassies from the East to build a temple in his honour as a way of acknowledging loyalty and the legitimacy of his office.

How the coded diplomatic statement of refusing divine honours was interpreted cannot be known in every instance. Price concludes, 'The Greek diplomatic advances to Rome with offers of cult are seen as elaborate ploys intended to gain Roman favour; the fact that the emperor might decline the honours did not discourage the Greeks and shows that there were no Roman pressures on the cults.'[130] This was not necessarily the case with some Roman officials in the East. (See pp. 168-71.)

The evidence cited indicates that this refusal was not taken at face value. In fact extant evidence points to a subsequent 'disregarding' of the imperial response. For example, Price records that in Asia Minor ten imperial cult temples or sanctuaries were erected between A.D. 1 and 50, a further seven for the remainder of that century and fifteen for the first half of the next.[131] He also cites Dio Cassius' comment that under Tiberius, Cyzicus lost its free status because its citizens had failed to complete an imperial cult temple to Augustus and in addition had also imprisoned some Roman citizens.[132]

Fishwick has rightly concluded, 'Despite Julio-Claudian "refusals" of divine honours for the emperor himself, this was a welcome extension

---

129. Oliver, *Greek Constitutions of Early Roman Emperors*, nos. 15, 19, 23.

130. Price, *Rituals and Power*, p. 65.

131. Price, *Rituals and Power*, p. 59.

132. Price, *Rituals and Power*, pp. 66, 83, and p. 251, citing as evidence Dio Cassius, *Roman History* 57.24.6.

of the ruler cult which official policy could afford to leave unchecked.'[133] When it came to establishing provincial, as distinct from local civic cults, Rome's official authorization was required. Tiberius gave permission for the setting up of a provincial cult in Asia in A.D. 23. It was dedicated not only to Livia and the personified Senate but also to himself, but no mention was made of *Roma* and the *Divus Iulius,* or Augustus.[134] Augustus' distinction between Roman citizens worshipping the Divine Julius Caesar and *Roma,* and provincials venerating Augustus and *Roma,* may have been set aside after the principate of Tiberius and gave rise to the Cult of the *Sebastoi.*[135] Such approval would be required for Nero's provincial-wide cult by the Achaean League located in Corinth, its capital. (See chapter 7.)

In the light of the above discussion on the 'refusal' of divine honours and temples, and the previous section on the widespread use of divine titles of the Julio-Claudian emperors, it certainly was not the case that imperial cultic activities lay dormant in any of their reigns. Almost all sources cited in this chapter are official ones, i.e., officially sanctioned inscriptions, plinths of statues and legal currency, and thus provide evidence of imperial endorsement of cultic veneration as a sign of loyalty. It was inevitable that the first Christians in the Roman Empire would have to deal with this reality. The Christian apologist Tertullian (A.D *c.* 160–*c.* 240) later noted that the emperor was clearly known as 'the god of the Romans' *(Romanorum deus).*[136]

When reflecting on the actual use of comparable divine titles for emperors and Jesus, it would be wrong to conclude Christians borrowed them from Rome. As already noted, one would have to ask what would ever have possessed Christians either in Judea or the Roman East to do this? Furthermore, there would be no advantages whatsoever for their movement if the first Christians themselves awarded titles to Jesus because it would be a highly confrontational move, indeed a treasonable one against Rome. Chapter 9 gives an example of the charge that recent converts in Thessalonica were acting contrary to the decrees of Caesar (Acts 17:6-7). (See pp. 250-55.)

---

133. Fishwick, *Imperial Cult in the Latin West,* I.2, p. 198, and citation p. 330. On the declining of honours, see Smallwood, *Documents of Gaius, Claudius and Nero,* no. 371; L. R. Taylor, "Tiberius' Refusal of Divine Honors," *TAPA* 60 (1929): 87-101; and M. P. Charlesworth, "The Refusal of Divine Honours: An Augustan Formula," *PBSR* 15 (1939): 1-10.

134. Tacitus, *Annals* 4.55-56.

135. Fishwick, "Provincial Cult," in *Imperial Cult in the Latin West,* III.1, p. 230.

136. Tertullian, *Apology* 24.9.

The precedent for the majority of divine titles used of Jesus rests either covertly or overtly in the Old Testament. There its prophetic aspects and honours were seen as promised, claimed and realized in the person of Jesus.[137] This unhappy coincidence would prove to be an enormous challenge for the first generation of Christians. Therefore, their giving of any divine titles to the Caesars was overtly acting contrary to Jesus' specific command — 'the things that are Caesar's you must render to Caesar and the things of God to God' (τὰ Καίσαρος ἀπόδοτε Καίσαρι καὶ τὰ τοῦ θεοῦ τῷ θεῷ) (Mark 12:17). They could not render to Caesar the things that are God's.

137. Fantin has amply demonstrated with the Old Testament of the use of the term 'Lord' in *Lord of the Entire World: Lord Jesus, a Challenge to Lord Caesar?* See for example terms such as 'son' Ps. 2:7, 'saviour' Isa. 49:26, 'priest' in perpetuity Ps. 110:4.

CHAPTER 5

Adopt, Adapt, Abstain:
Jewish Responses to Divine Honours

Were there any variations in acceptable cultic expressions of loyalty to the Caesars that took into account social, ethnic and cultic diversity across their vast empire? There was not total conformity, as an official distinction was observed between the veneration of *Roma* and the Divine Julius by Roman citizens and *Roma* and Augustus by provincials.[1] With respect to the customs of its conquered peoples, Rome did not have to endorse these nor did it require uniformity from those who were now part of its ethnically diverse empire. This certainly was the case with the Jews. Cicero (106-43 B.C.) delivered a speech in the Aurelian Forum in Rome in 59 B.C. on behalf of Flaccus following the Jews' subjugation to Rome by Pompey that reflects his accommodation yet disparagement of the Jews.

> Each city, Laelius, has its own peculiar religion; we have ours. While Jerusalem was flourishing, and while the Jews were in a peaceful state, still the religious ceremonies and observances of that people were very much at variance with the splendor of this empire, and the dignity of our name, and the institutions of our ancestors. And they are the more odious to us now, because that nation has shown by arms what were its feelings towards our supremacy. How dear it was to the immortal gods is proved by its having been defeated, by its revenues having been farmed out to our contractors, by its being reduced to a state of subjection.[2]

1. D. Fishwick, *The Imperial Cult in the Latin West* (Leiden: E. J. Brill, 1993²), I.1, pp. 129-30.
2. Cicero, *Pro Flaccus* 28.

Yet an official letter from Flaccus, the proconsul of Asia in 31 B.C., re-enforced Rome's policy concerning the temple tax and the concessions of Augustus to the Jews.

> Gaius Norbanus Flaccus, proconsul, to the magistrates of the Sardini-ans sends greetings. Caesar has written to me, and commanded me not to forbid the Jews, however many they are, from assembling together according to the custom of their forefathers, nor from sending their money to Jerusalem. I have therefore written to you, that you may know that both Caesar and I would have you act accordingly.[3]

Were the Jewish authorities able to find a way that was both theologically faithful to their cultic practices and an amicable sign of loyalty to Roman rule? If so, would it have created a credible precedent for the nascent Christian movement?

Rutgers made an important distinction in *The Hidden Heritage of Di-aspora Judaism* — 'Jews did not adopt non-Jewish ways, but they adapted such elements for their own purposes. They integrated foreign elements into their own way of life', having noted in the commencement of his monograph 'and perhaps, to a very limited extent, even religiously'.[4] The term 'adapt' is felt to be highly apposite because it describes how the Jews in Judea and in Jewish client kingdoms to its north responded without compromising their faith. It also had implications for Diaspora Jews. How-ever, 'adopt' has to be used of Herod the Great's policy because he built a temple within the kingdom of Judea for imperial cult veneration in his capital, Caesarea Maritima, for the use of provincials. It was dedicated to *Roma* and Augustus. When the Jews revolted against Rome in the time of Nero, they ceased from sacrificing daily in the temple in Jerusalem for the safety of the emperor; 'abstain' thus sent a very clear signal to Rome.

The findings in this chapter are an important prelude to the remain-der of this book, where the first Christians' responses to the entrenched

---

3. Josephus, *Jewish Antiquities* 16.117. He was appointed proconsul of Asia in 31 B.C. shortly after the battle of Actium when Augustus defeated Mark Anthony. The former is the one to whom he refers.

4. L. V. Rutgers, *The Hidden Heritage of Diaspora Judaism* (Leuven: Peeters, 1998[2]), pp. 227. R. S. Dutch, "The Greek Gymnasium and the Corinthian Christians," in *The Edu-cated Elite in 1 Corinthians: Education and Community Conflict in Graeco-Roman Context* (London: T. & T. Clark, 2007), pp. 147-67, discusses Jews in the Diaspora participating in first-century education.

imperial cultic activities are explored. Could it be that different Jewish responses would provide possible precedents for the first Christians in the Roman East given their movement derived from Judaism and the fact that they used the same Scriptures?

It is proposed to examine (I) the way that Herod the Great adopted the Roman imperial cult by building a temple in Caesarea Maritima for the use of provincials; (II) Rome's official endorsement of the traditions of the Jews and their astute adaptation without compromising their beliefs as an acceptable cultic expression of loyalty; (III) extant archaeological and other evidence from Diaspora synagogues of how the Jews showed their loyalty to the emperor; and (IV) the significance of the cessation of sacrifices for the safety of the emperor in the Jerusalem temple as the beginning of the Jewish revolt in A.D. 66 that finally led to its destruction. Given the epigraphic evidence from Rome relating to the Jews of this era cited as copies by Josephus, a short appendix will address the issue of their authenticity.

I. Herod the Great's Blatant Adoption of the Imperial Cultic Veneration

In the era of the birth of the founder of Christianity it is unlikely that Jews would ever have endorsed what had surely been the blatant compromise on the part of Herod the Great (c. 73-4 B.C.), who himself was only partly Jewish and a client king of Rome. He noted the long period of peace and prosperity Judah had enjoyed during his reign and said, 'the Romans are, so to speak, the masters of the world, and my loyal friends'.[5]

His three visits to Rome had a great impact on him.[6] He subsequently sent his sons to be educated there as part of his diplomatic strategy.[7] His building policy replicated Rome's architectural ethos with the construction of the city of Caesarea Maritima and other projects elsewhere in the East.[8] Herod's building obsession, even of pagan temples, was 'equalled or

---

5. Josephus, *Jewish Antiquities* 15.387.

6. On Herod the Great's strategic visits to Rome see J. Curran, "*Philorhomaioi:* The Herods between Rome and Jerusalem," *Journal for the Study of Judaism* 45 (2014): 496.

7. 'The Herodian family's presence in the city of Rome over more than three generations'. Curran, "*Philorhomaioi:* The Herods between Rome and Jerusalem," p. 493.

8. For a helpful discussion see P. Richardson, *Herod: King of the Jews and Friend of the Romans* (Columbia: University of South Carolina Press, 1996).

surpassed only by the Roman emperors'.[9] He undertook their construction in Greece, Asia Minor, Syria and the southern Levant, as Roller records.[10] He also instigated the huge project involving a vast number of Levites of re-building the Jewish temple in Jerusalem. Its construction was not completed until well after his death.[11]

Most surprising of all, Herod also constructed a temple to *Roma* and Augustus for imperial cultic celebrations in Caesarea Maritima, which became his capital. This was located in the Samaritan area but still within the ancient borders of Israel. This temple dominated the city and was constructed clearly for the purpose of cultic veneration by provincials and not specifically for Romans; otherwise the temple would have been named '*Roma* and Divine Julius' and not '*Roma* and Augustus'. In doing this Herod would certainly have been seen to be acting with blatant duplicity and blasphemy by orthodox Jewish standards of his day. In Philo of Alexandria's time that temple continued to function as an imperial cultic site. He records the Jews' appeal to Pontius Pilate, the governor of Judea, to 'take down the shields at once and have them transferred from the capital [Jerusalem] to Caesarea [Maritima] on the coast surnamed after your great-grandfather, to be set up in the temple of Augustus'. Philo confirms 'and so they were'.[12]

Was Herod's action the exception, or were there similar compromises by subsequent generations of Jews including those at the time of the rise of the Christian movement? One view suggests that in the East there was no alternative for Jews with respect to the imperial cult activities. They had to compromise their beliefs by participating in sacrifices in order to accommodate the cult of their conquerors, certainly in the kingdoms and provinces outside of Judah.[13]

After Rome's conquest of the Jewish kingdom, the Jews had no formal charter with the Roman authorities that outlined their rights and took into account their cultural and cultic traditions. Rajak notes that what they had

9. D. W. Roller, *The Building Program of Herod the Great* (Berkeley: University of California Press, 1998), pp. 259-60.

10. For his comprehensive discussion of Herod's enormous building programme within Judea and elsewhere in the Roman East, see Roller, "Catalogue of Herod's Building Program," in *The Building Program of Herod the Great,* pp. 125-238.

11. It is significant that John 2:20 records this and that it took forty-six years to complete.

12. Philo, *The Embassy to Gaius* 305.

13. See Roller, "Herod's Legacy," in *The Building Program of Herod the Great,* ch. 10.

secured was 'largely due to political pressure and diplomacy on the part of the Jewish representatives and especially of some powerful intermediaries, such as certain members and adherents of the Herodian dynasty whose other services were of manifest value to Rome'.[14] Evidence from official inscriptions indicates that Jews did find an acceptable solution whereby they could express loyalty to Rome through their own sacrificial system.

Augustus and Claudius affirmed their respect for ancient Jewish ritual traditions. This was part of the overall Roman policy of *mos maiorum*, literally the 'custom of the ancestors', i.e., respecting the established traditions of kingdoms that were 'incorporated' into their vast empire.[15] Extant official decrees issued by Roman emperors reflect this respect. For example on the Island of Chios, the Roman Senate *c.* A.D. 6 confirms their policy —

> the Senate specifically confirmed that they might enjoy the laws and customs and rights which they had when they entered into friendship with the Romans, that they should be subject to no ruling whatsoever of magistrates or promagistrates, [and that] those Romans among them should obey the laws of Chians. And a letter of Imperator, son of the god, Augustus, consul for the eighth time, written to the Chians ... concerning the freedom of the city.[16]

Roman citizens living on this island also had to respect local customs and abide by its civic laws.

II. Imperial Affirmation of the Jewish Cultic Adaptation

Sacrifices for the emperor were offered in the Jerusalem temple. This had important implications for the Jews in Judah as well as for their Diaspora compatriots throughout the Roman provinces.

14. T. Rajak, "Was There a Roman Charter for the Jews?" in *The Jewish Dialogue with Greece and Rome: Studies in Cultural and Social Interaction* (Leiden: E. J. Brill, 2002), p. 302.

15. O. F. Robinson, *The Criminal Law of Ancient Rome* (London: Duckworth, 1995), p. 80.

16. R. K. Sherk, *Roman Documents from the Greek East: Senatus Consulta and Epistulae to the Age of Augustus* (Baltimore: Johns Hopkins University Press, 1969), no. 70. I am grateful to B. Bitner who drew my attention to this inscription and gave me access to his paper, "Augustan *Iurisdictio Praesidis*: Procedure and Legal Documents in *CIG* 2222," read at the American Philological Association Annual Meeting, January 2011.

(i) Augustus' Endorsement of Jewish Cultic Rights

Smallwood notes that 'in completely unknown circumstances, Augustus sent an edict setting out Jewish rights in full to the proconsul of Asia to be posted in the temple of the imperial cult at Ancyra. It is the most comprehensive surviving statement of the rights granted by Julius Caesar and confirmed by Augustus'.[17]

His decree can be confidently dated *c.* 8 B.C., towards the end of Herod the Great's reign. It commences with the reason for its promulgation followed by the contents of this degree of Augustus.[18]

> Caesar Augustus, Pontifex Maximus with tribunician power, proclaims: Since the Jewish people have been found well disposed to the Roman people not only at the present time but (ἀλλά) also in the past, and especially in the time of my father, the emperor Caesar, as has their high priest Hyrcanus, it was decreed by me (ἔδοξέ μοι) and my council under oath (κατὰ ὁρκωμοσίας), with the consent of the Roman people, to proclaim the Jews may follow their own customs in accordance with the laws of their fathers, just as they followed them in the time of Hyrcanus, high priest of the highest god (ἀρχιερέως θεοῦ ὑψίστου).[19]

The Jews' long-standing loyalty to 'the Roman people' was commended first of all.

> ... and that their sacred monies shall be inviolable and may be sent up to Jerusalem and delivered to the treasuries in Jerusalem and that they need not give bond on the Sabbath or on the day of preparation for it after the ninth hour. And if anyone is caught stealing their sacred books or their sacred monies from a synagogue or an ark [of the law], he shall

17. E. Mary Smallwood, "The Diaspora and Jewish Religious Liberty," in *The Jews under Roman Rule from Pompey to Diocletian: A Study of Political Relations* (Leiden: E. J. Brill, 1981²), p. 143.

18. For the argument for dating, see C. Eilers, "The Date of Augustus' Edict on the Jews (JOS. *AJ* 16.162-165) and the Career of C. Marcius Censorinus," *Phoenix* 58, no. 1 (2004): 86-95.

19. Josephus, *Jewish Antiquities* 16.162, *ll.* 2-163, *l.* 11. The use of the superlative 'highest' (ὕψιστος) in the phrase was also used of Zeus, but this document accommodates the Jews' own description of their 'divinity'.

be regarded as sacrilegious, and his property shall be confiscated to the public treasury of the Romans.[20]

This confirms that they were authorized to follow their long-standing cultic traditions including the payment of the temple tax to their Jerusalem cultic site. It is significant that harsh punishments under Roman law were invoked for any profaning of the Jewish sacred scriptures, stealing the temple tax destined for Jerusalem or even the ark of the Law. A more severe penalty was applied for the confiscation of property. (See p. 273.)

Finally, Augustus noted that the details of their provincial honours to him and his decree were to be set up by the governor of the province in the most public part of the imperial cult temple for all non-Jews to see.

> As for the resolution that was offered by them in my honour concerning the piety which I show to all men, and on behalf of Gaius Marcius Censorinus, I order that it and the present edict be set up in the most conspicuous [part of the temple] assigned to me by the Koinon of Asia with plainly visible (lettering) [text variant]. If anyone transgresses any of the above ordinances, he shall suffer severe punishment.[21]

This shows not inconsiderable sensitivity on the part of Augustus. He took into account that when non-Jewish subjects were in the imperial cult temple specifically for cultic veneration to himself, they may well have been tempted to lash out at the Diaspora Jews for their failure to show similar loyalty in that sacred place or on other festive occasions. It also clearly spelt out substantial punishments that could be expected from those who failed to follow Rome's policy of showing respect for Jewish cultic procedures, sites and objects.

(ii) Claudius' Decree on Alexandrian Jews, Reaffirming Augustus' Decree

A later decree of Claudius to the Alexandrians in A.D. 41 that is independent of Josephus' copies of official sources affirms the rights Augustus gave

---

20. Josephus, *Jewish Antiquities* 16.163, *ll.* 11-165, *l.* 19.
21. Josephus, *Jewish Antiquities* 16.165, *ll.* 19-26.

to the Jews to worship their God and follow their customs.[22] Some of its concessions parallel those recorded in the Augustan decree.

Often an understanding of Claudius' attitude to the Jews throughout his rule is derived solely from his banishment of the Jews from Rome a decade later in A.D. 51 (Acts 18:2). However, his earlier attitude was influenced in part by the precedent set by Augustus. Claudius also had a long-standing friendship from early childhood with the grandson of Herod the Great, Marcus Julius Agrippa. He had been sent to Rome at the age of five and educated along with him and Drusus, the son of Tiberius. Claudius refers to him as 'my own Agrippa, whom I have reared and kept with me'[23] — a precedent established by Herod the Great for his sons.[24] He would become Herod Agrippa I, King of the Jews.

After the assassination of the emperor Gaius in January A.D. 41, 'Agrippa's role in the accession of the emperor [Claudius] should not be overlooked when these are assessed: according to Josephus it had been the Herodian who advised Claudius to accept the guards' offer of the empire', Rajak observes.[25] Dio Cassius explains the tangible reward that followed this.

> He [Claudius] enlarged the domain of Agrippa of Palestine, who happening to be in Rome, had helped him to become emperor, and bestowed on him the rank of consul; and to his brother Herod he gave the rank of *praetor* and a principality. And he permitted them to enter the Senate and express their thanks in Greek.[26]

So it was on the basis of their long friendship and also Agrippa's help with his accession that he reciprocated thus. Claudius gave him rule over what had been the Roman province of Judea, including Jerusalem with its temple. 'Agrippa I possessed the kingdom of his grandfather'.[27] Osgood

22. *P. Lond.* 1912.

23. J. Osgood, *Claudius Caesar: Image and Power in the Early Roman Empire* (Cambridge: Cambridge University Press, 2011), p. 76. Josephus, *Jewish Antiquities* 20.1.2.12; Curran, "*Philorhomaioi:* The Herods between Rome and Jerusalem," pp. 500, 505.

24. N. Kokkinos, *The Herodian Dynasty: Origins, Role in Society and Eclipse,* Journal for the Study of Pseudepigraphic Supplement Series 30 (Sheffield: Sheffield Academic Press, 1998), pp. 271-72, 285, n. 72.

25. Rajak, "Was There a Roman Charter for the Jews?" p. 321.

26. Dio Cassius, *Roman History* 60.8.2.

27. Curran, "*Philorhomaioi:* The Herods between Rome and Jerusalem," p. 508.

comments, 'The hope was that Agrippa, raised in Rome but Jewish, would be able to satisfy the Jewish people while staying loyal to Rome.'[28] He had exercised a very limited jurisdiction under Gaius. However, he did not live long to enjoy the much wider client kingdom but died two years later in A.D. 43.[29]

A further reason for the promulgation of the Alexandrian decree early in the Principate of Claudius was that it guaranteed the legitimacy of Jewish rights and safety in the capital of the province of Egypt. This followed the gruesome débacle with the torturing and murder of some of the Jews there. It had happened with the acquiescence of Aulus Avilius Flaccus, the Prefect of Egypt from A.D. 32 to 38. He had humiliated Alexandrian Jews by having them stripped naked and scourged in a public 'spectacle' in the theatre.[30] Following this, two embassies from Alexandria were sent to Claudius, one of Alexandrian officials and the other of Jewish representatives including Philo.

Claudius' decision was disseminated in Egypt by Lucius Aemilius Rectus, the Prefect subsequent to Flaccus. Imperial reciprocal honours were displayed publicly in Alexandria so that 'reading it one by one you may admire the majesty of our god Caesar and feel gratitude for his goodwill towards the city'. Claudius specifically cited as his precedent Augustus' policy towards the Jews.

> Therefore, even now I earnestly ask of you that on the one hand the Alexandrians show themselves forbearing and kindly towards the Jews who for many years have dwelt in the same city, and dishonour none of the rites observed by them in the worship of their god, but allow them to observe their customs as in the time of the deified Augustus which I also, after hearing both sides, have confirmed (ἐβεβαίωσα).[31]

Claudius was impartial in that he also placed certain restrictions on the Jews there. The ruling of Claudius also broadly stipulated how the

---

28. Osgood, *Claudius Caesar: Image and Power in the Early Roman Empire*, pp. 114, 120-21.

29. Some of Agrippa's actions such as strengthening the walls of Jerusalem and also assembling five other client kings from the region would raise concerns in Rome. Osgood, *Claudius Caesar*, p. 120.

30. Philo, *Flaccus* 74-75. See E. S. Gruen, "Caligula, the Imperial Cult, and Philo's *Legatio*," and D. R. Schwartz, "Philo and Josephus on Violence in 38 C.E.," *Studia Philonica Annual* 24 (2012): 135-47, 149-66.

31. *P. Lond.* 1912, *ll.* 82-88.

Jews were to function in their city. He made it very clear that they were not in any way to throw in their lot with Jewish agitators from Syria or the Egyptian hinterland. They were

> not to agitate for more privileges than they formerly possessed, and not in future to send out a separate embassy as if they lived in a separate city, a thing unprecedented, and not to force their way into gymnasiarchiac or cosmetic games, while enjoying their own privileges and sharing a great abundance of advantages in a city not their own, and not to bring in or be like Jews who come down the river from Syria or Egypt, a proceeding which will compel me to conceive serious suspicions; otherwise I will by all means take vengeance on them as fomenters of what is a general plague infesting the whole world.[32]

His imperial diplomatic skills come across in an even-handed ruling, but clearly he was determined to endorse respect for the long-standing rights of Jews. It is interesting that Herod Agrippa had already been active on behalf of the Jews in Alexandria. Philo notes that 'when King Agrippa visited Alexandria and when told of Flaccus's malignant action he intervened',[33] by 'explaining the date at which it [their resolution] was actually passed and testifying to the Alexandrian Judaeans' long-standing loyalty [to Rome]'.[34]

(iii) Claudius' Decree Affirming Jewish Rights Throughout the Empire

Herod Agrippa I and Herod of Chalcis, both grandsons of Herod the Great, subsequently lobbied Claudius to extend the confirmation of Jewish rights decreed for those in Alexandria to all Diaspora Jews living throughout his empire.

> King Agrippa and Herod, my dearest friends, having petitioned me to permit the same privileges to be maintained for the Jews through-

---

32. *P. Lond.* 1912, *ll.* 88-100. Curran, "*Philorhomaioi:* The Herods between Rome and Jerusalem," p. 507.

33. Philo, *Flaccus* 103.

34. J. B. Rives, "Diplomacy and Identity among Jews and Christians," in *Diplomats and Diplomacy in the Roman World,* ed. C. Eilers (Leiden and Boston: E. J. Brill, 2009), p. 117.

out the empire under the Romans as those in Alexandria enjoy, I very gladly consented, not merely to please those who petitioned me, but also because in my opinion the Jews deserve to obtain their request on account of their loyalty and friendship to the Romans. In particular, I hold it right that not even Greek cities should be deprived of these privileges, seeing that they were in fact guaranteed for them in the time of the divine Augustus.[35]

Claudius publicly refers to 'my dearest friends (τῶν φιλτάτων μοι) Agrippa [I] and Herod [of Chalcis]' and not the title 'Caesar's friend',[36] or the 'friend' (ὁ φίλιος) as he does with reference to Gallio.[37] The declaration continued —

It is right, therefore, that the Jews throughout the whole world under our sway should also observe the customs of their fathers unhindered (ἀνεπικωλύτως). I enjoin upon them also by these presents to avail themselves of this kindness in a reasonable spirit, and not to set at nought the beliefs about the gods held by other people but to keep their own laws. It is my will that the ruling bodies of the cities and colonies and *municipia* in Italy and outside Italy, and the kings and other authorities through their own ambassadors [in Rome] shall cause this edict of mine to be inscribed, and keep it posted for not less than thirty days in a place where it can be plainly read from the ground.[38]

This decree set parameters for the Jews in the light of the 'reasonable spirit' of Claudius. They were to reciprocate appropriately by not engaging in anti-polytheistic polemics — 'not to set at nought the beliefs about the gods held by other people' but 'keep their own laws'. As an imperial decree it was to be posted for a minimum of thirty days where it could be plainly read in the cities, presumably in the official centre of the city, i.e., the agora.

Of Claudius' policy in this decree, Rajak concludes —

---

35. Josephus, *Jewish Antiquities* 19.289-91.

36. Herod Agrippa II was also a named friend of Claudius and Vespasian. J. A. Crook, 'Prosopographical Index', in *Consilium Principis: Imperial Councils and Counsellors from Augustus to Diocletian* (Cambridge: Cambridge University Press, 1955), nos. 168-69.

37. A reference to the proconsul of Achaea L. Junius Gallio mentioned in Acts 18:12-17.

38. Josephus, *Jewish Antiquities* 19.289-91.

We are led to ascribe innovation to the emperor Claudius. Soon after his accession, he was evidently shaken by the pressures of those Greek-Jewish crises in both Palestine and Alexandria, which his predecessor Gaius had created and he had to resolve, to utter in his own inimitable way a general policy of toleration (if we may call it that) for Jewish observance.[39]

However, Pucci Ben Zeev argues that 'Claudius did not innovate. He is only giving formal expression to the policy already implemented by Augustus, who had granted religious freedom to the Jews of Rome, of Delos, of Alexandria and to those living in Asia'.[40]

(iv) Provincial and Sardinian Decrees Verifying Jewish Diaspora Rights

It is of interest that the city of Sardis that had so strenuously promoted imperial cultic honours on its imperial days in the Calendar (see p. 48) would become a location where provincial and civic authorities had affirmed Jewish rights, including legal ones, in some detail. As early as 49 B.C. the most senior Roman official in the province at the time, Lucius Antonius, reaffirmed them following a Jewish delegation to him.

> To the magistrates, Council, and People of Sardis, greetings. Jewish citizens of ours[41] have come to me and pointed out that from the earliest times they have had their own association (σύνοδον ἔχειν ἰδίαν) in accordance with their native laws and own place (καὶ τόπον ἴδιον) in which they decide their affairs and controversies with one another; and upon their request that it be permitted for them to do these things, I decided they might be maintained and permitted them to do so.[42]

They certainly had the right to meet as a Jewish association (σύνοδος). Lucius Antonius communicated this in detail to the civic authorities.

39. Rajak, "Was There a Roman Charter for the Jews?" p. 317.

40. M. Pucci ben Zeev, *Jewish Rights in the Roman World: The Greek and Roman Documents Quoted by Josephus Flavius* (Tübingen: Mohr Siebeck, 1998), p. 342.

41. Josephus, *Jewish Antiquities* 14.235. A textual variant has 'yours', which would be the specific reference to the Jewish citizens of Sardis.

42. Josephus, *Jewish Antiquities* 14.235.

The Jewish citizens living in our city have continually received many great privileges from the people and have now come before the Council and the People and have pleaded that their laws and freedoms be restored to them by the Senate and the People of Rome.[43]

Pucci ben Zeev suggests that this reference to the restoration of rights by Rome 'is of utmost importance for us, inasmuch as it constitutes the only instance we have in which it is stated explicitly that the Jews obtained from the Romans the return of the right to use their own laws.'[44]

The 'ancient traditions' *(mos maiorum)* that Rome respected were then spelt out in detail.

[T]hey may in accordance with their legal customs (κατὰ τὰ νομιζόμενα ἔθη) come together and have a communal life and adjudicate suits among themselves, and that a place (τόπος) be given them in which they may gather together with wives and children and offer ancestral prayers and sacrifices to the God (θυσίας τῷ θεῷ), it has therefore been decreed (δεδόχθαι) by the Council and the People that permission shall be given to come together on stated days (ἐν ταῖς προαποδεδειγμέναις ἡμέραις) to do those things that are in accordance with their laws, and also that a place be set apart by the magistrates for them to build and inhabit, such as they consider suitable for this purpose, and that the market officials of the city (ὅπως τε τοῖς τῆς πόλεως ἀγορανόμοις) shall be charged with the duty of having suitable food for them brought in.[45]

One of the surprising references is to 'sacrifices' (θυσίς). Pucci ben Zeev draws attention to the one who framed this resolution: 'We must remember who is speaking here, that is the council and people of Sardis, not the Jews. It is possible that the Greeks were not acquainted with Jewish peculiarities in matters of cult and sacrifices. Since the Jews had asked for a place in which they could gather together and pray, the Greeks may have taken it to mean what that would have meant for themselves.'[46] For Pucci ben Zeev, this provides yet further proof that had Josephus invented this

---

43. Josephus, *Jewish Antiquities* 14.259-60.
44. Pucci ben Zeev, *Jewish Rights in the Roman World,* p. 244.
45. Josephus, *Jewish Antiquities* 14.260-61.
46. Pucci ben Zeev, *Jewish Rights in the Roman World,* p. 223.

inscription he certainly would not have included the word 'sacrifices'. He preserved what was actually officially decreed.[47]

In addition to legal assemblies, the Jews also maintained the right of arbitration. Within the legal framework of cities was an official provision for private arbitration in civil cases by a person or persons officially appointed by the city for that task on an annual basis.[48] Inhabitants could elect to settle matters of dispute among themselves by this means rather than through a civic court with both a judge and juries. They were allocated this right by certain of the city authorities appointed to preside over such matters for them.[49] Their decision was final.[50]

The Romans also recognized kosher food of the Jews. For example, an inscription from Sardis in 47 B.C. restored Jewish rights following the Roman Senate's ruling before which they had lodged their petition. It had as the traditional concluding clause what the city itself would be responsible for — 'so that (ὅπως) the market officials of the city shall be charged with the duty of having suitable food for them [the Jews] brought in' for sale in the official market place.[51] All food was taxed and could only be sold there.[52] This further important aspect of Jewish traditions in daily life was respected in the Diaspora.[53]

(v) The Romans, the Jewish Temple and Imperial Sacrifices

In the Claudian inscription the Jews were to be allowed to observe 'the customs of their fathers unhindered'. The term 'unhindered' is a legal phrase, meaning there was no legal impediment that prevented them from

---

47. Pucci ben Zeev, *Jewish Rights in the Roman World*, p. 223.

48. *Lex Irnitana* ch. 86.

49. For a discussion see my "Civil Litigation, 1 Corinthians 6:1-11," in *Seek the Welfare of the City: Early Christians as Benefactors and Citizens* (Grand Rapids and Carlisle: Eerdmans & Paternoster, 1994), ch. 6.

50. For the Roman arrangement, see J. A. Crook, *Law and Life in Rome* (London: Thames & Hudson, 1967), pp. 78-79, and for the Jewish judicial practice see R. H. Fuller, "First Corinthians 6:1-11 — An Exegetical Paper," *Ex Auditu* 2 (1986): 103-4.

51. Josephus, *Jewish Antiquities* 14.261.

52. L. de Ligt, *Fairs and Markets in the Roman Empire: Economic and Social Aspects of Periodic Trade in a Pre-industrial Society* (Amsterdam: J. C. Gieben, 1993).

53. For further discussion and the implications for Christians see my "Kosher Food and Idol Meat (1 Corinthians 10:25-28)," in *After Paul Left Corinth: The Influence of Secular Ethics and Social Change* (Grand Rapids and Cambridge: Eerdmans, 2001), ch. 13.

doing this.[54] How did they officially relate imperial cultic sacrifices that in many ways epitomised divine honours and loyalty? Would they compromise their beliefs as the Stoic and Epicurean philosophers in Athens will be shown to have done? (See pp. 150-53.)

Smallwood makes this measured comment with respect to the Jews and imperial cultic activities.

[A] substitute for the direct worship of the emperor as a deity was devised for the Jews: in accordance with their Law, which countenanced prayer and sacrifice for temporal overlords, sacrifices of two lambs and a bull were to be offered up daily in the Temple to God for the emperor's well-being, to replace the offering of sacrifices to the emperor himself normal in other provinces.[55]

Rajak sees this as 'overt participation in emperor worship' for Diaspora Jews in the East.[56] But does this appropriately describe what occurred?

Philo, a Hellenized Jew from Alexandria who was a contemporary of the first Christians, was part of the embassy to Rome of the Alexandrian Jews to Gaius, Claudius' predecessor. He writes of Augustus —

he adorned our temple through the costliness of his dedications, and ordered that for all time continuous sacrifices of whole burnt offerings should be carried out every day at his own expense as a tribute to the Most High God. And these sacrifices are maintained to the present day and will be maintained forever to tell the story of a character truly imperial . . . another example no less cogent than this shows the will of Augustus. He gave orders for a continuation of whole burnt offerings every day to the Most High God to be charged to his own purse. These are carried out to this day. Two lambs and a bull are victims with which he added lustre to the altar.[57]

---

54. Josephus, *Jewish Antiquities* 19.290. See the entry on ἀνεπικωλύντως in L&S 'without let or hindrance, unhindered'.

55. E. Mary Smallwood, *Philonis Alexandrini Legatio ad Gaium* (Leiden: E. J. Brill, 1961), p. 240.

56. Pucci ben Zeev, *Jewish Rights in the Roman World*, p. 477, 'offering prayers to the Almighty in favour of the emperor'. For epigraphic evidence of *Deo Aeterno pro salute Augusti* in synagogues in Judea, Osia and Intercisa, see n. 72.

57. Philo, *Embassy to Gaius* 157. Tiberius followed suit, 157. It was Gaius 'not only saying but thinking that he was a god', 162.

Josephus later records that the Jews bore the cost of the sacrifice for the safety of the emperor.

> For them we also offer perpetual sacrifices *(continua sacrificia)* . . . we perform these ceremonies daily, at the expense of the whole Jewish community, but while we offer no other such sacrifices out of our common expenses . . . yet we do this as a peculiar honour to the emperors and to them alone, while we do the same to no other individual.[58]

Smallwood has satisfactorily reconciled the two accounts on the basis of Roman provincial financial procedures. 'Philo and Josephus may simply be viewing the matter in different lights, if the cost was actually defrayed out of the provincial taxes.'[59] Elsewhere she asks —

> Can this perhaps be reconciled with Philo by supposing that the institution of the sacrifices (for the precise date of which there is no evidence) occurred when the country became a province in A.D. 6, the natural time for the introduction of the imperial cult, and that the expense was met out of the taxes then paid by the province into the Emperor's treasury?[60]

Here was indeed a solution agreeable to both parties. The Jewish arrangement satisfied Rome in that they were undertaking cultic activities as a sign of their imperial loyalty that recognized Rome's suzerainty over their kingdom. At the same time their adaptation meant they did not have to compromise their cultic traditions by offering sacrifices to the emperor's statue as did the rest of the empire and thereby overtly participate in an idolatrous cultic activity. Within the parameters of their own sacrificial system in the Jerusalem temple a Jewish priest offered up a daily sacrifice to his God for the emperor's safety. Here is an important example of Rome showing it respected the Jewish *mos maiorum* in accordance with its policy towards other cultures within its empire.

---

58. Josephus, *Against Apion* 2.77.

59. Smallwood, "The Province of Judaea, A.D. 6-41," in *The Jews under Roman Rule from Pompey to Diocletian*, p. 148, n. 20.

60. Smallwood, *Philonis Alexandrini Legatio ad Gaium*, p. 241.

III. Diaspora Jews' Adaptation for Showing Imperial Honours

In the provinces where the worship of both Augustus and the goddess *Roma* for provincials was instituted in the time of Augustus, how did Jewish residents cope with the veneration of the divine Caesars?

In the late Hellenistic period half a shekel, equivalent to two Greek drachmae and two denarii in Roman currencies, had been levied on all Jewish males between twenty and fifty, as well as proselytes and freed slaves.[61] The Roman authorities showed their respect for Jewish customs. There had long been a 'temple tax' levied on Diaspora Jews for the support of their one and only centre for their priestly sacrificial system, i.e., the temple in Jerusalem. It was the subject of Augustus' letter to the proconsul of Asia *c.* 9-2 B.C. reminding him of the imperial ruling on this legitimate payment to Jerusalem.[62]

Smallwood notes —

> Augustus, aware that no practising Jew would ever agree to sacrifice to the Emperor himself or his *genius* [divine spirit], made no attempt to force the imperial cult in its usual form on them. The most a practising Jew could do was to sacrifice to God as a prayer for the Emperor's well-being . . . and Augustus accepted this as a substitute for the worship of *Roma et Augustus* carried out in other provinces.[63]

Is there evidence of the Jewish honouring of the emperor in the synagogues of the Diaspora? Inscriptions in Jewish synagogues in Judaea, Kadyoun, Ostia and Intercisa have the prayer addressed 'to the Eternal God for the safety of emperor' *(Deo Aeterno pro salute Augusti).*[64] It indicates that this is based on the precedent of the Jews in Jerusalem who offered up a sacrifice for the safety of the emperor in the only place where sacrifices were permitted in Jewish liturgical practices.

Philo of Alexandria (20 B.C.-A.D. 50) discussed the implications if the Diaspora meeting-houses or synagogues were destroyed. In doing so he revealed that they were places where they formally showed their loy-

---

61. Smallwood, *The Jews under Roman Rule from Pompey to Diocletian*, pp. 124-25 and 142-43.

62. Josephus, *Jewish Antiquities* 16.172-73.

63. Smallwood, *Philonis Alexandrini Legatio ad Gaium*, p. 240.

64. Pucci ben Zeev, *Jewish Rights in the Roman World*, p. 477, n. 72 for this epigraphic evidence.

alty to the emperor. This was recognised by others as giving appropriate honours to the Caesars.

> [The Jews] by losing their meeting-houses were losing also what they would have valued as worth dying many thousands of deaths, namely their means of honouring their benefactors (τήν εἰς τούς εὐεργέτας εὐσέβειαν), since they no longer had the sacred buildings where they could set forth their thankfulness. And they might have said to their enemies "You have failed to see that you are not adding to but taking from the honours given to our masters (τοῖς κυρίοις τιμή ἀλλ᾽ ἀφαιρούμενοι) and you do not understand that everywhere in the habitable world [the Roman Empire] the incentive of the Jews for the Augustan house (Ἰουδαίοις ὁρμητήρια τῆς εἰς τὸν Σαβαστὸν οἶκον) has its basis as all may see in the meeting-houses, and if we have these destroyed no place, no method is left to us for paying this honour (τιμῆς). If we neglect to pay it when our institutions permit we should deserve the utmost penalty for not tendering our requital with all due fullness.[65]

He declared that their 'sacred building' was to be seen as a place where 'they could set forth their thankfulness' to their imperial benefactors. The destroying of their meeting places would result in taking away the appropriate place for the public honouring of the Caesars by the Jews where 'all may see' this was done.

In recounting the violation of the Alexandrian synagogues Philo indicated what was in them related to 'the honours to the rulers',

> I omit to mention the imperial honours (τῶν αὐτοκρατόρων τιμάς) which were taken down and burnt such as (σιωπῶ τὰς συγκαθαιρεθείσας καὶ συμπρησθείσας τῶν αὐτοκρατόρων τιμάς) shields and gold crowns (ἀσπίδων καὶ στεφάνων ἐπιχρύσων) and the slabs [pillars] and inscriptions (στηλῶν καὶ ἐπιγραφῶν), consideration for which they ought even to have abstained from and spared the rest (δι᾽ ἃ καὶ τῶν ἄλλων ὤφειον ἀνέχχειν).[66]

---

65. Philo, *Flaccus* 48-50. For the concept of officially giving appropriate honours to benefactors by civil authorities in the Roman world, such as a golden crown, see my "The Public Honouring of Christian Benefactors: Romans 13.3 and 1 Peter 2.14-15," *JSNT* 33 (1988): 87-103.

66. Philo, *Embassy to Gaius* 133.

Harland, after citing this section from *The Embassy to Gaius,* rightly inserts this all-defining caveat 'but not images' with respect to what were appropriate expressions of loyalty to the reigning emperor for Jews in their synagogues.[67]

In addition, the Jews swore an oath of loyalty to the emperor. Josephus records one such occasion during the reign of Herod the Great when 'the whole of the Jewish people affirmed by an oath that they would be loyal to Caesar and to the king's government' (παντὸς γοῦν τοῦ Ἰουδαικοῦ βεβαιώσαντος δι' ὅρκων ἦ μὴν εὐνοήσειν Καίσαρι καὶ τοῖς βασιλέως πράγμασιν).[68]

When cognizance is taken of this evidence, it cannot be said that the Diaspora Jews lacked opportunities to be diligent in expressing their loyalty to the reigning Caesar. They adapted to honouring him within the parameters of their customs and cultic traditions, unlike Herod the Great, who simply adopted the imperial cultic worship of others in the empire. The reigning Caesar respected this; the one exception was Gaius who himself had proposed to have a statue of himself erected in the temple in Jerusalem. That understandably threatened to foment a major crisis had it occurred.[69]

The regular sacrifice in the temple in Jerusalem meant that Diaspora Jews did not have to participate in cultic veneration in imperial temples. Specific sacrifices according to the Torah could only be undertaken in their temple in Jerusalem. They could rightly point out, if challenged, that they were living according to their own traditions which Rome respected and had officially endorsed.

Furthermore, the Jews could argue that they had gone one better than their compatriots in the Greek East. Imperial cult priests offered up sacrifices only on the high and holy days specified. For example, 'Sacrifices were made to the emperor on his monthly birthday just as to Zeus.'[70] However, in the temple in Jerusalem a sacrifice was offered up on a much more regular basis for the safety of the emperor. This meant that the Jews had a strong argument that demonstrated their on-going loyalty to Rome and its ruler, more so than others whose offerings were on a less regular basis. (See pp. 26-27.)

As one of the delegates of the Alexandrian Jewish embassy to Gaius,

67. P. A. Harland, *Associations, Synagogues, and Congregations: Claiming a Place in Ancient Mediterranean Society* (Minneapolis: Fortress Press, 2003), p. 218.

68. Josephus, *Jewish Antiquities* 17.42.

69. Josephus, *Jewish War* 2.184-85.

70. D. Fishwick, *Imperial Cult in the Latin West,* II.1, p. 513.

Philo records the allegations of Isidorus, a bitter adversary present on this occasion.

> Isidorus, that bitter sycophant, realizing that Gaius enjoyed being of-
> fered titles beyond human nature, said: 'You are going to hate these
> Jews here, my Lord, and their fellow-countrymen more than ever
> when you hear about their ill-will and impiety towards you. For when
> all humanity was offering sacrifices of gratitude for your recovery,
> these were the only ones who could not bear to perform sacrifice. By
> 'these' I mean to include all other Jews as well.[71]

Philo also records their declaring the superiority of their cultic act.

> At that we all shouted out together, we did sacrifice and sacrifice hec-
> atombs too, and we did not just pour blood upon the altar and then
> take the flesh home to feast and regale ourselves with it as some do, but
> we gave the victims to the sacred fire to be entirely consumed and we
> have done this not once but three times already, the first time at your
> accession to the sovereignty, the second when you escaped the severe
> illness which all the inhabitable world suffered with you, the third as
> a prayer of hope for victory in Germany.[72]

Therefore it can be seen that the Diaspora Jews also adapted to Roman rule by showing honours that were appropriate to their faith but never
contrary to it. Philo attributed a copy of a letter from Herod Agrippa I to
Claudius that indicates how Jerusalem with its temple was also a critical
centre for Diaspora Judaism.

> [A]s I have said, the mother city not only of one country Judea but of
> most of the others in virtue of the colonies sent out of divers times to
> the neighbouring lands . . . so that if our home-city is granted a share
> of our goodwill the benefit extends not to one city but the myriads
> of the others situated in every region of the inhabited world whether
> in Europe or in Asia or in Libya, whether on the main lands or in the
> islands, whether it be seaboard or inland.[73]

71. Philo, *Embassy to Gaius* 355.
72. Philo, *Embassy to Gaius* 356.
73. Philo, *Embassy to Gaius* 281-83.

This letter notes that since the time of Augustus Jews in Rome collected their temple tax for Jerusalem.[74] This appears to be the prelude to Herod Agrippa's request to Claudius to circulate an edict requiring all throughout the empire to respect Jewish customs.[75]

(vii) A Statue in the Jewish Synagogue in Dora
and the Governor's Reaction

Publius Petronius, formerly proconsul of the province of Asia, was appointed Roman governor of Syria *c.* A.D. 39. Greeks in the city of Dora had desecrated the Jewish synagogue by placing a statue of him in it. This was not dissimilar to what Gaius, Claudius' predecessor, had proposed.[76] Josephus records that as a result Claudius issued an edict in A.D. 42 threatening criminal proceedings against the perpetrators for anti-Semitic actions by Greek citizens.

> Some of your number have been so perverse and audacious as to disobey the published edit of Claudius Caesar Augustus Germanicus on allowing Jews to continue their ancestral customs; they have done quite the contrary in preventing the Jews from having a synagogue by moving into it a statue of Caesar; they have sinned not only against the law of the Jews, but also against the emperor, whose statue is better placed in his own temple than in that of another, especially in a synagogue, for by natural law each must be lord of his own place, in accordance with Caesar's decree. For it would be ludicrous of me to refer to my own decree after the edict of the emperor who permitted Jews to follow their own customs yet also, be it noted, ordered them to live as fellow citizens with the Greeks in the community.[77]

The governor could not be accused of disloyalty to the emperor because he argued that the rightful place of the statue of Claudius was in the imperial cult temple. It was probably a nude statue of an uncircumcised

---

74. Philo, *Embassy to Gaius* 155-57.

75. P. Borgen, *Philo of Alexandria: An Exegete for His Time* (Leiden: E. J. Brill, 1997), pp. 20-21.

76. Philo, *Embassy to Gaius* 346.

77. Josephus, *Jewish Antiquities* 19.304-6.

emperor, as that was how they were portrayed as gods.[78] Therefore it was further repugnant to Jewish sensitivities. Claudius was even-handed in that he also emphasised that the Jews were required to live peaceably alongside the Greeks as specified in his edict.[79]

Petronius linked the contravention of Jewish rights with the decree of Augustus, not that of Claudius. Again he seeks to placate the situation by exonerating the magistrates of Dora, who were not the instigators of the riots but 'certain young men of Dora who set a higher value on audacity than on holiness and were by nature recklessly bold'.[80] It had not been planned, nor instantaneously begun by the mob.

> Since these men have so audaciously contravened the edict of Augustus, for which their leading members are themselves angry and state that it was not done by their particular plan but by the mob, on impulse, I have ordered them to be brought before me by Proculus Vitellius, the centurion, to account for their actions.[81]

Determined at all costs to bring the culprits to justice, he indicates the magistrates will be charged with guilt by association if they do not find out and indicate to the centurion stationed in Dora who the actual instigators of this desecration were.[82]

> To the leading magistrates, I give this warning: that unless they wish to have it thought that the wrong was committed with their consent and intent, they must point out the guilty men to the centurion, allowing no chance of riot or physical conflict; for this, in my judgement, is precisely what they hope to achieve by such actions.[83]

Herod Agrippa I's intervention from his neighbouring kingdom of

---

78. For a discussion of this see C. H. Hallett, "The Nudity of the Gods," in *Roman Nudity: Heroic Portrait Statuary 200 BC-AD 300* (Oxford: Oxford University Press, 2005), esp. pp. 172-83 and 223-24.

79. According to Josephus he had been very understanding of Jewish traditions and adherence to their law in the time of Gaius, *Jewish Antiquities* 18.261-88, 302-5.

80. Josephus, *Jewish Antiquities* 19.300.

81. Josephus, *Jewish Antiquities* 19.307.

82. B. Levick, "Tiberius and the Law: The Development of Maiestas," in *Tiberius the Politician* (London: Thames & Hudson, 1976), ch. 11.

83. Josephus, *Jewish Antiquities* 19.308.

Judah is understandable, as it was located north of Caesarea Maritima just on the other side of his domain in the southernmost part of the province of Syria.

> For both King Agrippa, my most honoured friend, and I have no greater interest than that the Jews should not seize any occasion under the pretext of self-defence, to gather in one place and proceed to desperate measure. And that you may be better informed of His Imperial Majesty's policy concerning this matter, I have appended his edicts which were published in Alexandria.[84]

The use of the superlative 'most honoured' (τιμιωτάτος) was an accolade appropriate for Agrippa to use, as the emperor had given him the official title of 'a friend of Claudius'.[85] He had earned this because of his assistance in helping facilitate the ascension of his life-long friend Claudius to the imperial office. (See pp. 101-3.) This helps to resolve the enigma of a ruler of a neighbouring kingdom assuming a governor's power that was clearly outside the jurisdiction given him by Claudius. Agrippa did this for the very purpose of pleading for the honouring of Jewish rights given by Augustus and confirmed, as we have noted, by Claudius in his important decree.

> Though they seem to be known by all, my most honoured friend, King Agrippa, read them out at my tribunal when he pleaded that the Jews ought not to be deprived of what Augustus had given them.[86]

The phrase 'known by all' indicates that the rights granted by Claudius to all Diaspora Jews had already been displayed in a public place in Dora. He concludes, 'For the future, I call upon you to seek no pretext for riot or disturbance but each to keep your own custom' (ἀλλ᾽ ἑκάστους τὰ ἴδια ἔθη θρησκεύειν).[87] Diaspora Jews like their compatriots in Jerusalem gave agreed honours to the Caesars.

---

84. Josephus, *Jewish Antiquities* 19.309-10 records Claudius' response to this.
85. J. A. Crook, 'Amici Principis', in *Consilium Principis: Imperial Councils and Counsellors from Augustus to Diocletian* (Cambridge: Cambridge University Press, 1955), no. 253.
86. Josephus, *Jewish Antiquities* 19.310-11.
87. Josephus, *Jewish Antiquities* 19.310-11.

IV. Abstention of Jerusalem Temple Sacrifices and the Jewish Rebellion

Pucci ben Zeev notes, 'According to Josephus, the suspension of the sacrifice [in the temple in Jerusalem] for the well-being of the emperor was the first tangible sign of the incipient rebellion against Roman rule in 66 C.E.'[88] The Jewish revolt ultimately saw the utter destruction of Jerusalem after a horrendous and prolonged siege by Rome. Josephus records —

> Eleazar, son of Ananias the high-priest, a very daring youth, then holding the position of captain, persuaded those who officiated in the Temple services to accept no gift or sacrifice from a foreigner. This action laid the foundation of the war with the Romans; for the sacrifices offered on behalf of that nation and the emperor were in consequence rejected.[89]

No longer sacrificing for the safety of the emperor sent a very clear signal to Rome of their abandonment of the long-standing and imperially endorsed act of loyalty. The Jews were in revolt against Rome, the consequences for which resulted in the prolonged four-year war with the siege of Jerusalem and the destruction of the temple in Jerusalem, the very heart of its sacrifices and liturgical practices.

In this chapter we have argued that after the era of Herod the Great, the Jews adapted in an appropriate way to give a public expression of loyalty to the Caesars on a daily basis but within the parameters of their own sacrificial system in the Jerusalem temple. It was permitted and in accordance with Rome's policy of recognising the ancient customs of its conquered peoples.

Hardin has argued 'that the [Diaspora] Jews did not have any such exemption or even special privileges from participating in the imperial cult. Neither did they claim special status'.[90] Is the converse of his argument correct — that Jews 'participated' in imperial cultic activities in the light of the evidence of their adaptation of expressing loyalty to the Caesars? Evidence has shown that the Diaspora Jews did not join in the

---

88. M. Pucci ben Zeev, *Jewish Rights in the Roman World, Texts and Studies in Ancient Judaism* (Tübingen: Mohr Siebeck, 1998), p. 472.

89. Josephus, *Jewish War* 2.409.

90. J. K. Hardin, *Galatians and the Imperial Cult: A Critical Analysis of the First-Century Social Context of Paul's Letter*, WUNT 237 (Tübingen: Mohr Siebeck, 2008), p. 110.

official local and provincial imperial cultic celebrations in the cities in the Greek East.

Hardin's conclusion is based in part on his interpretation of the comments of Philo of Alexandria on the ornamentation in the synagogue that related to the Caesars. By way of an analogy, in past decades in British Commonwealth countries it was a convention that a picture of the reigning monarch together with national flags be displayed in churches. The same was true in the United States of America, where a picture of the president could be hung along with official flags. In centuries ahead would it be a correct reading of this practice to say that Christians worshipped their monarch or president? It was done as an expression of loyalty, and Paul's stipulation in Romans 13:7 of giving appropriate honours to whom honour was due was consistent with Jesus' stipulation concerning 'giving to Caesar the things that are Caesar's'. Christians in the British Commonwealth and the United States would reject any notion of a blatant compromise of the Christian faith or of their divine and sole loyalty to Christ as their king or the one who presided over their affairs.

When cognizance is taken of what participation in imperial cultic activities really meant in terms of 'doing cult' before statues of the emperor and at times family members, and joining in festive activities, the right conclusion must surely be that the Jewish Diaspora did not participate in imperial cultic activities and the events that accompanied them. Like their Jerusalem compatriots they 'adapted', rather than 'adopted', to show loyalty and give appropriate honours to the Caesars.

Rives noted that Christians at that time, and even in a later period, had no such recognized identity, even though their movement derived from the Jewish faith.[91] The one exception could be in the province of Achaea. In chapter 7 it will be argued that Gallio ruled *de facto* that Christianity was Jewish and that the charges made by local Jewish antagonists were not within his remit as governor. Thus by implication they did not have to render divine honours to Caesar in the imperial cult temples within that province. In the remaining chapters of this book the different responses by individuals and churches from mixed ethnic Christian communities in the Julio-Claudian era are noted.

---

91. Rives, "Diplomacy and Identity among Jews and Christians," p. 117.

Appendix: Authenticity of the Official Decrees Cited by Josephus

On the issue of the credibility of the official degrees recorded in Josephus, it is important to be reminded who this author was. Flavius Josephus came from a wealthy aristocratic Jewish family of priestly descent. He first visited Rome *c.* A.D. 63 at the age of twenty-six to petition Nero to release some Jewish priests sent there for investigation by the procurator of Judaea, M. Antonius Felix, before whose court Paul also later appeared (Acts 24:1-21). Through Nero's wife, Poppaea Sabina, Josephus managed to secure the dropping of the investigation. She also gave him enormous gifts. Edmondson calls this his 'debut in the public affairs of Jerusalem'.[92]

Josephus had joined the Jewish revolt against Rome in A.D. 66 but later deserted to the Roman army. He subsequently witnessed the triumphal victory parade in Rome celebrating the Jewish defeat in A.D. 70. He was granted Roman citizenship, and changed his name from Yosef ben Mattityahu to Titus Flavius Josephus.[93] He actually saw himself as one of 'the most renowned of the Jews both in Alexandria and Rome',[94] even if he must have appeared a traitor to many of his Jewish contemporaries. He subsequently lived in Rome after its victory in Judea under the *aegis* of imperial privilege, residing as he did in a grace-and-favour imperial apartment.

A section of T. Flavius Josephus' *Jewish Antiquities,* a work comparable to *Roman Antiquities* by Dionysius of Halicarnassus (*c.* 60–*c.* 7 B.C.) and written in the time of Domitian (A.D. 81-96), reproduced copies of the official imperial and provincial resolutions spelling out Jewish rights. He had searched the official archives as he wrote his magisterial work on Jewish ethnic origins and history. Anticipating the response of any who refused to believe that the copies of them in his *Jewish Antiquities* were authentic, he asserted that they could be confirmed because they 'remain to this day and will continue to remain in the Capitol in Rome'.[95]

Of the authenticity of the official Roman documents that Josephus cites in his *Jewish Antiquities,* he himself states categorically —

---

92. J. Edmondson, "Introduction: Flavius Josephus and Flavian Rome," in *Flavius Josephus and Flavian Rome,* ed. J. Edmondson, S. Mason and J. Rives (Oxford: Oxford University Press, 2005), p. 3.

93. Josephus, *Jewish War* 1.1.

94. Josephus, *Jewish War* 7.447.

95. Josephus, *Jewish Antiquities* 14.266.

against the decrees nothing can be said — for they are kept in the public places of the cities and are still to be found engraved on bronze tablets in the [Roman] Capitol; and what is more, Julius Caesar made a bronze for the Jews in Alexandria, declaring that they were citizens of Alexandria — from these same documents I will furnish proof of my statements. Accordingly I will now cite the decrees passed by the Senate [Roman] and by Julius Caesar.[96]

He indicates they were engraved permanently on bronze pillars and marble tablets. Given that some modern scholars are not persuaded of their authenticity, it is appropriate to be reminded of what Josephus so strongly asserted.

> Now there are many other such decrees, passed by the Senate and by the Roman autocrats ... as well as resolutions of cities and rescripts of provincial governors in reply to letters on the subject of our rights, all of which those who read our work without malice will find it possible to take on trust from the documents we have cited. For since we have furnished clear and visible proof of our friendship with the Romans, indicating those decrees engraved on bronze pillars and tablets in the Capitol that remain to this day and will continue to remain in the Capitol.[97]

He emphasises the authenticity of his official sources and incredulity that anyone would be 'so stupid' as to reject the goodwill that Rome officially asserted to towards the Jews.

> I have refrained from citing all of them as being both superfluous and disagreeable; for I cannot suppose that anyone is so stupid (σκαιόν) that he will actually refuse to believe the statements about the friendliness of the Romans towards us, when they have demonstrated this in a good many decrees relating to us, or will not admit that we are making truthful statements on the basis of the examples given.[98]

In discussing the accessibility of notarised Roman documents, Ando notes that 'this has implications for the protocols of the *senatus consultum*

---

96. Josephus, *Jewish Antiquities* 14.188-89.
97. Josephus, *Jewish Antiquities* 14.265-66.
98. Josephus, *Jewish Antiquities* 14.267.

of 44 B.C. on the privileges of the Jews, the inscribed texts which were viewed and copied by Josephus more than a century later'.[99]

Insight into the official copying and dissemination of imperial communications is also revealed in a letter of Augustus to the Magistrates, Council and the People of Rhosos concerning privileges conferred on Seleukos of Thosos.

> The document written below has been excerpted from a stele [located] on the Capitol of Rome to file in your public records; send a copy also [to] the Council and the People of Tarsus, the Council and the People of Antioch, the Council and People [? Seleukeia], so that they may file it.[100]

A bronze tablet of a senatorial decree in both Latin and Greek that was found in Rome called on the consuls 'to send letters to our magistrates who are in charge of the provinces of Asia and Macedonia, and to their (city) magistrates'.[101] In the East the preservation of Roman documents is reflected in an official inscription from Chios.

> [S]ince following my general procedures of preserving the written documents of the proconsuls before me, I thought it sensible to keep safe also the extant letter of [Anstitius] Vetus [the previous consul] concerning these matters. . . . I found that in terms of time the oldest [was] a sealed decree of the Senate, passed in the second consulship of Lucius Sulla. . . . And a letter of Imperitor, son of the god, Augustus . . . concerning the freedom of the city.[102]

Furthermore, the seriousness with which Roman authorities viewed the changing of legal documents in their archives is found in the threat of

---

99. C. Ando, "A Religion for the Empire," in *Imperial Ideology and Provincial Loyalty in the Roman Empire* (Berkeley: University of California Press, 2000), p. 85. For a helpful discussion on the importance Rome attached to the preservation and copying of official documents by their own scribes, see his 'Notarised Documents and Local Archives', pp. 80-90.

100. Sherk, *Roman Documents from the Greek East*, no. 58, *ll.* 28-30, cited in a helpful discussion of procedures after the completion of the audience with the emperor or Roman Senate by J.-L. Ferrary, "After the Embassy to Rome," in C. Eilers, ed., *Diplomats and Diplomacy in the Roman World*, p. 129.

101. Sherk, *Roman Documents from the Greek East*, no. 22, *ll.* 28-30.

102. Sherk, *Roman Documents from the Greek East*, no. 70. Again I am grateful to B. Bitner for drawing attention to *P. Lond.* 103.

capital punishment in the decree of Quintis Veranius, who was appointed in A.D. 43 by Claudius as the governor of the newly constituted province of Lycia-Pamphylia. It was circulated to all the magistrates in the province so they are aware of the importance of the authenticity of official documents held in city archives.[103]

> T[ry]phon, public slave to the city of Telos, has not been taught either by my edicts or threats or even by punishment inflicted upon slaves who have committed like crimes, that he must not accept into the city archive documents of an official nature which contain interpolations and erasures. I led him to understand my feelings against people like him by having him flogged and I thus made it clear to him that if he again ignores my instructions about official documents, it will not be a simple beating but by exacting the supreme penalty from him that I will make the rest of the slaves forget their past sloppiness. . . .
>
> Further, in order that those concerned with issuing official documents . . . should cease working against their own security, I declare that any official document, of whatever sort, shall from the present day be invalid if it is written on a palimpsest or contains interpolations or erasures, whether it be a contract or a bond, whether a covenant . . . a declaration concerning a legal case . . . Let the magistrates . . . write up this decree throughout the entire province entrusted to my care.[104]

Given that Josephus could not envisage that 'anyone is so stupid' — to cite his own comment on any fabrication of legal decrees from the emperor to the provincial governors and civic authorities — one has to ask why he himself would be 'so stupid' to have actually forged, or even changed, these documents that could be verified from the Roman archives? To do so would attract the 'supreme punishment' under Roman law.[105]

It was certainly the case in the decree of Claudius to the Alexandrians where sources independent of Josephus make reference to the Augustan

---

103. Quintus Veranius Nepos (d. A.D. 57) was consul in A.D. 49, and elevated to patrician status by Claudius. In A.D. 57 he became governor of Britain, where he died.

104. R. K. Sherk, *The Roman Empire: Augustus to Hadrian: Translated Documents of Greece and Rome* (Cambridge: Cambridge University Press, 1988), VI, no. 48. See also D. C. Braund, *Augustus to Nero: A Sourcebook on Roman History, 31 B.C.–A.D. 68* (London and Sydney: Croom Helm, 1985), no. 587.

105. Sherk, *The Roman Empire: Augustus to Hadrian*, no. 48, *ll.* 17-18.

decree on the Jewish *mos maiorum*.[106] The same Roman policy is clearly enunciated for the people of Chios, and their customs were binding on Roman citizens residing there.[107] Furthermore, a decree in Josephus affirms the giving of worldwide Jewish rights by Claudius. It noted affirmations in his Alexandrian decree that were based on the assurance of respecting the *mos maiorum* for the Jews in the Augustan decree.[108]

Robello concludes that 'there is no reason to doubt upon the accuracy of any document cited by Josephus that deals with the Jews'.[109] Rajak also observes that 'the formal features of the documents quoted by Josephus are correct for genre and period, to a degree which makes it difficult to conceive of them as forgeries'.[110] Considering this evidence, it is rather surprising that the authenticity of Josephus' copies of official Roman inscriptions relating to the first-century period, especially those concerning the Jews that were promulgated in the Julio-Claudian and early Flavian period, has been questioned.[111] His extant evidence has been invaluable in providing a context for later discussions of the movement that sprang from the Jewish faith.

106. *P. Lond.* 1912.

107. Sherk, *Roman Documents from the Greek East,* no. 70.

108. Josephus, *Jewish Antiquities* 16.162, *ll.* 2-163, *l.* 11.

109. A. B. Rabello, "The Legal Condition of the Jews in the Roman Empire," *ANRW* 2, no. 13 (1980): 682.

110. Rajak, "Was There a Roman Charter for the Jews?" p. 305, citing in support in n. 9, 'Applebaum 1974, Smallwood 1976, Kasher 1978'.

111. See Pucci ben Zeev, "Greek and Roman Documents from Republican Times in the Antiquities: What Was Josephus' Source?" *Scripta Classica Israelica* 13 (1994): 47-59. Also her *Jewish Rights in the Roman World,* Texts and Studies in Ancient Judaism 74, where she indicates her scepticism as to their authenticity, p. 233, and "The Problem of Josephus' Sources," II, pp. 388-408, especially pp. 394-408. However, she does concede that archives were known to be kept in the Capitol and also in the Aerarium, a state archive in Rome, p. 232.

PART II

Divine Imperial Honours and the First Christians' Responses

CHAPTER 6

The Admission of New Gods to Athens: Rome's and Paul's

How would the Athenians relate to Rome's new imperial gods? Long before Roman times there had been ruler cults in Athens and in other cities in the East. The 'ruler cult had a very brief history. . . . Athens' two tries at ruler cult, the aborted one for Alexander [the Great] in 324 B.C. and that for Demetrios Poliocretes in 307/6 B.C. were both directed towards Macedonians and were both formal enactments of the *Ekklesia*' according to Mikalson in his extensive discussion of the religious world of Hellenistic Athens.[1] Would there be a similar response to Rome's imperial gods?

One of the long-standing legal functions of the Areopagus Council that continued under the Romans was the official admission of new gods to Athens once their promoters met the established criteria. In Acts 17:19-20 it was explained to Paul that he was required to appear before an official meeting of the Council to go through the due process of seeing whether his God met the criteria for recognition and thus formally be admitted (17:22-31).

Stoic and Epicurean philosophers had strong reservations about cultic practices in shrines and temples because they could engender superstitions among their followers. The issue of divine honours for the Caesars in Athens would not go away; hence their adherents would certainly need guidelines. By late Roman Republican times the philosophical school of the Stoics had developed what was, for them, a coherent theology called 'The Nature of the Gods' *(De natura deorum)* with proofs for their existence, rôles in creation and providential care that included that of humanity. (See pp. 159-62.) Zeno (335-263 B.C.) had founded Stoic philosophy

---

1. J. D. Mikalson, *Religion in Hellenistic Athens* (Berkeley, Los Angeles and London: University of California Press, 1998), p. 300.

in the Southwest Stoa of the agora in Athens, and its adherents were still active in this same central location when Paul dialogued with some of them along with followers from the rival school of the Epicureans (Acts 17:18). Would the Stoic and Epicurean adherents, some of whom were members of the Areopagus Council, have to compromise the tenets of their own beliefs when participating in imperial cultic acts as expressions of loyalty to Rome, as did other citizens?

Acts 17:34 notes that after Paul presented his case, Dionysius, an Areopagus Council member, Damaris and their entourage became Christians. Given the considerable number of shrines and temples dedicated to Rome's imperial gods, and the implication of Paul's speech, how did they deal with the imperial cult?

In order to evaluate the Athenians' reactions, it is proposed (I) to map the considerable archaeological and epigraphic evidence showing that imperial cultic temples, shrines and its priesthoods were extensive in Athens; (II) to examine ancient sources, including Acts 17:16-34, for evidence of the Areopagus Council's traditional legal protocol for officially admitting new gods to Athens including the imperial gods of Rome and Paul's; (III) to assess the attitudes of two Athenian philosophical schools towards imperial cult veneration and advice given to their adherents about participation; and (IV) to explore the different responses to Paul's official *apologia* by the Areopagus Councillors, including that of the Stoics and Epicureans, and the implications for giving divine honours to the Caesars for those who became Christians as a result of Paul's presentation.

I. Imperial Cult Places, Priests and the Public Veneration in Athens

Archaeological evidence of Athenian imperial cult sites shows how numerous and widespread they were. The names of imperial cult priests recorded on official inscriptions are indicators of the importance attached to cultic celebrations on imperial high and holy days in Athens.

(i) Athenian Politics and Rome

After conquests, Rome's strategy had been to leave cities largely self-governing except for criminal proceedings that came within the jurisdiction of the provincial governor.[2] Because of Athens' great and glorious past, her new Roman rulers took a special interest in this prestigious city from the time of its capture by Sulla in 86 B.C. They bestowed on it the privileged status of 'a freed and allied city' *(civitas libera et foederata).*[3]

Therefore Athens 'was technically outside the Roman Provincial governor's remit'.[4] As a result, 'the Areopagus [Council] retained its position of bygone years, with political powers as well as an important judiciary function, while the Council of Five Hundred had taken on a judiciary role', according to Lintoff.[5] For such concessions they would be expected to reciprocate with appropriate imperial divine honours to demonstrate Athenian loyalty to Rome.

In spite of its special status and the privileges it enjoyed, Athens did not always respond appropriately in terms of expected protocol for a city in the Roman Empire. For instance, she 'never gave precedence to business coming before the assembly from Roman authorities, as other states did, where such matters were given the first slate after the sacred ones'.[6]

Would the governing body of Athenians also seek to minimize the ruler cultic veneration in view of their intolerance of it in previous eras? Archaeological evidence reveals that the Athenians built a small imperial cult temple early in the time of Augustus next to the famous temple of Athena and close by the Altar of Zeus. Both in terms of size and splendour they completely overshadowed it. Did the small size of the imperial temple epitomise their attitude?

The Athenians did not always seem to have taken temple constructions seriously. Suetonius in his work, "The Deified Augustus," records that 'the friendly and allied kings, each in his own kingdom, founded a city named Caesarae.' He also noted that they resolved jointly to contribute

---

2. D. Johnston, *Roman Law in Context* (Cambridge: Cambridge University Press, 1999), p. 9.

3. Pliny the Younger, *Letters* 10.92.1.

4. A. J. S. Spawforth, "The Early Reception of the Imperial Cult in Athens: Problems and Ambiguities," in *The Romanization of Athens: Proceedings of an International Conference (1996),* ed. M. C. Hoff and S. I. Rotroff (Oxford: Oxbow Books, 1997), p. 192. This explains why the proconsul of Achaea would be located elsewhere, i.e., in the Roman colony of Corinth, the capital of the province.

5. A. Lintott, *Imperium Romanum: Politics and Administration* (London and New York: Routledge, 1993), pp. 147-48.

6. C. Habiht, "Roman Citizens in Athens (228-31 B.C.)," in *The Romanization of Athens,* ed. Hoff and Rotroff, p. 11. For βούλωνται πρώτοις μεθ' ἱερά καί τά 'Ρωμαίων, see *IG 12 Supplement* 645.

to the cost involved in completing the great temple of Olympian Zeus at Athens, on which work had begun in the sixth century B.C., and to dedicate it to his *genius* — this term would be used of the divine spirit of the Caesars.[7] (See pp. 214-21.) Some emperors, including Nero, had the title 'Zeus' used of them.

It had been intended to complete this important temple early in Augustus' reign, but work ceased. It was not until A.D. 131, and then only on the initiative of the emperor Hadrian, the great lover of Greek culture, that it was completed. Was their abandoning of the project for Olympian Zeus early in the Julio-Claudian period also indicative of indifference on the part of the Athenians towards Rome? In this 'land most dear to the gods',[8] the approval or disapproval of Athens had in the past also sent a powerful signal to other Greek communities to follow suit.[9]

In 'Empire of Honour' to cite Lendon's title, the local veneration of the ruling emperor, his predecessors and some living members of his family constituted tangible ways of officially expressing loyalty and gratitude in each city for the *pax romana*.[10] Athens knew it had to court Rome appropriately to retain its privileged status, and the giving of imperial cultic honours was an acceptable means of doing so.

Spawforth has concluded there was 'a muted quality in the installation of emperor worship at Athens' in the early years of Augustus.[11] Yet in the same essay he observes the best evidence for archaeological and epigraphic evidence of imperial cult honours in Greece apart from Corinth has been found in Athens, and includes the decade before and after Paul's visit.[12]

(ii) Athenian Imperial Cult Temples and Altars

The first imperial cult temple to *Roma* and Augustus was built on the Acropolis. It was supported by nine columns with a diameter of 7.36 me-

---

7. Suetonius, *The Deified Augustus* 60.

8. Aeschylus, *Eumenides* 869.

9. R. Garland, *Introducing New Gods: The Politics of Athenian Religion* (London: Duckworth, 1992), p. 8. For other 'foreign' divinities who also made it to the Acropolis in this period, see his chapters 1-7.

10. For an extensive discussion of this theme, see J. E. Lendon, *Empire of Honour: The Art of Government in the Roman World* (Oxford: Clarendon Press, 1997).

11. Spawforth, "The Early Reception of the Imperial Cult in Athens," p. 194.

12. Spawforth, "The Early Reception of the Imperial Cult in Athens," p. 183.

tres and had no interior walls. A third-century A.D. imperial bronze coin portrays this circular temple alongside the great temple of Athena.[13] When visiting the Acropolis one is still struck by how diminutive this temple would have been. It was placed twenty-three metres in front of the raised ancient temple to Athena, which measured 69.5 metres by 30.8 metres and towered over it. The dedication read —

The Demos (dedicates this) to the goddess Roma and Augustus Caesar (Θεᾶ ῾Ρώμῃ καὶ Σεβαστῷ Καίσαρι) when Pammenes, son of Zenon, of Marathon, Priest of the goddess Roma and Augustus Saviour (ἱερέως θεᾶς ῾Ρώμης καὶ Σεβαστοῦ Ζωτῆρος) on the Acropolis (ἐπ᾽ Ἀκροπόλει), was Hoplite General, and when Megiste, daughter of Asklepiades, of Halai, was Priestess of Athena Polias. In the Archonship of Areos, son of Dorion, of Paiania'.[14]

The construction of this imperial cult temple is dated somewhere between 27 and 18-17 B.C. Hoff has argued for 19 B.C., when Augustus returned to Athens after it had previously fallen out of favour with him, resulting in economic sanctions being imposed on the city.[15] He concludes, 'The institution of the cult to *Roma* and Augustus should be seen as an overt demonstration of their compliance.'[16]

Its location was not without some significance, as the Parthenon was more than a sanctuary to the goddess Athena, 'and its placement on the Acropolis echoes the visual allusions of historical Greek victories over the Persians'. 'It could be viewed as an all-purpose Panhellenic victory monument over the East.'[17]

There are other imperial cult sites. The temple of Ares, situated in the Athenian agora and opposite the Odeon, had the altar upon which Athenians offered up sacrifices on the emperor's birthday. It had an inscription hailing Gaius Caesar as the 'new Ares' (νέον ῎Αρη) and Drusus Caesar as

13. See M. C. Hoff, "The Politics and Architecture of the Athenian Imperial Cult," in *Subject and Ruler: The Cult of the Ruling Power in Classical Antiquity*, ed. A. Small, *JRA* Supplement 17 (Ann Arbor, MI: 1996): 188.

14. *IG* 2², 3173.

15. For a careful and detailed discussion of the visits and hostility of Augustus towards the Athenians and subsequent reconciliation, see M. C. Hoff, "Civil Disobedience and Unrest in Augustan Athens," *Hesperia* 58 (1989): 267-76.

16. Hoff, "The Politics and Architecture of the Athenian Imperial Cult," p. 193.

17. Hoff, "The Politics and Architecture of the Athenian Imperial Cult," pp. 193-94.

the 'new god Ares' (νέον θεὸν Ἄρη),[18] both of whom had been his nominated imperial heirs. Another dedication records 'the thank-offering for Ares and Sebastos (Augustus)' (χαριστήριον Ἄρει καὶ Σεβαστῷ), although there is insufficient evidence as Spawforth notes.[19]

In addition, seventeen known or possible altars have been located. Eleven have inscriptions indicating it is 'a god's' (θεοῦ), with some adding 'son of' (υἱοῦ).[20] This includes a shrine to the imperial gods in the Annex to the Stoa of Zeus. The presence of a cult site annexed to a building used for business or official civic activities was not without precedent in Greek cities.[21]

These are not the only places where cult would be done to the emperor on designated days in the city's calendar. There is also evidence of a major imperial cult temple situated at the end of the Roman forum in Athens. The forum itself would not only be a reminder to the Athenians of Rome's suzerainty but also of the emperors' generosity and their divinity.

The inscription on the propylion, the grand gateway to this forum, was also a constant reminder of the generosity of Rome's 'god' and his 'divine son', for it reads 'from the gifts given by Gaius Julius Caesar, god, and Imperator Augustus Caesar, son of god for the Athena Archegetis' (ἀπὸ τῶν δοθεισῶν δωρεῶν ὑπο Γαίου Ιουλία Καίσαρος θεοῦ καὶ Αὐτοκρατος Καίσαρπος θεοῦ υἱοῦ Σεβαστοῦ Ἀθηναῖ Ἀρχηγέτιδι).[22]

Being dedicated to both 'Athena Archegetis [Founder] and the Augustan gods' (Ἀθηναῖ Ἀρχηγέτιδι καὶ Θεοῖς Σεβαστοῖς),[23] it followed the convention of joint dedications of the chief divinity of a city and the Roman emperors. It was not something unique to Athens, as this was also the case in the Roman colony of Aphrodisias.[24] It had been thought that the use of the formula of the 'Augustan gods' and other gods occurred in state dedi-

---

18. *IG* 2², 3250 and 3257.

19. *IG* 2², 2953. For the weighing of the evidence see Spawforth, "The Early Reception of the Imperial Cult in Athens: Problems and Ambiguities," pp. 186-88.

20. A. Benjamin and A. E. Raubitschek, "Arae Augusti," *Hesperia* 28 (1959): 75-84 with seventeen plates pp. 86-87.

21. H. A. Thompson, "The Annex to the Stoa of Zeus in the Athenian Agora," *Hesperia* 36 (1966): 183-84.

22. *IG* 2², 3175.

23. *IG* 2², 3183. For the importance of *Athena Archegetis* see Mikalson, *Religion in Hellenistic Athens*, pp. 108-12.

24. Hoff, "The Politics and Architecture of the Athenian Imperial Cult," p. 196, citing as a precedent J. M. Reynolds, "The Origins and Beginnings of Imperial Cult in Aphrodisias," *PCPS* 26 (1980): 73.

cations only after Claudius deified Livia in A.D. 42 and elevated her to the status of an Augustan god'.[25]

The Roman forum had been built earlier on the site and was elevated above the ancient Greek agora. It was approximately 3.5 metres higher than the earlier Hellenistic road and certainly 'overlooked' all the activities undertaken in the famous Greek agora.[26] The choice of such an elevated location would not be without significance for Roman propaganda purposes. The forum also served as a major focus for imperial cult activities because the western façade of the arcuated building dominated it. It measured 18.02 metres across with three arch marble lintels and was at least forty-four metres in length. It was behind this façade that the imposing imperial cult temple was built that also dominated the Roman forum.[27]

Initially this building was identified as the Agoranomion, the office of the market officials, but this was subsequently rejected.[28] Standing today in front of the ancient Greek temple of Hephaistos built between 449 and 444 B.C. on the west side of the Greek agora, one can still see in the distance the Hellenistic Tower of the Winds in the Roman forum. Next to the tower to the right, but higher, are the remains of two of the three arched marble lintels of the imperial cult temple.

Its dominant position in this area of Athens parallels that of the imperial cult temple in Corinth, which also overlooked its Roman forum and was also built with steps leading up to it. Its foundations are at least three metres high above its forecourt. It was the tallest building in the Corinthian forum, and its elevation meant it rose above the prominent ancient temple of Apollo, the only preserved building from the Greek period. (See pp. 185-88.) In Ephesus one can stand on the actual site of the imperial cult temple of Domitian and its imperial predecessors that had earlier connections to *Roma* and previous emperors. It is on the highest section of that city overlooking the upper market, as was the case both in Corinth and Philippi.[29]

---

25. Hoff, "The Politics and Architecture of the Athenian Imperial Cult," p. 196.

26. Hoff, "The Politics and Architecture of the Athenian Imperial Cult," p. 196.

27. M. C. Hoff, "The Early History of the Roman Agora in Athens," in *The Greek Renaissance in the Roman Empire. Papers from the Tenth British Museum Classical Colloquium*, ed. S. Walker and A. Cameron, Bulletin Supplement 55 (London: Institute of Classical Studies, 1989), pp. 6-8.

28. See the refutation of this identification by M. C. Hoff, "The So-called Agoranomion and the Imperial Cult in Julio-Claudian Athens," *AA* 109 (1994): 93-117.

29. The temple in the Roman colony of Philippi was also built at the foot of the Acrop-

Hoff concludes of the Athenian temple that there is 'no compelling reason why the structure was considerably raised other than to provide an architectural prominence over the lower Market [the Roman forum], which itself serves as a magnificent forecourt to the building' except, he adds, 'as a focus for the early imperial cult'.[30]

That there should be more than one imperial cult site in a city is not without precedent. For example in the market building in Pompeii, a Roman colony, there is an altar to the imperial family that has statuary evidence of Britannicus and Agrippina II and dates from the beginning of Nero's reign. Standing to the right of it was the temple of Jupiter, and on the left the imperial cult temple as well as a sanctuary of the *genius* of Augustus.[31] So the convention of joint dedications to the chief divinity of a city and Roman emperors was not something peculiar to Athens.[32] The dedication on this Athenian temple reads — 'To Athena Archegetis [Founder] and the Augustan gods' (Ἀθηνᾶι Ἀρχηγέτιδι καὶ Θεοῖς Σεβαστοῖς).[33]

The imperial cult temple's prominent position in the Roman forum in Athens was highly symbolic. Its location was a silent but daily, visible reminder of the political reality of the Roman Empire, even in this famous 'free and allied' city. The conqueror wanted the conquered to be reminded that Rome ruled, and this on a daily basis, lest it somehow forget. Furthermore, the existence of altars elsewhere, temples on the Acropolis, the Greek agora and the Roman forum, all indicate how high a profile the imperial cult sites had in the commercial centre in Athens. Cult and commerce always sat comfortably together in the ancient world, not least of all in this famous city in the East of the Roman Empire.

---

olis. See C. Koukouli-Chrysanthaki, "Philippi," in *Brill's Companion to Ancient Macedonia: Studies in Archaeology and the History of Macedonia 650 B.C.–300 A.D.*, ed. R. J. Lane Fox (Leiden and Boston: E. J. Brill, 2011), p. 448.

30. Hoff, "The Politics and Architecture of the Athenian Imperial Cult," pp. 195-96.

31. J. J. Dobbins, "The Imperial Cult in the Forum at Pompeii," in *Subject and Ruler: The Cult of the Ruling Power in Classical Antiquity*, ed. A. Small, pp. 99-114.

32. Hoff, "The Politics and Architecture of the Athenian Imperial Cult," p. 196, citing as a precedent J. M. Reynolds, "The Origins and Beginnings of Imperial Cult in Aphrodisias," *PCPS* 26 (1980): 73.

33. *IG* 2², 3183. For the importance of *Athena Archegetis*, see Mikalson, *Religion in Hellenistic Athens*, pp. 108-12.

(iii) Imperial Gods, Priests and High Priests in Athens

Much information can be gleaned about the imperial gods and their cultic officials from inscriptions in Athens. The setting up of the cult of Augustus is usually dated in 27 B.C. This was after Octavian's victory at Actium, where the Athenians had sided with Mark Anthony, who had previously been officially received in Athens as 'the new god, Dionysius' (θεὸς Νέος Διόνυσος); 'Octavia "the Liberator" who accompanied him was identified with Athena Polias and therefore also received divine honours'.[34] Octavia the Younger (69-11 B.C.) was the sister of Augustus and the fourth wife of Mark Anthony, who later would be replaced by Cleopatra. The inscription reads, 'Antonius and Octavia, two benefactor gods' (Ἀντωνίου καὶ Ὀκραίας δυιν Θεων Εὐεργετων), and is dated 39-38 B.C.[35] In addition, the ancient Panathenaia Games were renamed Antonaia Games and dedicated to Mark Anthony as 'the new god, Dionysius' (θεὸς Νέος Διόνυσος). This is recorded in a decree honouring the Athenian *ephebes*.[36]

In Athens, Antonia Augusta, the grandmother of the future emperor Claudius, was declared the 'goddess, Antonia' (Θεὰ Ἀντωνία) during Tiberius' reign.[37] A high priest, Tiberius Claudius Novius, was appointed to do cult to her and was named 'a friend of Caesar'. (See pp. 29-30.) After her death on 1 May, A.D. 37, Antonia continued to be honoured in the time of Claudius.

> The Council of the Areopagus and the Council of 600 and the People honoured Tiberius Claudius Novius, son of Philinus, general of the hoplites for the fourth time and priest of Delian Apollo for life and President of the great Augustan Panathenaea and the Augustan Caesars and high priest of Antonia Augusta (ἀρχιερέα Ἀντωνίας

34. A. E. Raubitschek, "Octavia's Deification at Athens," *TAPA* 77 (1946): 149, cites Seneca the Elder's *Suasoriae* 1.6 when on his arrival in Athens they called him 'Dionysus', pp. 146-47.

35. Raubitschek, "Octavia's Deification at Athens," p. 149.

36. *IG* 2², 1043, *ll*. 22-23. For discussion see Raubitschek, "Octavia's Deification at Athens," pp. 146-50, and W. B. Dinsmoor, *Archons of Athens in the Hellenistic Age* (Amsterdam: A. M. Hakkert, 1966), pp. 285-86.

37. *IG* 2/3², 5095; N. Kokkinos, *Antonia Augusta: Portrait of a Great Roman Lady* (London: Routledge, 1992), p. 98. Cf. the People of Thasos dedicate an inscription to the wife of Augustus, Livia Drusilla 'a goddess and benefactor' (θεὰν εὐργέτιν), *ILS* 8784.

Σεβαστῆς), Novius friend of Caesar and friend of his country, for his virtue (ἀρετῆς ἕνεκεν).[38]

Novius, the holder of this office under Nero, was an Athenian citizen from among the élite, an ancestor of the famous orator and great future bene-factor of Athens and Corinth, Herodes Atticus.[39]

Nero, and Messalina his wife, would be added to the 'traditional gods' in cities in the East.[40] An inscription records Nero's speech deliv-ered at the Isthmian Games near Corinth on 29 November, A.D. 67. As a result of privileges he conferred on Greece, the decree was made by 'the magistrates and councillors and the people . . . to erect statues of Nero Zeus the Liberator and the goddess Augusta Messalina . . . to share with our ancestral gods' in the city of Acraephia. Epaminondas, a priest of Au-gustus, moved a resolution to 'the Council' for this new god and goddess to share the temple of Ptoian Apollo that housed that city's traditional divinities.[41]

When Nero appeared at the Athenian athletic games the dedication simply read, 'To Imperator Nero Caesar Augustus, the new Apollo'.[42] It was no less important than Acraephia's attribution but was rather greater because Augustus had attributed his victory in the East to Apollo.[43] The Athenian dedication read —

> Tiberius Claudius Herodes of Marathon, priest and high-priest of Nero Caesar Augustus for life, made this dedication to Dionysius [Zeus] the Liberator and Nero Claudius Caesar Augustus Germanicus and the Council of the Areopagus and the Council of the 600 and the people of Athens from his own resources when Tiberius Claudius Novius was general of the hoplites for the seventh time.[44]

---

38. *IG* 2/3², 3535. The inscription must be dated before 61-62, when he had been hoplite general for the ninth time.

39. For discussion see Spawforth, "The Early Reception of the Imperial Cult in Ath-ens," pp. 188-91.

40. *SIG*³, 814.

41. *SIG*³, 814 *ll.* 29-30, 44-51 (28 Nov., A.D. 67).

42. *IG* 2², 3278.

43. Suetonius, *Augustus* 70.

44. *IG* 2/3², 3182. J. H. Oliver, *The Athenian Expounders of the Sacred and Ancestral Law* (Baltimore: Johns Hopkins University Press, 1950), pp. 82-83.

This dedication to Nero by the high priest of the imperial cult was again linked to the divine Dionysius, the Liberator. Another inscription is dedicated 'To Imperator Nero Caesar Augustus, New Apollo'.[45] Six years prior, in A.D. 61, an Athenian bronze inscription by the ruling councils on the architrave on the Parthenon declared Nero, now twenty-four years old, to be 'the greatest emperor' and 'son of god'.

> The Council of the Areopagus and the Council of the Six Hundred and the People of Athens have honoured the greatest Imperator (Αὐτοκράτορ[α] μέγιστον), Nero Caesar Claudius Augustus Germanicus, son of god (Αὐτοκρατορα μέγιστον Νέρωνα Καίσαρα Γερανικὸν Θεοῦ υἱὸν) . . . and when the priestess of Athena was Paullina, daughter of Kapito.[46]

A further Athenian inscription linked the imperial goddess with the traditional instruments of government, 'Julia Divine Augusta Providence; the Council of the Areopagus and the Council of the 600 and the People dedicated [it]'.[47]

It was the same in the case of 'Julia Augusta Artemis Boulaea ('Ιουλίαν Σεβαστὴν Ἄρτεμιν Βουλαίαν) mother of Tiberius Augustus (Τιβερίου Σεβαστοῦ μητέρα) the Council of the Areopagus (ἡ βουλὴ ἡ ἐξ Ἀρείου Πάγου) [dedicated it]'.[48] βουλαῖος was the term used of certain gods having statues in the Council Chamber, in this case near that of the Council of the Areopagus. It shows that 'Livia (in her guise as Julia Augusta) had been assimilated to Artemis Boulaia'. This is yet another example of assimilation.[49] The statue was erected after A.D. 40, when Athens had its own particular instruments of government. First-century official inscriptions refer to 'The Council of the Areopagus and the Council of the 600 and the People'.

In the front row of the theatre of Dionysos situated below the Acrop-

45. *IG* 2/3², 3278.

46. *IG* 2², 3277.

47. 'Julia divine Augusta Providence; the Council of the Areopagus and the Council of the 600 and the People; dedicated by Dionysius, son of Aulus, of Marathon, from his own resources, when the *agoranomi* were the same Dionysius, of Marathon, and Quintus Naevius Rufus, of Melite.' *IG* ², 2.3, 3238.

48. M. Crosby, "Greek Inscriptions," *Hesperia* 6, no. 3 (1937): 464, *SEG* 20, 100.

49. S. E. Alcock, *Graecia Capta: The Landscapes of Roman Greece* (Cambridge: Cambridge University Press, 1993), p. 195.

olis is a chair from the Augustan era still bearing the inscription, [Seat] of 'priest and high priest of Augustus Caesar' (ἱερέως ὡς καὶ ἀρχιερέως Σεβαστου Καίσαρὸς).[50] It was not dedicated to *Roma* and Augustus but to the emperor. This was not without precedent, as there are other cities in the East where he allowed his name alone to be used.[51] The actual date of the inscription cannot be secured.

The priest of Augustus was a privilege traditionally open to Roman freedmen, but it was not so in Athens. The second title of 'high priest' was meant to give the office pre-eminence over the priests of other cults in the city, hence his place among the seats of honour in the theatre of Dionysus.[52]

No fewer than three priests during the principate of Tiberius are now attested. Whereas two bore the title 'priest (ἱερεύς) for life', the third was 'high priest' (ἀρχιερεύς) for life. Claudius as emperor was served by a 'priest for life', but during his reign the Athenians appointed a high priest for his mother, Antonia the Younger. Under Nero the same person, Tiberius Claudius Novius recurs, this time as 'high priest of the house of Sebastoi', i.e., the emperors.[53]

The Roman Senate granted the Achaean League the right to conduct federal imperial cultic celebrations annually in Corinth. This was initiated in late A.D. 54 or early in the following year. (See chapter 8.) The significance lies in the fact that even though this would always be celebrated in Corinth, the Athenians resolved to record officially that Gaius Julius Spartiaticus had been appointed the 'high priest of the divine Caesars and Caesar's family of the Achaean league, first [high priest] for life from its institution' (ἀρχιερεὺς Θεῶν Σεβαστῶν καὶ γένους Σεβαστῶν ἐκ τοῦ κοινοῦ τὴν Ἀχαΐας διὰ βίου πρῶτον τῶν ἀπ' αἰῶνος).[54]

Later, Athenian recognition would be given to Q. Trebellius Rufus from Narbonese in Gaul in the Latin West. He was the first person ever to hold the office of high priest, 'first high priest' (ἀρχιερεύς πρῶτος), in his

50. *IG* 3, 253. Spawforth, "The Early Reception of the Imperial Cult in Athens," pp. 183-85.

51. G. W. Bowersock, *Augustus and the Greek World* (Oxford: Clarendon Press, 1965), p. 116.

52. Spawforth, "The Early Reception of the Imperial Cult in Athens," p. 185.

53. *IG* 2², 1990, cited in Spawforth, "The Early Reception of the Imperial Cult in Athens," p. 185.

54. *IG* 3, 805; *IG* 5, 1, 463.

native Narbonese in the Flavian era.[55] He subsequently undertook the most prestigious office in Athens, the archonship. Now as a citizen, the Council of the Areopagus, the Council of Six Hundred and the People of Athens authorised the erecting of three statues to him in Athens.[56]

Athens did not incorporate the cyclical imperial games until the time of Claudius.[57] During his Principate Athenian priests could hold Roman citizenship. It was an Athenian, Tiberius Claudius Novius, 'with an unusually "Roman" outlook, who promoted the cult in the principates of Claudius and Nero'.[58] An official inscription from Claudius' era recorded a resolution of the Council of the Areopagus — 'Roman citizenship to be the greatest and most renowned of mankind' (τῇ μεγίστῃ καὶ παρὰ πασιν ἀνθρώποις διανομασμένῃ Ῥωμαίων πολειτείαι).[59]

The epigraphic material shows that imperial cult activities were presided over by officially appointed priests and is a further indicator of their high profile in Roman Athens.

(iv) Athenian Citizens' Cultic Participation

Finally, is there evidence of what ordinary Athenians thought and how they participated in the cult? While no extant inscription recording the annual calendar for cultic celebrations in Athens has been located to date, they were widespread in cities across the Roman world. (See pp. 26-27.) Celebrations on the imperial days were specified as 'non-work' days for everyone. Chapter 7 details epigraphic evidence of the calendar in the cities of Achaea and the allocated imperial holy days when everyone participated and no work was done. (See pp. 176-80.) Athens would have operated no differently.

One clear indicator was the Athenians' enthusiastic embracing of gladiatorial performances connected with imperial cultic celebrations and located in the theatre of Dionysos just below the Parthenon. Spawforth comments —

55. *IG* 2[2], 4193, *ll.* 5-6.

56. For an important discussion of Q. Trebellius Rufus see D. Fishwick, "Our First High Priest: A Gallic Knight at Athens," *Epigraphia* 60 (1998): 83-85, 88.

57. Spawforth, "The Early Reception of the Imperial Cult in Athens," p. 192.

58. Spawforth, "The Early Reception of the Imperial Cult in Athens," pp. 192, 193, 194.

59. *SIG*[3] 796, 3, *ll.* 32-33 cited by Spawforth, "The Early Reception of the Imperial Cult in Athens," p. 201, n. 80.

the Athenians were notoriously fond of the gladiatorial shows staged in this theatre. Given the well-demonstrated link in Greek subject cities between such shows and the Roman ruler cult, it is likely that, at Athens too, they were offered by priests of the imperial cult as part of the *munera* of their office.[60]

Such entertainment would override any aversion some philosophically minded Athenians might have had when they attended such celebrations connected with Rome's divine rulers.[61]

With respect to other forms of celebrations of the imperial cult, Fishwick makes a pertinent observation: 'The end result was that sacrifices became more and more a pretext for a good meal, religious anniversaries simply an occasion for a free dinner when one might indulge oneself in over-eating and over-drinking' and 'inscriptions and papyri confirm that games and banquets were a staple appurtenance of major festivals of the imperial cult throughout the empire.'[62]

It has been suggested that Athenian responses to the imperial cult were 'muted' in the period of Augustus,[63] but that could not be said at the time Paul visited Athens in the reign of Claudius. Reservations have also been expressed that the epigraphic evidence of imperial priests is not a complete indicator of enthusiasm for the imperial cult at a popular level and that those who undertook liturgies did so for their personal aggrandizement.[64] Whatever their motivation, on the basis of the primary sources cited above, one has to agree with Hoff that 'the cult to Augustus was highly active in Athens'.[65] This was more so in the Principates of Claudius and Nero, when there is a record that some Athenians became Christians in the reign of the former (Acts 17:34).

60. Spawforth, "The Early Reception of the Imperial Cult in Athens," p. 184, citing Dio Chrysostom, *Or.* 31.121 and A. H. M. Jones, *The Roman World of Dio Chrysostom* (Cambridge, MA: Harvard University Press, 1978), p. 32.

61. See S. E. Alcock, "The Problem of Romanization, the Power of Athens," in *The Romanization of Athens: Proceedings of an International Conference*, ed. Hoff and Rotroff, pp. 1-7.

62. D. Fishwick, *Imperial Cult in the Latin West* (Leiden: E. J. Brill, 1991), II.1, pp. 585, 587-88.

63. Spawforth, "The Early Reception of the Imperial Cult in Athens," p. 194.

64. Spawforth, "The Early Reception of the Imperial Cult in Athens," pp. 192-94.

65. Hoff, "The Politics and Architecture of the Athenian Imperial Cult," p. 194.

II. Official Protocol for Admitting New Gods to Athens

For centuries one of the official functions of the Athenian Council of the Areopagus was to examine any priest or, to use their word, 'herald' (καταγγελεύς) of a foreign god or goddess who came to their city promoting the veneration of their particular deity. The 'herald' was first required to provide proof of the existence of their divinity, then agree to build a temple dedicated to the veneration of the god or goddess and to provide for an annual feast day that would be integrated into Athens' religious calendar. These three essential requirements were needed for any divinity to be officially 'admitted' to Athens.[66]

(i) The Areopagus Council's Role in Assessing New Gods in Athens

In *Introducing New Gods: The Politics of Athenian Religion,* Garland traces the formal conventions whereby new gods were admitted to Athens from evidence with a *terminus ad quem* of 399 B.C. At his trial, Socrates was accused of having introduced new deities without authorization. The Romans had returned the original powers to the Areopagus Council, which would have included their formal acknowledgement of new imperial gods and the passing of resolutions to honour them.[67]

An unexpected first-century literary source confirms its on-going rôle, namely Luke in his account of Paul before the Council of the Areopagus (Acts 17:16-34).[68] It indicates that the Council formally continued to 'admit' to Athens new emperors as gods. This could include imperial family members.[69] From it we learn that Paul 'dialogued' (διελέγετο)

66. Garland, *Introducing New Gods.* Discussion of this ceased in 399 B.C. with the trial of Socrates.

67. Lintott, *Imperium Romanum: Politics and Administration,* pp. 147-48.

68. For reference to this see 'Acts 17:19-20 contains a crucial statement of the rights of the first-century Areopagus Council to examine heralds wishing to introduce gods to Athens' in my "*Christentum und Antike:* Acts and the Pauline Corpus as Ancient History," in *Ancient History in a Modern University,* ed. T. W. Hillard, R. A. Kersley, C. E. V. Nixon and A. Nobbs (Grand Rapids: Eerdmans, 1998), II, p. 130.

69. N. Evans, "Embedding Rome in Athens," in *Rome and Religion: A Cross-Disciplinary Dialogue on the Imperial Cult,* ed. J. Brood and J. L. Reed (Atlanta: Society of Biblical Literature, 2011), ch. 7, carefully documents much of the material evidence for imperial cultic activities and the 'intrusion' of Roman cultic ideology, yet remains agnostic on whether Paul actually delivered the speech, p. 94, n. 40. If he did not, it is strange that

with Jews, god-fearers and 'those who chanced to be there' in the Greek civic centre or agora (17:17), the original gathering place for the Stoics. Luke specifically adds 'and some of the Epicurean and Stoic philosophers also met with him', and after listening to him declared he was 'a charlatan' (σπερμολόγος) (17:18).[70]

When others witnessed Paul in action they suggested 'he appears to be a herald of foreign divinities' (καταγγελεύς ξένων δαιμονίων) (17:18).[71] Luke explains their reason for saying this, i.e., he 'was proclaiming Jesus and the resurrection' (ὅτι τὸν Ἰησοῦν καὶ τὴν ἀνάστασιν εὐηγγελίζετο).

The term 'herald' was also used of an imperial cult official in the time of Augustus.[72] Traditionally 'the herald' of the Areopagus Council appeared on the archon-list and possessed the seal of Athens.[73] There were those who perceived Paul to be such, announcing the existence 'of foreign deities' (ξένων δαιμονίων), i.e., non-Athenians with Paul 'proclaiming' two gods, 'Jesus and Anastasis', in the case of the latter 'the resurrection'.[74] Strabo in a well-known passage praises Athenian hospitality, including tolerance towards foreign gods, but he adds the negative caveat, 'For they welcomed so many of the foreign rites that they were ridiculed by comic writers.'[75]

It had long been thought that Paul delivered his address on the small slippery, rocky outcrop known as 'Mars Hill'. He was brought 'before the Areopagus' (ἐπὶ τὸν Ἄρειον πάγον) (17:19). This was the distinguished legal

---

Luke should have named two converts and their followers, one of whom was cited as an Areopagite, and also the specific occasion of their conversion in Acts 17:34.

70. He was a ragbag collector of scraps of learning and 'retails' them. Liddell and Scott cite Acts 17:18 as an example of the use of this term.

71. For a discussion of the use of the term δαιμόνια and its synonym θεοί, see pp. 214-21.

72. On the use of this term, see for example *OGIS* 456, a Mytilenean decree in honour of divine Augustus.

73. D. J. Geagan, *The Athenian Constitution after Sulla*, Hesperia Supplement XII (Princeton: American School of Classical Studies at Athens, 1967), pp. 24ff.

74. F. F. Bruce, *The Acts of the Apostles: Greek Text with Introduction and Commentary* (Leicester/Grand Rapids: IVP/Eerdmans, 1990), p. 377: '[T]hey might have thought that Anastasis was a new-fangled goddess.' *Contra* K. L. McKay, "Foreign Gods Identified in Acts 17:18?" *TynB* 45, no. 2 (1994): 411, who argues that 'Paul would not have introduced the idea of resurrection . . . by means of the abstract noun, ἀνάστασις' since he does not use it thus elsewhere in his letters and was unlikely to have used an abstract form here'. However, it is difficult to escape the implications that the reference to foreign 'gods' followed by ὅτι is what is being recorded *verbatim*.

75. Strabo, *Geography* 10.3.18.

entity that met in the setting appropriate to its authority, i.e., in one of the imposing official buildings in the Greek agora. He is recorded as standing 'in the midst of the Areopagus' (ἐν μέσῳ του Ἀρείου πάγου) (17:22), which implies a formal gathering of the Council. The phrase Luke uses of the Council is identical to that used in an Athenian inscription of officials who were 'the councillors of the Areopagus' (τῶν βουλευτῶν τῶν ἐξ Ἀρείου Πάγου).[76] Luke also records that Dionysius who was an Areopagite, i.e., a member of the Areopagus (Ἀρεοπαγίτης), became a convert (Acts 17:34). The reference is not to the slippery spot on the Acropolis looming over the Greek agora, but to the official meeting place in the agora of the Council of the Areopagus in Roman times.[77]

Luke's record states that 'they led (ἐπιλαβόμενοι) him to [the Council of] the Areopagus'.[78] The Western Greek text prefixes the sentence with 'after some days' and then adds that they were 'inquiring' as to his teaching. The statement 'after some days' could indicate that this occurred at a formal meeting of the Council. However, even if this variant is rejected, they brought Paul to the Council of the Areopagus to inquire of him further, since some of his hearers had cast him in the rôle of a herald of some 'foreign' cult, i.e., to Athens.

(ii) The Areopagus Council's Jurisdiction over New Gods Explained to Paul

This is further confirmed by the explanation that the Council of the Areopagus possessed the authority to assess Paul's claims (17:19). The standard translation of λέγοντες δυνάμεθα γνῶναι τις ἡ καινὴ αὕτη ἡ ὑπὸ σοῦ λαλουμένη διδαχή has been 'they said, "May we know what this new doctrine is that you are propounding?"' (17:19b). The use of the term δύναμαι within the Greek forensic semantic domain refers to the legal power that the Council possessed to examine Paul as the herald of his God. Δυνάμεθα can be translated as a present indicative, 'we have the power'. Justification for this rendering is found in a legal petition drafted by a lawyer. *P.Oxy.*

---

76. E.g., *SEG* 12, 87.

77. C. S. Keener, *Acts: An Exegetical Commentary 15:1–23:35* (Grand Rapids: Baker Academic, 2014), III, p. 2600.

78. The verb 'take' or 'take hold' gives the impression of 'seize' or 'arrest' (cf. Acts 21:33), but the subsequent discussion in verses 19-20 suggests that another meaning, 'lead', is appropriate.

899 (A.D. 200) cites a decree of Tiberius Alexander and the judgement of a court handed down on the basis of that degree and another legal ruling. It declares that the petitioner 'has the power (δύναται) [the legal right] to be released' (*l*. 31), like another person who had 'a legal right (δύναμις) to cultivate a field' (*l*. 9). Those of the Council before whom Paul was brought possessed the right to question him. There is sufficient literary and non-literary evidence to render δυνάμεθα as 'we have power or authority' and to conclude δυνάμεθα was a synonym for the legal term normally used, *viz.* ἔξεστιν.[79]

The infinitive γνῶναι that follows in the forensic domain means 'to form a judgement'. Herodotus records that an agreement was sworn and 'they adjudged' (ἔγνωσαν). Similarly, he writes elsewhere that the Lacedaemonians assembled a court and 'gave a judgement' (ἔγνωσαν). Other references also support the translation 'determine' or 'decree'.[80] Dio Chrysostom used both of these verbs to indicate the judicial right to make a judgement when he wrote, 'we shall not have the authority to judge (δυνησόμεθα γνῶναι) between the free man and the slave.'[81]

Good grounds exist, then, for arguing that in Acts 17:19 Paul was not simply being asked to provide an explanation. Instead these Council members were informing him at this initial interaction that 'we possess the legal right to judge what this new teaching is that is being spoken of by you'.[82] The reason to examine him officially was stated as — 'because you bring certain foreign things to our ears' (ξενίζοντα γάρ τινα εἰσφέρεις εἰς τὰς ἀκοὰς ἡμῶν) (17:20) — the 'certain "foreign" things' (ξενίζοντα τινα) was a reference to what was new to them.

The sentence following indicates further that they were guarding themselves against prejudicing the case because they were not conceding any attribution of divinity at this stage. The Council had to pass judgement on his so-called gods at a formal meeting. The neuter plural demonstrative pronoun 'these' (ταῦτα) refers to the *daimonia* in 17:20b. The usual

---

79. Bruce, *The Acts of the Apostles: Greek Text,* p. 378, made the important observation, which he left undeveloped, that Attic Greek would prefer ἔξεστιν here to the use of δυνάμεθα, which is used in Koine Greek in the forensic semantic domain.

80. Herodotus, *Histories* 1.74, 6.85. Liddell and Scott, *Greek-English Lexicon,* also cite Herodotus 9.3 and Isocrates, *Orations* 17.6 for this meaning.

81. Dio Chrysostom, *Or.* 14.24.

82. Dio Chrysostom, *Or.* 14.24, '[W]e shall not be able to judge (δυνησόμεθα γνῶναι) between the free man and the slave', although in this case it relates more to a matter of outward appearance.

translation is 'we therefore wish to know what these mean' (βουλόμεθα οὖν γνῶναι τίνα θέλει ταῦτα εἶναι). The nature of their inquiry indicates they are fulfilling one of the functions of the 'Council (βουλή) of the Areopagus', hence the cognate βουλόμεθα indicates 'we wish to take counsel'.

Literary sources show that the verb θέλω is best rendered 'to claim' when it is followed by the accusative and the infinitive, as occurs in Acts 17:20b. Pausanias provides two comparable examples — 'they were claiming to be Arcadians' (Ἀρκάδες ἐθέλουσιν εἶναι), and 'they are claiming Zeus was born (θέλουσι γενέσθαι) and brought up among them'. Plutarch uses the same construction, i.e., 'proclaiming to be the People' (δῆμον ἐθελοῦντας εἶναι).[83]

The verb followed by the same construction can also mean 'to decree'. An official inscription records, 'He decreed the danger of the case to be . . .' (ἠθέλησεν τὸν κίνδυνον τῆς προβολῆς εἶναι).[84] Octavian expressed an imperial wish in a private letter that would certainly carry the same import — τούτους θέλω φυλαχθῆναι, as the following line confirms that Augustus is decreeing what must be done.[85]

It is therefore appropriate to render the clause τίνα θέλει ταῦτα εἶναι as 'what it is claimed these gods *(i.e., daimonia)* are'. What Paul as a herald was doing in the agora in the perception of his hearers was seen to be 'decreeing'.[86] On the basis of the meaning of γνῶναι (v. 19) and other forensic terms, the sentence would read, 'We therefore wish to take counsel to judge what these divinities decreed [by you] are.' In "Hailing New Gods in Athens," Versnel concludes, 'Foreign gods could be admitted, it is true, but admission as an official cult was only granted on condition that the new god submitted to the local *nomoi* of the *polis*.'[87]

The tone of these sentences in Acts was polite, for this was not a criminal prosecution. The translation suggested for Acts 17:19-20 would

83. See Liddell and Scott, *Greek-English Lexicon*, ἐθέλω or θέλω #8, citing Pausanias, where 'they say' (φασίν) in contrast to 'they claim' refers to a conviction concerning, in this case, their civic status, *Description of Greece*, I.4.6; cf. also 4.33.1 and Plutarch, *Romulus* 3.4.3.

84. *CPR* 20, *l.* 17 (third century A.D.).

85. J. Reynolds, *Aphrodisias and Rome*, JRS Monograph 1 (London: The Society for the Promotion of Roman Studies, 1982), no. 10, *l.* 4 (39-38 B.C.).

86. Cf. Acts 2:12, where the speakers determine the meaning of the verb θέλει: 'They were all amazed and were perplexed, saying one to another "what do you think this is?" [τί θέλει τοῦτο εἶναι].'

87. H. S. Versnel, "Hailing New Gods in Athens," in *Ter Unus: Isis, Dionysos, Hermes: Three Studies in Henotheism,* Inconsistencies in Greek & Roman Religion I (Leiden: E. J. Brill, 1990), p. 102.

confirm they were intent on exercising their rights to determine whether these were new gods and thus to be admitted. Here was an initial meeting with some of the Council members, held after they had perceived what Paul was doing. They would know that, if he gained the authorization of the Areopagus Council, his divinities would secure a rightful place either in the Athenian Pantheon, the Greek agora, or possibly even in the Roman forum.

The hearing summarized in Acts 17 reflects Paul's sensitivity to what was not merely of religious importance but could also have had political consequences. Such a distinction could never be valid in Athens or elsewhere in the Roman East. This was no criminal court case as has been suggested.[88] It was one that sought to ascertain whether there really had been an epiphany of Paul's 'divinities'. Did his 'gods' exist? If so, what official recognition was the Council to give, what temple location or altar, what statues and divine honours would be appropriate, and when would be the annual official holiday and feast?

(iii) Paul's Presentation of Evidence to the Council

The opening part of Luke's summary of Paul's *apologia* reflects the convention for introducing new gods to Athens. His 'introduction' *(exordium)* to this formal presentation before a properly convened meeting of the Areopagus Council must have surprised them. His opening assertion was that he did not have to establish the existence of this 'new' divinity in Athens. The fact was that the Athenians had already recognized that there was the 'unknown god' (Ἀγνώστῳ θεῷ) (Acts 17:23a), and they had already erected an altar to him.

In his *Description of Greece* Pausanias records his tour of the temples and religious sites of Athens and surrounding areas in the second century A.D. He records that in Phaleron, which was one of the ancient ports of Athens, he saw 'altars of gods named "unknown"' (βωμοὶ θεῶν τε ὀνομαζομένων Ἀγνώστων).[89] Van der Horst has suggested that the phrase βωμοὶ θεῶν refers to altars each of which is dedicated to the 'unknown

---

88. T. D. Barnes, "An Apostle on Trial," *JTS* 20 (1969): 407-19; p. 419 suggests Paul seems to have been put on trial in Athens, that this theory 'possesses intrinsic plausibility', but he felt that it was a 'clearly impossible task of providing proof positive'.

89. Pausanias, *Description of Greece* 1.1.4. See Diogenes Laertius, *Lives of Philosophers* 1.110. For Athenian altar-inscriptions to emperors, see *IG* 2, 3, 4960-5020.

god'.[90] Following his discussion with the young man Timasion, Apollonius, who was educated in rhetoric in Athens and later in Rome, wrote, 'it is a much greater proof of wisdom and sobriety to speak well of all the gods, especially at Athens, where also altars are set up in honour even of unknown gods' (οὗ καὶ ἀγνώστων δαιμόνων βωμοὶ ἵδρυνται).[91]

The Stoics and Epicureans among Paul's hearers would have no difficulty with the use of the singular for 'god' or 'gods'. Diogenes Laertius records that 'worshippers of god . . . have acquaintance with the rites of the gods . . . how to serve the gods'.[92] Therefore debates as to whether there was or was not an actual inscription using the term 'God' in the singular is misplaced, given the interchangeable use of the singular and plural in theological discussion.[93]

Paul's affirmation that he was not the herald of something nonexistent would have secured the attention of the Council. Barnes notes, 'Paul replies that his audience already acknowledges his God.'[94] He has met the first criterion required in the due process of official recognition. Paul proceeds to tell them what this God whom 'you [officially] venerate

90. P. W. van der Horst, "The Altar to the 'Unknown God' in Athens (Acts 17:23) and the Cults of 'Unknown Gods' in the Graeco-Roman World," in *Hellenism-Judaism-Christianity* (Kampen: Kok Pharos, 1994), p. 167, citing Homer, *Iliad* 11.808 and Juvenal, *Satires* 3.145.

91. Philostratus, *Life of Apollonius of Tyana* 6.3.5. Evans, "Embedding Rome in Athens," p. 94, argues surprisingly concerning the cult of the unknown god, 'There is no archaeological or epigraphic evidence for such a cult.' While that is true, one cannot rule out the possibility of uncovering such in the future; one cannot summarily dismiss Pausanias' evidence describing religious sites throughout Athens and the reference to altars within its jurisdiction to unknown gods. See *Description of Greece* 1.1.4. His description of Greek travels to religious sites has long been seen to be a genuine record and supplements primary onsite evidence. See Alcock, *Graecia Capta: The Landscapes of Roman Greece,* and the excellent paper effectively using this literary source as well as archaeological and epigraphic evidence by Barbara S. Spaeth, "Pausanias and the Cults of Roman Corinth," delivered at the SBL conference in San Francisco, 19-21 November 2011.

92. Diogenes Laertius, *Zeno* 7.119. Paul was not, as Barnes, "An Apostle on Trial," p. 418, suggested, 'using the sophistical trick of slightly misrepresenting the evidence in his own favour'.

93. See B. Gärtner, "The Altar Inscription," in *The Areopagus Speech and Natural Revelation* (Uppsala: Gleerup, 1955), pp. 242-47, where he surveys the very considerable literature generated by this discussion up to his time of publication. He does suggest that the inscription could be 'To the god who is in fact nameless', arguing that 'Paul's adaptation of the words to his own ends need not coincide with the actual meaning of the inscription', p. 247. However, that is not how ancient sources outside of Paul's speech are translated.

94. Barnes, "An Apostle on Trial," p. 418.

(εὐσεβεῖτε) as "unknown" is like' (17:23). Again it would have surprised them that the second requirement for approval in the process of admitting new gods to Athens was not needed. His God 'does not dwell in temples (ναοῖς) made with hands' (17:24b). Paul would not need to erect one dedicated to this divinity as Athenian custom required.

Furthermore, no endowment would be required to establish an obligatory feast day in the Athenians' annual religious calendar because, Paul asserts, 'He has no need of anything, because it is he who gives life and breath and all things to all of his creation' (17:25). This 'unknown' God does not need anything from the Athenians because it is He who provides everything for their needs, including their life and their sustenance, not only for them but for the whole created order as the 'Lord of heaven and earth'.

Barnes deduces that 'the Areopagus seems to be the effective government of Roman Athens and its chief court. As such, like the imperial Senate in Rome, it could interfere in any aspect of corporate life — education, philosophical lectures, public morality, foreign cults'.[95] He then surprisingly concludes, 'Hence there is no need to suppose that the Areopagus had special "surveillance over the introduction of foreign divinities"', adding as a footnote, 'As appears to be implied by Geagan' who categorically stated that '[t]he account of Paul's speech before the Areopagus illustrates its surveillance over the introduction of foreign divinities'.[96]

When the wording in Acts 17:19-20 is examined within the forensic semantic domain, the case of first-century jurisdiction of the Council of the Areopagus over this matter is established and coalesces with other external evidence. The summary of Paul's speech to this point covers the three traditional proofs needed by any herald seeking to introduce a new god into Athens. So there was still, in the Roman period, a due process for the admission of a new god or gods to Athens by the governing Council. When a new emperor was announced it can be assumed the Council formally recognized his divinity and, as a consequence, authorized the giving of divine honours to the new Caesar, including at times his family members.

---

95. Barnes, "An Apostle on Trial," p. 413. There is also the Council of 600 and the People.

96. Geagan, *The Athenian Constitution after Sulla*, cit. p. 50. Barnes noted, and indeed used, Geagan's work as an important treatment of the constitution of Athens after Sulla (138-78 B.C.).

III. Athenian Philosophers and Priests and the Public

What further light might there be on imperial cultic activities in Athens? The philosophy and practices of the teachers and adherents of both philosophical schools concerning Athenian gods and goddesses including imperial ones are reflected in extant sources.

(i) Philosophers, Politics and Popular Piety

Both Epicureans and Stoics addressed the issue of involvement in the political processes of the Roman world. An ancient Epicurean *dictum*, 'live unnoticed' (λαθέ βιώσας), was an escapist exhortation to its followers to withdraw from *politeia*.[97] The Stoics' approach was the opposite, for they promoted active involvement in it. The Stoics' *dictum* was 'The wise man never stays outside politics'.[98] Seneca the Younger cites a close friend's view of Stoic teaching.

> I will follow the commands of our teachers and throw myself into politics. I will accept honours and their insignia, not attracted by the purple or the fasces, but in order to be of greater service to my friends, my fellow citizens and humanity.[99]

Wistrand's discussion of the Stoic philosophers' attitudes to the Principate notes their reputation for delivering lectures on morality without fear or favour of the emperor.[100] They clearly did this to the point where Seneca the Younger (*c.* 4 B.C.–A.D. 65), the brother of Gallio, proconsul of Achaea, who was Nero's personal tutor and 'friend of the emperor' *(amicus principis)* and later occupied the rôle of chief advisor to the young emperor, censured his fellow Stoics.

> Use your philosophy to get rid of your own faults, not to decry those of others. The philosopher should not dissociate himself from the

97. For a full discussion see G. Roskam, *'Live Unnoticed' λαθέ βιώσας: On the Vicissitudes of an Epicurean Doctrine*, Philosophical Antique, vol. 111 (Leiden: E. J. Brill, 2007).

98. Cited by Cicero, *Tusc.* 4.51.

99. Seneca the Younger, *De tranquillitate animi* 1.10.

100. E. Wistrand, "The Stoic Opposition to the Principate," *Studii Clasice* 15 (1979): 96-97.

usages and customs of the Society; he must not seem anxious to appear to condemn whatever he avoids doing himself. It is possible to be a philosopher and avoid pompousness and invidious criticism of others.[101]

The Stoics were preoccupied in the political domain with 'frankness of speech' *(libertas)* and 'uncompromising firmness of principle' *(constantia)*. As such it brought those of its adherents operating in the public square into conflict with emperors at various times.

The contrast between the Imperial ideology and reality was patent and the contrast between Imperial propaganda and the Stoics' censure of vices prevalent in the contemporary world became plainly discernible. The preaching and the disapproving attitude of the Stoic philosophers were interpreted as criticism of the reigning emperor and his regime.[102]

When they withdrew from public life as a silent condemnation of the Principate, it was rightly interpreted as a highly visible protest.[103] 'Loyal writers like Seneca the Younger, Martial and Quintilian responded by ridiculing the philosophers and praising the blessings of the emperor's government. Affronted emperors even punished critical philosophers by exile or death.'[104]

Early Stoicism had been opposed to the worship of idols and the erection of temples, but by the time of Posidonius (*c.* 135–*c.* 51 B.C.), and certainly by the early Roman Empire, it had accommodated practices of popular piety.[105]

There was, however, a measured compromise. Attridge comments that 'there is some evidence that this was done in the early years of the school, although the classical Stoic position was one of accommodation to ordinary cult and beliefs'. He also cites Balbus, who was appointed by

---

101. Seneca the Younger, *Letters* 105.3.

102. E. Wistrand, *Felicitias Imperatoria*, Studia Graeca et Latina Gothoburgensia XLVIII (Arlölv: Berlings, 1987), p. 64.

103. Wistrand, "The Stoic Opposition to the Principate," pp. 94-96, for evidence.

104. Wistrand, *Felicitias Imperatoria,* p. 64.

105. D. L. Balch, "The Areopagus Speech: An Appeal to the Stoic *Historica Posidonius* against Later Stoics and Epicureans," in *Greeks, Romans and Christians: Essays in Honor of Abraham J. Malherbe,* ed. D. L. Balch, E. Ferguson and W. Meeks (Minneapolis: Fortress Press, 1990), p. 71.

Augustus as proconsul of Africa and provided an apology for Stoic participation in popular religion recorded in Cicero's *De natura deorum*.[106]

> [T]hough we repudiate these myths with contempt, we shall never-
> theless be able to understand the personality and the nature of the
> divinities pervading the substance of the several elements, Ceres per-
> meating earth, Neptune the sea and so on; and it is our duty to revere
> and worship these gods under the names which custom has bestowed
> upon them.[107]

A *rapprochement* with cults in the later development of post-
Posidonian Stoicism (*c.* 135–*c.* 51-52 B.C.) would include a 'defence of temples and explanation of religious images and temples' by Dio Chrysostom
(A.D. *c.* 40-50–*c.* 110) in his Olympian oration, 'On Man's First Concep-
tion of God' delivered before an ancient statue of Zeus *c.* A.D. 101. It provides an example from the Flavian period.[108] As Price notes, 'Thus Dio
[Chrysostom] of Prusa could argue that images and sacrifices might not be
strictly necessary, but that they point as manifestations of man's goodwill
and disposition towards the gods'.[109] Strabo, who lived in the Principates
of Augustus and Tiberius, supported the 'orthodoxy' of Zeno, the founder
of the Stoic school, on images stating categorically that 'the Greeks were
wrong in modelling gods in human form'.[110]

Both pagan and later Christian apologists would also draw attention to Zeno's comments on popular piety. Plutarch (*c.* A.D. 50–*c.* 120)
declared Zeno's teaching was not to construct temples 'because a temple
is not worth much, is also sacred and no work of builders and mechanics
is worth much'.[111] Diogenes Laertius (third century A.D.) would go on to
note the exact place in Zeno's (335-263 B.C.) *Republic* when he wrote, 'line
200 prohibits the building of temples, law courts and gymnasia in cities'.[112]
Clement of Alexandria, a second-century Christian apologist, refers to

---

106. H. W. Attridge, "The Philosophical Critique of Religion under the Early Empire,"
ANRW 2, no. 16.1 (1978): 66, and Cicero, *De natura deorum* 2.23-28, 59-72.

107. Cicero, *De natura deorum* 2.2.71.

108. Dio Chrysostom, *Oration* 12.

109. S. R. F. Price, *Rituals and Power: The Imperial Cult and Asia Minor* (Cambridge:
Cambridge University Press, 1984), p. 228.

110. Strabo, *Geography* 16.2.35-39 cited by Balch, "The Areopagus Speech," p. 69.

111. Plutarch, "Stoic Self-contradictions," *Moralia* 1034B.

112. Diogenes Laertius, *Lives of the Eminent Philosophers, Zeno* 7.33.

this, citing the same source — 'we ought to make neither temples nor images; for no work is worthy of the gods.'[113]

Epicurus himself had believed that popular piety was not correct — 'For the utterances of the multitude about the gods are not true preconceptions but false assumptions.'[114] In spite of this commonly held conviction, Epicurean philosophers made no endeavour to discourage their adherents from participating in popular cultic activities. In mid-first century A.D., an important Epicurean directive from Oxyrhynchus, Egypt, declared that the proof of piety could not be measured by offering up sacrifices, and therefore one was free to do so but with a caveat that would embrace imperial cultic activities as a compromise.

> It is of course open to you to offer sacrifices to the gods . . . you conform in some sense to religious traditions. Only be careful that you do not permit any admixture of fear of the gods or of the supposition that in acting as you do you are winning the favour of the gods.[115]

Are there any critiques of the duplicity of the Stoic philosophers' participation in such cultic activities? Plutarch (A.D. 46–c. 120) in 'Stoic Self-contradictions' makes this telling indictment.

> Moreover, it is a doctrine of Zeno's [the founder of this philosophical school] not to build temples to the gods, because a temple, not worth much, is also not sacred. . . . The Stoics, while applauding this as correct, attend the mysteries in the temples, go up to the Acropolis, do reverence to statues, and place wreaths upon the shrines, though these were works of builders and mechanics. Yet they think that the Epicureans are confuted by the fact that they sacrifice to the gods, whereas they are themselves worse confuted by sacrificing at altars and temples that they hold do not exist and should not be built.[116]

There were strong social and political pressures that resulted in Stoic adherents feeling compelled to participate in imperial cultic veneration,

---

113. Clement of Alexandria, *The Stromata* 5.11.

114. Epicurus, *Epistle* 124.

115. *P.Oxy.* 215, and for a discussion see Attridge, "The Philosophical Critique of Religion under the Early Empire," pp. 45-47, and A. J. Festugière, *Epicurus and His Gods* (Oxford: Blackwell, 1955), pp. 64-65.

116. Plutarch, "Stoic Self-contradictions" 1034B-C.

even though it compromised their teaching. Plutarch saw this as highly hypercritical given their condemnation of their opponents, i.e., the Epicureans, for this very same thing.

What had the philosophers done intellectually? Van Neffelen notes, 'Political thought of the Post-Hellenistic period is rarely deemed original and seems only interesting to the extent that it attempts to legitimise Roman rule and the emperors in trite categories and rehashed arguments.'[117] He observes there were 'two important shifts in emphasis: the idea of "natural leaders" and the description of kingship as part of a cosmic structure'[118] and further shows that —

> Stoics such as Dio Chrysostom and Epictetus integrate gods and men in a single, universal hierarchy, which turns worship into an expression of honour due to a superior. The explicitly political images used for comparison with the pantheon such as . . . the Roman emperor, and their respective subordinates, are not, however, sufficiently explained by seeing them as mere attempts to ascribe coherence and unity to traditional religion: they indicate a much more profound link between religion and political hierarchies, which is the projection of the ideal hierarchy onto the divine world.[119]

These Stoic philosophers had integrated into their thinking the two spheres of imperial politics — the Caesars and the gods. Those who were at the centre of civic life as members of the Areopagus Council were amenable to referencing emperors in the 'cosmic structure', as is evidenced by the divine honours bestowed on them. It may well be that some of those whom Paul was addressing in Athens had been at the vanguard of assimilating the divine imperial 'reality' into their philosophical systems. Were they among those who voted for formal resolutions by the Council of the Areopagus bestowing divine honours on Claudius and Nero?

117. P. van Nuffelen, *Rethinking the Gods: Philosophical Reading of Religion in the Post-Hellenistic Period,* Greek Culture in the Roman World (Cambridge: Cambridge University Press, 2011), p. 112.

118. Van Nuffelen, *Rethinking the Gods,* p. 113.

119. Van Nuffelen, *Rethinking the Gods,* p. 119. Epictetus' concern was with the sheer extravagance of the entertainment side of imperial cultic celebrations, and not the status of the emperors.

(ii) Philosophers and Priesthoods

It is known what at least one philosopher said about imperial cult priest-hoods. Epictetus, a Stoic philosopher (A.D. 55–c. 135) who had been schooled in Rome under the leading Stoic philosopher, Musonius Rufus, was very clear. Although he had close imperial court connections, he was banished from Rome along with all other philosophers by Domitian in A.D. 93 and settled in Nicopolis. At times he proved to be highly counter-cultural in his teachings to young students and to others as well. Records reveal his advice to a person who was entertaining the thought of becom-ing a priest of the imperial cult.

> Epictetus: 'Drop the business: you will spend a lot of money for nothing'.
> The man: 'But', said the man, 'they will write my name on contracts'.
> Epictetus: 'And you will be present to say to those who read them out "That is my name they have written"? And even if you can be pres-ent every time now, what about when you are dead?'
> The man: 'My name will live after me.'
> Epictetus: 'Write it on stone and it will live after you. Who will remem-ber you outside of Nicopolis?'
> The man: 'But I shall wear a crown of gold'.
> Epictetus: 'If you want a crown at all, take a crown of roses and wear it; you look more elegant in that'.[120]

Bowersock notes of this particular section, 'This whole exchange contains not a word about the *divus,* about any emotion connected with worship, about any divine intercession, about anything we should want to call religious sentiment. Nor is there the slightest suggestion of impiety in Epictetus's dissuasion of the priestly candidate. The only thing at stake is the man's reputation and career; and it is acknowledged that the priest-hood will cost him dear.'[121] This dialogue of Epictetus was not untypical of him because he did not hesitate to teach his students to evaluate and reject some of the cultural trends of his day.[122]

120. Epictetus, "How we ought to bear ourselves towards tyrants" 1.26-29.

121. Bowersock, "Greek Intellectuals and the Imperial Cult in the Second Century A.D.," in *Augustus and the Greek World,* p. 183.

122. For his stinging critique of the widely lauded sophistic movement of his day, see my "Epictetus and the Corinthian Student of the Sophists," in *Philo and Paul among*

Stoic philosophers noted this priestly office would be a position held for life, and they regarded it as a total waste of one's own financial resources.[123] The costs incurred by the provincial priests were enormous, including financing the gladiatorial and other spectacular annual events.[124] But it was regarded as important because of its social significance and, after all, it was the pinnacle of one's public career.

Millar comments on this advice by Epictetus, 'The man's priesthood in the passage illustrates perfectly the political functions of Emperor-worship, in providing for the wealthy classes honorific positions which gave them prestige and identified them with the regime.'[125] Fishwick nuanced this, based on the extant inscriptions of provincial priesthoods in Hispania Citerior. For him they reflect the rank and status of a local upper class that was located in the hierarchy immediately below the upper equestrian and senatorial classes and the pinnacle of a public career.[126] Bowersock notes other cases where the provincial priesthoods were viewed as civic duties for the 'wealthy and ambitious', but there were those who refused to offer themselves for this liturgy.[127]

In discussions relating to emperors, neither Plutarch (*c.* A.D. 50-120) nor Dio Chrysostom (*c.* A.D. 40-112), who wrote on the imperial cult *per se,* denounced the later period of the Flavian emperors. Dio delivered four orations. In "On Kingship," to Trajan on his accession, Dio tells him, 'you have him [Heracles] as a helper and guardian of your rule, as long as it is determined that you reign'.[128]

Earlier Dio in the garb of a philosopher, i.e., 'clad in a mean cloak', delivered an oration to the Alexandrians. He declared that he had been appointed to this task, coming as 'Hermes on behalf of Zeus', and is there 'by the will of some deity'.[129] According to Jones, the reigning emperor was

---

the Sophists: Alexandrian and Corinthian Responses to a Julio-Claudian Movement (Grand Rapids and Cambridge: Eerdmans, 2002²), ch. 7.

123. See the provincial priesthood of Spartiaticus for life in Corinth, pp. 200-205.

124. D. Fishwick, *The Provincial Priesthood: Imperial Cult in the Latin West* (Leiden: E. J. Brill, 2002), III.1, p. 302.

125. F. Millar, "Epictetus and the Imperial Court," *JRS* 55 (1965): 147.

126. Fishwick, *The Provincial Priesthood: Imperial Cult in the Latin West,* III.2, pp. 87, 95-96. This was not atypical, as his exploration of other sites reveals where the provincial cult was observed.

127. Bowersock, "Greek Intellectuals and the Imperial Cult in the Second Century A.D.," p. 183.

128. Dio Chrysostom, "On Kingship," *Or.* 1-4 and *Or.* 1.84.

129. Dio Chrysostom, "On Kingship," *Or.* 1-4; 32.21-22.

'the living image of Zeus', which was also a Ptolemaic image of kingship.[130] While the Alexandrians had been the first to bestow divine honours on Vespasian (A.D. 69-79) immediately on his accession to the Principate, Dio came to seek to heal the rift that occurred when, in return for bestowing divinity upon the emperor, he 'repaid' this by levying a heavier tax burden on Egypt.[131] In this oration there was a clear accommodation to the mindset of the Alexandrians concerning the imperial cult as he spoke on behalf of his emperor, Vespasian.

Both philosophical schools in Athens had embraced this 'principle' of accommodation in the first century A.D., adjusting their beliefs to contemporary practices for themselves and their followers. It therefore gave a green light to Athenian citizens to participate in the imperial cult, bearing in mind the philosophers' caveats for those who were their adherents. It is clear that Stoicism and Epicureanism had endorsed imperial cultic activities, and part of their motives may have been to retain their followers.

It would be hard to conceive of members of the Council of the Areopagus who were adherents of the Stoic and Epicurean schools absenting themselves from the official august celebrations on major imperial cult days. Evidence suggests that in the Roman Empire the Stoic and Epicurean philosophers and their adherents participated in the imperial cult by accommodating their teaching, whether it meant joining in prayers to the gods for the emperor or doing cult to an image of the reigning emperor in an imperial temple. Athenians participated, but would the first Christians in that city likewise simply 'go with the flow'?

IV. Paul's Confrontation, God's Amnesty and the Audience's Responses

Paul's citation in Acts 17:27-28 of Epimenides of Crete, a fifth-century B.C. Greek prophet and poet, would be a telling rebuke to the philosophers' compromise. Epimenides had written 'in him [the "unknown" God] we live and move and have our being', and its implication 'for we are also his

---

130. Jones, *The Roman World of Dio Chrysostom*, pp. 44, 174, n. 83; and for a detailed treatment of the visit, see A. Henrichs, "Vespasian's Visit to Alexandria," *ZPE* 3 (1968): 58-80.

131. For a discussion of their reaction, see Dio Cassius, *Roman History* 65.8, 'Six obols more you demand of us', they taunted, and in a crowded assembly they shouted in unison at Titus, Vespasian's son, 'We forgive him; for he does not know how to play the Caesar'. Suetonius, *Vespasian* 19.2 noted that they called Vespasian 'a fishmonger'.

offspring'.[132] Paul spelt out the logical consequence of this for his audience — 'being therefore the offspring of God we are compelled not to think (οὐκ ὀφείλομεν νομίζειν) that the Deity is like gold or silver or stone, an image formed by the art and imagination of man' (Acts 17:29). Given that his audience operated on the premise that poets were divinely inspired, it was a major rejection of any veneration of images, including those of imperial gods.

The Council had been assembled to pass judgement on Paul's 'gods', but in his *apologia* he turned the tables and declared that their actions would ultimately come under the scrutiny of his God. At the same time Paul presented another option. God offered an amnesty. 'The times of ignorance God overlooked but He now commands all men everywhere to repent' (17:30). His audience had to respond because God had fixed the actual day for their final judgement. The judge had already been appointed to carry out the great assize, and the basis of his judgements would be righteousness (17:31). That explained the necessity for all people everywhere to repent of their culpable guilt, and not least those whom Paul was addressing, including members of the Council.

What proof could Paul offer that there would be a final day of judgement? He declares, 'God raised him [the judge] from the dead' (17:31). 'Jesus and the resurrection' (Ἰησοῦν καὶ τὴν ἀνάστασιν) was the essence of his message in the agora (17:18).

Acts 17 records three responses of those present at the hearing. One group said they would hear Paul again about this. Another mocked because he mentioned the issue of raising their judge from the dead (17:32). The latter reaction is entirely explicable because Aeschylus (*c.* 525-*c.* 456 B.C.) in his account of the founding of the Council of the Areopagus by the city's patron god, Apollo, had long ago declared that 'when a man dies, the earth drinks up his blood; there is no resurrection' (ἀδρὸς δ' ἐπειδὰν αἷμ' ἀνασπάσῃ κόλις ἅπαξ θανάτος, οὔτις ἐστ' ἀνάστασις).[133] The implication was the *raison d'être* for the Areopagus Council's judicial rôle from very ancient times, for after death there would be no calling to account. Therefore they had to dispense justice to offenders in their lifetime, as only in this life could punishment on the guilty be administered.

A third response was that some accepted the offer of the amnesty that concluded Paul's *apologia*. Luke records that 'some people joined him [Paul] and believed among whom also were Dionysius, the Areopagite' (ὁ

132. Citing Aratus, *Phaimomena* 5.
133. Aeschylus, *Eumenides* 647ff.

Ἀπεοπαγίτης) and a woman named Damaris and others who were with them'. Dionysius was a member of the Council, while the 'others with them' were presumably clients (17:34).

The content of Paul's address to the Council of the Areopagus would have been highly instructive for these Athenians who became Christians (17:34). When thinking about the implications of their conversion, they were no longer to attribute providence to the gods nor speak of the 'divine being' in terms of a plurality of gods. Neither could they venerate statues of gods before Athens' imperial altars, nor in the temples of other gods on the allotted days. That would be idolatry, for this 'unknown' God could not be replicated in any human likeness (17:29).

Their 'unknown God' did not share his throne with any other god, including imperial or Athenian; they could not be incorporated in the pantheon and worshipped with them. The Old Testament forbade monolatry, i.e., the worship of the God of Israel along with other divinities — 'you shall have no other gods alongside me' (Exod. 20:3).

Spawforth's examination of the extant Athenian evidence leads him to this conclusion: 'It was only under Claudius and Nero that the imperial cult became much more prominent in Athens itself, chiefly as a result of initiatives by Tiberius Claudius Novius, including above all the incorporation of the cult into the Athenian cycle of major religious festivals.'[134] The archaeological and epigraphic evidence from the eras of both emperors helps us understand the enormous pressure on everyone to conform. However, the first Athenian converts in the time of Claudius could not, for the reasons Paul gave in his *apologia* before the Aeropagus Council.

Would Christians in Athens and other places in the Roman East heed the dominical injunction binding and restricting them to 'render to Caesar the things that are Caesar's and to God the things that are God's' (Mark 12:17)? Certainly the essence of Paul's Areopagus address gave no leeway for those converts to Christianity to rationalise any compromises or to render divine honours to the Caesars as their compatriot philosophers and others might continue to do with whatever caveats they might stipulate.

This investigation has also revealed Paul's theological framework and arguments against religious pluralism that had a bearing on the issue

---

134. Spawforth, "The Early Reception of the Imperial Cult in Athens," p. 194. Paul's defence before the Areopagus Council occurred prior to his time in Corinth and can be dated around A.D. 51, as Acts 18:2 refers to the expulsion of the Jews from Rome by Claudius. Gallio's proconsulship of Achaea can be dated in the same period, see pp. 192-93.

of divine honours for the Caesars and its challenge for converts in other communities where the Christian message took root through his missionary endeavours.

Appendix: *De natura deorum* for Stoics and Epicureans and Paul

(i) *The Stoics and Paul*

The summary of Paul's speech suggests he seems to have consciously followed the sequence of the traditional presentation of the nature of divinity used by the Stoics. Balbus' debate with opposing schools of philosophy *c.* 77-78 B.C. presents a standard order of the Stoic *apologia* on the immortality of the gods — "The Nature of the Gods" *(De natura deorum)*. 'First they prove that the gods exist; next they explain their nature; then they show that the world is governed by them; and lastly, that they care for the fortunes of mankind.'[135]

Paul's speech assumes their belief in God's existence and his rôle as the creator of the world — 'Lord of heaven and earth' (v. 24a). Paul also affirms that 'He gives life and all things to all his creation' (v. 25b) and that his providential care is intrinsically bound up with the needs of all mankind (v. 26). He develops this theme on the nature of the known God. Traditional Christian apologetics later continued this same progression, arguing as the Greeks did with their 'natural theology'.[136]

The Stoics would not have been at all concerned that Paul used the term 'God' and not 'gods'. Gerson remarks that there is 'a curious feature of the language in which Cicero [who records the debate of Balbus] expressed the Stoic position, namely the shifting back and forth from talk about "God" to "gods" — a common feature as other sources record. God is one but called by many popular names'.[137] Cleanthes, who succeeded Zeno as head of the Stoic school, wrote his hymn to Zeus that likewise expressed this interchangeable use of the terms.

---

135. Cicero, *De natura deorum* 2.3.

136. Attridge, "The Philosophical Critique of Religion under the Early Empire," pp. 45-78.

137. L. P. Gerson, *God and Greek Philosophy: Studies in the Early History of Natural Theology* (London: Routledge, 1990), p. 155. Cf. Diogenes Laertius, "Zeno," *Lives of Eminent Philosophers* 7.119, '. . . worshippers of God; for they have acquaintance with the rites of the gods . . . how to serve the gods.'

Of gods most glorious, known by many names,
Power supreme, O Lord of Nature's changes,
Law-giving pilot of the universe,
I hail you, Zeus, with whom there is no man
Forbidden converse: we are of your race;
Of all the beasts that live and walk the earth
Only we have a semblance of thy reason. [138]

Balbus also presents the Stoic's view on the existence of the God/
gods without any *apologia* — '*the* main issue is agreed among all men of
all nations, inasmuch as all have engraved in the minds an innate belief
that the gods exist', citing with approval Chrysippus' arguments for God's
existence and the latter's conclusion 'therefore God exists'.[139]

While the Stoics were comfortable with the interchangeable use of
the terms 'God' and 'gods', Paul would never have been. Such an ambiguity had already arisen in the minds of his hearers in the agora in Athens
when he was perceived by his audience to be proclaiming 'foreign deities',
viz. 'Jesus and ἀνάστασις', (17:18). His message could only be communicated by discussing specifically the nature and work of God. The Stoic
perception concerning the nature of 'god' did not necessarily make him
personal but rather pantheistic. Cleanthes, Chrysippus and Posidonius
declared with Zeno — 'the substance of God to be the whole world and
the heavens'.[140]

There are also important resonances with the Stoic concept of providence. This may well have been Paul's most important bridge to that group
in his audience. Balbus sets out the Stoic thesis as he sees it — 'the world
is ruled by divine providence . . . of the gods', 'only familiarity blinds us
to nature's marvels'. Providential government of the world can be in-
ferred, firstly from divine wisdom and power, secondly from the nature
of the world, thirdly from a detailed review of the wonders of nature, and
fourthly from the care of man.[141]

It is also based on the belief that 'all the things in this world . . . have

---

138. *Stoicorum Veterum Fragmenta* 1.537.

139. Cicero, *De natura deorum* 2.13, 16.

140. Diogenes Laertius, "Zeno," *Lives of Eminent Philosophers* 7.14, Cicero, *De natura deorum* 1.39. God is said by some to be 'breath' (πνευμα), i.e., a mixture of air and fire, and sometimes the whole world is called 'God'. See F. H. Sandback, *The Stoics* (London: Chatto & Windus, 1975), p. 35.

141. Cicero, *De natura deorum* 2.95, 76-80, 81-97, 98-153, 162.

been created and provided for the sake of men' and 'the things that it contains were provided and contrived for the enjoyment of men'. The sun and moon are seen to contribute to the 'maintenance and structure of the world and the seasons and the bounty of the earth have been given for him'.[142] Balbus sees some confluence with an Epicurean idea. He asks, 'Why should I speak of the teeming swarm of delicious fish . . . which affords us so much pleasure that our Stoic Providence appears to have been a disciple of Epicurus?' Then he states that 'an abundance of commodities was created for men's use and which men alone discover'.[143]

The Stoic doctrine was not restricted to mankind in general but applied as much to the individual.

> Nor is the care and providence of the immortal gods bestowed only upon the human race in its entirety, but is also wont to be extended to individuals. We may narrow down the entirety of the human race and bring it gradually down to smaller and smaller groups, and finally to single individuals.[144]

Seneca the Younger (*c.* A.D. 1-65), a contemporary of Paul and brother of Gallio, developed this point in *De Providentia* written during Claudius' reign. This work, which is Stoic in essence but tempered by his experience of life including a former period of imperial exile from Rome and mellowed by eclecticism, seeks to answer a question raised by his friend, Lucilius, a procurator of Sicily. 'Why, if a Providence rules the world, it still happens that many evils befall good men?' Seneca made it clear that he preferred to place this question within a more coherent framework, i.e., the traditional Stoic treatment of the nature of God proving 'that a Providence does preside over the universe, and that God concerns himself with us'. He continued with an immediate reference to 'gods' and used the terms interchangeably in this letter while remaining true to his Stoic tradition.[145]

Not only does Seneca argue that the sufferings of the just are consistent with Providence, but he speaks of God as 'father' — like a teacher who tests just men with hardship. It would be easy to draw the conclusion that Seneca believed in a personal God and therefore represented normative

---

142. Cicero, *De natura deorum* 2.154, 156.
143. Cicero, *De natura deorum* 2.162.
144. Cicero, *De natura deorum* 2.164.
145. Seneca, *De Providentia* 1.1.

first-century Stoicism. He dealt with subjects such as God, prayer, divine justice and immortality and was able 'to invest with emotions ideas and concepts which are in themselves [for Stoics] impersonal and unexciting'.[146] However, it has been shown that his characteristic method was to work from the premise of the recipient of his letter and to develop a more orthodox Stoic view as he proceeded.[147]

After a careful analysis of the basic contrast between Paul and Seneca on this point, Sevenster concluded that 'Seneca is in the last resort not serious when he speaks of the personal god'.[148] However, there would have been sufficient common ground to begin a dialogue had Seneca the Younger and Paul been in Athens at the same time.[149]

Resonances with Stoicism are not only to be found in the general structure of Paul's presentation, but in particular with providence derived from the Old Testament — 'God who made the world and things in it' (e.g., Genesis 1–2; Deut. 10:14; Ps. 115:16). 'He has made from one all the nations of earth to dwell on all the face of the earth' (Gen. 3:20). 'He Himself gives life and breath and all things to all . . . having determined their appointed seasons and the bounds of their habitation' (Job 12:23; Acts 17:24a, 25-26a).

It should be noted that, when Stoics discussed God's providence, it tended to be 'impersonal'. Gerson warns, 'Virtually all of the Stoic theological language must be transposed to take account of their physics. Divine providence is here just the contribution of particular laws and parts of the cosmos to the whole'.[150] This was a crucial difference between Paul's doctrine of God's providence and that of the Stoics. The theme of judgement also found common ground between Paul and his Stoic audience, according to Van Nuffelen.[151]

It can be concluded, in seeking to understand how the Stoics would have perceived Paul, that it was clear to them that he was following their traditional sequence used when presenting an apologetic on the existence and nature of the gods.

146. Seneca, *De Providentia* 1.5. J. H. W. G. Liebeschuetz, *Continuity and Change in Roman Religion* (Oxford: Clarendon Press, 1979), p. 115.

147. J. R. G. Wright, "Form and Content in the Moral Essay," in *Seneca Medea*, ed. C. D. N. Costa (Oxford: Oxford University Press, 1973), pp. 48-49.

148. J. N. Sevenster, *Paul and Seneca* (Leiden: E. J. Brill, 1961), p. 37.

149. For a discussion of the spurious letter from Seneca to Paul, see Sevenster, *Paul and Seneca*, pp. 11ff.

150. Gerson, *Gods and Greek Philosophy*, p. 166.

151. Van Nuffelen, *Rethinking the Gods*, p. 112.

(ii) The Epicureans and Paul

Paul's speech also addressed the adherents of Epicurean philosophy, whose 'code of behaviour' dealing with happiness was spelt out in the forty famous epitomes of its founder, Epicurus.[152]

The cardinal truth, he declared in a letter to Menoeceus, was 'First believe that God is living, immortal and blessed (πρωτον μεν τον θεον ζωον απητηαρτον και μακαριον νομιζων)'. He proceeded to encourage his readership to believe this and 'not to affirm anything that is foreign to his immortality or that agrees not with blessedness, but believe about him whatever upholds both his blessedness and immortality'.[153] As Paul uses all these terms elsewhere of God, *viz*, he is a 'living' God (1 Thess. 1:9), he is 'immortal' (Rom. 1:23) and he is 'the blessed God' (1 Tim. 1:11), the Epicureans in the audience would have agreed with what Paul said.

Epicurus believed that the knowledge of the divinity was clear to all; he said that it was 'according to the notion of God indicated by the common sense of mankind. For there are gods, and the knowledge of them is manifest'.[154] Just as with the Stoics, the terms 'God' and 'gods' could be interchanged, the Epicureans would have understood this when Paul declared that the character of the unknown God could be known.

There was also a consensus between Paul and the Epicureans on the idea that God does not live in man-made temples. For the latter, the dwelling place of God or the gods was not this earth — divinity was far removed from it and lived in perfection. The Epicureans were notionally opposed to all forms of superstition. They discussed 'the interior, psychological effects of improper belief and demeaning practice, which characterize what they consider to be superstition'.[155] Both they and Paul agreed that God has no need of anything (17:25a) because the Epicureans also held that 'God had no need of human resources'.[156]

There were clearly philosophical and practical departure points between Paul and the Epicureans, who denied that 'God's providential relationship with the world entertains a just judgement of mortals, especially a judgement that takes place after death, where rewards and punishments

---

152. Diogenes Laertius, *Epicurus* 10.139-54.

153. Diogenes Laertius, *Epicurus* 10.123.

154. 'The gods exist, the knowledge which we have of them is clear vision,' Epicurus, *Epistles* 3.123.

155. Attridge, "The Philosophical Critique of Religion under the Early Empire," p. 64.

156. Philodemus, *Πρὸς εὐσεβείας* fr. 38.

are allotted'.[157] Epicurus in his 'catechism' affirmed that 'Death is nothing to us; for the body, when it has been resolved into its elements, has no feeling and that which has no feelings is nothing to us'. He asserted elsewhere, 'Accustom yourself to believe that death is nothing to us.'[158]

In concluding, it might well be asked — did Paul engage in accommodating Stoic and Epicurean beliefs in Athens in the same way that these philosophers accommodated themselves to the imperial cult for their hearers for pragmatic reasons? Paul later declared that he had become 'all things to all men that by all means I might win some' (1 Cor. 9:20-23). However, while he found common ground in general revelation with the Old Testament, he knew that there were lines that could not be crossed.

In Acts 17 Paul made six important affirmations about the nature of God. These derive from the Old Testament and contrast with Stoic and Epicurean standard teaching on 'the Nature of the gods'.

(i) On the subject of God and the created order: God 'made the world and everything in it, being Himself Lord of heaven and earth . . . gives life and breath and all things to all his creation' (vv. 24-25, cf. Genesis 1).

(ii) On God and the nations: God 'determined allotted periods and the boundaries of their habitations [the nations]' and 'the times of ignorance therefore God overlooked' (vv. 26, 30, cf. Deut. 32:8 and Ps. 74:17).

(iii) On God and general revelation: In the Athenian speech the created order is also the signal from God (cf. Ps. 19:1-4) that they should 'seek after God, in the hope they might feel their way toward him, and find him' (v. 27, cf. Job 23:3, 8, 9).

(iv) On the immanence of God: 'He is not far from each one of us,' a statement that was confirmed by their divinely inspired poets. Epimenides the Cretan wrote 'in him we live and move and have our being' (v. 27, cf. Job 12:10).

(v) On the living God and humanity: Because the poets were seen to speak definitively, the citation 'For we are also his offspring',[159] rules out any inanimate configuration of this living and life-giving deity replicated in 'gold or silver, graven by art and device of man'. Being then the offspring of God, 'we ought not to think that the godhead is like gold, or silver, or stone, graven by art and device of man' (vv. 28-29, cf. Isa. 40:18-19).

(vi) On God and repentance: the judge, the day and the standard

---

157. Diogenes Laertius, *Epicurus* 10.139, 124.

158. J. H. Neyrey, "Acts 17, Epicureans and Theodicy: A Study of Stereotypes," p. 129ff.

159. Cf. Aratus, *Phainomena* 5 and Cleanthes, *Hymn to Zeus* 4.

of judgement are all fixed. In his great mercy God provides a window of opportunity for all people everywhere to repent because that is the only way to avoid condemnation on the day of judgement. The proof that this day is coming is the resurrection of Jesus from among the dead (vv. 31-32).

Paul's affirmations in the Athenian speech about God's providence and his activity in creation were clearly taught in the Old Testament. In Isaiah 40:28 this God is 'the everlasting God, the Lord, the Creator of the ends of the earth'. It is He who 'has measured the waters in the hollow of His hand, and meted out heaven with the span, and comprehended the dust of the earth in a measure, and weighed the mountains in scales, and the hills in a balance' (Isa. 40:12). There is a resonance, if not a direct connection, with Jeremiah 5:24 — 'Let us now fear the Lord our God, who gives rain for the former and the latter, in its season; who reserves for us the appointed weeks of the harvest.' Psalm 50:9-12 declares that God owns all of his creation.[160]

Here, then, it has been demonstrated that there was important common ground between certain beliefs of the Stoics, Epicureans and those in the Old Testament. Paul's knowledge of their belief systems enabled him to engage with them. Acts 17:18 records that he had already done so in the agora prior to coming before the Areopagus Council. While there was some confluence with what he believed about God, there were real dissonances with certain philosophical traditions of both schools of thought. Furthermore, there was culpability on their part because they had indicated to their followers they could participate in cultic activities, including imperial ones 'tongue-in-cheek' while at the same time warning them not to be superstitious when they went into the temple. This was duplicitous on their part, but the earliest converts to Christianity in Athens could not do this.

---

160. Gärtner, *The Areopagus Speech and Natural Revelation*, pp. 85-87.

CHAPTER 7

Promoting Cultic Honours in Achaea and Exemption for Christians

A senior Roman official, Publius Cornelius Scipio, assiduously promoted divine honours for Augustus in the leading cities of the province of Achaea, which would have included its capital, the Roman colony of Corinth. A lengthy inscription dated *c.* A.D. 1 or 2 from the ancient city of Messene in Achaea some 150 kilometres from Corinth records what cultic activities he promoted province-wide.[1]

Price saw this inscription as the best officially documented case of a Roman governor enthusiastically promoting the imperial cult in any Roman province.[2] Spawforth also concluded it is 'a prime document for the richness of Augustan Messene's imperial cult'.[3] Likewise Millar recorded its importance: '[T]he games and sacrifices carried out for Augustus cast significant new light on the ceremonial and diplomatic aspects of the relations between Greek cities and the emperor.'[4]

The official resolution by the city of Messene commended Scipio for undertaking three significant cultic actions relating to the imperial family that are unfolded sequentially in the inscription. He offered thanks to the gods, made sacrifices to Augustus, and personally sponsored the Caesarean games. He persuaded other leading cities to follow his example by doing the same.

---

1. *SEG* 23, 206. For a discussion of this text and its dating, see J. E. C. Zetzel, "New Light on Gaius Caesar's Eastern Campaign," *GRBS* 11 (1970): 263-66.

2. S. R. F. Price, *Rituals and Power: The Imperial Cult and Asia Minor* (Cambridge: Cambridge University Press, 1984), p. 70.

3. A. J. S. Spawforth, *Greece and the Augustan Cultural Revolution* (Cambridge: Cambridge University Press, 2012), p. 212. One can supplement this with that of his predecessor, Paullus Fabius Maximus, governor of the province of Asia.

4. Fergus Millar, "Two Augustan Notes," *CR* 18 (1968): 264-65.

The Achaeans later lauded Augustus' successors, Tiberius and Gaius, on becoming emperors in A.D. 14 and A.D. 37 respectively, with official embassies to Rome that outlined the divine honours they would render to them.

In Corinth archaeological and epigraphic evidence survives confirming that, in the subsequent reigns of the Julio-Claudian emperors when Paul established the church there, the veneration of the imperial gods was alive and well. How would the Christians cope with the expectation of their having to give divine honours to the Caesars?

This chapter will examine (I) significant information in the Messene inscription on Scipio's energetic promotion of imperial cultic celebrations in the era of Augustus; (II) later celebrations associated with the accession of both Tiberius and Gaius that provide evidence of the continuation of imperial cultic activities in Achaea; (III) important archaeological evidence of local imperial cultic activities in Corinth from its foundation as a Roman colony in 44 B.C. to Paul's time there; and (IV) Gallio's official ruling on the status of the first Christians in Corinth with its implication for their non-participation in local imperial cultic activities (Acts 18:12-16).

I. Imperial Cultic Activities in the Province of Achaea A.D. 2

The epigraphic evidence for city-based imperial cultic veneration in the province of Achaea was recorded almost half a century before Paul's arrival in Corinth. The Council and People of Messene passed an official decree containing a number of highly revealing features of imperial cultic activities.

It recorded that Publius Cornelius Scipio himself had organized and actually financed these city-wide celebrations and spectacles in Messene. The inscription notes that he was also 'preparing most of the cities in the province to do the same with him' (*ll.* 9-10). His achievements were spelt out in considerable detail by Philoxenidas, the secretary of the Messene Council in this official resolution during the magistracy of Theodoros (*ll.* 1-2). There are twenty lines in the main clause of this decree listing all Scipio's imperial cultic activities before indicating what reciprocal honours the Council had 'decreed' (ἔδοξε) for this Roman benefactor (*l.* 21).[5]

---

5. The details of the latter are no longer extant, but they would have been commensurate with his gift, given the convention of awarding appropriate honours based on the size of the benefaction.

What particular circumstances provided the justification for such sponsorship and veneration? When Scipio learnt that Gaius, the adopted son of Augustus and by then an appointed heir, had defeated a dangerous enemy of Rome in the East, he marked this victory with provincial-wide celebrations. These included offering up a sacrifice to the gods for his continuing safety, sponsoring a lavish festival, and making sacrifices to Augustus as well. He encouraged all the cities in the province to do the same. Furthermore he actually changed the imperial provincial calendar, deducting two imperial cult days from 'the days of Augustus' festival', and in their place established annual celebrations with sacrifices on the anniversary of when Gaius was first elected consul in Rome.

(i) The Motivation Behind Scipio's Imperial Cult Involvement

Zetzel states that 'one would like very much to know why Scipio, the Roman magistrate, is performing games and sacrifices in Greece, rather than letting the natives themselves honour the emperor'.[6] His view is that the only explanation as to why Scipio did this was because 'the province of Achaea was so disorganized, without a κοινόν [province] and stricken with στάσις [discord], that official guidance was needed for any extraordinary festivals'. He concedes this solution is 'not really satisfactory' and admits 'this problem too awaits its solution'.[7]

Spawforth has recently rejected Zetzel's tentative solution based on Herz's discussion of significant details about Scipio's origins, his career and his relationship with Augustus.[8] He was technically a half-brother of Gaius.[9] Scribonia, Scipio's mother by a previous marriage, subsequently married Augustus in 40 B.C. She had been 'required' for dynastic reasons to divorce his father, but she would later find herself divorced by Augustus on the very day she gave birth to their daughter, Julia the Elder, the following year. Hence Scipio was a half-brother to Julia the Elder and he was by law a stepson of Augustus by reason of his mother's second marriage.[10]

6. Zetzel, "New Light on Gaius Caesar's Eastern Campaign," p. 263.

7. Zetzel, "New Light on Gaius Caesar's Eastern Campaign," p. 263.

8. Spawforth, *Greece and the Augustan Cultural Revolution*, p. 212.

9. P. Herz, 'Die Adoptivsöhne des Augustus und der Festkalender Gedanken zu einer Inschrift aus Messenes', *Klio* 75 (1993): 284-86.

10. E. Fantham, *Julia Augusti: The Emperor's Daughter* (London and New York: Routledge, 2006), p. 19.

Syme singles out the Scipio family as one example of 'the schemes devised by Augustus in the ramification of family alliances [that] were formidable. . . . Of his allies among the young *nobiles* . . . he subsequently ensnared the house of Cornelii Scipiones. . . . [T]he young generation of *nobiles* grew up and passed through the avenue of political honours to the consulate'.[11]

Scipio's career was a significant one, having previously been appointed *consul ordinarius* in Rome along with Lucius Domitius Ahenobarbus. Both held these posts in Rome for a year from 1 January, 16 B.C.[12] Scipio was subsequently appointed to the important post of proconsul of Asia somewhere between 9 and 3 B.C.[13] and prior to taking his position in Achaea. Paullus Fabius Maximus had held this office from 10 to 9 B.C. Given the on-going celebrations in province-wide Asia, Scipio would have been well aware of the initiatives of its previous proconsul. The latter had made the birthday of 'the most divine Augustus' the beginning of each New Year. (See pp. 28-29.) It was in this last position that Scipio would be proactive in encouraging imperial cultic honours and veneration.

Grant notes the evidence of Scipio being honoured in his provincial appointment in Asia — '*c.* 7 B.C. a new era began in which portraiture on coins in Asia was restricted to any governor who was "a friend of Caesar" *(amici principis)'.*[14] A coin survives from Pitane with the laureate head of Augustus and on the reverse an image of Scipio, as its governor.[15]

He also had official status as a trusted person close to the emperor and signified by the official title bestowed on him as 'a friend' *(amicus)* of Augustus.[16] As 'Caesar's friend' he had obligations to promote his interests. Syme pointed out that he was one of the 'inner circle of Augustus' associates'.

---

11. R. Syme, *The Roman Revolution* (Oxford: Clarendon Press, 1939), pp. 378-79.

12. V. Ehrenberg and A. H. M. Jones, "The Fasti," in *Documents Illustrating the Reigns of Augustus and Tiberius* (Oxford: Clarendon Press, 1976²), p. 37.

13. K. M. T. Atkinson, "Governors of the Province of Asia in the Reign of Augustus," *Historia* 7 (1958): 326, and R. K. Sherk, *Roman Documents from the East: Senatus Consulta and Epistulae to the Age of Augustus* (Baltimore: Johns Hopkins University Press, 1969), p. 339 and n. 4, locates it between 10 and 6 B.C., but he does come after Maximus. See pp. 29-31.

14. M. Grant, *From* Imperium *to* Auctoritas*: A Historical Study of* Aes *Coinage in the Roman Empire* (Cambridge: Cambridge University Press, 1946), p. 387.

15. *RPC* no. 2392.

16. J. A. Crook, '*Amici Principis*', in *Consilium Principis: Imperial Councils and Counsellors from Augustus to Diocletian* (Cambridge: Cambridge University Press, 1955), p. 161, no. 124.

This was another strategy of Augustus to extend his power and influence through marriages, as was the case with Maximus.[17] (See pp. 32-33.)

Scipio then became *de facto* governor of the province of Achaea with the designation of *quaestor pro praetore*.[18] 'The *quaestor* was not merely a financial official . . . but a deputy to the governor in all respects.'[19] He was 'left in the position of authority, in case of the death or early departure of a governor and until a successor arrived'.[20]

Governors were known to have promoted imperial cult veneration. One has only to ask why it was that Pontius Pilate as a governor of Judaea under Tiberius from A.D. 26 to 36 subsequently erected a shrine in Caesarea Maritima, the capital of that province. (See p. 84.) Its inscription read, 'the temple of Tiberius Marcus Pontius Pilate gave and dedicated it' ([————]s *Tiberieum [Po]ntius Pilatus [praef]ectus Iud[ae]e [dedit dedicavit]*). The editors of the inscription note that 'temples connected to theatres are common in Roman architecture' and it was not uncommon to have 'instant shows of loyalty to the emperor' especially after the treason trial of Sejanus in the reign of Tiberius.[21]

Q. Marcius Barea, proconsul of Africa in A.D. 41-43 whose capital, Carthage, was founded as a Roman colony at the same time as Corinth, dedicated a shrine to *Diva Augusta* after the Senate in Rome formally deified Livia in January, A.D. 42, and built a small temple that he also dedicated *Di Augusti* to Claudius.[22] Rives suggests that 'Barea may have had a personal interest in promoting the imperial cult but does not indicate

17. Grant, *From Imperium to Auctoritas,* citing R. Syme, *The Roman Revolution,* pp. 378-79, 382.

18. Zetzel, "New Light on Gaius Caesar's Eastern Campaign," pp. 262-63, weighs the alternative that either he was an official with the *imperium,* commanding a province, or he was no more than the holder of the provincial quaestorship.

19. A. Lintott, *Imperium Romanum: Politics and Administration* (London and New York: Routledge, 1993), p. 50.

20. R. K. Sherk, *Rome and the Greek East to the Death of Augustus* (Cambridge: Cambridge University Press, 1984), p. 151, explains that this is the significance of the additional phrase *pro praetore* with respect to this inscription.

21. C. M. Lehmann and K. G. Halum, *Joint Expedition to Caesarea Maritima: Excavation Reports, the Greek and Latin Inscriptions of Caesarea Maritima* (Boston: ASOR, 2000), no. 43, and discussion on pp. 67-70. See also J. Patrich, *Studies in the Archaeology and History of Caesarea Maritima: Caput Judaeae, Metropolis Palaestinae* (Leiden and Boston: E. J. Brill, 2011), p. 30, n. 104, who suggests that the Tiberium was adjacent to the compound of the Roman authorities.

22. *ILA* 2.550; *CIL* 11002; J. M. Reynolds and J. B. Ward Perkins, *The Inscriptions of Roman Tripolitania* (Rome, 1952), no. 273.

either the exercise of a particular religious authority or an institutionalized role in the foundation of imperial cults'.[23]

Later the action of Publius Celerius, another proconsul of Asia, is commemorated in a bilingual inscription — 'procurator of the god Claudius and of Nero Claudius Caesar Augustus Germanicus, set up the base of this monument and the statues from his funds and dedicated them'.[24] The four-metre-long base bore statues of these two emperors.

Therefore, the view that the proconsuls' remit was only to exercise the *imperium* in criminal courts and oversee the collection of taxes for Rome is not the full story. Rives cites a Roman law where 'it was the duty of a governor to inspect sacred temples and public works alike to ensure that they were completed if begun, and kept in repair once constructed'.[25]

P. Cornelius Scipio, P. Fabius Maximus and Q. Marcius Barea and possibly Publius Cererius as proconsuls actively promoted imperial divine veneration. So it was not just leading provincial citizens or Roman resident businessmen who did this.[26] Therefore Scipio's endeavours were by no means unique in the Julio-Claudian era.

The Messene inscription records part of Scipio's motivation.

> [H]aving being endowed with unsurpassed goodwill towards Augustus and his whole house, having made a very great and highly honorific vow, to preserve him (Augustus) safe for all time, as is shown by his deeds on every occasion. (*ll.* 3-7)

Given these two grandsons of Augustus whom he adopted as sons and named as his successors, it is significant that Scipio spearheaded such

23. J. B. Rives, *Religion and Authority in Roman Carthage from Augustus to Constantine* (Oxford: Clarendon Press, 1995), pp. 81-82.

24. R. A. Kearsley, *Greeks and Romans in Imperial Asia: Mixed Language Inscriptions and Linguistic Evidence for Cultural Interaction until the End of AD III*, Inschriften Griechischer Städte aus Kleinasien 57 (2001), no. 156.

25. Rives, *Religion and Authority in Roman Carthage from Augustus to Constantine*, p. 82, and in n. 131 citing Ulpian, *The Digest*, 1.16.7.1. See also J. Rogan, *Roman Provincial Administration* (Stroud, UK: Amberley Publishing, 2011), chs. 4-5, for a discussion of their diverse responsibilities.

26. 'To *Roma* and to Imperator Caesar, son of the god, Augustus, Pontifex Maximus, holder of the tribunician power for the nineteenth time, to their own saviour (τῷ ἰδίῳ σωτῆρι), the Milyadeis and the Roman businessmen among them and the Thracians living among them dedicated this.' G. H. R. Horsley, *The Greek and Latin Inscriptions in the Burdur Archaeological Museum*, The British Institute at Ankara Monograph 34 (2007), no. 328.

divine honours for Augustus as his 'friend'. It was a public affirmation of his 'unsurpassed goodwill towards Augustus and his whole house', including Gaius and Lucius, to whom technically he himself was related as step-grandsons of Augustus. In so doing he could well have had an eye on his future, knowing his distinguished career path already in Rome, the province of Asia and now in Achaea. 'Dio Cassius points out that not all the flattery was sincere, because many people were intent only on furthering their careers by means of their supposed attachment to Gaius and Lucius.'[27] Whatever his motive, he would not have breached imperial protocol.

(i) Sacrifices for and to Augustus and Celebrating the Caesarean Games

Secretary of the Council was Philoxenidas in the magistracy of Theodoros. Decree: Since Publius Cornelius Scipio, *quaestor pro praetorian,* being endowed with unexcelled goodwill toward Augustus and all his house, having made one great and highly honorific vow to guard him against all harm, as displayed by his deeds on each occasion conducting the Caesarea Games (τὰ Καισάρεια) and sparing neither expense (ἐνλείπων) nor honour (φιλοτιμία), nor the thanksgiving to the gods for the sacrifices to Augustus at the same time (μηδὲ τὰς ὑπὲρ τᾶν διὰ τοῦ Σεβαστοῦ φυσιᾶν εὐχαριτίας ποτί τοὺς θεους ἅμα), and preparing the great cities of the province (καὶ τὰς πλείστας τῶν κατὰ τὰν ἐπαρχείαν πόλεων) to be ready to do the very same thing along with him (σὺν ἑαυτῷ τὸ αὐτὸ τοῦτο ποιεῖν κατασκευασάμενος). (*ll.* 1-10)[28]

This inscription records imperial cultic activities involving 'the thanksgiving to the gods for the sacrifices to (διά) Augustus at the same time' (τὰς ὑπὲρ τᾶν διὰ τοῦ Σεβαστοῦ φυσιᾶν εὐαριστίας ποτί τοὺς θεοὺς ἅμα) (*ll.* 8-9). How to render the phrase διὰ τοῦ Σεβαστοῦ is a critical

---

27. P. Southern, *Augustus* (London and New York: Routledge, 1998), p. 173, citing in n. 10; Dio, *Roman History* 55.6.5, 8.3, 9.2-4; and Tacitus, *Ann.* 1.3, who also commented on the motives of Augustus.

28. *SEG* 23, 206, and R. K. Sherk, *The Roman Empire: Augustus to Hadrian* (Cambridge: Cambridge University Press, 1988), no. 18. See Zetzel, "New Light on Gaius Caesar's Eastern Campaign," pp. 259-60, with corrections of earlier editions. A further correction is suggested in *l.* 9 as the subsequent discussion will argue.

issue for understanding one imperial cultic practice. Millar states that the sacrifice was 'for Augustus', as does Sherk,[29] both of whom do so without comment. Fishwick is uncertain and inserts a question mark but does not pursue the matter, stating the city was 'celebrating lavishly the festival of the Caesarea with sacrifices for (?) Augustus'.[30] Zetzel in his translation renders the phrase 'to Augustus' without comment.[31] Price makes no specific observation concerning this phrase, but he does devote an important section of his book to sacrifices to the emperor that has made good the deficiencies in understanding that particular aspect of imperial cultic activities.[32]

To appreciate his sacrifices in relation to Augustus, several points need to be noted about the actual phrases used for divine sacrifices and veneration to others in this inscription. The inscription records a sacrifice 'for (περί) the safety of Gaius with an oxen' (αὐτός τε βουθυτῶν περὶ τᾶς Γαίου σωτηρίας) (*l.* 15) and another 'to be made on behalf (ὑπέρ) of Gaius' (Γαίου θυσιᾶν ποιήσασθαι) to celebrate annually the date of his appointment as consul in Rome (*l.* 18).

In the inscription the term 'for' (περί) is used of sacrifices for Gaius and 'on behalf of' (ὑπέρ) for the safety of Gaius, but neither is used with respect to 'the thanksgiving' (τᾶς . . . εὐαριστίας) 'to the gods' (ποτὶ τοὺς θεοὺς) in relation to Augustus (*l.* 8). In the case of the thanksgiving 'to' (ποτί) in Doric Greek in which this inscription was written, ποτί is the same as πρός with the accusative in Classical Greek and Koine Greek.[33] Hence the phrase should be rendered as 'thanksgiving to the god'.

Why was 'for' (ὑπέρ) not used if the sacrifice being noted was to the gods 'for' Augustus in *l.* 8? The phrase in *l.* 8, 'the sacrifice διά Augustus' (τᾶν διὰ τοῦ Ζεβαστοῦ Φυσιᾶν), cannot refer to Augustus' actual involvement in sacrifices performed in Achaea in his rôle of *pontifex maximus*

29. F. Millar, "Two Augustan Notes," *CR* 18 (1968): 264, and Sherk, *The Roman Empire: Augustus to Hadrian*, p. 33.

30. D. Fishwick, *The Imperial Cult in the Latin West: Studies in the Ruler Cult of the Western Provinces of the Roman Empire* (Leiden: E. J. Brill, 1991), II.1, p. 514.

31. Zetzel, "New Light on Gaius Caesar's Eastern Campaign," p. 260.

32. Price, "Sacrifices," in *Rituals and Power,* ch. 8, and p. 70 for the importance he attaches to the evidence in this inscription under the subheading 'A system of exchange', pp. 65ff.

33. J. Méndez Dosuna, "The Doric Dialects," in *A History of Ancient Greek,* ed. A.-F. Christidis (Cambridge: Cambridge University Press, 2007), p. 450, cf. Polybius, *Historicus* 1.36.1.2-3, διά τε τῆς πρὸς τὸν θεόν εὐχαριστίας, cited by Liddell and Scott.

because he was in Rome. Nor was it 'concerning' him to other gods, for this occurs in the context of thanksgiving to the gods. In an official inscription one would expect the same construction if the reference was to the same activity.

How then are we to understand διά in relation to the phrase concerning Augustus? It is contingent upon a grammatical construction in Doric Koine Greek. Pausanias (c. A.D. 150) noted of the Messenes that 'even to our day they have retained the purest Doric in the Peloponnese', so it does not surprise us that this inscription has Doric Greek characteristics.[34] Buck notes διά tends to be used not only with the concept of time but also of 'the matter or person involved'.[35] When used with verbs of direction, the genitive indicates the object aimed at, and here the verb 'to omit' (ἐνλείπειν) was used to indicate Scipio was sparing neither expense, nor display, nor thanksgiving for the sacrifice 'to' Augustus.

How should we understand the reference in ἅμα καί, 'at the same time' (l. 9)? The usual approach has been to reverse the word order 'and at the same time preparing also the great cities of the province to do the same' (ll. 9-10) as Scipio was recorded doing thus. The translation should not read 'at the same time even causing most of the cities in the province to do the same'. Rather the thanksgiving to the gods and the sacrifice to Augustus are recorded as being done as liturgical acts at the same time.

These combined cultic acts were not without parallels. In the same year, 2 B.C. in Neapolis, the port of Philippi, imperial games were instituted in honour of both *Roma* and Augustus. The official inscription was directed to all its inhabitants, who were commanded 'you must go to the temple of Augustus' (ἀγέτωσαν τὸ Καισαρεῖον). Later there is a reference to 'sacrificing to Augustus Caesar' (θύσαντες Σεβαστῷ Καίσαρι) that was found in the same location.[36]

---

34. Pausanias, *Description of Greece* 4.27.11, cited in S. E. Alcock, "The Peculiar Book IV and the Problem of the Messenian Past," in *Pausanias: Travel and Memory in Roman Greece,* ed. S. E. Alcock, J. F. Cherry and J. Elsner (Oxford: Oxford University Press, 2001), ch. 8, p. 293, n. 29. For most recent discussion of Doric, see Méndez Dosuna, "The Doric Dialects." See also Doric Greek in J. M. Hall, *Ethnic Identity in Greek Antiquity* (Cambridge: Cambridge University Press, 1997), p. 180.

35. C. D. Buck, *Introduction to the Study of the Greek Dialects* (Chicago: Chicago University Press, 1955²), pp. 136-37.

36. Olympia V, *Die Inschriften* (1896, no. 56), *ll.* 48, 52. I. Gradel, *Emperor Worship and Roman Religion,* Oxford Classical Monographs (Oxford: Clarendon Press, 2002), p. 82,

Another example comes from the speech Aelius Aristides delivered to the imperial court in Rome in A.D. 155. He noted a person 'stands up, praises and reverences him [the emperor]' (ἀλλ' ἀναστὰς ὑμνεῖ καὶ σέβει) 'and offers a twofold prayer' (καὶ συνεύχεται διπλῆν εὐχὴν) 'on the one hand to the gods on the emperor's behalf' (τὴν μὲν ὑπὲρ αὐτοῦ τοῖς θεοῖς) 'and on the other concerning his personal affairs to the emperor himself' (τὴν δὲ αὐτῷ ἐκείνῳ περὶ τῶν αὐτοῦ).[37] In such a formal setting as the imperial court he saw no inconsistency in declaring 'twofold' (διπλός) cultic activities of praying to the gods for the emperor and at the same time to the emperor for one's personal needs. It was not just two prayers to one god — otherwise 'two' (δύο) would be the appropriate term — but a prayer to each god.

The activities recorded in the Messene inscription were not unique with thanksgiving to the gods and sacrifices to Augustus. This agrees with the word order 'the thanksgiving for the sacrifice to Augustus to the gods at the same time' (μηδὲ τᾶς ὑπὲρ τᾶν διὰ τοῦ Ζεβαστοῦ Φυσιᾶν ποτί τοὺς θεους ἅμα). The phrase τᾶν διὰ τοῦ Σεβαστοῦ φυσιᾶν εὐαριστίας occurs between the article τᾶς and εὐχαριτίας to the gods. Scipio is undertaking multiple cultic activities in Messene and is using his efforts as a paradigm for other leading cities in Achaea to follow, as the next section of the inscription indicates.

Therefore the references in the Messene inscription in Doric Koine Greek are to the giving of thanks to the other gods and sacrifices being offered to Augustus. Scipio, we are told, did this on 'every occasion', i.e., on the days of Caesar's festival 'performing the Caesareas (τὰ Καισάρεια) without falling short' (*l.* 7), i.e., not failing to perform both of these cultic activities at the same time.

(iii) New Sacrifices for Gaius, an Adopted Son and Heir of Augustus

The reason that Scipio required all in Messene and elsewhere in Achaea to undertake further cultic veneration is spelt out in the inscription —

---

notes that 'the same inscription mentions a sacrifice to Augustus'. *Contra* M. Pucci ben Zeev, *Jewish Rights in the Roman World: The Greek and Roman Documents Quoted by Josephus Flavius,* Texts and Studies in Ancient Judaism 74 (Tübingen: Mohr Siebeck, 1998), p. 475, who cites what she sees as 'only one instance from Cos of a sacrifice to an emperor known to have been performed by an imperial high priest'.

37. Aelius Aristides, *Or.* 26.32.

and when he learned that Gaius, the son of Augustus (υἱὸς τοῦ Σεβαστοῦ), involved in battle against the barbarians on behalf of all men, was in good health, had escaped the dangers, and had taken vengeance on the enemy, with exuberant joy at this best news (ἐπὶ ταῖς ἀρίσταις ἀνγελίαις) he directed all both to wear wreaths and to sacrifice (στεφαναφορεῖν τε πάντοις διέταξε καὶ θύειν) on 'undisturbed' holidays, and he himself both sacrificed an ox for the safety of Gaius (αὐτός τε βουθυτῶν περὶ τᾶς Γαίου σωτηρίας) and was lavish in various spectacles so that what took place rivalled what had come before those given in the past on one hand, but the solemnity remained balanced. (*ll.* 10-17)

Significantly there are two imperial sacrifices described in this one inscription. There were sacrifices to the gods 'for (περί) the safety of Gaius' (*l.* 15) — the sacrifice of an ox was very much a Roman custom — and sacrifices on 'behalf of' (ὑπέρ) Gaius (*l.* 18). (See Section *iv.*)

A similar inscription in Koine Greek from Sardis also makes reference to the imperial cultic practice concerning prayers offered for him — 'sacrifice for Gaius to the gods for his [Gaius'] safety' (ὑπὲρ τῆς σωτηρίας αὐτοῦ) with 'most splendid sacrifices performed to the gods' (θυσίας τοῖς θεοῖς ἐκπρεπεστάτας ἐπιτελέσαι).[38]

The great importance of Gaius and Lucius as successors is reflected in a frieze in the Sabastion leading to the imperial cult temple in Aphrodisias. Gaius is portrayed naked holding an orb of the world in his hand as a symbol of world rule, but Lucius, likewise naked, has a ship's stern in his hand representing a naval victory.[39] When statues of members of the imperial family appear naked, it is an indication that they are gods. (See pp. 189-90.)

Dio Cassius records that

Agrippa again acknowledged the birth of a son who was named Lucius; Augustus immediately adopted him together with his brother Gaius, not waiting for them to become men, but appointing them then and there successors in his office, in order that fewer plots might be formed against him.[40]

---

38. *IGR* 4, 1756, *ll.* 11-12, 15.

39. Reproduced by Mesut Ilgim, *Aphrodisias Sebastion Sevgi Gönul Hall* (Istanbul: Kayis, 2008), p. 59.

40. Dio Cassius, *Roman History* 54.18.1.

A personal letter from Augustus to Gaius, written after he officially reached manhood by Roman reckoning, shows how fond he was of his now adopted son and heir, for he used very affectionate terms.

> [M]y most delightful donkey, whom I always miss, by all that's holy, whenever you are absent . . . I beg the gods that whatever time I have left I might pass with (all of) us in good health and with the State in the happiest condition, and with (the two of) you [Gaius and his brother, Lucius Caesar] behaving like men and succeeding to my post of honour.[41]

For good reasons Scipio well understood the aspirations of Augustus for Gaius. It explains one of his three cultic acts being rigorously promoted in this decree. It was the sacrifice 'for the safety of Gaius' against enemies of the empire and at the same time reflected his endorsement of Gaius as a successor of Augustus. The nexus between political loyalty to Augustus and his household and imperial cultic activities aiming to preserve their safety was there for all to see. The concept of 'the safety' (σωτηρία) of the emperor and his family would develop further in the Julio-Claudian era with cultic actions to the gods for 'the safety of the emperor' *(pro salute imperatoris)*.[42]

The citizens of Rome had already shown their support for Augustus by choosing Gaius as consul when he was only fourteen years old and had just assumed the *toga virilis*. Augustus being an astute politician showed his formal 'displeasure' with this election, but it is doubtful that his protestation was genuine as the election would have been arranged with his knowledge. Southern has suggested that 'it may have been an elaborate way of testing the reactions of the people or it may have been a spontaneous gesture in response to the fact that Gaius was not legally a man'. In the meantime he was given a priesthood and permitted to attend meetings of the Senate in Rome.[43]

Coins of Augustus were struck depicting his adopted sons Gaius and Lucius Caesar, with honorific shields and a spear. The inscription on the coins identifies them as 'sons of Augustus, consuls designate, and leaders of youth *(principes iuventutis)*'. Augustus himself, not the Senate of Rome,

---

41. Aulus Gellius, *Attic Nights* 15.7.3.

42. D. Fishwick, *The Imperial Cult in the Latin West: Provincial Cult* (Leiden: E. J. Brill, 2004), III.3, pp. 359-69.

43. P. Southern, *Augustus* (London: Routledge, 1998), pp. 170-77, 180.

struck the gold and silver coins affirming who his successors were. Triumphal arches, public buildings, altars and even temples were erected in their honour.[44] However, Augustus deferred Gaius taking up the consulship until A.D. 1, when he would have reached the age of twenty-one.

This information helps in the dating of the inscription to between 6 B.C., when Gaius was 'designated consul', and A.D. 1, when he assumed the office as consul because of the use of the term 'designated'. It is possible then to date the inscription from details concerning Gaius to A.D. 1 or 2.

Who was expected to participate in these celebrations in the province of Achaea? This is a question that would be important for the first Christians half a century later. Scipio clearly 'directed all inhabitants both to wear wreaths and to sacrifice' (στεφαναφορεῖν τε πάντοις διέταξε καὶ θύειν) to celebrate Gaius' escape from danger (*ll.* 13-14). He specifies 'all' were to wear crowns and offer sacrifices and, in the future, to keep themselves 'free from work', i.e., 'undisturbed' (ἀπράφμονος) (*l.* 14) for the anniversary of Gaius' entry to the consulship. The celebrations were not just for the ruling élite, but it was intended that every citizen in the provincial cities should participate on these imperial high days.

(iv) Alteration to the Calendar Celebrating Imperial Days

[A]nd he made a great effort, in leaving two days from the days of Augustus' festival and made the beginning of the sacrifices on behalf Gaius (τὰν ἀρχὰν τᾶν ὑπὲρ Γαίου θυσιᾶν ποιήσασθαι) from the day on which for the first time he was designated consul and he also instructed us to annually celebrate this on each day with sacrifices and the wearing of wreaths as graciously and [———] as we can; and therefore the council-members decreed on the fifteenth day before the Calendars of [———]. (*ll.* 17-21)

Scipio not only commanded annual sacrifices but also actually adjusted the imperial calendar in the province, omitting 'two days from the days of Augustus'. These were to make the beginning 'of the sacrifices for Gaius from the day on which for the first time he [Gaius] was designated

44. See P. Zanker, *The Power of Images in the Age of Augustus* (Ann Arbor: University of Michigan Press, 1987), plate 173, and pp. 217-26 for discussion of Augustus' promotion and honours for them and also plate 201 of the temple in Nimes built for Gaius and Lucius.

consul' (*ll.* 16-17). He 'instructed us' (διετάξατο ἁμῖν) (*l.* 19), i.e., 'set in place' — a verb also used of setting an army in battle formation (διάγειν ὅσοις δυνάμεθα) 'to annually celebrate this day on each day' (διετάξατο δὲ ἁμῖν καὶ καθ' ἕκαστον ἐνιαυτὸν τὰν ἁμέραν ταύταν διάγειν) (*l.* 20).[45] Zetzel's translation of the final extant sentence in the inscription is 'he instructed us to observe this day annually'. This does not bring out the point clearly that it was to be observed over the two days set aside in the calendar.

Elsewhere Gaius was fêted with 'the Games of the Imperial Family and established for Gaius Caesar (victor) in the Isthmian boys stadion-race[46] and pentathlon on the same day' around the same period on the island of Cos.[47] Corinth had minted a coin showing Gaius and Lucius facing each other and on the obverse side an image of Augustus inscribed 'Caesar, Corinth' dated around this period, i.e., 2-1 B.C.[48]

We also learn that Apollonodotus, a magistrate in Eresus on the island of Lesbos, 'dedicated to the sons of Augustus a sanctuary and temple from his own money in the most prominent part of the square' as well as 'a temple to Augustus at the harbour of the market . . . so that no notable place should lack his goodwill and piety to the god [Augustus]'.[49]

Scipio's promotion of the cause of Gaius should not be seen as in any way detracting from the veneration of Augustus but rather clearly affirming his total loyalty to the emperor and commending his decision on his succession. Gaius had successfully taken vengeance on Rome's enemy somewhere beyond the eastern frontiers of the empire, and the sacrifices for the preservation of his future rôle in the empire is explicable.

Scipio used his office in Achaea to see that divine honours to the Caesars were firmly implemented and established province-wide, for we are told he was 'also causing most of the cities of the province (τὰς πλείστας

45. A comparable phrase καθ ἑκάστην τὴν ἡμέραν is in Classical Greek from Isocrates, *Panathenaicus* 211, referring to 'every single day'.

46. For a discussion of the stadion-race of 600 feet see E. N. Gardiner, "The Stadium and the Foot-Race," in *Athletics in the Ancient World* (Newton Abbot: Dover, 2002), ch. 9, and plate 91 for an illustration of a boys' race.

47. *SIG*³ 1065 (Cos).

48. A. Burnett, M. Amandry and P. P. Ripollès, *Roman Provincial Coinage: From the Death of Caesar to the Death of Vitellius (44 B.C.-A.D. 69)* (London and Paris: British Museum Press and Bibliothèque nationale de France, 1998), cited in *RPC* no. 1136. For a list of cities in the empire where coins were struck bearing Gaius and Lucius, the joint heirs, see *RPC* nos. 1, 2, p. 733.

49. *IG* 12, 124, cited in Price, *Rituals and Power,* pp. 3, 249.

τῶν κατὰ τὰν ἐπαρχείαν πόλεων) to do the same thing with him' (*ll.* 10-11). The inscription gives an indication of what occurred in some of the celebrations — 'sacrifices and crown-wearing' (θυσια καὶ στεφάαφορια) 'as graciously and . . . as we can' (*ll.* 19-20). It was not to be done 'theatrically' so that the balance between spectacles and solemnity was disturbed, but with appropriate decorum as had been the case on Scipio's celebration of the victory of Gaius (*l.* 17).

Here is a reference in the imperial calendar, literally 'the days of Caesar's festival' (τὰν Καίσαρος ἁμερᾶν), where a holiday was 'taken off' Caesar's calendar and replaced with one devoted to the celebration of his son's consularship in the Principate of Augustus which spoke of 19 August 'on this day', the birthday of Augustus being 23 September.[50]

Subsequent to this inscription being decreed, Gaius was fatally wounded in battle in A.D. 4 in Lycia. His brother, Lucius, suffered a similar fate. A decree from Pisae in Etruria marked the deep sense of mourning empire-wide. The anniversary of this catastrophe was to be observed as 'a day of grief and so it was marked down [in the calendar]' that 'all should change into mourning clothes, that the temples of the immortal gods and public baths and taverns should all be closed'.[51] This was in stark contrast to the joyful celebrations wearing wreaths and offering sacrifices that Scipio had decreed for Achaea. This tragic setback for Augustus' succession plans for the empire would have been commemorated in Corinth.

This Messene inscription also testifies to the fact that cities were already celebrating the imperial holy days before Scipio's innovations. As we shall see, there is earlier evidence in Corinth of the veneration of Julius Caesar and Augustus. This reveals that it was an official from Rome who greatly enhanced the existing celebration of imperial cultic activities. It shows that, in spite of any formal imperial 'declining of temples' that occurred on accessions (see pp. 77-80), the veneration of the emperor on designated holidays was not only a city initiative in the Roman East, but it also set the scene for continuing provincial imperial celebrations.

This official civic inscription encapsulates a wealth of information about the trilogy of imperial cultic activities and resonates with what is known elsewhere. Sacrifices to the emperor, thanksgiving to the gods for him, annual sacrifices for one of the emperor's adopted sons and a named

---

50. *CIL* 10, 8375, cited in Fishwick, *Imperial Cult in the Latin West,* II.1, 490.
51. *ILS* 140.

successor were to take place in all the major cities in the province. In addition, all inhabitants of Achaea were required to participate in the celebratory activities of the games and imperial cultic venerations and, not least of all, those in its capital, Corinth.

II. Accession Celebrations for Tiberius and Gaius

Not only had Scipio so assiduously promoted imperial cultic activities (*c.* A.D. 1-2), but on the actual accession of Tiberius in A.D. 14 another decree records the celebration of 'all those who live in the city', i.e., Messene.

> For divine Caesar Augustus and Tiberius Caesar Augustus . . . [lead] . . . all those who live in the city . . . leisure for three consecutive days, to celebrate contests — a gymnastic one for the children and the *ephebes,* and an equestrian one for the *neoi* — on the anniversary, and the victors' weapons to be dedicated by the priest of that year, and to send an embassy to Rome to the emperor Tiberius Caesar. This (embassy) is to deplore that the god is no longer manifest among us, to greet the emperor Tiberius and to rejoice together that he who is worthy and who, according to our wish, has become the ruler of the entire world and also to lament bitterly the adversities that have overcome the city, and to supplicate so that we may obtain some mercy.[52]

This inscription makes it clear that there were to be three days of imperial celebrations, the equivalent to 'on undisturbed days' as in the Scipio inscription and involving 'all who live in the city'.

It records the local celebrations relating to the apotheosis of 'the divine Caesar Augustus', i.e., this god's ascension to heaven and Tiberius' accession. In addition, the embassy to Rome mourned 'the god no longer manifest among us', while formally recognizing Tiberius' rule over 'the entire world' and the appropriate honours brought to him by an embassy from Messene.

At the same time they would seek to redress an unknown incident related to the city's enemies. This was an acceptable convention of official embassies bringing greetings on the accession and seeking something by way of imperial favour or redress for a felt injustice inflicted on their city

---

52. *SEG* 39, 378.

as was the case here. What it was is uncertain. If this were a dispute with Sparta over the control of a temple, Messene would later win.[53]

That such an embassy should also make reference to 'the adversaries that have overcome the city' may seem entirely inappropriate at a time of celebrating the accession of a new emperor. But conventionally delegations regularly could come to Rome to seek concessions and privileges. In *Empire of Honour*, Lendon discusses at length this concept of 'reciprocity'. The fact that embassies also came with requests was no breach of protocol.[54] Prior to A.D. 15 Achaea had been administered as a province by the Senate, but because of the revolt at the end of the Principate of Augustus to which this inscription alludes, Tiberius took over its administration.[55] They celebrated his successor's ascension.

Caligula, known as Gaius Julius Caesar Augustus Germanicus, authorized all the ancient Greek Leagues to meet for the celebrations of his accession on A.D. 37.

> The rescript of Gaius to the Pan-Hellenic League of the Achaeans, Boeotians, Locrians, Phocians and Euboeans. I have read the decree given to me by your ambassadors and have recognized that you have spared no extravagance in your zeal and devotion to me, in that you have both each personally offered a sacrifice for my security and have joined in a common festival and decreed the greatest honours you could; for all this I both praise you all (ἐφ' οἷς ἅπασι ἐπαινῶ ὑμᾶς) and give my approval. And remembering the distinction from ancient times of each of the Greek republics, I permit you to meet as a League. But as for the statues you voted me, if you please, reduce the great number and be content with those that will be placed at Olympus and Nemea and at the Pythian sanctuary and at the Isthmus. By doing this you will [venerate me] and burden yourself less with expense.[56]

Two important facts emerge from this inscription. Each person in the province sacrificed personally for the new emperor, i.e., Gaius'

---

53. B. Levick, *Tiberius the Politician* (London: Thames & Hudson, 1976), p. 126.

54. J. E. Lendon, *Empire of Honour: The Art of Government in the Roman World* (Oxford: Clarendon Press, 1997), p. 168.

55. Tacitus, *Annals* 1.76.2. It was restored to the Senate in A.D. 44, Dio Cassius, *Roman History* 40.24.1.

56. *IG* 7, 2711.

safety — 'in that each one of you have both personally (ἰδίᾳ τε ἕκαστος) offered a sacrifice for my safety' (θυσάμενοι ὑπὲρ τῆς ἐμῆς σωτηρίας) and 'joined in the common festival' (καὶ κοινῇ ἑορτάσαντες) — hence his praise for all.[57]

This important imperial rescript records that this ancient League was now permitted to meet officially 177 years after its rebellion against, and its defeat by, the Roman Army in 146 B.C.[58] This restoration was their reward for organizing such an outpouring of loyalty by the citizens of the province of Achaea to the emperor, Gaius.

Philo of Alexandria (*c.* 20 B.C.-A.D. 50) provides further information on how the accession of Gaius was lavishly celebrated.

> There was nothing to be seen throughout the cities but altars, victims, sacrifices, people in white clothes, garlanded and cheerful, showing their goodwill by their joyous faces, banquets, festivals, musical competitions, horse-races, revelling, night-celebrations to the music of flutes and the lyre, enjoyment, recreation, holidays, and every kind of pleasure appealing to every sense.[59]

We can assume that this also applied to the individual and corporate activities that occurred on the occasion of the accession of Claudius in A.D. 42 because Scipio had laid down for Achaea that 'all to both wear wreaths and to sacrifice' (στεφαναφορεῖν τε πάντοις διέταξε καὶ θύειν). (See p. 195.)

As Scheid argued in "Epigraphy and Roman Religion," inscriptions are invaluable because of the great deal of information encoded in them. They were also displayed publicly for the purpose of shaping the citizens' understanding of, and the requirement to give, divine honours for emperors.[60] The Scipio inscription certainly constructs a helpful profile of the nature of the imperial cultic activities that were promoted in leading cities in the province of Achaea.

---

57. *IG* 7, 2711, *ll.* 26-27.

58. A. Lintott, *Imperium Romanum: Politics and Administration* (London and New York: Routledge, 1993), pp. 9-10.

59. Philo, *The Embassy to Gaius* 11-12.

60. J. Scheid, "Epigraphy and Roman Religion," in *Epigraphy and the Historical Sciences*, ed. J. Davies and J. Wilkers, Proceedings of the British Academy no. 177 (Oxford and New York: Oxford University Press, 2012), p. 31.

III. Imperial Cultic Veneration in Roman Corinth[61]

Aulus Gellius later observed that colonies were 'offshoots of Rome, with their laws and customs dependent on the Roman people'.[62] Corinth was the centre for the promotion of Romanization in Achaea. Spawforth notes, 'the colony's assertive *Romanitas* in the early Principate is one of its most striking features'.[63]

Julius Caesar authorized Corinth's foundation as a Roman colony in 44 B.C. just prior to his assassination. Two years later the Roman Senate deified him. An early record of the veneration of Julius Caesar was inscribed on a grey marble block in the theatre in Corinth affirming his perpetual divinity — 'sacred to the deified Julius Caesar' (*divo Iul[io] Caesari [sacrum]*).[64] Walbank has argued that this indicates a date prior to the Senate's formal deification because

---

61. R. DeMaris, "Cults and the Imperial Cult in Early Roman Corinth: Literary *Versus* Material Record," in *Zwischen den Reichen: Neues Testament und römische Herrschaft: Vorträge auf der ersten Konferenz der European Association for Biblical Studies*, ed. M. Labahn and J. Zangenberg, Texte und Arbeiten zum neutestamentlichen Zeitalter 36 (Basel: A. Francke Verlag, 2002), pp. 73-91. In spite of the title of the essay and his justified criticisms of a catalogue of inappropriate attempts to tie archaeological evidence to 1 Corinthians, he devotes only two paragraphs to the imperial cult and then only to the identifying of Temple E with the cult. More recently C. Miller, "The Imperial Cult in the Pauline Cities of Asia Minor and Greece," *CBQ* 72 (2010): 314-22, likewise discusses Corinth and cites epigraphic evidence but without exploring its important implications, and then surprisingly concludes, 'The evidence for the cult in Corinth is a bit dicey and fragmentary' and 'the lack of evidence in Corinth for the imperial-cult-saturated environment is perhaps more striking as well as more historically telling than for any other Pauline city' (pp. 329-31). *Contra* Spawforth, who concluded that the best evidence, i.e., archaeological and epigraphic, for imperial cultic activities in Greece is in Corinth followed by Athens. "The Early Reception of the Imperial Cult in Athens: Problems and Ambiguities," in *The Romanization of Athens: Proceedings of an International Conference*, ed. M. C. Hoff and S. I. Rotroff, Oxbow Monograph 94 (Oxford: Oxbow Books, 1997), p. 183.

62. Gellius, *Attic Nights* 16.13.

63. A. J. S. Spawforth, "Roman Corinth: The Formation of a Colonial Élite," in *Roman Onomastics in the Greek East: Social and Political Aspects*, ed. A. D. Rizakis, Meletemata 21 (Athens, 1996), p. 175. The term *Romanitas* is to be avoided, even though it has recently gained currency among ancient historians. The term is not found in the *Oxford Latin Dictionary*, which cites works occurring in sources up to A.D. 200. I owe this observation to Emeritus Professor E. A. Judge. The first occurrence of this term I could locate is in Tertullian (*c.* A.D. 155-230), "On the Pallium" 4, where he used it pejoratively to describe those in Carthage who 'aped' Roman culture.

64. J. H. Kent, *Corinth: Inscriptions 1926-1950* (Princeton: American School of Classical Studies at Athens, 1966), VIII.3, no. 50.

the inclusion of Caesar in the dedication is unusual and suggests a date early in the life of the colony, before the new title, *Divus Iulius*. . . . It is also possible that the Corinthians pre-empted this official ceremony [in Rome] in giving Julius Caesar divine honours after his death but before his apotheosis at Rome.[65]

Corinth's use of *divus* dates it after the Roman Senate's decision in 42 B.C. to award perpetual divinity. The term was also correctly used in other Corinthian inscriptions, i.e., 'to the deified Augustus' *(divo augusto),*[66] and 'to the deified Augusta, the grandmother of [Tiberius] Claudius Caesar Augustus Germanicus' *(divae Augustae avae Ti Claudi Caesaris Augusti Germanici).*[67] On the significance of the term *divus* and its selected use for emperors, see pp. 62-66.

(i) Corinthian Imperial Cultic Sites

The mid-second-century A.D. traveller to Corinth, Pausanias, recorded that 'above the market place is a temple of Octavia, the sister of Augustus who was emperor of the Romans after Caesar, the founder of present Corinth'.[68] She had also been deified in Athens.[69] He later details aspects of the layout of the forum after relating something of the history of the Greek period.

Now the sanctuary of Athena Chalinitis is by their theatre, and near is a naked wooden image of Heracles, said to be the work of Daedalus. . . . Above the theatre is a sanctuary of Zeus Capitolinus (Διὸς Καπετωλίου) named in the Latin tongue, which might be rendered into Greek Coryphaeos (Κορυφαῖος).[70]

---

65. M. E. H. Walbank, "Evidence for the Imperial Cult in Julio-Claudian Corinth," in *Subject and Ruler: The Cult of the Ruling Power in Classical Antiquity, Papers Honouring D. Fishwick*, ed. A. Small, JRA Supplement 17 (Ann Arbor: Journal of Roman Archaeology, 1996), p. 201.

66. Kent, *Corinth*, VIII.3, nos. 51-53.

67. Kent, *Corinth*, VIII.3, no. 56.

68. Pausanias, *Description of Greece* 2.3.1.

69. For Octavia's deification in Athens, see A. E. Raubitschek, "Octavia's Deification at Athens," *TAPA* 77 (1946): 146-50, and K. W. Arafat, *Pausanias' Greece: Ancient Artists and Roman Rulers* (Cambridge: Cambridge University Press, 1997), p. 108.

70. Pausanias, *Description of Greece* 2.4.5.

The term κορυφαῖος would be an obvious choice, given that it refers to a 'head man, chief, or leader and the apex of the Roman priesthood, a high priest'. Liddell and Scott also note it was an epithet for the Roman Jupiter Capitolinus, citing this reference in Pausanias. At that time there was uncertainty about another temple outside of Corinth on the road to Sicyon that had been destroyed by fire. Some attributed it to Apollo, according to Pausanias, who went on to say, 'Subsequently I heard another account, that the Corinthians built the temple for Olympian Zeus, and that suddenly fire from some quarter fell on it and destroyed it.'[71] While there may have been uncertainty concerning this one, there is no doubt concerning what is known in archaeological circles as Temple E.

A feature of this temple is that its foundations were substantially raised above ground level.[72] As a result, it stood higher than the ancient Greek temple of Apollo, which was the only structure the Roman colonists had preserved from Greek Corinth. The latter was changed internally to conform with Roman interior temple design. Augustus had attributed a major victory to Apollo.[73]

It is suggested that this temple dedicated to Octavia, the sister of Augustus who had also been deified in Athens, was the focus of Corinth's imperial cultic activity. Walbank has argued against this as being either 'a' or 'the' major imperial cult site, and relegates imperial cultic activities to a minor temple that stood alongside other small temples at the south end of the Roman forum.[74] However, Williams did not endorse this as the location of the imperial cult celebrations but rather in the Octavian temple.[75]

In the East imperial temples traditionally dominated the civic and

71. Pausanias, *Description of Greece* 2.5.5.

72. Having stood on the raised section of Temple E, it is clear that it was intended to be higher than that of Apollo and to tower over the official Roman forum as in other cities. See pp. 130-31.

73. Suetonius, *Augustus* 70; D. Fishwick, *The Imperial Cult in the Latin West* (Leiden: E. J. Brill, 1993²), I.1, p. 81.

74. E. Mary Walbank, "Pausanias, Octavia, Temple E," *Annual of the British School at Athens* 84 (1989): 361-94. She says it was the Capitoline, but Pausanias, *Description of Greece* 2.4.5, records in Corinth that 'above the theatre is a sanctuary to Zeus surnamed in the Latin tongue *Capitolinus*'; and later "Evidence for the Imperial Cult in Julio-Claudian Corinth," in *Subject and Ruler*, ed. A. Small, pp. 201-13.

75. C. K. Williams II, the former head of the American excavations in Corinth, "A Re-evaluation of Temple E and the West End of the Forum," in *The Greek Renaissance in the Roman Empire*, ed. S. Walker and A. Cameron, BICS Supplement 55 (London: 1989), pp. 156-62.

commercial centres of cities. This was the case in the Roman forum in Athens in relation to its famous ancient Greek agora. As we have seen, it was higher than the latter and the imperial cult temple was its highest point.[76] Mitchell has noted that in Anatolia imperial temples were also built in the most central and conspicuous location in the civic space.[77] This is certainly true in Ephesus, where Domitian's temple and its important imperial predecessors occupied the highest vantage point overlooking the official northern agora, or what is called 'the administrative district'[78] that towered over the rest of the city.[79]

The Roman colony of Pompeii in Italy provides an example of more than one imperial cult temple in the forum and its surrounds. Next to it stood a temple to the *genius* of Augustus and at the far end of an adjoining food market *(marcellum)* a sanctuary to the imperial family. The remains of a temple to the *Fortuna* of Augustus are just blocks away on the same road. 'The inhabitants of Pompeii viewed with awe the shrines associated with the imperial cult, but they could also see the proximity and relevance to their own lives of the imperial family.'[80] Given the extent of imperial cultic sites in Pompeii, it is unnecessary to postulate that there was only one such temple in the forum in Corinth.

Williams noted that 'the escalation of the Imperial Cult in Corinth from the time of Tiberius onwards' resulted in the reconstruction of the Temple E and its considerable enhancement.[81] Alcock in her work on the landscapes of Greece observes that '[i]mperial sanctuaries became major landmarks within a city'.[82] The identity of small temples or shrines in front of Temple E and lower in the forum cannot be definitely established. Just

76. In the case of Athens the Roman forum was built separately and higher than the Greek agora so that it was dominated. See pp. 132-33.

77. S. Mitchell, *Anatolia: Land, Men, and Gods in Asia Minor* (Oxford: Clarendon Press, 1993), I, p. 100.

78. For a photograph of the model of the temple in Ephesus Museum in Vienna, see P. Scherrer, ed., *Ephesus: The New Guide* (Turkey: Graphics Ltd, 2000), p. 85.

79. P. Trebilco, *The Early Christians in Ephesus from Paul to Ignatius* (Grand Rapids and Cambridge: Eerdmans, 2004), pp. 35-37.

80. R. Laurence, *Roman Pompeii: Space and Society* (London and New York: Routledge, 1994), p. 137.

81. C. K. Williams II, "The Refounding of Corinth: Some Roman Religious Attitudes," in *Roman Architecture in the Greek World*, ed. S. Macready and F. S. Thompson, Occasional Papers 10 (London: Society of Antiquities, 1987), p. 30.

82. S. E. Alcock, *Graecia Capta: The Landscapes of Roman Greece* (Cambridge: Cambridge University Press, 1993), p. 198.

because one or more may have been an imperial cult shrine, it in no way rules out that the large, raised temple at the end of the forum was used for major imperial cult activities.

It is inconceivable that the dominant temple in Roman Corinth was bypassed on high and holy imperial cult days for celebrations to be held only in front of small temples like shrines in the forum thought to be dedicated to imperial veneration. Certainly the Octavian temple would have enabled imperial cult feasts days to be celebrated there, as it was the only one in the forum of any significant size with a substantial precinct for dining surrounding it.[83] A provincial cult required a major temple to be the focus of the important celebrations. Chapter 8 will show that the Roman Senate in late A.D. 54 authorized provincial imperial cultic celebrations to be located in Corinth.

In addition, official coins minted in Corinth feature two types of temples. One has a hexastyle temple on a mountain, i.e., the Acrocorinth;[84] the other also has six columns, representing the temple of Apollo.[85] The laureate head of Nero is portrayed on another coin with the obverse 'the Genius of the Colony', who is Venus, the Greek equivalent being Aphrodite.[86]

Another Corinthian coin portrays a temple viewed from the corner with four columns and steps leading up to it. It is identical to the raised Temple E located at the end of the forum.[87] A coin from Nero's Principate shows Tyche crowning him, presumably in the small temple located at the west end of the forum.[88] Another, the Octavian temple, has him standing

---

83. Walbank has yet to address this major innovation. She has continued to argue her case, "Evidence for the Imperial Cult in Julio-Claudian Corinth," pp. 201-13. The numismatic evidence from the Julio-Claudian period is not addressed, although for her ongoing interest in numismatics in a later period see more recently M. E. H. Walbank, "Aspects of Corinthian Coinage in the Late 1st and Early 2nd Centuries A.C.," in *Corinth the Centenary 1896-1996*, ed. C. K. Williams and N. Bookidis, Corinth Volume 20 (Athens: The American School of Classical Studies at Athens, 2003), ch. 20, p. 337. In this latter chapter she cites a coin that has a temple as 'Capitoline (?)', Figures 20.1, 11; another has four columns, 20.4, 1; and 20.4, 1 and 20.14, 1 are cited simply as a 'temple façade'.

84. *RPC* no. 1180 (Claudius, A.D. 41-54) Amandry, pp. 193-94.

85. *RPC* no. 1151 Amandry, pp. 169-73 and 1157 (Tiberius, A.D. 14-37); Amandry, pp. 174-75. For a discussion of the temple of Apollo, see N. Bookidis and R. S. Stroud, "Apollo and the Archaic Temple," *Hesperia* 73 (2004), n. 42, of the six columns.

86. *RPC* no. 1189 Amandry, pp. 203-4 (Nero A.D. 54-68).

87. *RPC* nos. 1218-21 Amandry, pp. 234-35 (Galba, A.D. 68-69).

88. *RPC* no. 1207 (Nero, A.D. 54-68) Amandry, pp. 224-25. For a discussion of this

in the middle of four columns. It was struck by the same magistrates and celebrates Nero's famous visit to Corinth when he granted the abolition of taxes for Greece.[89] This was a much-celebrated event with 'honours' bestowed on him for 'winning' all the competitions he entered in the Isthmian Games — as he did in all other important games in Greece. (See pp. 136, 298-300.)

The numismatic evidence further supports Williams' identification of Temple E as the one used for imperial cultic activities. In addition, its precinct would enable a person to observe another Christian 'reclining in the idol temple' (ἐν εἰδωλείῳ κατακείμενον) in a feast day of the 'so-called gods in the heavens and on earth' (1 Cor. 8:5, 10).[90]

(ii) Corinthian Inscriptions and Statues of the Divine Family

Apart from the theatre, the greatest concentration of extant imperial statues has been found in the Julian Basilica in Corinth, where court cases were heard. Those of the deceased heirs of Augustus, Gaius and Lucius, were located together and portrayed as gods with a dedication to the imperial family both living and deceased.[91] It is not unexpected that after their deaths statues of them both were erected in Corinth.

They are portrayed naked, indicating that they are to be seen as gods in the guise and posture conventionally assigned to Hermes.[92] Hallett in his discussion of "The Nudity of the Gods" concluded, 'The emperors never appear nude. . . . When nude or partly nude figures do occur in the *genre,* they are immediately identified as gods.'[93] This was no less true of the

---

temple, see C. M. Edwards, "Tyche at Corinth," *Hesperia* 59, no. 3 (1990): 529-42. See *RPC* no. 1207-9 for coins issued by the magistrates T. Claudius Anaxilaus and P. Ventidius (A.D. 67-68).

89. *RPC* no. 1208 (Nero, A.D. 54-68) Amandry, pp. 224-25.

90. κατάκειμαι 'recline at a meal'.

91. Paul D. Scotton, "A New Fragment of an Inscription from the Julian Basilica at Roman Corinth," *Hesperia* 74, no. 1 (2005): 99-100.

92. E. H. Swift, "Imperial Portraits at Corinth," *AJA* 25, no. 4 (1921): 336. They are preserved in the Corinthian museum.

93. For the official outpouring of grief in Roman Pisae in Etruria at his death, see the lengthy inscription where it was resolved that there would be an annual festival of the Family Dead 'to his departed spirit', cited in C. H. Hallett, "The Nudity of the Gods," in *Roman Nudity: Heroic Portrait Statuary 200 BC-AD 300* (Oxford: Oxford University Press, 2005), pp. 223-24.

adopted sons of Augustus, given what is known of the honouring of Gaius from the Messene inscription discussed earlier.[94]

Scotton concluded that in the light of the imperial statues and an inscription to the *Caesares Augusti* located in the Julian Basilica — a clear reference to the living and deceased emperors in Corinth — that there was 'the presence of some manifestation of the imperial cult' not only in the imperial cult temple but also in this court of justice.[95]

(iii) Corinthian Imperial Cult Priests and Monuments

Because it was a Roman colony, aspects of the cult in Corinth differed from those in Greek cities of the province. For example, only in a Roman colony could freedmen be eligible to be appointed a priest of Augustus *(augustales)* and also designated *flamen.*[96]

There were in Corinth priests of the local imperial cult. 'To [———], priest of [———] and priest of the Tutela Augusta. The colony awarded a golden crown [———]'.[97]

An inscription dedicated to a priestess in the Principate of Tiberius has also been located in Corinth. Callicratea, daughter of Philesus, was a 'priestess in perpetuity of Augustan Providence and Public Safety' *(Providentiae Aug. et Salitus publicae).* The Corinthian tribe of Agrippia erected another 'to one who well deserves this' *(bene meritae),* Callicratea. '[Diana] Bringer of the Light of Peace, Augusta, a dedication, for the safety of Tiberius Caesar Augustus, Licinius . . . freedman of Publius . . . Philosebastus, had this made at his own expense'.[98] Both are thought to celebrate the unmasking of the plot by Lucius Aelius Sejanus against the emperor Tiberius in A.D. 31.[99]

---

94. In Aphrodisias in the Sebastion leading to the Imperial Cult temple there is a frieze with a naked Claudius as emperor holding the hand of Agrippina. An Ephesian coin was struck with the heads of Claudius and Agrippina the Younger facing each other with the inscription 'marriage of gods' (θεογαμία) on the obverse side, and on the reverse side there was a statue of Artemis with the word 'Ephesian' ('Εφεσια) indicating its provenance, *RPC* no. 2620.

95. Scotton, "A New Fragment of an Inscription from the Julian Basilica at Roman Corinth," pp. 99-100.

96. Price, *Rituals and Power,* p. 88.

97. Kent, *Corinth,* VIII.3, nos. 193, 198.

98. A. B. West, *Corinth: Results of Excavations conducted by the American School of Classical Studies at Athens 1896-1926* (Cambridge, MA: Harvard University Press, 1931), VIII.2, nos. 110 and 15.

99. West, *Corinth,* VIII.2, pp. 14, 90-91, where he refers to the treason of Sejanus.

Gaius Julius Spartiaticus was '*flamen* of the Deified Julius' in the time of Claudius, indicating that priesthoods were not only undertaken by Roman freedmen and women but also by Roman citizens.[100] Tiberius Claudius Dinippus was priest of the Britannic Victory in Corinth following the Roman conquest of Britain in A.D. 44.[101]

'Epigraphic evidence likewise exhibits the Corinthian aristocracy's devotion to — even its obsession with — the imperial cult: for the first century or so of the colony's existence "the majority of extant dedicatory inscriptions or records of priesthoods are aimed at Roman gods and to imperial cult"'.[102] This primary evidence endorses Alcock's observation.

There were numerous monuments erected to emperors as gods reading '[sacred] to the deified Julius Caesar', '[sacred] to the deified Augustus', 'sacred to [the deified] Augustus. Gnaeus [Corneliu]s Speratus, Augustalis [dedicated this monument]', and '[Sacred to the deified] Augustus'. This building was dedicated 'to the deified Augusta, the grandmother of [Tiberius] Claudius Caesar Augustus Germanicus'.[103] This refers to the official deification of Livia by her grandson, the emperor Claudius, in A.D. 42.[104]

Now located in the Museum in Ancient Corinth is a slightly larger-than-life statue of Augustus with the *toga* drawn over his head called *capite velato*. He is portrayed offering up a sacrifice and is one of twenty such statues that have survived in different cities in the Roman Empire. Augustus is sculptured in 'the manner of a Roman magistrate' making a sacrifice. It incorporated in his person headship of the civil and cultic activities as the *pontifex maximus* of the empire.[105] The sacrifice would have been to the gods on behalf of the empire.

The inscriptions recording priestly imperial cultic activity 'directed everyone to wear crowns and to sacrifice', and they were to 'observe this day annually with sacrifices and wearing of crowns'. On the accession of the emperor Gaius 'each one of you personally offered up a sacrifice'. It is also clear from the inscription to Scipio that there were other days

---

100. West, *Corinth*, VIII.2, nos. 68 and 100.

101. Kent, *Corinth*, VIII.3, nos. 158-63.

102. Alcock, *Graecia Capta: The Landscapes of Roman Greece*, p. 169, citing D. Engles, *Roman Corinth: An Alternative Model for the Classical City* (Chicago: University of Chicago Press, 1990), pp. 72, 101-2, 106.

103. Kent, *Corinth*, VIII.3, nos. 86, 50-55.

104. Suetonius, *The Deified Claudius* 11.2.

105. For a discussion of this evidence see D. Gill, "The Importance of Roman Portraiture for Head-coverings in 1 Corinthians 11:2-16," *TynB* 41, no. 2 (1990): 246-48.

throughout the year when there were cultic celebrations. This would have been true for Claudius when he became emperor in A.D. 41.

All the extant evidence assembled here indicates that the Corinthians were deeply involved with imperial cultic activities long before Paul evangelized there, and not long after the foundation of the colony in 44 B.C.

IV. Christians Given *De Facto* Cultic Exemption

The Christian community began in *c.* A.D. 51 in Claudius' reign. Individual Jews in the Diaspora were excused from local imperial cultic participation in pagan temples.[106] Could this in any way pose problems for Jews in Corinth who acknowledged that Jesus was the Messiah?

Those who believed Paul's gospel message did not have to renounce their ethnic identity, and Christian Jews were not required to participate in comparable imperial activities. We have noted that the reason for Jewish non-participation was the daily offering up of a sacrifice in the temple in Jerusalem on behalf of the reigning emperor. It was an extremely important adaptation that was acceptable to the authorities in Rome.

When Paul began his mission in Corinth, he initially devoted himself to evangelizing in the synagogue, reasoning every Sabbath, seeking to persuade both Jews and Greeks who were present (Acts 18:4-5).[107] The second phase of his ministry was undertaken after he had abandoned his evangelism in the synagogue when they openly rejected his message. Much to the great ire of the Jewish community, he gathered the converts and met next door to their synagogue in the house of Titus Justus, whose name implies Roman citizenship, as does that of Crispus, the ruler of the synagogue who 'believed in the Lord with all his household' (Acts 18:8).[108]

It is understandable that the Corinthian Jews attempted to initiate a criminal action against Paul but failed before Junius Annaeus Gallio, a

---

106. Josephus, *Jewish Antiquities* 19.287-91.

107. Kent, *Corinth*, VIII.3, p. 20, n. 9, makes the important observation that '[t]he only episode in the colony's history known in some detail from the literary sources is the visit of St. Paul in A.D. 51 (Acts 18:1-18)'.

108. E. A. Judge, "The Roman Base of Paul's Mission," in *The First Christians in the Roman World,* WUNT 229, ed. J. R. Harrison (Tübingen: Mohr Siebeck, 2008), p. 562. In the case of Crispus it was not essential for him to have been Jewish to be the head of a synagogue, as demonstrated from extant evidence in the East by T. Rajak and D. Noy; see *"Archisynogogoi:* Office, Social Status in the Graeco-Roman World," *JRS* 83 (1993): 75-93.

competent Roman jurist, and then proconsul of the province of Achaea.[109] He had become a Roman Senator in A.D. 37, and was appointed as proconsul of Achaea in the time of Claudius. Suetonius records that when Claudius restored Achaea to the Senate's control 'he would note that this province was dear to him because of the exchange of shared heritage'.[110] Gallio was a trusted 'friend *(amicus)* of Claudius', as the emperor himself officially recorded in an inscription to the inhabitants of Delphi when he entrusted the restoration of the welfare of the ancient city to him.[111] After his appointment to this provincial position in Corinth, Gallio went on to be elected one of the suffect consuls of Rome in A.D. 56, and subsequently became Nero's 'herald'.[112]

After Paul abandoned attending the synagogue, Acts records that the Jews 'unanimously' (ὁμοθυμαδὸν) brought a case against him to Gallio. They implemented legal proceedings alleging that 'contrary to the law this man is "deceptively" persuading' (παρὰ τὸν νόμον ἀναπείθει οὗτος)[113] 'the men [of Corinth] to worship God' (τοὺς ἀνθρώπους σέβασθαι τὸν θεόν) (Acts 18:13).[114]

It is significant that 'when Paul was about to open his mouth' in his defence (Acts 18:14a), Gallio immediately ruled there was no case to answer.[115] He explained why. The accused was not guilty because he had

---

109. For his legal and rhetorical training under the watchful eye of his father, Seneca the Elder, see J. Fairweather, "The History of Declamation," in *Seneca the Elder* (Cambridge: Cambridge University Press, 1981), ch. 2.

110. Suetonius, *The Divine Claudius* 42. Suetonius, *Divus Claudius,* ed. D. H. Hurley (Cambridge: Cambridge University Press, 2001), p. 231.

111. *Syll.*³ 801 D. For a detailed discussion see my "Rehabilitating Gallio and His Judgement in Acts 18:14-15," *TynB* 57, no. 2 (2006): 291-308.

112. Seneca the Younger, *Dialogues* 12.7. For the dating of his rôle as one of the two suffect consuls of Rome see G. Comedeca, "I consoli del 55=56 e un nuovo collega di Seneca nel consolato: P. Cornelius Dolabella," *ZPE* 63 (1986): 208-10.

113. ἀναπείθω, unlike Acts 18:4, where Luke uses πείθω to describe Paul's reasoning method of seeking to 'persuade' people. The term implies he is seductive or deceitfully doing so. For forensic examples, see *P.Magd.* 14 (221 B.C.) and *P.Ryl.* 114 (A.D. 280).

114. For the arguments for the veracity of the forensic summaries in Acts, see my "The Rôle of the *captatio benevolentia* in the Speeches of Tertullus and Paul in Acts 24," *JTS* 42, no. 2 (Nov. 1991): 505-31, and "Official Proceedings and Forensic Speeches in Acts 24–26," in *The Book of Acts in Its Ancient Literary Setting,* ed. A. D. Clarke and B. W. Winter (Grand Rapids: Eerdmans, 1993), ch. 11. For a detailed discussion of Acts 18:14-15 see my "Gallio's ruling on the legal status of early Christianity (Acts 18:14-15)," *TynB* 50, no. 2 (Nov. 1999): 213-24.

115. For a discussion of his legal competence and the implications of this legal ruling, see also my "Rehabilitating Gallio and His Judgement in Acts 18:14-15," pp. 291-308.

not committed a 'felony' nor 'a political misdemeanour' (ἀδίκημα τι ἢ ῥᾳδιούργημα πονηρόν) (Acts 18:14b). The 'claims' (ζητήματα)[116] of the accusers were over three issues. They related firstly to περὶ λόγου, a phrase consistently rendered in translations and commentaries as 'words' but it is in the singular. The editors of the ninth edition of Liddell and Scott's *Greek English Lexicon* have inserted a new classification of λὸγος that referred to 'a declaration of immunity', citing legal texts in support of this rendering of the term.[117] Was one of the charges against Paul that the group meeting each Sabbath next to the Corinthian synagogue was a *collegium illicitum* (Acts 18:7) and therefore did not qualify for the 'declaration of immunity'?[118] Furthermore, did this also include the Jewish exemption from local imperial cultic honours?

Because of heightened political activity among different groups and societies during his rule, Augustus initiated legislation that made it illegal for any association to meet more than once a month. It would be a case of *collegium illicitum*. In that same piece of legislation, the Jews alone were specifically given immunity from monthly meetings and were permitted to meet once a week.[119]

Secondly, Gallio refers to 'names' (ὀνόματα). 'Roman law held a person liable for actions and not for any name they professed.'[120] This was no different for Christians who would be interrogated by Pliny the Younger in Bithynia early in the next century. They were not executed just because they bore the name but because they refused to perform a cultic act before the statue of Trajan.[121]

Lastly, Gallio categorically ruled that the substance of their case against the accused was about 'the law, that of yours' (νόμου τοῦ καθ'

116. Cf. Porcius Festus' use of the term 'points of dispute' in another case of the Jews *v.* Paul, Acts 25:19, cf. *P.Ryl.* 117, 14 (3 A.D.), *SIG* 785, 8 (1 A.D.).

117. Liddell and Scott, *Greek English Lexicon* 9th ed., λὸγος as 'a declaration of immunity' in *A Revised Supplement to Liddell and Scott* (1996), VII.6, citing Justinian, *Novellae* 17.6 and *Edicta* 2 pr. as examples.

118. J. Hardin, "Decrees and Drachmas at Thessalonica: An Illegal Assembly in Jason's House (Acts 17.1-10a)," *NTS* 52, no. 1 (2006): 29-49, has argued that this legislation was used against Jason. See pp. 254-55 for a discussion of that charge. In Corinth they moved to the house of Titus Justus, with 'some Jews and Greeks' who had already believed (Acts 18:4, 7). Later it is Gaius who will host Paul and all the church in Corinth (Rom. 16:23).

119. O. F. Robinson, *The Criminal Law of Rome* (London: Duckworth, 1995), p. 80.

120. Robinson, *The Criminal Law of Rome*, p. 17.

121. M. Sordi, *The Christians and the Roman Empire* (London: Routledge, 1994), p. 62, citing Pliny, 10.96.6.

ὑμᾶς), i.e., Jewish law, and not Roman criminal law. Therefore it was purely an internal Jewish issue and did not come within his jurisdiction as governor.

What were the implications of his ruling for the early Christians in Corinth? It must have been totally unexpected because they were declared to be *de facto* a Jewish gathering, and thereby legally able to meet weekly. It would also mean that they were excused from participation in imperial veneration on specified holy days in the temple in Corinth, when 'all are both to wear wreaths and to sacrifice (στεφαναφορεῖν τε πάντοις διέταξε καὶ θύειν) on "undisturbed" holidays,' which were prescribed in Scipio's decree. (See p. 176.)

Gallio's important legal ruling has consequences for the enigma expressed by Millar, Price and Mitchell concerning the early Christians and the regular local imperial cultic celebrations and helps resolve the problem for those in Corinth at this stage of the church's growth.[122] As a result, Paul's movement in Corinth was seen as coming within the teaching and the aegis of Jewish customs or laws, i.e., the *mos maiorum,* living in accordance with their ancient traditions.[123] This would mean that these Christians did not have to offer divine honours to Claudius or any other imperial gods, as Jews had secured a concession from such participation.

The imperial cultic observances in Corinth from 44 B.C. profiled in this chapter have referenced archaeological, epigraphic and numismatic evidence in Achaea from its foundation. This is further understood in the era of Augustus and on the accession of the next two emperors, confirming that it faithfully continued in the rest of the Julio-Claudian era. From the inception of the colony, official evidence bears witness as to how intrusive these activities were in the lives of those who resided in Corinth as well as in other cities in the province.

122. F. Millar, "The Imperial Cult and the Persecutions," in W. den Boer, *Le Culte des Souverains dans l'empire romain* (Genève: Vandoeuvres, 1972), p. 163. Price, *Rituals and Power,* pp. 123-24, citing Eusebius, *Ecclesiastical History* 4.8-9 and S. Mitchell, *Anatolia: Land, Men and Gods in Asia Minor* (Oxford: Clarendon Press, 1993), II, p. 10.

123. Robinson, *The Criminal Law of Rome,* p. 80, on the *mos maiorum.*

CHAPTER 8

New Imperial Honours:
Some Corinthian Christians Compromise

After the departures of Paul and Gallio, a week of provincial imperial celebrations by the major cities of the Achaean League was officially approved
and located in Corinth. This was initiated by Rome, as was the case for all
provincial imperial cultic celebrations elsewhere. Leading citizens from
major cities in the League attended the week of celebrations.

Epigraphic evidence reveals this was a recent development in the
imperial cult veneration inaugurated in late 54 or early 55 A.D. and involved
the whole of the province of Achaea. While Paul does not name who were
'the so-called gods in heaven and on earth' (8:5), the latter phrase implied
they could be living ones. A Corinthian inscription along with another in
Athens secures the *Sitz im Leben* of the provincial imperial cultic celebration in Corinth.

This innovation in the giving of divine honours to the Caesars confronted Christians there, leaving them divided as to how they would respond. It emerged that some actually decided to participate in the imperial
cult celebrations by dining in its temple precincts (1 Cor. 8:10). This was in
spite of the fact they were not under any obligation to do so as a result of Gallio's ruling. (See pp. 193-94.) They actually justified their decision to those
who disagreed with them on theological grounds. 'We know an idol in the
world is nothing' and 'there is no God but One' (8:4). These possessed the
civic 'right' (ἐξουσία) to join in such privileged celebrations, possibly on the
grounds of social status (8:9). Others in the church were so deeply perturbed
by this that it became one of the issues raised in their letter to Paul.[1] It was

---

1. Paul wrote in response to their letter, cf. 1 Cor. 7:1, 'now concerning things about
which you wrote'. For an example of a letter responding to issues raised by the recipient that

related to 'things offered to idols' (8:1, 4) and feasting in the temple (8:10; 10:21). Paul addressed this issue in a lengthy response in 8:1–11:1.

Acts recorded that Paul had remained in Corinth teaching the word of God 'many days longer' after Gallio's decision (Acts 18:11). It may seem somewhat enigmatic that Paul himself could not fall back on any traditions he had taught about this particular issue. His long discussion in 1 Corinthians 8:1–11:1 continues with, 'Now I am praising you (ἐπαινῶ δὲ ὑμᾶς) because you remember me in all things, and hold fast the traditions, just as I delivered them to you (καθὼς παρέδωκα ὑμῖν)' (11:2).[2] Subsequently he would remind them of the implications of the tradition of the Lord that he had previously delivered to them regarding the Lord's Supper (1 Cor. 11:23-25). This implies they were in new territory facing a cultic innovation that was introduced after Paul's departure.

The purpose of this chapter is (I) to explore important epigraphic and other official evidence witnessing the implementation of this new federal imperial cult; (II) to identify 'the so-called gods in heaven and on earth' (1 Cor. 8:5), as well as the table and cup of the 'demons' *(genii)* referred to later in 10:20-1; and (III) to examine the nature of the Corinthian imperial cultic activities that included 'sacrifices', 'tables' and 'cups', and also how Paul dealt with the compromising Christians who were *de facto* giving divine honours to Nero.

I. The New Achaean League's Imperial Cult in Corinth (A.D. 54)

In A.D. 44 Corinth's status among provincials had already risen with the creation of a separate, senatorial province of Achaea that Tiberius had previously removed from the jurisdiction of the Senate in A.D. 15 because of internal strife.[3] Corinth had also experienced enormous eco-

---

used the form περὶ δέ, see *BGU* 1141 (10. B.C.), *ll.* 31, 40; cf. *l.* 1, 'you wrote this to me' (μοι τουτο ἔγραψας). Other matters were signalled by Paul in 1 Cor. 7:1, 25; 8:1, 4; 12:1; 16:1 and 12.

2. According to the earliest manuscript of Paul's letters, P[46], his response to this issue would take 237 lines, comparable to the number in 1:10–4:21 and only exceeded in length by nine lines for chapters 12–14 in the whole letter. For a discussion see the statistical details in my "The 'Underlays' of Conflict and Compromise in 1 Corinthians," in *Paul and the Corinthians: Studies on a Community in Conflict, Essays in Honour of Margaret Thrall*, ed. T. J. Burke and J. Keith Elliott (Leiden: E. J. Brill, 2003), p. 140.

3. Tacitus, *Annals* 1.76.2 and Suetonius, *The Deified Claudius* 26. See G. W. Bowersock, *Augustus and the Greek World* (Oxford: Clarendon Press, 1965), pp. 106ff.

nomic growth under Claudius.[4] Evidence of leading Greek families moving from elsewhere in the province to reside in this prestigious Roman colony further indicates its importance as a desirable location of the rich and powerful.[5] The authorization of the province-wide annual imperial cult celebration in Corinth was now an imperial 'gold leaf' placed in its crown, making it even more prestigious in the eyes of both its Roman citizens and provincials.

With these celebrations, considerable financial benefits flowed to Corinth as a substantial annual levy was fixed on all the participating cities in the League to finance them.[6] A sizable influx of dignitaries from cities in the League came to participate in the official week-long celebrations, games, gladiatorial combats, wild animal shows and banquets held in the temple precincts. (See pp. 24-25.)

Those possessing Roman citizenship had already been given dining privileges during the Isthmian Games around A.D. 51.[7] This enabled them to dine in the temple precincts as well as participate in other festivities.[8]

4. C. K. Williams II, "Roman Corinth as a Commercial Center," in *The Corinthia in the Roman Period,* ed. T. E. Gregory, Journal of Roman Architecture Supplementary Series 6 (Ann Arbor, MI: 1993), pp. 31-46, who demonstrates the rapid expansion needed to meet the demands of new empire-wide trading patterns based on archaeological evidence in Corinth, including its harbour facilities.

5. A. J. S. Spawforth, "Roman Corinth: The Formation of a Colonial Élite," in *Roman Onomastics in the Greek East: Social and Political Aspects,* ed. A. D. Rizakis, Meletemata 21 (Athens, 1996), pp. 173-74.

6. For a later complaint by the city of Argos of the costs levied on it as a city in the League participating in the cultic celebrations in Corinth, see A. J. S. Spawforth, "The Achaean Federal Imperial Cult I: Pseudo-Julian Letters 198," *TynB* 46, no. 1 (1995): 151-68.

7. I argued previously that the *Sitz im Leben* for this passage was the imperial games held in nearby Isthmia. This view was challenged by J. Potopoulos, *Food Offered to Idols in Roman Corinth* (Tübingen: J. C. B. Mohr, 2003), pp. 218-19, who wrote that there was no evidence of temple dining rooms at the temple of Poseidon at the time of the writing of 1 Corinthians. He appears to assume that dining rooms *per se* were set inside the temple building. Archaeological evidence shows a large temple precinct similar to the space surrounding the imperial cult temple in the forum in Corinth. Dinners given by the president of the games were in Isthmia. However, I now renounce this view argued in "The Imperial Cult, the Games, and Dining in a Temple (1 Corinthians 8-10:21)," in *After Paul Left Corinth: The Influence of Secular Ethics and Social Change* (Grand Rapids and Cambridge: Eerdmans, 2001), ch. 12, that the specific reference was to the temple of Poseidon, given the fact that, in the East, imperial cult temples were placed in the agora and the archaeological evidence for the large imperial cult temple in Corinth that dominated it.

8. See J. H. Kent, *Corinth: Inscriptions 1926-1950* (Princeton: American School of

However, all Corinthians could attend the spectacles, including those in the circus, as citizens did in cities in the East in the context of provincial imperial cultic activities. Long before, in the era of Augustus, Corinth's Roman circus had been constructed next to the gymnasium and between *decumanus* IV North and *decumanus* V North. It was 400 metres in length and 65 metres wide and it could hold up to 12,000 spectators. Four-horse chariots *(quadrigae)* and two-horse chariots *(bigae)* raced in the circus in the Panhellenic Isthmian Games, the Caesarean games and the Penteateric Corinthian Caesaeras festival.[9] It was an ideal location for such events that were part of the provincial celebrations.

Other equestrian contests were held there, and sometimes athletic events and gladiatorial shows as well.[10] The latter had become a characteristic of provincial imperial cultic celebrations.[11] It is recorded how one imperial high priest was 'acclaimed by the crowd and responded by further munificence; "the spectacle, especially of the gladiators, caused the greatest astonishment and even credulity as roses and gifts were thrown into the amphitheater where the variety of the gladiators' arms were wondered at"'.[12] Gladiatorial shows were also associated with Roman imperial birthdays and the dedication of temples;[13] hence Corinth could readily include them in provincial imperial cultic celebrations.

The forerunner to this new development had been the celebration by the Pan-Achaean assembly of festivals held on the accession of both Gaius and Claudius. (See pp. 181-83.) The provincial imperial cult was established with the cities in the ancient Achaean League that became part

Classical Studies at Athens, 1966), VIII.3, no. 153, and my *After Paul Left Corinth*, pp. 276-78. Kent incorrectly translated *colonii* as 'inhabitants' of the colony, although he did so in no. 151, where he rendered the same term as 'colonists', i.e., Roman citizens.

9. For the location of the circus, see D. G. Romano, "A Roman Circus in Corinth," *Hesperia* 74, no. 4 (2005): 585-611. He notes it measured 388 metres by 43 metres and was built in the Augustan period. It bordered *decumanus* IV and V north and south of the gymnasium and the temple of Asklepieion.

10. Romano, "A Roman Circus in Corinth," pp. 586, 599, 603, 608.

11. For gladiatorial games sponsored by the high priests at provincial imperial cultic celebrations in the Roman East, see D. Fishwick, *Imperial Cult in the Latin West: Studies in the Ruler Cult of the West* (Leiden: E. J. Brill, 1991), II.1, 577; and *Imperial Cult in the Latin West: The Provincial Cult. Part 3 The Provincial Centre: Provincial Cult* (Leiden: E. J. Brill, 2004), III.3, pp. 307-20.

12. S. R. F. Price, *Rituals and Power: The Roman Imperial Cult in Asia Minor* (Cambridge: Cambridge University Press, 1984), p. 116, citing *BCH* 12 (1888): 11.

13. Fishwick, *Imperial Cult in the Latin West: Studies in the Ruler Cult,* II.1, p. 576.

of what Spawforth calls the 'younger' one, i.e., the post-146 B.C. Achaean League.[14]

The League had had an unfortunate history. Its confrontation with, and ultimate defeat by Rome in 146 B.C. had resulted in the subsequent sacking of Corinth. Given complications in Achaea at the end of Augustus' life, there would certainly have been consultations with the Roman Senate before it approved the creation of the League's imperial cult located in Corinth.[15] This move saw Corinth's final restoration with Rome. The penultimate step had occurred on the accession to the throne of Gaius where he decreed, 'And remembering the distinction from ancient times of each of the Greek republics, I permit you to meet as a League' (p. 182).

It is important to note that Claudius is recorded as having expressed a special affection for the province of Achaea, which he conveyed to the Roman Senate. Suetonius wrote that while 'commending to the Senators the province of Achaia, he declared that Greece was dear to him because of their exchanged heritage'.[16] Immediately after his death it proved to be an opportune moment for the Senate to permit the Achaean League to preside over imperial cultic celebrations in Corinth.

(i) Spartiaticus, the First Federal Imperial High Priest A.D. 54-55

We possess four separate and important pieces of first-century evidence from which it is possible to understand aspects of this federal cult, including the date when it was inaugurated. The first high priest of the federal imperial cult was the great Corinthian benefactor Gaius Julius Spartiaticus, who was honoured with a statue erected by the Corinthian tribe of Calpurnian. The accompanying inscription, first published in 1926, contains information about the prestigious public offices he held, but more importantly of his involvement in the imperial cult both at a local and provincial level, together with the adulation he received because of this new rôle in Corinth's affairs.[17]

14. A. J. S. Spawforth, "Corinth, Argos, and the Imperial Cult: A Reconsideration of Pseudo-Julian, Letters 198," *Hesperia* 63, no. 2 (1994): 218.

15. Fishwick, "The Provincial Priesthood," in *Imperial Cult in the Latin West: Provincial Cult,* III.2, p. 301.

16. Suetonius, *The Divine Claudius* 42. Suetonius, *Divus Claudius,* ed. D. H. Hurley (Cambridge: Cambridge University Press, 2001), p. 231.

17. L. R. Taylor and A. B. West, "The Euryclids in Latin Inscriptions from Corinth,"

Gaius Julius Spartiaticus, son of Laco, grandson of Eurycles, of the Fabian tribe, procurator of Caesar and the Augusta Agrippina, military tribune, decorated with the public horse by the deified Claudius, flamen of the Deified Julius, magistrate of the fifth year twice *(quinquennial duovir iter.)*, president of the Isthmian and Caesarean Sebastean games, high priest for life of the Augustan house, the first of the Achaeans to hold this office on account of his excellence and unsparing and most lavish generosity both to the divine family *(domus divina)*[18] and to our colony: the tribesmen of the Calpurnian tribe (set up this statue) for their patron.[19]

Traditionally the one who held the federal high priesthood had to be 'the most distinguished available candidate of the day', for it was 'the summit of a man's career' in the East.[20] Certainly, no other person in Achaea better matched this requirement than Spartiaticus as the evidence reveals.

His father, C. Julius Laco, had long ties with Corinth's civic life. He built the luxurious baths in Corinth and, according to Pausanias, 'beautified it with various kinds of stone, especially the one quarried at Croceae in Laconia. On the left of the entrance stands a Poseidon, and after him Artemis hunting'.[21] An inscription to him records that he held some of the public offices that his son would subsequently occupy.[22] Laco, who

---

AJA 30 (1926): 393-400, and revised in 1931 by A. B. West, *Corinth: Results of Excavations Conducted by the American School of Classical Studies at Athens 1896-1926* (Cambridge, MA: Harvard University Press, 1931), VIII.2, no. 68.

18. For a discussion of this concept see Fishwick, "*Domus Divina,*" in *Imperial Cult in the Latin West,* II.1, ch. 4.

19. West, *Corinth,* VIII.2, no. 68, and E. Mary Smallwood, *Documents Illustrating the Principates of Gaius, Claudius and Nero* (Cambridge: Cambridge University Press, 1967), no. 264. Spawforth, "Corinth, Argos, and the Imperial Cult," p. 218, has restructured his translation of the inscription by placing lines 10-15 at the beginning of the text. In doing this he has followed the second-century A.D. inscription from the Greek city of Messene, *IG* 5, 1, 1451 (A.D. 139-61) by which time official inscriptions in Corinth were no longer in Latin but in Greek as part of the Hellenistic revival in Hadrian's period. However, reordering of the Latin text detracts from the intended nexus that stressed his life-long rôle as imperial priest and his great benefactions to the 'divine family' with this new office as the pinnacle of his liturgies in ascending order of importance.

20. Fishwick, *Imperial Cult in the Latin West,* III.2, p. 306, and Spawforth, "Corinth, Argos, and the Imperial Cult," p. 219.

21. Pausanias, *Description of Greece* 2.3.5.

22. '[P]rocurator of Tiberius Claudius Caesar Augustus Germanicus, priest *(augur)*, president of the Isthmian and Caesarean Games, magistrate in the fifth year, curio, priest

originally lived in Sparta, belonged to one of the long-standing and most distinguished families in Achaea.[23] His grandfather was Eurycles, the famous Spartan dynast who was given the prestigious title of 'Caesar's friend' by Augustus.[24]

So distinguished were the father and grandfather of Spartiaticus that they were remembered annually on specific festive days associated with imperial cultic activities in Gyntheum, the port for Sparta in the south of Achaea. These were named in an inscription indicating the regulations for the celebration of the various festivals. Under the section for days for 'the gods and rulers', two days were for thymelic games, which were for music festivals with dancing but not drama. The first was 'one to the memory of Gaius Julius Eurycles, many times benefactor of our nation and city, and a second day in honour of Gaius Laco, protector of the security of our nation and city'.[25]

(ii) Senior Civic and Imperial Posts of Spartiaticus

The statue and the inscription record the career of Spartiaticus, a very important player in Achaea who had been made a member of the Equestrian order. He was 'decorated with the public horse by the deified Claudius' — the horse being Claudius' symbol of knighthood.[26]

He had been elected on two occasions to Corinth's most important magistracy *(II quinquennial duovir)* noted at the beginning of the inscription. Every five years new members, nominated by the two magistrates for that year, were added permanently to the governing council (βουλή) of Corinth, hence the strategic importance politically of this post every fifth year.

Spartiaticus became 'president of the Isthmian and Caesarean Sebastean games'. These famous games were restored to Corinth from Sykion,

---

(flamen) of Augustus . . . to the well deserving one *(bene merenti)'*. West, *Corinth,* VIII,2, no. 67.

23. On the evidence assembled of the coming of the wealthy Greek élite to Corinth, see A. Spawforth, "Roman Corinth: The Formation of a Colonial Elite," *Melethemata* 21 (1996): 174.

24. P. Cartledge and A. Spawforth, *Hellenistic and Roman Sparta: A Tale of Two Cities* (London and New York: Routledge, 1989), pp. 98-104.

25. *SEG* 11, 923.

26. Fishwick, *Imperial Cult in the Latin West: Provincial Cult,* III.2, p. 302.

where they had been held after Rome's defeat of the Corinthians in 146 B.C. and soon after its re-founding as a colony in 44 B.C. They were not fully housed in Isthmia until possibly A.D. 51. In Roman times the presidency of these games had become the highest of the honorary public offices to which one could be elected because of the great prestige of these ancient games in the East. Normally the running of the games in any city was the responsibility of the city's 'administrator', the *aedile*. The sheer cost of financing the imperial games in nearby Isthmia meant its presidency became the most senior of all the liturgies in Corinth to which one could be elected by popular vote.[27]

From the *cursus honorum* cited above, Spartiaticus had both rank and status, as had his father and grandfather. This is reflected in a distinguished public career in which he held all the important honorary civic offices in Corinth by election.

He also had another extremely important imperial connection in that he was responsible for the imperial estates in Achaea as 'procurator of Caesar and the Augusta Agrippina', i.e., Nero and his mother, Agrippina the Younger, a responsibility he undertook in late A.D. 54. His father, C. Julius Laco, had held the same post under Claudius as 'procurator of Tiberius Claudius Caesar Augustus Germanicus'.[28] His grandfather, Eurycles, was the ruler of Sparta and a 'friend' of Caesar Augustus. So he had inherited much of his father's and grandfather's political influence, as happened with some leading families in the East who enjoyed imperial patronage.[29]

(iii) Imperial Cult Priesthoods in Spartiaticus' Family

The inscription records Spartiaticus' previous imperial cult involvement as 'priest *(flamen)* of the Deified Julius'. Like his father, he was the priest of

27. In Corinth the duties of the *aedile* had been divided. He retained the responsibility for the financial affairs of the colony and disputes connected with commercial matters. The expense of running the Isthmian Games including feasts on several occasions in the precincts of the temple of Poseidon meant that only a very rich citizen could be elected as president of the games. The cost for him staging them was enormous. For a discussion, see my "An Early Christian Benefactor and Prominent Citizen," in *Seek the Welfare of the City: Christians as Benefactors and Citizens,* First Century Christians in the Graeco-Roman World (Grand Rapids and Carlisle: Eerdmans and Paternoster, 1994), ch. 10.

28. West, *Corinth,* VIII.2, no. 67.

29. G. W. Bowersock, "Eurycles of Sparta," *JRS* 51 (1961): 112-18, for a discussion of this provincial family's political role, in particular p. 118 for his family tree in Sparta, especially C. Julius Eurycles.

local Corinthian imperial cult celebrations. The inscription erected to Laco in the time of Claudius records that he was *flamen Augusti*.[30] Price provides evidence that *flamines,* i.e., 'priests on the Roman model are found only in Roman colonies'.[31] The phrase '*flamen* of the Deified Julius' according to Fishwick 'appears in provinces where worship was originally addressed to the deified emperor — that is, a deceased ruler raised to the rank of a state god'.[32]

Recorded in the Spartiaticus inscription was the office that would become exceedingly important in Corinth and the province, i.e., 'high priest of the Augustan house for life' *(Sebasteon, archiere domus Aug. in perpetuum).* It is made clear that he was 'the first of the Achaeans to hold this office' *(primo Achaeon).*

While it might be thought that on the basis of this inscription he had been the first Achaean to hold this office, which others had previously held elsewhere, another inscription confirms that he was the first from the time of the creation of this federal imperial cult. An Athenian inscription resolves any ambiguity. It records that he was 'the high priest of the divine Caesars and Caesar's family of the Achaean League first [high priest] for life from its institution' (ἀρχιερεὺς Θεῶν Σεβαστῶν καὶ γένους Σεβαστῶν ἐκ τοῦ κοινοῦ τὴν Ἀχαξιας διὰ βίου πρῶτον τῶν ἀπ' αἰῶνος). The word order stresses that he was the first to hold this prestigious and life-long office.[33] From his native city of Sparta it was recorded that he was the 'high priest of the Caesars' (ἀρχιερεὺς τῶν Σεβαστῶν).

Syme notes, 'When religion is the care of the State in an oligarchical society, it is evident that sacerdotal preferment will be conferred, not upon the pious and learned, but for social distinction and for political success.'[34] Fishwick also observed that the career of a provincial priest in the Latin West 'is marked by a full roster of municipal posts served as a rule before the crowning honour of the provincial priesthood'[35] and a permanent office.[36] This was certainly true of Spartiaticus.

---

30. West, *Corinth,* VIII.2, no. 67, *l.* 7.

31. Price, *Rituals and Power,* p. 88.

32. Fishwick, "The Provincial Priesthood," in *The Imperial Cult in the Latin West,* III.2, p. 294.

33. *IG* 3, 805 (Dittenberger, *Syll.*³ 790) and *IG* 5, 1, 463.

34. R. Syme, *The Roman Revolution* (Oxford: Clarendon Press, 1939), p. 382.

35. Fishwick, *Imperial Cult in the Latin West,* III.2, p. 299.

36. He would fall out of favour later in Nero's reign; Cartledge and Spawforth, *Hellenistic and Roman Sparta,* p. 103.

His duties included presiding over the assembly that acted on behalf of the province. The rôle of the high priest in the provincial cult was important, for he was also responsible for arranging all the accompanying festive activities. If his office ended after a year, a statue was mounted on a plinth outlining his liturgies and erected with the approval of the Achaean League and the 'Council and the People' of Corinth.[37] In the case of Spartiaticus, the Corinthian tribe to which he belonged honoured him with an inscription while he was still holding this office and not after its completion or his demise. He was their 'patron', as they recorded at the conclusion of the inscription.

The Greek benefaction inscriptions had a traditional structure for the person being lauded, although this was not the Roman tradition. Latin inscriptions noted only the liturgies the person had held, and that in an abbreviated form. However, in the case of Spartiaticus, his inscription contained a unique feature that broke with this convention. After citing his liturgies, it recorded their praise of him with the following accolades, 'his excellence and unsparing and most lavish generosity', and then indicated that the beneficiaries of these were 'both to the divine family *(domus divina)* and in our colony' *(ll.* 11-12). The former phrase was considered to be 'an elastic term that included all the members of the Imperial house'.[38]

Price notes the prestigious nature of this position. 'To be an imperial priest was a mark of distinction, as was true of priesthoods in general, according to Artemidorus (II, 30), while to be a provincial priest was the pinnacle of achievement. A Roman astrologer, Firmicus Maternus counts such dignitaries of the province of Asia among those famed throughout the world.'[39]

For Rome, the high priest for life of the provincial or federal imperial cult had to be a person of the highest social status with a good track record of public liturgies.[40] The epigraphic evidence shows that Spartiaticus certainly qualified.

---

37. Fishwick, "The Provincial Priesthood," in *The Imperial Cult in the Latin West,* III.2, p. 302.

38. D. Fishwick, *"Domus Divina,"* in *The Imperial Cult in the Latin West,* II.1, ch. 4 and p. 423 for a discussion of the term. See also D. Wardle, "Valerius Maximus on the *Domus Augusta,* Augustus, and Tiberius," *CQ* 50, no. 2 (2000): 479-93.

39. Price, *Rituals and Power,* p. 122 commenting on *Matthesis* 4.21.5.

40. Fishwick, *Imperial Cult in the Latin West,* III.2, p. 298, notes, 'Alongside personal merit, affinity with a distinguished, well-to-do family was a key ingredient in the background of provincial priests.'

(iv) Dating the Federal Imperial Cult of Achaea

Significantly for our purposes, the inscription of Spartiaticus also helps in dating the creation of this imperial federal cult. He is named 'procurator of Caesar and the Augusta Agrippina' of the imperial estates in the province. The rôle of Nero's mother, Agrippina II was *de facto* co-regent with her son in the immediate period following the accession of Nero and before her 'fall from power'. Spawforth comments that this title indicates 'the extraordinary prominence of Nero's mother'.[41] We know the *terminus ad quem* for the dating of this inscription because of her downfall in February the following year. (See p. 209.) This secures the dating of the inauguration of the federal imperial cult in Corinth because her name disappeared from coins and from the public domain in A.D. 55. Claudius died on 13 October, A.D. 54. Augusta Agrippina was immediately declared the priestess of Claudius; her deceased husband was immediately 'deified' by the Senate and Nero was designated as 'son of the Deified [Claudius]'.

Commemorative coins were struck bearing Nero's image and recording his connection to his predecessor.[42] The coin, an *aureus,* had the highest value in Roman currency and was worth twenty-five *denarii.* On the obverse side of one minted in Rome in late A.D. 54, Nero and his mother faced each other, so that neither was seen as subordinate to the other.[43] It read, 'Agrippina Augusta (wife) of the deified Claudius, mother of Nero Caesar' (Obverse): 'To Nero, son of the deified Claudius, Caesar Augustus Germanicus, emperor, of tribunician power; in accordance with a decree of the senate' (Reverse). The legend on the coin stated that it was issued 'in accordance with the senate's decree' (*S.C. = Senatus consulto*). The Senate issued bronze coins while the emperor traditionally issued gold and silver, so this issue was unprecedented.[44] The message this *aureus* sent to the inhabitants of Rome was that the Senate recognized the 'official'

---

41. Cartledge and Spawforth, *Hellenistic and Roman Sparta: A Tale of Two Cities,* p. 103.

42. B. Levick, *Claudius* (London: Batsford, 1990), p. 187.

43. H. Mattingly, ed., *Coins of the Roman Empire in the British Museum* (1923), I.1, p. 200. Cf. the relief panel from the north portico of the Aphrodisias Sebasteion with Nero aged sixteen crowned by Agrippina. T. P. Wiseman, *Myths of Rome* (Exeter: University of Exeter Press, 2004), p. 260.

44. B. W. Jones and R. D. Mills, *The Use of Documentary Evidence in the Study of Roman Imperial History* (Sydney: Sydney University Press, 1984), pp. 6-7, in commenting on this particular coin.

rôle of Nero's mother. Never before had the mother of a reigning emperor appeared facing him.[45] This informed everyone of her position as *de facto* 'co-regent' with her son, whose accession occurred three months before his seventeenth birthday.[46]

In Corinth, the image of Agrippina had already been struck on an *aureus* in the Claudian period[47] — the colony possessed the right to mint its own coins up until A.D. 68. Local deities were normally placed on the reverse of coins, but here in a chariot is Venus, the divine patroness of Corinth. Another had a male togate figure with a draped female, possibly referring to Claudius following his marriage to Agrippina. The laureate head of Claudius and the draped bust of Nero on the reverse appeared on a coin struck in Syrian Antioch between A.D. 50 and 54 as well as another with Agrippina II on the obverse side and her son on the reverse.[48]

In the great Sebastion at Aphrodisias that led up to the imperial cult temple is a frieze of Agrippina holding the hand of Claudius, who is portrayed naked, i.e., a god.[49] An Ephesian coin with the heads of Claudius and Agrippina facing each other has the inscription 'marriage of gods' (θεογαμία) on the obverse side. On the reverse was a statue of Artemis with the word 'Ephesian' ("Εφεσια).[50] She was a well-known and venerated goddess in the East.

Two other striking friezes have been located in Aphrodisias. They illustrate two attempts by the sculptor to reflect the political reality of Agrippina's power. The first has Agrippina actually placing the laurel crown on Nero's head, which was the task of the Roman Senate confirming his office as Caesar and not one for her. The other depicts the same but with Nero giving a trophy or something similar to the Senate.[51]

---

45. A. A. Barrett, *Agrippina: Sex, Power, and Politics in the Early Empire* (London: Routledge, 1996), p. 153, sees this as 'a striking piece of documentary evidence which brings her very close to the status of co-regent'.

46. Smallwood, *Documents Illustrating the Principates of Gaius, Claudius and Nero,* no. 106. The obverse side of the coin: AGRIPP. AVG. DIVI CLAVD. NERONIS CAES. MATER.

47. *RPC* nos. 1183-88.

48. *RPC* nos. 4169-70.

49. B. Kovulmaz, *Aphrodisias Sebasteion Sevgi Gönöl Hall* (Istanbul: Yapi Kredi Publications, 2008), p. 45.

50. *RPC* no. 2620.

51. R. R. R. Smith, "The Imperial Relief from the Sebastion at Aphrodisias," *JRS* 77 (1987): 88-138. For Nero and Agrippina, see pp. 127-32. It was 'most likely taken down after A.D. 68 and reused as a floor slab', p. 128. For Claudius and Agrippina 'handshaking' = marital harmony *(Concordia),* see p. 107; cf. for the coin of Rome crowning Augustus, S. J. Friesen,

Even during Claudius' reign Agrippina had possessed considerable political clout. When Claudius adopted Nero in A.D. 54, the year in which the latter died, a coin was struck in Corinth with two full-length males, presumably Nero and Britannicus, the latter being the natural son of Claudius.[52] Other Corinthian coins issued after Nero's accession named her Agrippina Augusta, with one having 'Julia Agrippina Augusta, mother of Caesar'.[53] Subsequently Britannicus was poisoned, possibly by Agrippina, on 11 February, A.D. 55, in order to further secure Nero's position as emperor.

Early in the Principate of Nero numerous coins were struck bearing Agrippina's image. On the obverse side of one in Synaus is a draped female figure on the right facing the bare head of Nero. It read, 'Agrippina, goddess, Nero, god' (Ἀγριππεῖνα θεὰ Νέρως θεός), thus providing evidence of attributing divinity to her as well. On the reverse side is the god Apollo, whom Augustus venerated and to whom he had accredited a major victory. He is depicted firing an arrow.[54]

Nero subsequently and abruptly stripped his mother of her power because she sought to rule his empire. She was removed from the palace proper to a house owned by her grandmother on the Palatine in Rome.[55] In the following year the Roman mint continued to portray her behind Nero with the reverse depicting her still in her official rôle as priestess of *Divus Claudius* and with another male figure, probably Augustus. It declared her to be 'Agrippina Augusta, wife of the Deified Claudius and mother of Nero Caesar'. They are shown riding in a chariot drawn by four elephants that was traditionally driven into the Circus Maximus in Rome carrying the

---

Twice Neokoros: Ephesus, Asia and the Cult of the Flavian Imperial Family (Leiden: Brill, 1993), p. 14.

52. *RPC* no. 1182.

53. *RPC* nos. 1190, 1193-94. See also S. E. Wood, *Imperial Women: A Study of Public Images, 40 B.C.–A.D. 68* (Leiden: E. J. Brill, 1999), p. 292, n. 121.

54. *RPC* no. 3107, 'presumably dated about 55'.

55. See A. A. Barrett, *Agrippina: Sex, Power and Politics in the Early Empire* (New Haven: Yale University Press, 1996), pp. 164-80, for a detailed discussion of the eroding of her power base, and for sources of coins struck portraying her in Rome and the empire, pp. 224-29. See J. Ginsburg, "Visualizing Agrippina," in *Representing Agrippina: Constructions of Female Power in the Early Roman Empire,* American Classical Studies 50 (Oxford: Oxford University Press, 2006), ch. 2, where she assembles statues, cameos and coins as part of her argument that credence must be placed on non-literary sources over against 'biased' literary sources; S. Freisenbuch, "Witches of the Tiber: The Last Julio-Claudian Empresses," in *The First Ladies of Rome: Women behind the Caesars* (London: Jonathan Cape, 2010), ch. 4.

portrait of the Deified Augustus. It signified her connection with the imperial cult.[56] She would soon disappear from all coins.[57]

As Spartiaticus held the title of 'procurator of Caesar and the Augusta Agrippina', Spawforth has rightly argued that 'the striking reference to Nero's mother can only belong to the brief period of political ascendancy in 54-55' before her power was broken.[58] Griffith has suggested that 'her control of the business of government ceased at the end of 54'.[59] The *terminus ad quem* could well be soon after the poisoning of Britannicus in early A.D. 55, when Nero no longer felt the need of his mother's 'protection'.

In the light of the above evidence, Spawforth has argued that the establishment of a federal imperial cult in Corinth by the cities in the Achaean League coincided with the accession of Nero. This would have resulted in the Christians in Corinth witnessing for the first time, and then annually, imperial cultic activities far more spectacular than they had previously known, with senior representatives from the Achaean League descending on their city. Corinthian citizens would have seen the locating of the federal imperial cult in their city as an enormous honour, adding further to its prestige and importance while it seemed to pose a problem for some of the Christians.

II. Identifying 'the So-Called Gods' and the Imperial *'Genii'*

(i) The So-Called Gods in Heaven and on Earth

Are there any clues confirming that imperial divinities were actually being venerated in 1 Corinthians 8:1–11:1? Having quoted the arguments of those who justified their participation in the temple feast based on the premise 'an idol is nothing' and 'that there is no God except one' (ὅτι οὐδεὶς θεὸς εἰ

---

56. Barrett, *Agrippina: Sex, Power and Politics in the Early Empire*, p. 226, no. 54.

57. Wood, *Imperial Women: A Study of Public Images, 40 B.C.–A.D. 68*, p. 265, 'her disappearance from coinage of the Roman mint after the second year of his Principate'.

58. Spawforth, "Corinth, Argos, and the Imperial Cult," p. 218. For her rôle as *de facto* 'co-regent' see Barrett, *Agrippina: Sex, Power and Politics in the Early Empire*, pp. 164-80; Griffin, *Nero: the End of a Dynasty* (London: Batsford, 1984), p. 38; and Freisenbuch, "Witches of the Tiber: The Last Julio-Claudian Empresses," ch. 4.

59. M. T. Griffin, *Nero: The End of a Dynasty* (New Haven: Yale University Press, 1984), p. 38.

μὴ εἷς) (8:4), Paul's response was, 'For, even though there are the so-called gods either in heaven or on earth; just as indeed there are many gods and many lords' (8:5).

The statement 'in heaven (ἐν οὐρανῷ) or on earth' (ἐπὶ γῆς) resonates with an important, recently discovered fragment of an inscription that was dedicated to 'Caesares Augusti and the colony of Corinth' (Caesaribus Augustis et Colonia Laus Iulia Corinthiensis).[60] It was located in the Julian basilica built in the time of Augustus.[61] Scotton concludes that it was 'a generic dedication to the Caesares Augusti, living and dead emperors'.[62] This was the official Roman convention for referring to present and deceased emperors, in the same way Paul refers to the phenomena 'gods either in heaven or on earth'.

Who were the gods in heaven and on earth? The Senate officially deified Julius Caesar, Augustus and Claudius.[63] This is the only passage in the Pauline corpus where he refers to gods 'on earth'. In a single inscription both Augustus and Tiberius were addressed in Cyprus as 'gods' while living. Between 9 b.c. and a.d. 2 there was inscribed to the former, 'To Imperator Caesar Augustus, god, son of a god' (Θεός, Θεοῦ υἱῷ θεῷ). The same phrases, 'To Tiberius Caesar Augustus, god, son of a god', were added, referring to the apotheosized Augustus in the heavens.[64] This was in contrast to 'those in heaven' such as Julius Caesar, Augustus and Claudius who had already undergone an apotheosis.[65] 'The Caesar [Claudius] who had to pay his debts to his ancestors, god manifest, has joined them', i.e., the gods.[66]

Why does Paul use the plural for those on the earth? Living members of the imperial family were identified as divinities. An inscription in Athens reads to 'Julia divine Augusta Providence' ('Ιουλίαν θεὰν Σεβαστὴν

60. Paul D. Scotton, "A New Fragment of an Inscription from the Julian Basilica at Roman Corinth," *Hesperia* 74, no. 1 (2005): 96-97.

61. For the dating of the building see the discussion of C. K. Williams II and P. Russell, "Corinth: Excavations of 1980," *Hesperia* 50 (1981): 1-44.

62. Scotton, "A New Fragment of an Inscription," p. 100.

63. V. Ehrenberg and A. H. M. Jones, *Documents Illustrating the Reigns of Augustus and Tiberius* (Oxford: Clarendon Press, 1976²), no. 115 a and b. See also no. 108 (Acanthus, Macedonia) 'to Caesar Augustus, a god, son of a god' (θεῷ Θεοῦ υἱῷ).

64. See Suetonius, "The Deified Julius," "The Deified Augustus," and "The Deified Claudius," in *The Lives of the Caesars*.

65. On the *apotheosis* of the emperor, see I. Gradel, *Emperor Worship and Roman Religion*, Oxford Classical Monographs (Oxford: Clarendon Press, 2002), pp. 305-24.

66. *P.Oxy.* 1021.

Πρόνοιαν),[67] and one in Ephesus with an edict of the proconsul of Asia is even more fulsome.

> And since the long-due divine honor has been conferred upon Julia Augusta by our most pious imperator Augustus, her hymnodes must be granted the same rights as those of the divine Augustus, since the Senate and Divine Augustus — after she had been honored with sacred laws before her immortality — considered her worthy of divinity and conferred it upon her.[68]

Elsewhere she was described as 'mother of Tiberius Caesar Augustus, princeps and savior . . . mother of the world *(genetricis orbis)*' and Quintus Julius Plotus was 'priest of Julia in perpetuity' *(Flamini Iuliae Aug. in perpetuum).*[69]

Either in Corinth or Patria, the other Roman colony in Achaea, a bronze coin was struck that was inscribed 'Divine Claudia, daughter of Nero' and on the reverse 'Divine Poppaea Augusta', i.e., her mother.[70] Earlier the city of Thasos dedicated an inscription to 'Livia Drusilla, the wife of Augustus Caesar, as a goddess and benefactor'.[71] In Athens Antonia Augusta, the grandmother of Claudius, was deified in her own lifetime, *c.* A.D. 18 in the reign of Tiberius, and she continued to be venerated after her death.[72] A building in Corinth was dedicated 'to the deified Augusta, the grandmother of [Tiberius] Claudius Caesar Augustus Germanicus'.[73] Aphrodite was sometimes addressed as 'lady', and in other instances as 'god' or 'lord'.[74] Therefore deified emperors and living members of the imperial

---

67. *IG²* 2.3, 3238.

68. Smallwood, *Documents Illustrating the Principates of Gaius, Claudius and Nero,* no. 380, Col. 8, *l.* 25–Col. 9, *l.* 7.

69. Ehrenberg and Jones, *Documents Illustrating the Reigns of Augustus and Tiberius,* nos. 123 and 131.

70. Smallwood, *Documents Illustrating the Principates of Gaius, Claudius and Nero,* no. 148. Claudia died when four months old in A.D. 63 and her mother in A.D. 65, when she was given divine honours.

71. *ILS* 8784.

72. *IG* 2/3, 2, 5095. During Tiberius' reign *c.* A.D. 18-37, Antonia Augusta, the living grandmother of the future emperor, Claudius, was declared the goddess, Antonia (Θεὰ Ἀντωνίᾳ) in Athens. For a discussion see N. Kokkinos, *Antonia Augusta: A Portrait of a Great Lady* (London and New York: Routledge, 1992), p. 98.

73. Kent, *Corinth,* VIII.3, no. 55.

74. See my "Theological and Ethical Responses to Religious Pluralism: 1 Corinthians 8–10," *TynB* 41 (1990): 214, for evidence.

family, including women, were covered by the generic description of the divinities in heaven and on earth.

This is further substantiated from the Athenian inscription to Spartiaticus that mentions the gods to whom he will perform cult as the high priest of the Achaean League. It records that these are 'the divine *Augusti* and Caesar's family' (Θεῶν Σεβαστῶν καὶ γένους Σεβαστῶν).[75] The term γένος was used of 'family' or 'clan'.[76] The phrase γένους Σεβαστῶν parallels that of the Spartiaticus inscription in Corinth. It refers 'to the divine family' *(domus divina)* (*ll.* 11-12).[77] Fishwick sees this term as encompassing all the family, who were honoured in the same way — 'a development of considerable significance for the history of the Roman ruler cult'.[78] At this stage these would have included Nero's mother and Britannicus, the natural-born son of Claudius and Nero's half-brother.

The description of imperial divinities that Spartiaticus venerated and performed sacrifices to fits well with the declaration that the activities in Corinth were 'to the gods in heaven' and also 'gods on the earth' (8:5). These extant inscriptions verify Paul's identification of the apotheosized gods and the living members of the imperial household in Corinth as 'gods in heaven and on earth'.

(ii) The Significance of Paul's Selection of the Phrase 'So-Called'

Paul's participial construction, 'the so-called' (οἱ λεγόμενοι), was also used of kings, philosophers and sophists when false claims were being made of their actual status. The Old English term 'commonly' could mean 'popularly but incorrectly' and serves as a comparable example for this Greek conventional phrase, as also found in Dio Chrysostom.[79] The *Hermetic*

---

75. *IG* 5, 1, 463 and discussion in Taylor and West, "The Euryclids in Latin Inscriptions from Corinth," p. 395.

76. See Liddell and Scott, *Greek English Dictionary,* III.b.

77. Taylor and West, "The Euryclids in Latin Inscriptions from Corinth," p. 395, state that γένους Σεβαστῶν refers to 'the living Augustus', but it is clear that the phrase covers more of the imperial family than the reigning emperor.

78. See Fishwick, *"Domus Divina,"* in *The Imperial Cult in the Latin West,* II.1, ch. 4 and pp. 423, 435, for full discussion of the term. See also D. Wardle, "Valerius Maximus on the *Domus Augusta,* Augustus, and Tiberius," *CQ* 50, no. 2 (2000): 479-93.

79. On an important discussion of the construction in the latter writer, see J. L. Moles, "The Career and Conversion of Dio Chrysostom," *JHS* 98 (1978): 91, citing examples *Or.* 31.11, 77/78.34 and also Epictetus, *Discourse* 4.1.51.

Writings likewise reflect this convention when it refers to 'neither other so-called gods . . . only God'.[80] Tertullian, the Christian apologist (*c.* A.D. 150-222), also wrote that 'the so-called gods are of course mere names', for they were not divine.[81]

Paul here refers to the popular but inappropriate designations by Corinthian citizens who venerated the Caesars as gods and lords. He is indicating they are definitely erroneously designated as such.[82] Therefore the description of the gods 'so-called' does not mean that Paul was acknowledging their divinity but rather that these human beings were popularly but wrongly so designated.[83] The use of 'either' 'or' (εἴτε . . . εἴτε) with respect to the gods meant that the reference was to deceased as well as to living members of the imperial family. The term 'lord' enjoyed substantial use in this era.[84]

Then follows the clause 'for even as (καὶ γὰρ ὥσπερ) there are many gods and many lords' (8:5). The connectives, καὶ ὥσπερ, are to be translated 'even as'.[85] At this point Paul draws a clear distinction between 'the so-called gods in heaven and on earth' and the multiplicity of gods with their cults and statues reflecting the pluralism of cultic life of Corinth. The latter are, as he says, 'many gods and many lords'.[86] Therefore Paul had specific gods in mind (8:5).

Furthermore, some Christians as a matter of their 'right' (ἐξουσία) were reclining while feasting as was the custom, and doing so in a specific temple or in its precincts that were connected to the veneration of imperial divinities and not just those in any temple. They were not there to offer up sacrifices on an altar but were reclining at a meal in a particular temple. Later we will return to a discussion of known locations, but here we explore the possible further identification of imperial 'gods in heaven and on earth'.

---

80. *The Hermetic Writings* 2.14.

81. Tertullian, *De idolatria* 15.

82. λέγω, Liddell and Scott, *Greek English Dictionary,* #10.

83. Paul's statement cannot be taken to mean 'a concession of the existence of many gods and lords [which] was not necessarily incompatible with Jewish monotheism'. It was not 'as emphatic a qualification of the monotheism of [v. 4] as Paul could have made as a Christian', *contra* P. A. Rainbow, *Monotheism and Christology in 1 Corinthians 8:4-6* (Oxford University D.Phil., 1987), p. 132, and J. C. Hurd, *The Origins of 1 Corinthians* (London: SPCK, 1965), p. 125.

84. J. D. Fantin, *"Kyrios Christos* and *Kyrios Kaisar:* Christ's Challenge to the Living Caesar," in *Lord of the Entire World: Lord Jesus, a Challenge to Lord Caesar? New Testament Monograph* 31 (Sheffield: Sheffield Phoenix Press, 2011), ch. 5.

85. See καὶ ὥσπερ in the Liddell and Scott entry under ὥσπερ.

86. Pausanias, the second-century traveller of religious sites who visited Corinth, records the proliferation of statues and temples. *Description of Greece* 2.3.1.

(iii) Identifying the 'Genius/δαίμον'

To whom was Paul referring when, in his response to their questions about 'food offered to idols', he later wrote, 'But that which they offer, they offer to δαιμονίοι and not to God. I do not want you to be participants with δαιμονίων. It is not possible to drink the cup of the Lord and the cup of the δαιμονίων. You cannot partake of the table of the Lord and the table of δαιμονίων' (10:20-21). He is contrasting the 'cup' and the 'table' of the Lord with our Greek term 'demons'. Was the latter a non-specific reference or just encompassing pagan divinities generally in Corinth?

The significance of the term δαιμονίον has been discussed on the grounds of an implied or stated connection with the demonic world that was the referent also in the Gospels.[87] Should the terms 'god' (θεός) and 'demon' (δαιμονίον) be taken as synonymous in this discussion (1 Corinthians 8 and 10)? Is the reference to 'demons' correct as is implied in the generally accepted rendering in English? There are a number of indications in the text that would suggest the answer is in the negative and the latter term refers to the imperial *genii*.

Δαίμων and its diminutive δαιμονίνον were used positively in the Graeco-Roman world, over against some in the Jewish world of Paul's day who saw the term having a 'demonic' reference. Varneda notes that when used in a good sense, 'the idea of δαίμων was intimately linked to that of god or his providence over mankind. Naturally, when one says that the δαίμων is positive, one means that it helps people in a favourable fashion'.[88] Josephus, the Jewish historian writing in Rome, also used the term positively. When he wished to speak negatively, he chose κακοδαίμων and its cognate (κακοδαμενέω).[89]

---

87. See G. J. Riley, "Demon," in *The Dictionary of Deities and Demons in the Bible,* ed. K. van der Toorn, B. Becking and P. W. van der Horst, DDD (Leiden: E. J. Brill, 1999²), pp. 235-40, esp. p. 235, for a cursory treatment of the use of the term from Homer and Plato onwards. Riley quickly identifies the δαίμων with evil spirits (1 Cor. 10:21-2). Cf. P. Lampe, "Die dämonologischen Implikationeen von 1 Korinther 8a und 10 vor dem Hintergrund paganer Zeugnisee," in *The Demonology of Israelite-Jewish and Early Christian Literature in Context of Their Environment,* ed. H. Lichtenberger, A. Lange and K. F. D. Römheld (Tübingen: J. C. B. Mohr Siebeck, 2003), pp. 584-99, where he argues that Paul's prohibition was rooted in his idea that the meat was inhabited by demons.

88. P. V. I. Varneda, "The Theory of Historical Cause," *The Historical Method of Flavius Josephus* (Leiden: E. J. Brill, 1986), ch. 1, p. 45, n. 211.

89. For positive references in Josephus, *Jewish War* 2.457, 3.341, 485, 4.217, 622, 5.502, 6.59, 252, 296, 7.318, *JA,* 16.210 and also his use of the negative term κακοδαίμων, *Bellum*

This term and its cognates in extant literature of the Graeco-Roman world were not used pejoratively. Dio Chrysostom (*c.* A.D. 40-112) wrote an oration, "Concerning the guiding spirit" (περὶ τοῦ δαιμονος) in which he referred to the good *daimon* (ἀγαθὸν δαίμονα), cf. 'felicity' (εὐδαίμονων). In another discourse entitled, "The wise man is blessed" (ὅτι εὐδαιμων ὁ σοφος), the use of εὐδαίμων was followed by a discussion of δαίμων. To the interlocutor Dio asks of a person being discussed whether he is 'fortunate' or 'unfortunate' — 'Then when a man's spirit is good (ὁ δαίμων ἀγαθός ἐστι), you maintain that a man is "fortunate" (εὐδαίμονα), but when he is bad, that he is "unfortunate" (κακοδαίμονα), do you?' He also asserts that 'the guiding spirit is divine (τὸ δαιμόνιον θεῖν) and good'[90] and went on to argue elsewhere that

> [a]ll things that happen to men for their good are without exception of divine origin (δαιμόνια) and he proceeds to affirm this is true for a seafarer who finds an experienced pilot or a nation or city that finds good leaders. This also applies when a physician arrives in time to save a patient. We must believe that he is a helper come from the god (παρὰ θεοῦ) and if one hears words of wisdom, one must believe that they too were sent by god. For, in general, there is no good fortune (εὔδαιμον), no benefit, that does not reach us in accordance with the will and the power of the gods.[91]

Dobbin, in his edition of Epictetus, suggested, '*Daimon* is a word that resists translation. No English word has its range. Attempts to inventory the different meanings have been made. . . . For the sake of convenience, three can be distinguished: (1) beings intermediate between man and the gods, especially (2) guardian spirits; (3) the faculty of reason, the portion of god implanted in man, his true self.'[92] However, it is clear that Dio Chrysostom, Epictetus and Josephus, all of whom wrote in the same era, did not use it as a pejorative term. Dobbin did not take cognizance of the fact that this term was adopted for divine emperors.

Judaicum, Jewish War 1.545, *Jewish Antiquities* 1.97, *Contra Apion* 1.204, to be possessed by an evil spirit.

90. Dio Chrysostom, *Or.* 25.7, 23.6, 10.

91. Dio Chrysostom, *Or.* 32.14-15 (Vespasian).

92. R. Dobbin, *Epictetus, Discourses Book 1* (Oxford: Clarendon Press, 1998), pp. 153-54, citing Epictetus, *Discourses* 1.15 section 1.11-17.

(iv) Paul Perceived as the Herald of Daimonia *in Athens*

In Athens Paul had 'appeared to be [to some to be] the herald of foreign *daimonia*' (οἱ δὲ ξένων δαιμονίων δοκεῖ καταγγελεὺς εἶναι) (Acts 17:18). The term used here has no pejorative overtone. Luke uses the term δαιμόνιον nineteen times in his Gospel to refer to 'demons' in the negative sense,[93] but because of that it does not *ipso facto* have to be rendered 'foreign demons' given its context here as to who said it and what happened subsequently (17:18). In English translations it has been correctly rendered as 'foreign gods' or 'foreign divinities'. The reason given is 'because he was preaching Jesus and the resurrection' (ὅτι τὴν Ἰησοῦν καὶ τὴν ἀνάστασιν εὐηγγελίζετο) (17:18), and the context suggests the term was not being used in any pejorative sense.

In the famous Athenian trial in 399 B.C. Socrates was accused of 'introducing new *daimonia*'. The charge brought against him by Meletos was that 'Socrates has broken the law by not acknowledging the gods whom the state acknowledges and introducing other new *daimonia*'.[94] Religious issues even in the period of the Roman era were politically sensitive, and therefore the issue needed to be assessed by the Council of the Areopagus.[95] (See pp. 143-46.)

In the case of the Jews *versus* Paul in Caesarea Maritima, the governor, Festus, refers to the Jewish cult as δεισιδαιμονία (Acts 25:19), and it may have had a derisory tone. Given the context it would seem most appropriate now to render it as 'cult' or even 'religion'. Some translators have chosen 'superstition', although more recently 'religion'.[96] Outside the Gospels the term is seldom used.[97] Here the reference is to 'divinities'.[98]

93. Luke 4:33, 35, 41; 7:33; 8:2, 27, 29, 30, 33; 9:1, 42, 49; 10:17; 11:14, 15, 18, 19, 20; and 13:32.

94. Diogenes Laertius (2.40).

95. R. Garland, "Socrates and the New *Daimonia*," in *Introducing New Gods: The Politics of Athenian Religion* (London: Duckworth, 1992), ch. 7.

96. Today, however, the term would be rendered 'religion' in Acts 25:19 as in the New International Version and the English Standard Version.

97. It is used in 1 Tim. 4:1; James 2:19; and Rev. 9:20; 16:14; 18:2, all in a pejorative sense.

98. *Contra* T. Knöppler, "Paulus als Verkünder fremder δαιμόνια. Religionsgeschichtlicher Hintergrund und theologische Aussage von Act 17,18," in *The Demonology of Israelite-Jewish and Early Christian Literature in Context of Their Environment,* ed. Lichtenberger et al., pp. 577-83, who argues that this address cannot be Pauline but should be seen as the product of Hellenized Jews who had converted to Christianity.

(v) The Genius *or* δαίμων *of Corinth*

In this search to identify to whom Paul is referring, it is appropriate to ask how the inhabitants of Corinth, where Latin was the language of officialdom, would have understood this term.[99] Corinthian coins struck early in the Principate of Nero provide evidence that the Latin term *genius* had common currency. The obverse of one coin has the bust of 'Nero Claudius Caesar Augustus', and the reverse side has the names of the two Corinthian magistrates holding that office in A.D. 54-55, M. Acilius Candidus and Q. Fulvius Flaccus. They were customarily named on Corinthian coins with the abbreviation *Gen. Col.*, meaning 'the Genius of the Colony', standing holding a *patera* and *cornucopia*. Another coin has the bust of Agrippina and Augustus with the identical obverse 'Genius of the Colony'.[100]

Octaviae Neronis Augusta was inscribed on a Corinthian coin with a bust of Octavia, along with the same magistrates named on the reverse side and the words 'Genius of the Colony'. The same abbreviation also occurs in the nearby Roman colony of Patria on a coin struck in Nero's time, *'Gen. Col.'*[101] In these circumstances the term would not be understood as 'demon of the colony' by its citizens, but a reference to the 'divine guardian spirit' of Corinth.

(vi) The δαίμων *or* Genius *of Emperors*

On the death of Claudius an edict was issued in Egypt announcing his apotheosis, and Nero on his accession to the Principate was referred to without explanation as the good *daimon*.

> The Caesar who had to pay his debt to his ancestors, god manifest (ἐνφανὴς θεός), has joined them, and the expectation and hope of the world has been declared emperor (αὐτοκράτωρ), the good *genius* of the world (Ἀγαθὸς Δαίμων δὲ τῆς οἰκουμένης) and the source of all

99. All official Corinthian inscriptions in the first century were in Latin, and it was not until the Hellenistic revival under emperor Hadrian that they were rendered in Greek.

100. A. Burnett, M. Amandry and P. P. Ripollès, *Roman Provincial Coinage: From the Death of Caesar to the Death of Vitellius (44 B.C.-A.D. 69)* (London and Paris: British Museum Press and Bibliothèque nationale de France, 1998), cited in *RPC* nos. 1189-91.

101. *RPC* no. 1257.

good things (ἀρχὴ ὤν [μεγιστε] τε πάντων ἀγαθῶν), Nero has been declared Caesar. Therefore ought we all to be wearing garlands and with sacrifices of oxen to give thanks to all the gods.[102]

In the context of the official announcement of the death of Claudius and the accession of Nero, the phrase certainly does not have any negative connotations. This laudatory phrase 'good' *genius* is the apposite translation. This not-yet seventeen-year-old is declared to be 'the expectation and hope of the world and the sources of all good things'. In the light of those accolades in an official edict it would be inappropriate to render the term as 'demon' but rather that of Latin's *genius*.

This is further supported with an official inscription also from the same era as 1 Corinthians.

> With good fortune. Since Nero Claudius Caesar Augustus German-
> icus, imperator, the good *genius* of the world (ὁ ἀγαθὸς δαίμων τῆς
> οἰκουμένης), in addition to all the other benefactions he has conferred
> on Egypt, has exercised his most brilliant foresight (πρόνοια) by send-
> ing us Tiberius Claudius Balbillus as prefect. . . . For it is fitting that his
> god-like favours (ἰσόθεος) inscribed in sacred writings, be remem-
> bered for all time.[103]

So the term was not restricted to Nero's accession but was used during his Principate and that of other emperors.[104] It is of interest that the term 'honours equal to the gods' is either ἰσόθεος or ἰσοδαίμων in Greek.[105]

Usage is further supported from numismatic evidence from Alexandria, where Nero was promoted as the good *daimon*. A number of coins were issued there annually from A.D. 56 to 60 with the abbreviations Νεο. ἀγαθ. δαιμ. In between A.D. 66 and 68 the elided term ἀγαθαδαιμον was used, which is further evidence of its positive connotations. It was also part of propaganda promoting the good 'genius' (δαίμων) for the imperial cult.[106]

---

102. *P.Oxy.* 1021 (A.D. 54), *Select Papyri* 2. 235.

103. *OGIS* 666 (Memphis, Egypt). The godlike favours are those of the prefect Tiberius Claudius Balbillus, appointed by Nero.

104. There are ninety-three examples of the phrase ἀγαθὸς δαίμων in *Duke Documentary Papyri*.

105. For evidence, see entries cited in Liddell and Scott, *Greek English Dictionary*, 9th edition.

106. *RPC* nos. 5210, 5219, 5230, 5240, 5249, 5260, 5305, 5320.

In Caria in Asia, the cult to the *Agathoi Daimones* had long existed, so the term was not seen as a negative one in the East even before Roman times.[107]

> Among imperial issues, the coins of Nero (54-68 A.D.) excel all others, never to be surpassed for their variety and importance, as well as their artistic quality. It is interesting to note that for the first time in imperial numismatics, the *genius* of the emperor, sacrificing at the altar, takes the form of a youth, like the *genius* of the Roman people.[108]

Fishwick also has made important observations on the use of this term in relation to his discussion of the imperial cult — 'the *genius* is a divinity, much resembling the Greek δαίμων, which is worshipped along with other deities.'[109] Orr also notes that 'the earliest references in literature make it abundantly clear that the *genius* is a divinity, much resembling the Greek δαίμων'.[110] Gradel has argued that Claudius and not Nero introduced the cult of the *genius* of the living emperor.[111]

Tertullian (*c.* A.D. 150-222) provides important second-century evidence confirming the nexus between the Latin and Greek terms and its diminutive in relation to the emperor because, he asserts, this was widely understood.

> [W]e [Christians] make our oaths, too, not by 'the *genius* of the Caesar' but by his health, which is more august than any *genius (augustior omnibus geniis)*. Do you not know that *genius* is a name for *daemon*, or

107. Price, *Rituals and Power,* p. 36, translates the phrase as 'Good Spirits' because that is how this cult that was exclusive to Caria was named. *P.Mich.* 203 (A.D. 98-117) is a letter from Saturnilus to his mother informing her 'that I have another son whose name, the gods willing, is *Agathos Daimon*'.

108. F. Alves, *Portugal from Its Origins through the Roman Era* (Lisbon: Mosaico, 1989), p. 73.

109. Fishwick, "Genius and Numen," in *The Imperial Cult* II.1, ch. 1, p. 382. See also his "Genus and Numen," *Harvard Theological Review* 62 (1969): 358ff., and earlier E. Owen, "Δαίμων and Cognate Words," *JTS* 32 (1931): 133-53. D. Fishwick, "Addendum," in *The Imperial Cult in the Latin West* (Leiden: E. J. Brill, 2005), III.4, states, 'the Hellenistic practice of pouring a libation to the ruler's *daimon* at meal times rather suggests an offering to his *genius*', p. 249.

110. D. G. Orr, "Roman Domestic Religion: The Evidence of the Household Shrines," *ANRW* 16, no. 2 (1978): 1570, n. 77, with bibliography.

111. Gradel, "The Emperor's *Genius* as a State Cult," in *Emperor Worship and Roman Religion,* ch. 7.

in the diminutive *daemonium*? *(Nescitis genios daemonas dici et inder diminutiva voce daemonia.)*. . . . We respect the judgment of God in the Emperors, who has set them over the nations . . . but [he adds ironically] *daemons* or *geniuses,* we are accustomed to exorcise, in order to drive them out of men — not to swear by them and so give them the honor of divinity *(divinitatis).*[112]

As a Christian writer, Tertullian reverts in his concluding statement to the gospel meaning of 'demons'. It is significant that he indicates it is obvious what the Greek equivalent is for the Latin term. He also comments that Christians did not swear oaths on 'the genius' or *daemonium* of the emperor but shows clearly that others did so as the norm in the culture.[113] When Tertullian was but a youth, Saturninus, proconsul of Africa, declared in the face of claims made by Christians whom he interrogated, 'Our religion is a simple one: we swear by the *genius* of our lord the emperor and we offer prayers for his health, something you too should do.'[114]

There is certainly substantial extant evidence to require the reconsideration as to whether the term δαιμονίον in 1 Corinthians 10:20-21 should not be rendered as *'genius'* with reference to the divine imperial family on earth, in particular Nero. Gradel has argued that while the *genius* of Augustus was not a state god, the entry of such into a cult of the living emperor occurred under Claudius rather than Nero.[115] In "The Emperor's Genius in State Cult," Gradel shows that the veneration of the *genius* of the *paterfamilias* of Roman households was transposed into the *genius* of Augustus and then, in the time of Claudius, into the imperial cultic celebrations.[116]

This was confirmed on the anniversary of the accession of Nero in A.D. 58. The Arval Brothers, a college in Rome consisting of twelve mem-

---

112. Tertullian, *Apology* 32.2-3.

113. J.-M. Carbon, 'ΔΑΡΡΩΝ ΔΑΙΜΩΝ: A New Inscription from Mylasa,' *Epigraphica Anatolica* 37 (2005): 1-6.

114. Cited by C. Ando, *Imperial Ideology and Provincial Loyalty in the Roman Empire* (Berkeley: University of California Press, 2000), pp. 394-95.

115. Gradel, *Emperor Worship and Roman Religion,* pp. 162ff., 187ff.; Fishwick, *Imperial Cult in the Latin West: Provincial Cult,* III.3, p. 363, argued for Nero but in Fishwick, *Imperial Cult in the Latin West: Provincial Cult,* III.4, p. 250, he supports the redating to the time of Claudius.

116. Gradel, *Emperor Worship and Roman Religion,* ch. 7.

bers elected annually from senatorial families, offered up the following imperial sacrifices.

> L. Salvius Otho Titianus, chairman of the college, sacrificed in the name of the Arval Brothers on the Capitol for the [anniversary of the] accession of Nero Claudius Caesar Augustus Germanicus: to Jupiter a steer, to Juno a cow, to his [i.e., Nero's] *Genius* a bull *(Genio ipsius taurum),* to *Divus Augustus* a steer, to *Diva Augusta* a cow, to *Divus Claudius* a steer.[117]

Here a distinction is drawn between sacrifices 'for the accession' of Nero and at the same time a bull sacrificed 'to his genius'.[118] Furthermore —

> under the mastership of the Imperator Nero Claudius Caesar Augustus for the second time, father of the fatherland, the deputy-master, Marcus Aponius Saturninus in the name of the college of Arval brethren sacrificed . . . for the laurel of Imperator Nero Claudius Caesar Augustus Germanicus in the temple for the divine Augustus; to the new divine Augustus a male ox, to the divine Augusta a male ox, to the divine Claudia the virgin a cow, to the divine Poppaea Augusta a cow, a bull to the *genius* of the emperor, Nero Claudius Caesar Augustus Germanicus, to Juno Messalina a cow.[119]

This means that now the *genii* or *daimonia* of the living but not the deceased emperor Claudius would be formally venerated and sacrificed to. This was an innovation for a state god, as the concept of *genius* had formerly been applied in a different way to Augustus.[120]

This survey provides substantial evidence that δαιμόνια or *genii* was used of the emperors in imperial cultic activities in the time of Claudius and had become grist for the mill in the new federal imperial cult incorporated in Corinth.[121]

---

117. *CIL* 6, 2041.

118. Gradel, *Emperor Worship and Roman Religion,* p. 179.

119. *Acta fratrum arvalum,* Fragments (c) col. II, (e).

120. Fishwick, *Imperial Cult in the Latin West: Provincial Cult,* III.4, p. 250.

121. This discussion does not exclude the possibility that this may not have 'demonic' implications in Paul's thinking. Nowhere does he use this term of the nondescript 'principalities and powers'.

III. Corinthian Federal Imperial Cultic Activities

Having established to whom Paul was referring, what then went on at the federal imperial cult celebrations? The Spartiaticus inscription from Corinth is not the only indicator of provincial cultic activities.

Banquets restricted to the privileged were celebrated within the proximity of the temple. It is recorded that, in addition to games, a banquet was given to celebrate Livia's birthday and was attended by the magistrates and priests of Augustus who had been freed and had secured this status by means of a financial consideration.[122] In fact, these freedmen were expected to provide for such occasions. As Fishwick notes, 'To provide feasts and distributions on imperial days was a benefaction to be expected of rich men in general (cf. *IG* 12, *Suppl.* 124) and of imperial priests in particular.'[123]

In 1 Corinthians 8:9 Paul refers emphatically to 'this right of yours' (ἡ ἐξουσία ὑμῶν αὕτη) as the word order shows, having previously explained where it was exercised, i.e., in the temple of the 'so-called gods in heaven and on earth' (8:5). He argues further, 'if anyone [a fellow-Christian] sees you [singular] having this knowledge reclining in an idol temple' (ἐὰν γάρ τις ἴδῃ σὲ ἔχοντα γνῶσιν ἐν εἰδωλείν κατακείνενον) he may be encouraged to do the same, with dire consequences to his or her spiritual life (8:10-12).[124] Paul later charged that some Christians 'sat down to eat and drink and rose up to play', thus involving themselves in 'idolatry' (10:14). So clearly they were feasting in an idol temple.

In the East this feasting took place in the precincts of the imperial temple on what were actually designated as 'the imperial days'.[125] The provincial Council of Asia recorded the holding of banquets.[126] Eighteen

---

122. *CIL* 6, 29682. For discussion see Fishwick, *Imperial Cult in the Latin West*, II.1, p. 587.

123. Fishwick, *Imperial Cult in the Latin West*, II.1, pp. 585-86.

124. Κατάκειμαι refers to reclining to eat at the table. For evidence of the use of the cognate δειπνῆσαι εἰς λείνην τοῦ κυρίου Σεραπιδος 'asks you to dine at a banquet of the Lord Serapis' and discussion of the presence of the god on such occasions, see G. H. R. Horsley, "Invitations to the *kline* of Sarapis," in *New Documents Illustrating Early Christianity: A Review of Greek Inscriptions and Papyri Published in 1971* (Sydney: The Ancient History Documentary Research Centre, Macquarie University, 1981), pp. 5-9.

125. For examples see *SEG* 13, 258, 39-40 (Sytheum) *OGIS* 524 = IGR 4, 1257 (Thyatira), cited in Price, *Rituals and Power*, p. 105.

126. Friesen, *Twice Neokoros: Ephesus, Asia and the Cult of the Flavian Imperial Family*, pp. 22-23.

priests of the Divine Augustus and *Roma* from A.D. 19-20 to 36-37 are each recorded as having given public banquets.[127] Livy noted that tables were set up in the forum. The 'table' (τραπέζης) Paul refers to in 1 Corinthians 10:21 proves it was a banquet.[128]

Pergamum also had a provincial imperial cult, and the decree cited below indicates that sacrifices were offered to imperial gods as well as to 'festivals and feasts'. The information agrees basically with what we know happened during the provincial imperial cult in Pergamum with an official decree of the Assembly of Asia.

> Since one should annually make clear display of one's piety and of all holy, fitting intentions towards the imperial house, the choir of all Asia, gathering at Pergamum on the most holy birthday of Sebastos Tiberius Caesar god, performs a task that contributes greatly to the glory of Sebastos in hymning the imperial house and performing sacrifices to the Sebastean gods and conducting festivals and feasts.[129]

Fishwick's observation may well explain why it was so desirable for the Roman citizens of Corinth to indulge themselves at such feasts. 'The end result was that sacrifices became more and more a pretext for a good meal, religious anniversaries simply an occasion for a free dinner when one might indulge oneself in over-eating and over-drinking' and records that 'inscriptions and papyri confirm that games and banquets were a staple appurtenance of major festivals of the imperial cult throughout the empire'.[130] This certainly resonates with the festive mood of Israel's indulgence that Paul parallels in Exodus 32:6 — 'as it is written, "The people sat down to eat and drink and rose up to amuse themselves"' (10:7).

The established convention in imperial cult feasts of inviting the *genii* to be present is witnessed at the feast of a departed emperor and the reigning Tiberius. In A.D. 18 an inscription written after the death of Augustus and the awarding of his perpetual divinity in the reign of Tiberius records the protocol for such imperial feasts. 'And that celebrating the birthdays of Augustus and Tiberius, before the magistrates (*decurions*) go to eat, their

---

127. S. Mitchell, "The Celts and the Impact of Roman Rule," in *Anatolia: Land, Men, and Gods in Asia Minor* (Oxford: Clarendon Press, 1993), I, p. 108.

128. Livy, 39.46.3. For an example in Ancyra, see Fishwick, "Banquets," in *Imperial Cult in the Latin West*, II.1, p. 586.

129. *IGR* 4, 1608c = *I.Eph.* VII 2, 3801, cited in Price, *Rituals and Power*, p. 105.

130. Fishwick, *Imperial Cult in the Latin West*, II.1, pp. 585, 587-88.

geniuses (genii) [the emperor's] should be invited to feast with incense and wine at the altar of Augustan divinity.'[131]

Paul's explicable objections to this are further reflected in his statement, 'I do not wish you to be in partnership with *daimonia* (κοινωνοὺς τῶν δαιμονίων)' (10:20). Such a compromise would bring Corinthian Christians into confrontation with their Lord, as it had done in Old Testament times, hence the reason to 'flee' idolatry by not attending these temple feasts (10:7-22).

Important evidence of these festivities comes from a later first-century source. A copy of an official petition from the city of Argos, a member of the Achaean League, concerned these same celebrations in Corinth. It refers to the expensive purchase of bears and panthers for its 'hunting shows' and not for gymnastic or musical contests as was the preference of Argos. Its importance also rests in the disclosure of annual levies imposed on Argos as a share of the costs of these lavish celebrations, which continued to be held in Corinth.[132]

All the cities of the Achaean League were levied with a contribution towards the costs of staging these events. That later became a point of official complaint by another the city in the League, Argos, because of the financial burden they felt, having already incurred the costs for their local imperial cult celebrations. Its citizens formally objected in particular to the extravagance of the wild beast shows that accompanied the celebrations, given their own financial situation and their prior obligations to host their own local games. An unnamed but notable Greek provincial who had connections with the governor agreed to use his influence to secure an audience with the governor, whether through friendship or as part of the governor's legal retinue.[133] Argos had lost its opportunity to appeal against the levy because its city advocate had been remiss, missing the cutoff date, hence the attempt to seek to redress this through a provincial official. The costs have been seen to be substantial by imperial priests, and the example cited is from the local imperial cult as in Camulodunum (Colchester), where there was a temple to Claudius according to Tacitus. He noted that 'the priests [in Camulodunum], chosen for its service, were bound under

131. *ILS* 154. The reference in the invitation is to the emperors and not the magistrates.

132. See Spawforth, "Corinth, Argos, and the Imperial Cult," pp. 211-32, for this neglected evidence of their complaint.

133. See *Letter* 198, 409. Spawforth, "Corinth, Argos, and the Imperial Cult," pp. 228-30, for the funding of the cult.

the pretext of religion to pour out their fortunes like water'.[134] With respect to the expenses incurred in the extravagant Corinthian celebrations, they are clearly borne not by the high priest but by the cities in the League as the extant evidence has shown.

It is understandable, given the prestige and the sheer extravagance of such celebrations, that some Christians whose social status entitled them to participate rationalized their participation, justifying their decision on the theological premise that 'an idol is nothing, and that there is no God but one . . . but for us there is one God the Father . . . and one Lord, Jesus Christ' (8:4, 6). While they could not be accused of monolatry, i.e., acknowledging that other gods existed alongside of theirs, they were guilty of severely compromising their faith by drinking from the cup to the divine *genii* of the Caesars 'in heaven and on earth' who were regarded by their compatriots as present and feasting with them at the table (10:20-22). Hence Paul's binding commands: 'Wherefore my beloved, you must flee idolatry' (Διόπερ ἀγαπητοί μου, φεύγετε ἀπὸ τῆς εἰδωλολατρίας) (10:14) and 'whether you eat or drink, or whatever you do, you must do all to the glory of God' (πάντα εἰς δόξαν θεοῦ ποιεῖτε) (10:31) — something they clearly could not have claimed to be doing by attending these imperial cultic feasts and the entertainment provided in conjunction with the wider celebrations in Corinth.

---

134. Tacitus, *Annals* 14.31. Fishwick, *Imperial Cult in the Latin West: Provincial Cult,* III.1, pp. 77-82, questions the interpretation that the expenses were incurred by the high priest and not a wider constituency in this city.

CHAPTER 9

Avoiding Divine Honours:
Some Galatian Christians' Strategy

Of the province of Galatia, Mitchell in his *Anatolia: Land, Men, and Gods in Asia Minor* has argued that it has yielded the most detailed archaeological evidence on this cult in the Anatolian provinces. A major imperial temple dating from the middle to late Augustan period has been excavated in Pisidian Antioch, the capital of Galatia. Another imperial cultic site in Iconium was also a centre of Paul's missionary endeavour.[1] Friesen records

---

1. S. Mitchell, *Anatolia: Land, Men and Gods in Asia Minor, the Celts in Anatolia and the Impact of Roman Rule* (Oxford: Clarendon Press, 1993), I, p. 104.

This chapter is a revision and expansion of my "The Imperial Cult and the Early Christians in Pisidian Antioch (Acts 13 and Galatians 6)," in *Actes du 1er Congrès International sur Antioche de Pisidie*, ed. T. Drew-Bear, M. Tashalan and C. M. Thomas (Lyon: Université Lumière-Lyon, 2002), pp. 67-75. It adds primary evidence of the Gentiles' total abhorrence of circumcision and the Jewish defence of the practice. It also evaluates and incorporates some aspects of the interpretations of Justin K. Hardin, *Galatians and the Imperial Cult: A Critical Analysis of the First-Century Social Context of Paul's Letter*, WUNT 237 (Tübingen: Mohr Siebeck, 2008), especially the threat of the agitators to break ties with uncircumcised Gentile believers unless they underwent circumcision and the imperial cultic activities, pp. 111ff., and for A. V. Prokhorov's critique of his discussion, "Taking the Jews out of the Equation: Galatians 6:12-17 as a Summons to Cease Evading Persecution," *JNTS* 36, no. 2 (2013): 172-88, in which he rejects Hardin's interpretation. He adds a section, "Suggested Improvements to Winter's Theory," pp. 180-84, arguing it was 'not a Jewish Christian and Gentile Christian conflict but an 'intra-Gentile' one that revolved around the Roman imperial cult veneration and their fomenting the Galatian Christians' crisis. It is conceded that these Christian agitators could be both Jews and proselytes prior to becoming Christians or the latter after their conversion who argued for the observance of the Torah for the preservation from persecution of the Christian communities but primarily for their own protection. The focus of this chapter is on the nexus between divine honours for the Caesars and the Galatian Christians' response.

that since 25 B.C., some seventy years before the arrival of Christianity, a provincial temple had operated in Galatia for *Roma* and Augustus and not just local temples in its cities.[2] Furthermore, an inscription recording imperial cultic activities incorporated into diverse festive occasions in Ancyra in Galatia over a long period of time bears witness to the fact that feasts, games, bull fights, gladiatorial contests, and chariot and horse races were at the forefront of imperial cult celebrations.[3] (See p. 24.)

Paul and Barnabas had spearheaded the first Christian mission to Pisidian Antioch that resulted in Gentiles, as well as Jews, embracing the Christian message. This stirred up those who were loyal Jews, some of whom had access to 'women of high status and the chief men of the city', with the latter orchestrating the evangelists' eviction from this Roman colony (Acts 13:50). Thus later, when Paul was returning to Antioch via Lystra and Iconium encouraging converts to continue in the faith, he forewarned them 'that it is necessary also through many tribulations to enter the kingdom of God through many difficulties' (καὶ ὅτι διὰ πολλῶν θλίψεων δεῖ ἡμᾶς εἰσελθεῖν εἰς τὴν βασιλείαν τοῦ θεοῦ) (14:21-22).[4]

Gentile Christians were under great pressure to embrace an ethnic Jewish identity as proselytes. This manipulation came not from without but from within the Christian community. The Letter to the Galatians records a summary of the arguments that some Christians had mounted in order to pressure all Gentile Christians to undergo the rite of circumcision. Jews had skilfully adapted to the reality of their Roman conquerors by offering up a daily sacrifice to their God in their temple in Jerusalem for the emperor's safety that was within the parameters of their sacrificial system. (See pp. 98-100.) Diaspora Jews did the same by showing loyalty to the Caesars in their synagogues. (See pp. 110-11.) This strategy would secure for all Christians living in the province, and not least of all the agitators themselves, the avoidance of any possible persecution for not participating in rituals connected with imperial cult veneration.

2. S. J. Friesen, *Twice Neokoros: Ephesus, Asia and the Cult of the Flavian Imperial Family* (Leiden: E. J. Brill, 1993), p. 27.

3. *OGIS* 533.

4. S. Mitchell concludes rightly that 'there is virtually nothing to be said for the north Galatian theory'. The letter 'was certainly addressed to the Galatian churches which Paul had evangelised in the south of the province'. "Christian Origins," in *Land, Men, and Gods in Asia Minor*, II, pp. 3-4, *pace* the South Galatian theory intensively argued by C. Breytenbach, *Paulus und Barnabas in der Provinz Galatien: Studien zu Apostelgeschichte 13f: 16,6: 18,23 und der Adressaten des Galaterbriefs* (Leiden: E. J. Brill, 1996).

It only emerges at the end of the Galatian letter that Paul exposed the motive of the Christians who were putting the pressure on other believers. He declared emphatically they were doing this for one sole reason — 'only' (μόνον) and then explains why 'in order for the cross of Christ they would not be persecuted' (ἵνα τῷ σταυρῷ τοῦ Cριστοῦ μὴ διώκωνται) (6:12). By providing Gentile converts with an officially recognized *persona* these Christians were thereby securing the requisite self-protection by belonging to ethnically identifiable Jewish groups.

The avoidance tactic suggested here will be explored by examining (I) extant evidence for the reaction of the wider society to Jewish circumcision as a totally repugnant rite; (II) traditional first-century Jewish arguments promoting and defending this rite recorded by Philo of Alexandria, a Hellenistic Jew (*c.* 20 B.C.-*c.* 50 A.D.); (III) indicators of the arguments for, and actions taken by, some Christians aimed at compelling all Gentile fellow believers to be circumcised and keep the Torah in order to give them a legal identity; and (IV) Paul's exposure of their real motive behind forming ethnically identifiable 'associations' of Christian Jews and proselytes in Galatia.

I. Reactions to Jewish Circumcision in First-Century Roman Society

The one major social stigma associated with being Jewish men in the first-century world was male circumcision. Traditionally non-Jews had long regarded the foreskin of the male genitals as a sign of beauty, not only in the Greek period but also in the Roman era. Hodges explores the primary evidence for this in his seminal article, "The Ideal *Prepuce* in the Ancient Greece and Rome: Male Genital Aesthetics."[5] He has shown the importance of the genitals as 'iconographic representation of male excellence'.[6]

In his medical textbook Galen (129 A.D.-*c.* 200) records something of the idealized Greek perception of the male image.

Nature out of her abundance ornaments all the members, especially in man. In many parts [of the body] there is manifest ornamentation,

---

5. F. M. Hodges, "The Ideal *Prepuce* in Ancient Greece and Rome: Male Genital Aesthetics and Their Relation to *Lipodermos,* Circumcision, Foreskin Restoration and the *Kynodesme,*" *Bulletin of the History of Medicine* 75 (2001): 376-405.

6. Hodges, "The Ideal *Prepuce* in Ancient Greece and Rome," p. 376.

though at times this is obscured by the brilliance of their usefulness. The ears show obvious ornamentation, and so, I suppose, does the skin called the prepuce at the end of the penis.[7]

The foreskin was seen to be of such importance that, when damaged, ancient medical textbooks provided details of surgical procedures for its restoration. Antyllus, a second-century writer, refers to this operation being done 'as a result of some accident'.[8] Aulus Cornelius Celsus (*c.* 25 B.C.–*c.* A.D. 50) noted that the foreskin was sometimes damaged in the rigors of sporting activity and detailed how it could be repaired.[9] He also conceded that surgery for its removal was necessary in certain instances of severe complications from disease.

> Sometimes through such ulceration the penis is so eaten away underneath the foreskin that the glans falls off; in which case the foreskin itself must be cut away all round. It is the rule, whenever the glans or any part of the penis has fallen off, or has been cut away, that the foreskin should not be preserved.[10]

Given the evidence that the foreskin was seen as a sign of male beauty, it is understandable that contemporaries of a Jew whose circumcision was exposed naturally ridiculed him. Martial (A.D. 40-*c.* 102) records that Menophilus always wore a large sheaf (*fibula*) to disguise his circumcision in the gymnasium.

> I had supposed, as we often bathe together, that he was anxious to spare his voice, Flaccus. But while he was in a game in the middle of the sports ground with everybody watching, the sheath slipped off the poor soul; he was circumcised.[11]

Elsewhere he refers in derogatory terms to an unnamed poet, twice calling him the 'circumcised one' — the person was clearly Jewish because Martial adds he was 'born in Jerusalem'.[12]

---

7. Galen, *On the Usefulness of the Parts of the Body* 2.529.
8. Paul of Aegena, 6.53, citing the lost work of Antyllus.
9. Celsus, *De Medicina* 2.275.
10. Celsus, *De Medicina* 2.275.
11. Martial, *Epigram* 7.82. For other highly derogatory comments see 7.35.55.
12. Martial, "On a Jew, a rival poet," *Epigram* 94.

Circumcision was the distinguishing mark of male Jews and the cause of demeaning comments as evidenced in Paul's day. Petronius (*c.* A.D. 27-66) in his *Satyricon* reveals his racial prejudice when he states ironically, 'please circumcise us so that we look like Jews' and adds a further derogatory comment, 'He has only two faults, and if he were rid of them he would be simply perfect. He is a Jew and he snores.'[13]

Tacitus (A.D. 56-117), a Roman Senator, reveals his racial prejudice in a lengthy tirade against Jewish distinctiveness, their monotheism and not only the distinguishing mark of circumcision but also their unwillingness to flatter their kings by setting up statues to them.

> [O]ther customs of the Jews are base and abominable and owe their persistence to their depravity. . . . They adopt circumcision to distinguish themselves from other peoples by this difference. Those who are converted to their ways follow the same practice, and the earliest lesson they receive is to despise the gods, to disown their country and to regard their parents, children and brothers as of little account. . . . The Jews conceive of one god only. . . . Therefore they set up no statues in their cities, still less in their temples; this flattery is not paid to their kings, nor this honour given to the Caesars.[14]

In singling out this glaring omission — the requisite 'honour given to the Caesars' — Tacitus refers to the standard ritual act before imperial statues in cities throughout the empire. He indicates the lengths to which Jews went not to replicate rulers in stone, let alone any divine representation of them. Jews disapproved of imperial statues. This was more so because the traditional portrayal of them nude signified they were gods. The portrayal of either category in marble was an anathema because it was idolatrous, as Hallett in "The Nudity and Divine Symbols" of emperors records —

> the emperors never appear nude in Roman historical reliefs. When nude or partly nude figures [in statues of emperors or the deified imperial family] do occur in this genre, they are immediately identified as gods or personifications. . . . [N]ude or part nude images of emperors

---

13. *The Satyricon* 102.13-14, 68.4-8.

14. Tacitus, *Histories* 5.5. Josephus, *Contra Apion* 1.137, 143 records how Apion 'derides the practice of circumcision' but as a 'penalty' had an ulcer that resulted in his having to be circumcised, but the medical operation was not successful and gangrene set in and he died 'in terrible pain'.

are among the best known surviving examples of Roman nude portraiture, and these are quite often furnished with divine attributes, like the eagle, aegis, and the thunderbolt of Jupiter.[15]

A good example of this was located in Corinth, where naked statues of the two adopted sons and nominated heirs of Augustus, Gaius and Lucius Caesar, in a cultic setting have survived.[16] (See p. 189.) In a much later period, after Constantine 'Christianized' the Roman Empire, a bronze statue was cast with him nude as had been the Roman tradition.[17] Philo notes that idols which the Gentiles deified included imperial gods. This ran counter to Jewish instincts reflected in his *Special Laws* and in another discussion of idolatry as the alternative to God.[18]

Juvenal, the Roman poet (the late first century A.D. and early second century), records that circumcision was part of the process by which Gentiles became Jewish proselytes. He saw this as actually 'despising of the laws of Rome'.

> [T]hey get rid of their foreskin. And with their habit of despising the laws of Rome, they study, observe, and revere the Judaic code, as handed down by Moses in his mystic scroll, which tells them not to show the way to anyone except a fellow worshipper and if asked, to take only the circumcised to the fountain.[19]

In the reign of Hadrian (A.D. 117-38) the focus was on the revival of Greek culture. It included the withdrawal of the right even of the Jews to perform circumcision, which was classified under the laws forbidding castration.[20]

---

15. C. H. Hallett, "The Nudity of the Gods," in *Roman Nudity: Heroic Portrait Statuary 200 BC–AD 300* (Oxford: Oxford University Press, 2005), esp. pp. 172-83 and 223-24.

16. Hallett, "The Nudity of the Gods," plate 98. For a recent discussion of the Julian basilica as an imperial cult veneration site, see Paul D. Scotton, "A New Fragment of an Inscription from the Julian Basilica at Roman Corinth," *Hesperia* 74, no. 1 (2005): 99-100.

17. J. Bardill, *Constantine, Divine Emperor of the Christian Golden Age* (Cambridge: Cambridge University Press, 2011).

18. Philo, *Special Laws* 1.344 with reference to those who ascribe divinity to their respective idols and 'deify reason'. This form of ἐκθειόω is used elsewhere in Philo in *The Posterity of Cain* 115.l.5 and *Confusion of Tongues* 173.l.2.

19. Juvenal, *Satire* 14.100-104. The fountain refers to baptism as part of the initiation of proselytes.

20. In a later period, circumcision of Gentiles was illegal; see E. Mary Smallwood, "The Legislation of Hadrian and Antonius Pius against Circumcision," *Latomus* 18 (1959): 347.

The Digest of Justinian recorded later in the time of Antonius Pius (A.D. 138-61),

> Jews are permitted to circumcise only their sons on the authority of a rescript of the Divine *(divi)* Pius; if anyone shall commit it on one who is not of the same religion, he shall suffer the punishment of a castrator *(castrantis)*.[21]

A legal Roman code of the third century outlined the dire consequences for doing this.

> Roman citizens who suffer themselves or their slaves to be circumcised in accordance with the Jewish custom, are exiled perpetually to an island and their property confiscated; the doctors suffer capital punishment. If Jews shall circumcise purchased slaves of another nation, they shall be banished or suffer capital punishment.[22]

While excising the foreskin of males was long held to be repugnant except for medical reasons, the Romans had tolerated the rite of circumcision on Jewish males, along with their keeping the Sabbath and observing Jewish laws. It was part of Rome's policy of allowing, but not necessarily endorsing, the ancient traditions of the nations it conquered and incorporated into its empire.

II. Traditional and First-Century Arguments Promoting Circumcision

Paul's Christian adversaries in Galatia mounted arguments that were meant to be so compelling that Gentile Christians capitulated. Before searching for clues from the Letter to the Galatians, it is helpful to explore other evidence from that period as to how circumcision had been traditionally defended and promoted by Jews. This is best preserved in the works of Philo, a well-educated, Hellenized Jewish apologist from Alexandria, the capital of the prefecture of Egypt.

21. *The Digest* 48.8.11, cited in A. Linder, ed., *The Jews in Roman Imperial Legislation* (Detroit: Wayne State University Press, 1987), p. 100.

22. Paulus, 'Prohibition of Circumcision of Gentiles', *Sententiae* 5.22.3-4.

He embarked on a lengthy discussion of what he called 'the particular ordinances' in the Mosaic Law, having completed a treatise on that which Israel so valued as the basis of all its laws, i.e., the ten great commands, literally 'words' from God. He argued that the Decalogue encapsulated 'the summaries of the special laws that . . . run through the whole of the legislation'[23] and as the second command, forbidding idolatry or more specifically monolatry, i.e., the worship of one God without denying the legitimate existence of other gods. The Roman Empire's inclusive ideology had serious implications for Jews.

However, there clearly was the need to begin *The Special Laws,* Book I, by first addressing a major issue, namely circumcision. In adopting this strategy Philo was well aware that, for his audience of non-Jewish contemporaries, it was a major impediment for them to come to realize the great value of all instructions in the Mosaic Law not only for the Jewish race but also for all humanity.

Philo acknowledged that his fellow citizens were highly derisory of it. Therefore he asks them to lay aside their prejudice and listen to the traditional arguments of the benefits derived from circumcision as well as the two further ones he added of his own. Hence his salutatory remarks in the introduction.

> I will begin with that which is an object of ridicule among many people. Now the practice that is thus ridiculed, namely circumcision of the genital organs is zealously observed by many other nations, particularly by the Egyptians, a race regarded as pre-eminent for its populousness, its antiquity and its attachment to philosophy. . . . And therefore it would be well for the detractors of which to desist from childish mockery and to inquire in a wiser and more serious spirit into the causes to which the persistence of this custom is due, instead of dismissing the matter prematurely.[24]

'The principal reasons are four in number' according to Philo, who concludes that 'these are the explanations handed down to us from the ancient studies of divinely gifted men' (ἀρχαιολογούμενα παρὰ θεσπεσίοις ἀνδράσιν). He does not identify them by name but indicates that they 'researched deeply the writing of Moses', literally 'no superficial research'

---

23. Philo, *The Decalogue* 29.
24. Philo, *The Special Laws* 1.1-2.

(οὐ παρέργως διηρεύνησαν) and were the most gifted interpreters of the Torah.[25]

The first was that circumcision prevents certain medical conditions.

One is that it secures exemption for the severe and almost incurable malady of the prepuce called anthrax or carbuncle, so named, I believe from that slow fire which it sets up and to which those who retain the foreskin are more susceptible', i.e., the persistent agony it brought to the sufferer.[26]

Next, Philo records the argument that circumcision ensures genital cleanliness.

Secondly, it promotes cleanliness of the whole body as befits the consecrated order, and therefore the Egyptians carry the practice to a further extreme and have the bodies of their priests shaved. For some substances that need to be cleared away collect and secrete themselves in the hair and the foreskin.[27]

Within this argument Philo has an addendum that was particularly relevant to the province of Egypt. The Jewish circumcision procedure was in fact more restrained, or rather not as extreme as that of the Egyptians, who also shaved the whole body as part of the initiation process of those entering their order of priesthood.[28] Long before, Herodotus (c. 484-425 B.C.) commented that some Egyptian religious practices with regard to cleanliness were excessive. 'They practice circumcision for the sake of cleanliness, considering it better to be clean than comely. The priests shave their whole body every other day, in order that no lice or other impure

25. Philo, *The Special Laws* 1.8; N. E. Livesey, *Circumcision as a Malleable Symbol,* WUNT 2, no. 295 (Tübingen: Mohr Siebeck, 2010), p. 46, n. 20, notes the use of this phrase and comparable ones elsewhere in Philo's *corpus*. She suggests that the reference may be to the Jewish patriarchs, Abraham and Isaac. There is no evidence in the Pentateuch that they did so. The possibility is that, like Philo, these were Jewish teachers who before his era defended what would be seen by non-Jews as mutilation of something that in the Greek period was regarded as a sign of beauty.

26. Philo, *The Special Laws* 1.4; F. M. Hodges, "Phimosis in Antiquity," *World Journal of Urology* 17, no. 3 (1999): 133-36, argues it referred to the condition where the foreskin cannot be retracted or stretched over the glans penis. The term φιμός means 'contraction'.

27. Philo, *The Special Laws* 1.5.

28. Philo, *The Special Laws* 1.5.

thing may adhere to them when they engage in the service of the gods.'[29] Philo continues —

> Thirdly, it assimilates the circumcised member to the heart. For as both are framed to serve for generation, thought being generated by the spirit force in the heart, living creatures by the reproductive organ, the earliest men held that the unseen and superior element to which the concepts of the mind owe their existence should have assimilated to it the visible and apparent, the natural parent of things perceived by sense.[30]

Livesey explains this. 'The third reason is that circumcision creates a likeness between the reproductive organ and the heart . . . the circumcised member for the generation of living beings, the heart for the generation of thoughts.' She notes the Old Testament reference to the nexus between the male member and the heart with the metaphor of 'the circumcision of the heart'.[31]

The fourth and final traditional argument was that nations practicing circumcision have a much greater reproduction record. Although Philo does not indicate specifically who they were, he clearly would have included the Jewish race.

> The fourth and most vital reason is its adaption to give fertility of offspring, for we are told that it causes semen to travel aright without being scattered or dropped into the folds of the foreskin and therefore the circumcised nations appear to be the most prolific and populous.[32]

Livesey concludes that 'The first four reasons justify its benefits for health and fertility, over against the charge of ridicule'.[33] Having recorded

29. Herodotus, *Histories* 2.37.

30. Philo, *The Special Laws* 1.6.

31. Livesey, *Circumcision as a Malleable Symbol*, p. 51, citing Lev. 26:41; Deut. 10:16; Jer. 4:4; 9:26; and Ezek. 44:7, 9, and also pp. 111-13 in relation to Paul's discussion in Rom. 2:29.

32. Philo, *The Special Laws* 1.7.

33. Philo, *The Special Laws* 1.7.57. Livesey in ch. 3, "Circumcision in Philo," in *Circumcision as a Malleable Symbol,* p. 44, suggests this discussion is most likely addressed to fellow Jews. However, one cannot ignore the fact that he felt the need to address the enormous prejudice against it at the commencement of this work. It is suggested that this is part of

the wise men's reasons and arguments from the past justifying and defending circumcision, Philo has two further ones.

> To them I would add that I consider circumcision to be a symbol of two things most necessary to our well-being. One is the excision of pleasures that bewitch the mind. For since among the love-lures of pleasure the palm is held by the mating of man and woman, the legislators thought good to cut off the organ which ministers to such intercourse, thus making circumcision the figure of excessive and superfluous pleasure.[34]

The implication is that circumcision was seen as a remedy for sexual indulgence rampant in his day and strongly defended in Philo's day.[35] He records these arguments *verbatim* in his *The Migration of Abraham*.

> It is true that receiving circumcision does indeed portray the excision of pleasure and all passions, and the putting away of the impious conceit (καὶ δόξης ἀναίρεσιν ἀσεβοῦς ἐμφαίνει), under which the mind supposed that it was capable of begetting its own power: but let us not on this account repeal the law laid down for circumcising.[36]

He does not further explain the last comment, which hints at the possibility of rescinding 'the law'. Livesey suggests that Philo refers to it as a law rather than a Jewish custom, and therefore it would be binding on all Jews.[37]
His second argument states —

> The other reason is that a man should know himself and banish from the soul the grievous malady of conceit. For there are some who pride themselves on their power of fashioning as with a sculptor's cunning the fairest of creatures, and in their bragging pride 'consecrated', closing their eyes to the Cause of all that comes into being, though they might find in their families a corrective for their delusion. . . . The evil

---

Philo's broader agenda to convince non-Jews that the Old Testament in its LXX translation is God's gift to all the nations and adopting its precepts brings such blessing to life.

34. Philo, *The Special Laws* 1.8.9.
35. Livesey, *Circumcision as a Malleable Symbol*, pp. 54-55.
36. Philo, *The Migration of Abraham* 16.92.
37. Livesey, *Circumcision as a Malleable Symbol*, p. 70.

belief, therefore, needs to be excised from the mind with any others that are not loyal to God.[38]

Philo's reference to 'consecrated' (ἐξεθείωσαν), a derivative from θεῖος, provides a clue to the attribute of divinity that was given to statues of gods carved in the schools of the skilled sculptors in his day.[39]

His six arguments defending circumcision both ancient and contemporary show that this was a high-profile, contentious issue among Philo's contemporaries in Alexandria. It is not without significance that he felt his last argument was needed in addition to the previous traditional ones. It had implications for imperial statues that were the object of regular veneration in the cities of Galatia.

He concludes with the statement 'so much for these matters' (τούτων μὲν δὴ πέρι τοσαῦτα).[40] Given that his last argument was not unconnected with themes unfolded in his *Special Laws* that deal with Jewish cultic matters in the Torah, the first issue of the 'sole sovereignty of God' is reasonable.[41] However, his *apologia* for circumcision and the priority he knew he had to give to it indicate just how widespread was the prejudice and denigration of the Jews because of it. Why then would Gentile Christians ever consider undergoing circumcision in the light of social consensus revealed in this primary evidence?

III. Pressuring Gentile Christians to Be Circumcised

Before exploring this issue among Galatian Christians, it is important to note that part of Paul's standard apostolic teaching in all the churches was that if one was circumcised on becoming a Christian 'he must not be uncircumcised' (μὴ ἐπισπάσθω). The inverse also applied — that if 'any one was called uncircumcised he must not be circumcised (ἐν ἀκροβυστίᾳ κέκληταί τις μὴ περιτεμνέσθω) (1 Cor. 7:17-18). This teaching was clearly stated — 'only to each as the Lord distributed, each as God called he is to walk' (εἰ μὴ ἑκάστῳ ὡς ἐμέρισεν ὁ κύριος ἕκαστον ὡς κέκληκεν ὁ

---

38. Philo, *The Special Laws* 1.10.

39. Philo's views on statues of gods is negative; see K.-G. Sandelin, "Philo's Ambivalence towards Statues," in *Attraction and Danger of Alien Religion,* Studies in Early Judaism and Christianity (Tübingen: Mohr Siebeck, 2012), p. 67.

40. Philo, *The Special Laws* 3.1.

41. Philo, *The Special Laws* 1.12ff.

θεός), adding, 'and this I ordained in all the churches' (καὶ οὕτως ἐν ταῖς ἐκκλησίας πάσαις διατάσσομαι) (7:17). He explained that 'circumcision is nothing and uncircumcision is nothing; but keeping of the commandments of God' (ἡ περιτομὴ οὐδέν ἐστιν ἀλλὰ τήρησις ἐτολῶν θεοῦ) (7:19). Paul affirms again, 'Each in the calling in which he was called, brothers, in this he must abide with God' (ἕκαστος ἐν ᾧ ἐκλήθη ἀδελφοί ἐν τούτῳ μενέτω παρὰ θεῷ) (7:24).[42] While the *Sitz im Leben* in Galatians was different from that in 1 Corinthians, Paul's teaching on this issue remained unchanged.

Only in the closing section of Paul's Letter to the Galatians does it emerge why this had become such a pressing and major issue for some of the Christians in that province. In Galatians 6:12 what was happening comes to light — 'they themselves are contending it is essential to be circumcised' (οὗτοι ἀναγκάζουσιν ὑμᾶς περιτέμνεσθαι). Paul uses the verb ἀναγκάζω to indicate what was happening to Gentile Christians. It is usually rendered "compel" you to be circumcised'. Liddell and Scott's *Greek English Lexicon* records that when this particular verb, ἀναγκάζω, is followed by the accusative and infinitive it means 'contend that such a thing is necessarily so'.[43] So the action indicates that it was an inevitable and in fact compulsory step that every male Gentile Christian had to take.

The two verbs 'contending to be circumcised' had been used together to describe how Gentiles became and were subsequently seen to be Jews in the time of Herod the Great. Ptolemy in his work "On Herod the King" records of the Idumaeans (who were actually Syrians and Phoenicians) that there were those 'contending as a matter of necessity [they had] to be circumcised' (ἀνακασθέντας περιτέμνεσθαι).[44]

Josephus also writes of the same conquest, that Hyrcanus 'captured all the subdued Idumaeans, allowed them to remain in their country if

---

42. He goes on to declare that Christians must not sell themselves into household servitude for seven years but they must take manumission after this contractual period. He does not indicate any further reasons for asserting that the Corinthian Christians retain their social status but, given the desire of some to climb the social ladder, he rules that such an ambition must not be that of the Christians; see my "St. Paul as a Critic of Roman Slavery in 1 Corinthians 7:21-23," Proceedings of the International Conference on St. Paul and European Civilization, Παύλεια 3 (1998): 339-54.

43. They cite as supporting evidence Plutarch, *Lycurgus* 17.4, Isocrates, *Panegyricus Or.* 4.124, Demosthenes, *Philippica* 40, Xenophon, *Cynegeticus* 10.21.4, Dionysius Halicarnassus, *Roman Antiquities* 6.4.4, Josephus, *Jewish Antiquities* 13.196, and Dio Chrysostom, *Or.* 7.106.

44. Ptolemy, "On Herod the King," fragment n. 28.

they would circumcise the genitals (εἰ περιτέμνοιντο τὰ αἰδοῖα) and would wish to observe the laws of the Jews' (καὶ τοῖς Ἰουδαίων νόμοις χρήσασθαι θέλοιεν). He notes that as they were keen to continue to reside there, the resetting of their way of life was necessary so that 'from that time on they are Jews' (ὥστε εἶναι τὸ λοιπὸν Ἰουδαίους), and 'the Jews kept pressuring these men to be circumcised' (τούτους περιτέμνεσθαι τῶν Ἰουδαίων ἀναγκαζόντων).[45]

This linguistic construction together with Paul's use of the same words provides further clarification of the Galatian Christians' *Sitz im Leben.* Luke records Paul, stating *verbatim,* 'I was constrained to appeal (ἠναγκάσθην ἐπικαλέσασθαι) to Caesar' (Acts 28:19). Translating the verb as 'compelled' in that context would be inappropriate if it implied any external physical constraints either by Porcius Festus or Herod Agrippa II. Rather Paul, on reflection, was aware that it was the only option open to him in his legal case, although later Agrippa is reported to have said to Festus that there was an alternative course of action, i.e., for him to go free if he had not appealed to Caesar, implying there was no case to answer (Acts 26:32).[46] Acts 15:24 records that some Christians who were Pharisees had argued specifically, 'It is necessary [divinely ordained] to circumcise (δεῖ περιτέμνειν αὐτούς παραγγέλλειν τε τηρεῖν τὸν νόμον τοῦ Μωυσέως), and also for them to keep the law of Moses' (15:5).[47]

Within the Letter to the Galatians itself there are two other examples, one of which has the identical verbal construction relating to Jewish customs. It helps reveal the nature of the constraint some Christians were exercising on Gentile fellow believers (6:12). One concerns the absence of any pressure whatsoever being exerted on Titus, who was with Paul and ethnically part Greek, to be circumcised while they were in Jerusalem. 'But not even Titus who was with me, being a Greek, was compelled to be circumcised' (ἀλλ' οὐδεν σὺν ἐμοί Ἕλλην ὤν ἀναγκάσθη περιτμηνθῆναι) (2:3). The other is Paul's use of ἀναγκάζω in his confrontation with Peter in

---

45. Josephus, *Jewish Antiquities* 13.257-58.

46. For a discussion see my "Official Proceedings and Forensic Speeches in Acts 24-26," in *The Book of Acts in Its Ancient Literary Setting,* ed. A. D. Clarke and B. W. Winter (Grand Rapids: Eerdmans, 1993), ch. 11, concerning the integrity of these summaries of legal proceedings.

47. See G. G. Porton, *The Stranger within Your Gates,* Chicago Studies in the History of Judaism (Chicago and London: University of Chicago Press, 1994), chs. 2-6, for a discussion from the Mishnah, Tosefta, early Midrashic Texts, the Palestinian Talmud and the Babylonian Talmud on the centrality of male circumcision for conversion, and "The Conversion Ritual," ch. 8, and "Converts as Newborn Children," ch. 9.

Antioch. He recorded *verbatim* in Galatians 2:14 relating to an important Jewish custom concerning Gentiles — 'if you being a Jew live as do the Gentiles, and not as the Jews, how do you contend [it is necessary] for the Gentiles to live as Jews (πῶς τὰ ἔθνη ἀναγκάζεις ἰουδαιζεξιν)?' In both these instances the pressure was not physical *per se,* but arguments were presented as to why it was absolutely essential for them to undergo circumcision. Peter is reported as having withdrawn from sharing table fellowship with the Gentile Christians, 'fearing the circumcision party' (φοβούμενος τοὺς ἐκ περιτομῆς). His action was a catalyst because 'the rest of the Jews acted insincerely (συνυπερκρίθησαν αὐτῷ) with him, so that even Barnabas was carried away by their insincerity (ὑποκρίσει)' (2:12-13).[48]

When combined with the identical *Sitz im Leben* of the Idumaeans, it can be concluded that in Galatia certain Christians mounted arguments specifically aimed at persuading all male Gentile Christians that it was absolutely essential for them to undergo this rite in order to be in right standing with the authorities in the province of Galatia. There is no evidence that the traditional arguments of the advantages of circumcision of the 'wise' men as recorded by Philo were put forward. It would seem from Paul's arguments in 2:15ff. that the issue was the keeping of the Jewish law, including the rite of circumcision traditionally regarded in other Jewish sources as central. Porton's extensive discussion of substantial evidence from the Mishnah, Tosefta, early Midrashic Texts, the Palestinian Talmud and the Babylonian Talmud clearly shows this.[49] Circumcision was unavoidable.

IV. The Motive and Method of the Circumcision Party Exposed

Is there a precedent for Gentiles being pressured into undergoing circumcision in order to become Jews in a previous era of Jewish history? In the time of Herod the Great (74/73 B.C.-4 B.C.), there was a choice to be made by the Idumaeans. They 'were not Jews originally but . . . having been subjugated by them [the Jews] and as a matter of necessity being circumcised (ἀνακασθέντας περιτέμνεσθαι), contributing taxes of the nation and following the same laws, they were named Jews (ἐκλήθησαν Ἰουδαῖοι)'.[50]

---

48. If the earliest Pauline manuscript reading, P[46], is preferred then the reference to 'certain things' (τίνα) came from James, a reference to the Jerusalem Council's decision (Acts 15:22-29).

49. See Porton, *The Stranger within Your Gates,* chs. 2-6.

50. Ptolemy, "On Herod the King," fragment 28.

Josephus also records that while some of his compatriots were pressuring Gentiles to be circumcised, it was something he never did and he explains why.

> [T]he Jews kept pressuring them to be circumcised (τούτους περι-
> τέμνεσθαι τῶν Ιουδαίων ἀναγκαζόντων) if they wished to live among
> them. I however would not allow any compulsion to be put on them,
> declaring to them 'Everyone ought to worship God in accordance with
> the dictates of his own conscience and not to have any force put upon
> them; and that these men, who had fled to us for protection, ought
> not to be so treated'.[51]

Josephus cites Strabo's account of Aristobulus — 'this man was a kindly person and very serviceable to the Jews, for he acquired additional territory for them, and brought over to them a portion of the Ituraean nation, whom he joined to them by the bond of circumcision.'[52]

The quotations cited above from Ptolemy and Josephus use verbs identical to those Paul uses to describe the pressure being brought to bear on Gentiles by the Christian agitators to undergo the rite of circumcision. The result would mean that Galatian Christians as a whole would have a recognized legal entity that was distinctly Jewish. If all male Christians were circumcised, they could legitimately meet once a week, be seen to be Jewish by following the Torah as a canon by which they lived and also claim that appropriate cultic honours were being given to the Caesars in the temple in Jerusalem within the legitimate parameters of the Jewish faith. (See pp. 99, 109.) Hence, they would not be required to give divine honours in the imperial temples in the province of Galatia.

(i) Tactics Used by Some Galatian Christians

Does Paul throw further light on the strategy adopted by some Christians to persuade fellow believers? Galatians 4:17 records that 'they are zealously seeking you (ζηλοῦσιν) with no good motive (οὐ καλῶς) but they

---

51. Josephus, *The Life of Flavius Josephus* 113, where the reference is to the two nobles from the region of Trachonitis. See also *Jewish Antiquities* 13.318-19; if Itureans wished to remain in Judaea they were 'to be circumcised'.

52. Josephus, *Jewish Antiquities* 13.318-19.

are shutting you out (ἀλλὰ ἐκκλεῖσαι ὑμᾶς) in order that you may seek them' (ἵνα αὐτοὺς ζηλοῦτε).[53] Liddell and Scott record that ζηλόω was also used with respect to persons meaning 'pay zealous court to', citing Galatians 4:17 as an example.

The verb 'to strive after' (ἐκκλεῖσαι) can mean 'to exclude from' and 'to shut out'. They were marginalizing uncircumcised Gentile Christians either literally from their weekly meeting, or socially from fellowship. The ploy of holding them at arm's length was done to make them know that they are not yet fully part of the Christian community. It may not have been dissimilar psychologically to the division in the Jewish temple that had a court for the Gentiles and another for Jews with a sign implying that it excluded those who were not fully proselytized. Not being 'Jewish' meant that Galatian Christians would have to operate in the wider culture without enjoying the identity and concessions that the Claudian decree had recently verified as the right of all Diaspora Jews. (See pp. 103-4.) Hence the manipulative action referred to in 4:17 was deliberately meant to marginalize and isolate the non-circumcised Christians.

Most importantly, they were in no man's land with respect to how acceptable imperial honors were to be given that would fulfill Jesus' edict only 'to render to Caesar the things that were Caesar's' (Mark 12:17). Would they not have to show their loyalty in the imperial cult temples by doing cult to the Caesars past and present as gods? The only alternative open to these Christians was to capitulate to the strong arguments of other Christians, and enter into the Jewish safe-haven through circumcision, operating within the Jewish customs of the 'inner circle'.

Paul had already made reference to the exclusion from Jewish table fellowship when Peter withdrew from eating with Gentiles, as he feared the circumcision party. Such tactics were apparently not dissimilar to those now being employed. Paul records that he had argued with Peter, 'If you, though a Jew, live like a Gentile and not a Jew, how can you force Gentiles to live like Jews?' (Gal. 2:14).[54]

---

53. For this important discussion, see Hardin, *Galatians and the Imperial Cult*, p. 143, who endorses J. M. G. Barclay, *Obeying the Truth: A Study of Paul's Ethics in Galatians* (Edinburgh: T & T Clark, 1988), pp. 59-60.

54. If the reading from the earliest manuscript of Galatians, P[46], is accepted, then the reference is not to 'certain men' but 'certain things' (τίνα) as per James (2:12). This reference is to the rulings of the Jerusalem Council recorded in Acts 15:22-29. It rejected the demand that Gentiles had to be circumcised. The only stipulations they laid on them were 'no greater burden than these requirements: that you abstain from idols, and from blood,

Arguments for essential steps for Galatian Christians to be 'Jewish' had to be substantial and the Torah would be the tool that encompassed the wider observations of the law as 'binding' on Christians. Any social stigma and derision in the baths that were frequented by every stratum of society in the Roman Empire would not outweigh the protection afforded by being Jewish Christians.

(ii) Exposing the Motive of the 'Circumcision' Party

The Christians in Galatia who were involved were doing so as a preventative move. Paul emphasizes that they did it for one purpose and one only. 'Only' (μόνον), i.e., solely — 'in order that they would not be prosecuted for the cross of Christ' (ἵνα τῷ σταυρῷ τοῦ Χριστοῦ μὴ διώκωνται) (6:12). It is important to note that the verb διώκω used in the forensic semantic domain meant to 'prosecute'.

Robinson in his comprehensive work *The Criminal Law of Ancient Rome* records that while it was illegal under Roman law for any association to meet more than once each month, Jews had been specifically exempted in the same legislation enacted by Augustus. They were permitted to meet weekly. Robinson then observes that 'This is one reason why the Christians could hardly have formed legal *collegia*, since they needed to meet weekly for worship; Jews had an exemption'.[55]

Thus to escape possible criminal prosecution in the Roman province of Galatia, the 'circumcision party' would have to be able to show they qualified as a legitimate Jewish 'association'. However, a mixed group of Christian Jews and Gentiles, not Gentile proselytes, provided a reason to take legal action against all Christians as they did not in reality constitute a legal Jewish meeting. If all Gentile Christians could be persuaded to become Jews, then this would protect all Diaspora Christians in the province from any possible breach of Roman law. They had become a homogenous Jewish entity with all its males circumcised. Acts 13:50 records that it was

---

and from what has been strangled, and from sexual immorality. If you keep yourselves from these, you will do well' (15:29).

55. O. F. Robinson, *The Criminal Law of Ancient Rome* (London: Duckworth, 1995), p. 80. For the extensive phenomena of such associations in the East see S. G. Wilson, *Voluntary Associations in the Graeco-Roman World* (London: Routledge, 1996) and O. M. van Nijf, *The Civic World of Professional Associations in the Roman East* (Amsterdam: J. C. Gieben, 1997).

the Jews who stirred the intense public hostility in Antioch against Paul and Barnabas. This was also the case in Iconium (14:5). Again in Lystra they came from Antioch and Iconium specifically to persecute them and bring their mission to a close. It is significant that on returning to Antioch, Paul did not in any way minimize the many tribulations in store for the Galatian Christians (Acts 14:22).

Given the history of the initial Jewish harassment of the emerging Christian movement in Galatia, one can understand the reason for wanting to compel all Christian males to be circumcised. If only all Gentile Christians would observe the Jewish rites and operate within the parameters in daily life, the Christian communities as a whole would not be put in jeopardy, but could gather to meet weekly and personally be exempt from performing imperial cultic honours.

(iii) The Benefits Accruing to Circumcised Gentile Christians

In 6:12 Paul describes the benefits that the circumcision party argued would accrue to all Gentiles undergoing the rite of circumcision. It is normally rendered as 'as many as wish to make a fair show in the flesh' (ὅσοι θέλουσιν εὐπροσωπῆσαι ἐν σαρκί). The verb θέλω was used to indicate a decree or something ordained that had a legal implication. There is a comparable example in an inscription from Ephesus 'and as many as wished to become citizens' (ὅσοι δ᾽ ἂν θέλωσιν πολῖται γενέσθαι).[56]

The intended outcome of this action is indicated as εὐπροσωπῆσαι ἐν σαρκί. This phrase has normally been rendered somewhat enigmatically 'to make a fair show in the flesh'. Given that the foreskin was regarded as a sign of beauty and circumcision was the complete opposite, making the male member 'ugly' by doing something what was equated with castration, it is difficult to see how the outcome of circumcision could ever have been construed as a 'fair show' in the flesh with the male genital organ bereft of its adorning foreskin.

Cognates of εὐπροσωπέω have legal connotations and relate to one's social status and identity. It would support the contention that circumcision would bring about a recognized status for the whole Christian community. Nguyen has undertaken an extensive investigation outside of Galatians into the cognate of 'appearance' based on Paul's dichotomy of

56. I.Eph. 2003.

'the face' (πρόσωπον) also exploring its Greek equivalent in Latin *persona,* as a reference to one's status in society, in contrast to the 'heart' (καρδία), i.e., the real person. The evidence in 2 Corinthians 5:12 highlights this — 'We are not commending ourselves to you again but giving you cause to boast about us, so that you may be able to answer those who boast about your *persona* and not about what is in the heart' (ἵνα ἔχητε πρὸς τοὺς ἐν προσώπῳ καυχωμένους᾿ καὶ μὴ ἐν καρδίᾳ).[57]

The term 'face' (πρόσωπον) originally carried the meaning of 'mask', but by the early first century it was widely used to describe the status of a person. Its Latin equivalent was *persona.* Lohse has suggested that the legal use of the term πρόσωπον for 'person' does not occur in the first century.[58] However, Dionysius of Halicarnassus writing in the time of Augustus used it in its legal sense of the persons whom he represented in court.[59] The idea of 'legal personality', *juristische person* (πρόσωπον), is derived from the word Paul uses in Galatians 6:12.[60]

Schlossmann, whose work formed the basis of Lohse's word study, acknowledged Dionysius of Halicarnassus' use of the term but wrongly dismissed it by attributing it to the influence of Latin.[61] That, however, constitutes no reason for rejecting such a meaning in the Graeco-Roman world of the early empire with its bilingualism. Nédoncelle, in a careful study on πρόσωπον and *persona,* has shown that the Latin term *persona* had this legal connotation in Cicero (106-43 B.C.), and that the range of Latin meanings in Cicero is already found in the Greek works of Polybius (*c.* 200-*c.* 118 B.C.).[62]

Lucian states, 'I do not know what answer you can make to give you

---

57. On Paul's usage in 1 and 2 Corinthians, giving the first-century central function of *persona*/πρόσωπον, see V. Henry T. Nguyen, "Social Identity and Persona," in *Christian Identity in Corinth: A Comparative Study of 2 Corinthians, Epictetus and Valerius Maximus,* WUNT 2, no. 243 (Tübingen: Mohr Siebeck, 2008), ch. 2, and pp. 117-18 for the reference to the legal/social status in Galatians 6:12.

58. E. Lohse, "πρόσωπον," *TWNT* 6, 770.

59. Dionysius of Halicarnassus, *Lysias* 24. See also Demosthenes 13, Thucydides 34, 37.

60. To cite Preisigke's translation. See Diogenes Laertius, *The Lives of Eminent Philosophers* 4.46 and also *BGU* 5114, *l.* 49. Cf. Aristotle, *Politics* 1263b.15, 'Such legislation therefore has an "appropriate appearance",' i.e., it was good legislation.

61. S. Schlossmann, *Persona* und πρόσωπον *im Recht und im christlichen Dogma* (Kiel, 1906), p. 42.

62. M. Nédoncelle, "Prosopon et persona dans l'antiquité classique," *Revue des Sciences Religieuses* 22 (1948): 277-99, at 296, citing Cicero, *De Oratore* 2.102.

a good "face" (εὐπρόσωπός σοι) before your accusers' because of the impossibility of defending the indefensible.[63] Liddell and Scott suggest that the term in Plutarch could refer to a legal personality — 'Why I thought my face to be handsome' (καὶ ἐδόκοον εὐπρόσωπος εἶναι), which is seen as a pun because of physical deformity.[64] Polemon wrote to Menches requesting him to hasten in collecting taxes. 'Regarding the *komogrammateis* whom you mention [a discussion of overcharging for taxes] you will be right in not diminishing the report compared to the first one, in order that we may make a good show (εὐπροσωπῶμεν)'.[65] Given the fact that Polemon was engaged in official business and that his superior had apparently charged more, the verb carries the idea of making the report appear legal.

Having 'a good legal face' was the antonym to having no legal status at all. Diogenes Laertius records that Bion was by birth a citizen of Borysthenes (Olbia). His father was a native of Borysthenes (γένος Βορυσθωνίτης), who 'had no face' (ἔχων οὐ πρόσωπον), i.e., legal status, but only the writing 'on his face' (ἐπὶ τοῦ προσώπου) as he had been branded a slave. It emerges that Bion's father, as a freedman, had cheated the government of revenue and was thus sold into slavery.[66]

Papyri record the use of πρόσωπον to refer to legal persons whether in connection with the laws concerning the division of property according to households and 'not individuals' (μὴ κατὰ πρόσωπον),[67] or with the authorized person in a public liturgy — someone duly elected to office or 'some other [qualified] person', i.e., possessing legal status, a citizen.[68]

The phrase 'having a face' (ἔχων πρόσωπον) is widely used in non-literary sources, especially public inscriptions. There are three hundred examples of the use of this term in the Packard Humanities Institute Classical Inscriptions. When πρόσωπον is combined with the verb 'to have', the references are to the 'legal status' of the person or persons referred to. The phrase 'having legal status' was an indicator of status or rank in the structure of Roman society.[69]

---

63. Lucian, "Apology for the 'Salaried Posts in Great Houses'," 3.
64. Plutarch, *Moralia* 2.458F.
65. *P.Tebt.* 19, *l.* 12.
66. Diogenes Laertius 4.46.
67. *P.Ryl.* 76 *l.* 12 (second century A.D.).
68. *P.Oxy.* 904.l.8; see also *P.Oxy.* 1033.l.8.
69. Nguyen, "Social Identity and *Persona*," ch. 2. On the linguistics for a good legal face see the discussion justifying this approach in my "A Cambridge Lexical Handbook of

If this term is rendered thus in Galatians 6:12, how does circumcision give all Christians a recognized legal status in the first-century Graeco-Roman society? If circumcision epitomized being a Jewish male, then Gentile Christians persuaded to undergo this rite were now legally and socially recognized as Jews in the eyes of the law. We know this from the declaration recorded in the time of Herod of circumcised Idumaeans that 'they were called Jews' (ἐκλήθησαν Ἰουδαῖοι).[70] In that particular instance it was not necessarily that they were calling themselves Jews, but others saw them as such, hence the use of the passive tense to express kinship or legal status, having met the requirements of being Jewish.

Furthermore, if all Gentile Christians in Galatia gave in to the pressure to become Jews and keep the Jewish law, then Christian communities would have the legal right to gather weekly, being rightly identified as a legal Jewish entity. It meant that in any legal challenge they would meet the criterion of being Jewish and thus all Galatian Christians would avoid 'persecution' from legal 'prosecution' (6:12).

Here Paul has given a clue when he states the sole reason 'only' (μόνον) was an avoidance tactic so that a legal case could not be mounted against them. The verb διώκω has traditionally been rendered as 'persecute', but it has a dual meaning. In fact the major entry in Liddell and Scott for διώκω is 'to prosecute' through the due process of the law in a court.[71] Hence it is credible to translate this passage 'in order that they may not be prosecuted for the cross of Christ' (ἵνα τῷ σταυρῷ τοῦ Χριστοῦ μὴ διώκωνται). All Christians there would be exempt from individually rendering divine honours to the Caesars on imperial cultic and festive occasions.

Is it that some Galatian Christians feared this possibility? They knew that in the early days of the Christian mission some had suffered at the hands of officials. Furthermore, Paul and Barnabas were severely treated and expelled from all the centres in Galatia where they preached (Acts 13:50; 14:5, 19). Luke records that Paul had also issued a warning that troubles lay ahead and that it was through much suffering that they would enter

---

New Testament Greek: Social Settings, Semantic Domains and First-Century Synonyms," in *Actas do Colóquio Lexicography and Lexical Semantics: Questions at Issue in the Making of a Greek Lexicon* (Lisbon: Centro de Estudos Clàssicos, 2008), pp. 93-105.

70. Josephus, *Jewish Antiquities* 13.258.

71. It is of interest that in the discussion of διώκω in Liddell and Scott's major entry, they indicated it was used as a legal term 'to prosecute', ὁ διώκων, the prosecutor, opp. ὁ φεύγων, the defendant.

the kingdom. His warnings had been taken on board and lingered in the minds of those Christians referred to in Galatians 6:12.[72]

Paul then makes a telling statement in 6:13-14. 'May it never be' (μὴ γένοιτο) that he would do that, i.e., boasting in a culturally acceptable *persona* to avoid any persecution and not glorying in 'the cross of Christ', even through it was totally ignominious for Jews and Greeks. One cannot but be arrested by his derogatory dismissal of this issue after exposing the singular motive of Jewish Christians — 'for neither circumcision or non-circumcision is anything but a new creation' (6:15). So how could this be a non-issue in the Galatian Christian context when it was such a major issue in the wider world of the province when one's *persona* was, in effect, one's real identity in society?

In the concluding section of Galatians, Paul reveals that these Christians themselves were not keeping the Jewish Torah (6:13). Furthermore, what motivated them was something to be deplored. What they were promoting shows they were self-serving, or better still self-preserving, rather than being gospel-honouring and orientated. They were being deflected away from the cross of Christ into this legal safety-net in order to secure a uniform Jewish *persona* (6:14), as 'proselytes and native-born Israelites are equal with regard to all laws which are mentioned in the Torah'.[73]

The results of this masterful solution proposed and so strongly promoted by some Galatian Christians, if accepted, meant that all Christians in Galatia had a legal status in the eyes of their fellow citizens. They would be considered Jewish either by birth or by proselytisation. They would be exempt from having to give divine honours to the Caesars and participation in other events that Rome had so skilfully linked into cultural events. Along with all Diaspora Jews and proselytes they would be able to indicate the daily sacrifice offered up for the safety of the reigning Caesar

---

72. It has been argued that a party from Jerusalem was responsible for the difficulties in Galatia, although nothing in the text actually demands that conclusion, rather the opposite. *Contra* R. Jewett, "The Agitators and the Galatian Congregation," *NTS* 17 (1971): 198-212, who argued that circumcision would thwart the zealots' threat, which had pushed Jewish Christians into a nomistic campaign among fellow Christians in Palestine. Cf. earlier G. W. Burton, *Galatians*, ICC (Edinburgh: T & T Clark, 1921), p. 349, who argued that Christian Jews wished to remain in good standing in their Jewish community by being able to point to converts from the Gentile world who have not only accepted Jesus as the Messiah, but also were observing the Jewish law. For a discussion see Barclay, *Obeying the Truth: A Study of Paul's Ethics in Galatians*, p. 45ff.

73. Porton's comment in his chapter on "Converts and Conversion in Mishnah," in *The Stranger within Your Gates*, p. 62.

in Jerusalem. However, their meeting places in Galatian homes would not have 'shields and gold crowns' and 'slabs [pillars] and inscriptions' as there were in Diaspora synagogues.[74]

Paul had to engage in intense and extended arguments against the maneuver involving the churches he had founded in Galatia. His apostolic teaching was consistent on this issue — 'this is my rule in all the churches' (1 Cor. 7:17-18). His response to the Galatian crisis indicates the enormity of the pressure brought to bear on the first Gentile Christians for them to take this despised but evasive action for the sake of all Christians in the province. Again, Mitchell's enigma with respect to the first Christians and the highly intrusive presence of the imperial cult can be well understood.[75]

74. Philo, *Embassy to Gaius* 133.

75. Galatians 4:10 alluded to by Mitchell, *Anatolia: Land, Men, and Gods in Asia Minor: The Rise of the Church,* II, p. 10, and explored fully by Hardin, "Days, Months, Seasons, Years and the Imperial Cult (Gal. 4:10)?" in *Galatians and the Imperial Cult: A Critical Analysis of the First-Century Social Context of Paul's Letter,* ch. 5.

CHAPTER 10

Confrontation for Thessalonian Christians and the Most Divine Caesar

From the very foundation of the Christian community in Thessalonica in the reign of Claudius, the challenge of the imperial claims of divinity confronted its members. Antagonistic Jews made serious allegations that Paul and Silas were known Jewish revolutionaries — 'These men who have turned the world upside down have come here also' (Acts 17:6). It was with men such as these that Claudius had forbidden any Jews to associate. Hence all the Thessalonian Christians would be guilty by reason of association with 'these men'.

Thessalonian Jews made another serious charge against every new Christian, stressing that 'these all are acting against the decrees of Caesar' (οὗτοι πάντες ἀπέναντι τῶν δογμάτων Καίσαρος)[1] — explaining further that the crime of each and every Christian was 'saying there is another king, Jesus' (βασιλέα ἕτερον λέγοντες εἶναι Ἰησοῦν) (17:7). Having given their allegiance to him, they were by implication seen as repudiating the validity of imperial decrees, and thus the jurisdiction of Claudius over them. He had been declared 'the most divine Caesar and truly our saviour' (τοῦ θειοτάτου Καίσαρος καὶ ὡς ἀληθῶς σωτῆρος ἡμῶν).[2] Earlier coins minted in Thessalonica had shown the crowned head of Julius Caesar with the inscription θεός, and on the reverse side the bare head of Augustus with the word 'Thessalonica'.[3]

In seeking to understand the confrontation these Thessalonian Chris-

---

1. The term ἀπέναντι. Liddell and Scott translate this as 'against', i.e., with the genitive, citing Acts 17:7 as an example.

2. *IGRR* 1, 1118, *ll.* 34-35.

3. *RPC* nos. 1554-55.

tians experienced over giving their loyalty to Jesus Christ and therefore no longer rendering to Claudius what they were now rendering to Jesus, it is proposed to explore (I) the charges against Paul and Silas as known revolutionaries opposing Roman rule; (II) the accusation of treason against their new converts, who were said to have rejected Caesar's decrees by affirming their allegiance to a rival king (Acts 17:7); (III) the reaction of civic officials in dealing with such serious charges (Acts 17:8); and (IV) later eschatological claims that arose by 'the man of lawlessness' in 2 Thessalonians 2:3-4, who declared himself superior to all other gods.

I. Paul and Silas as Jewish Revolutionaries Against Rome (Acts 17:6)

Paul and Silas were accused of being known Jewish revolutionaries opposed to Roman rule and undermining the *pax romana* — 'the ones who have turned the world upside down' (οἱ τὴν οἰκουμένην ἀναστατώσαντες). It was alleged that 'these also have now come here' (οὗτοι καὶ ἐνθάδε πάρεισιν) (17:6). It was against such Jews that Claudius had given a most serious warning to the Alexandrian Jews at the very beginning of his reign in A.D. 41. He warned them to avoid at all costs 'certain Jews from Egypt and Syria' who had rejected Roman rule, and sought support for their cause from their compatriots. Hence his dire warning that they were

> not to invite in as allies or approve of (μηδὲ ἐπάγεσθαι ἢ προσίεσθαι)[4] Jews who come down the river from Syria or Egypt, a proceeding which will compel me to conceive serious suspicions; otherwise I will by all means take vengeance on them as fomenters of what is a general plague infesting the whole world.[5]

There are good grounds for identifying 'the ones who have turned the world upside down' with the 'fomenters of . . . a general plague' that Claudius saw as infesting the whole of his empire.

Nero, the successor of Claudius, would see the outworking of such

---

4. The verbs ἐπάγεσθαι used to describe to 'bring in, invite as aiders or allies' and προσείεσθαι used in the passive 'to be like', i.e., 'identify with', 'approve'.

5. *P. Lond.* 1912, *ll.* 96-99.

treasonable Jewish activists who eventually stirred up revolt against Roman rule resulting in the disastrous war for the Jews in Judaea (A.D. 66-70). It would result in the conquest of Jerusalem, the total destruction of its temple and the Jews no longer a recognized nation with specific privileges and exemptions.

It was alleged before the 'politarchs' (πολιτάρχαι) that those whom Claudius had denounced to the Alexandrian Jews had now surfaced in Thessalonica.[6] Furthermore, these were those 'whom Jason and others harboured' (οὗ ὑποδέδεκται Ἰάσων), as had some of the Jews and 'a large number of devout Greeks and not a few of the leading women [in civic affairs]' (Acts 17:4).[7] Claudius' degree had strictly forbidden any 'to invite [them] in as allies or approve of', i.e., 'harbour' them (l. 96). In so doing these new Christians were not only defying his decree but under Roman Law were guilty of 'treason' (maiestas) by reason of their associating with Paul and Silas.[8]

II. 'Another King, Jesus' and 'the Decrees of Caesar'

The charge levelled against the Christians in Thessalonica was that by giving their allegiance to another king, Jesus, they rejected the rule of the present Caesar, Claudius (17:7). They were thereby seen as denying their oath of loyalty to him and rejecting the legitimacy of his official decrees. When both the citizens and the authorities heard these things they were naturally very disturbed (17:8).

Such a reaction is understandable when cognizance is taken of the annual oath of loyalty sworn to the emperor in Rome. The one sworn to Augustus on 6 March, 3 B.C., provides evidence of this.

6. For a thorough discussion on Thessalonian archaeological evidence, see G. H. R. Horsley, "Appendix: The Politarchs," in *The Book of Acts in Its Graeco-Roman Setting*, ed. D. W. J. Gill and C. Gempf, The Book of Acts in Its First Century Setting (Grand Rapids and Carlisle: Eerdmans and Paternoster, 1994), II, pp. 419-31.

7. The word ὑποδέχομαι used here carries the meaning of 'harbouring' someone who is involved in criminal activities. On the high-profile rôles of women in civic life in this era, see my "The Appearance of Women in the Public Sphere," in *Roman Wives, Roman Widows: The Appearance of 'New' Roman Women and the Pauline Communities* (Grand Rapids: Eerdmans, 2003), ch. 9.

8. For this innovation in Roman law, see B. Levick, "Tiberius and the Law: The Development of maiestas," in *Tiberius the Politician* (London: Thames & Hudson, 1976), ch. 12.

I swear by Zeus, Earth, Sun, all the gods and goddesses, and Augustus himself that I will be favourably disposed towards Augustus, and his children and descendants all the time of my life. . . . I will spare neither my body nor my soul nor my life nor my children but in every way for things that affect them I will undergo every danger, and whatever I will perceive or hear against them being said or plotted or done, I will report it and I will be an enemy to the person saying or plotting or doing any of these things. . . . If I do anything against this oath . . . I pray that there may come upon myself, my body, my children and all my family destruction, total destruction to the end of my line and of all my descendants, and may neither the bodies of my family nor or of my descendants by earth or sea be received, nor may they bear fruit for them. In the same words was this oath sworn by all the inhabitants of the land in the temples of Augustus by the altar of Augustus.[9]

In Acts 17:3 Luke explains the nature of the alleged crime of the rejection of 'the decrees of Caesar' by the Thessalonian Christians (τῶν δογμάτων Καίσαρος) — they were 'saying there is another king, Jesus' (βασιλέα ἕτερον λέγοντες εἶναι Ἰησοῦν). Paul and Silas had declared in the synagogue that 'Jesus is the Messiah' who had been crucified and was raised from the dead. The charge by the Jews was therefore not unwarranted, given the messianic claim of kingship.

They were accused of plotting against 'the decrees of Caesar' (ἀπέναντι δογμάτων Καίσαρος πράσσουσιν),[10] indicating not just one but a plurality of 'decrees'. It is significant that the reason for the implied rejection of his decrees is 'saying there is another king, Jesus' (Acts 17:7). Scholarly discussion has assumed that the accusers had a specific legal decree or decrees in mind, as Judge has argued.[11] More recently Hardin questioned this explanation and proposed as an alternative that the de-

---

9. *IGRR* 3, 137, *ll.* 6-11, 15-24, 26-30, 37 (ET). See R. K. Sherk, *Roman and the Greek East to the Death of Augustus* (Cambridge: Cambridge University Press, 1993), no. 105.

10. The verb has a number of meanings, i.e., 'plotting' or 'passing over' with the latter meaning 'only found in the present' according to Liddell and Scott. Also ἀπέναντι 'against' with the genitive 'opposite', with Liddell and Scott also citing Acts 17:7. A clear rejection of the decrees is implied.

11. E. A. Judge, "The Decrees of Caesar in Thessalonica," in *The First Christians in the Roman World: Augustan and New Testament Essays,* ed. J. R. Harrison (Tübingen: Mohr Siebeck, 2008), ch. 32.

crees had to do with the law regulating associations that were seen as hotbeds of sedition.[12] It is certainly well documented that since the time of Augustus, his successors legislated to curtail the politicization of associations by restricting the registered monthly meetings. The same legislation specifically permitted Jews to hold weekly meetings. Subsequent Julio-Claudian emperors also addressed similar problems regarding unruly and disloyal associations.[13]

Hardin argued that the fine imposed by the politarchs was for breaching the law relating to illegal assemblies.[14] He cites in support of this a later, important Spanish city constitution from the Flavian era where a fine was imposed for the illegal gathering of associations.[15] However, if Christians in Thessalonica continued to meet after Paul and Silas departed, they would continue to be in breach of this Roman law because they would still be an illegal assembly. This would only confirm their clandestine activity against the emperor and thus they would be guilty of treason. Neither of the letters — 1 or 2 Thessalonians — gives any indication that they were not meeting together or that there were legal complications in so doing.

It could be argued that the synagogue in Thessalonica where Paul originally preached on three Sabbath days was composed of both Jews and God-fearers. The ethnic mix had not changed with the converts. Acts 17:4 records that 'certain of them [Jews] were persuaded and "joined" Paul and Silas,[16] as did a great many of devout Greeks and also of the leading women not a few' (τινες ἐξ αὐτῶν ἐπείσθησαν καὶ προσεκληρώθησαν Παύλῳ καὶ Σιλᾷ τῶν τε σεβομένων Ἑλλήνων πλῆθος πολύ γυναικῶν τε τῶν πρώτων οὐ ὀλίγαι). Could they subsequently have been seen in the eyes of the officials as another synagogue? We know from first-century literary evidence that there could be more than one synagogue in a city, as was the case in Rome in this period.[17]

---

12. J. J. Hardin, "Decrees and Drachmas at Thessalonica: An Illegal Assembly in Jason's House (Acts 17.1-10a)," *NTS* 52, no. 1 (2006): 29-49.

13. For a summary of Julio-Claudian emperors' responses to associations, see my "Roman Law and Society in Romans 12–15," in *Rome in the Bible and the Early Church,* ed. P. Oakes (Carlisle and Grand Rapids: Paternoster and Baker, 2002), pp. 71-74.

14. For the review, see Hardin, "Decrees and Drachmas at Thessalonica," pp. 33-38.

15. Hardin, "Decrees and Drachmas at Thessalonica," p. 46, citing J. González, "The *Lex Irnitana:* A New Flavian Municipal Law," *JRS* 76 (1986): 172.

16. The passive of προσκληρόω, 'to be attached to', according to Liddell and Scott, who cite Acts 17:4 as an example of this rendering of the verb.

17. Philo, *Embassy to Gaius* 155-57, calls them 'Houses of Prayer'.

There is an important link between the initial accusation of rejecting imperial decrees and the explanation that immediately followed. It was a long-standing legal and literary convention to begin official imperial decrees by indicating the emperor's name followed by his titles. One common feature of decrees was that all used 'a god' followed by the phrase 'a son of a god'. They then added *imperator* — the Latin term for the Greek equivalent was αὐτοκράτωρ that is rendered in the English as 'emperor', i.e., 'king'.[18] In Republican times this term was used of a victorious Roman commander, but Augustus adopted it as his *praenomen* 'Imperator Caesar' rather than 'Caesar Imperator'. It became an official formal title adopted by all subsequent rulers of the Roman Empire.

As a consequence of endorsing a rival king it is understandable that the Christians could be seen to be rejecting not only the divine, imperial titles but *ipso facto* the validity of all his official imperial decrees that were sent from Rome, in this case, by Claudius. The Jewish charge was not unrelated to Paul's declaration in the synagogue that Jesus was the Messiah. Given this explanation of the charge in Acts 17:7, it is understandable that the Christians were seen to be over-riding the validity of all imperial decrees *per se* because they were now subjects of another king, Jesus and his 'decrees', having abandoned their former allegiance.

A far-reaching implication of the Thessalonian Christians' loyalty to Jesus from the very beginning of their conversion would later be reported back to Paul by Christians in other cities in the provinces of Macedonia and Achaia. From the days of first embracing the Christian gospel they had seen the need to reject all forms of idolatry. The reports also indicated 'how you turned to God from idols to serve the living and true God and to wait for his Son from heaven' (καὶ πῶς ἐπεστρέψατε πρὸς τὸν θεὸν ἀπὸ τῶν εἰδώλων δουλεύειν θεῷ ζῶντι καὶ ἀληθινῷ καὶ ἀναμένειν τόν υἱὸν αὐτοῦ ἐκ τῶν οὐρανῶν) (1 Thess. 1:9). This implied that they had ceased giving any divine honours before the statue of Claudius in the imperial cult temple or at other events connected with imperial divine honours in Thessalonica because of their exclusive allegiance to Jesus as 'his [God's] Son' (τὸν υἱὸν αὐτοῦ) (1:10).

---

18. For evidence of titles of Nero in a bilingual decree from him in Latin and Greek, see M. P. Charlesworth, "Nero," in *Documents Illustrating the Reigns of Claudius & Nero* (Cambridge: Cambridge University Press, 1939), no. 4.

III. The Civic Authorities' Response
to the Allegation of Treason

A confrontation occurred between new Christians, the civil authorities and some of the Thessalonians almost immediately after they had embraced the gospel message that Paul and Silas preached. Some enraged Jews from the local synagogue colluded with 'some wicked men of the rabble' to create a riot, disturbing the city and attacking the house of Jason (Acts 17:5). They dragged him along with some other Christians before the city authorities, the politarchs, having already created a volatile situation and 'shouting' the most serious allegation against the Christians (17:6-7). Harrison sees this allegation as a legal charge on the basis of the 'seditious' message of Paul and Silas.[19]

The politarchs (πολιτάρχας) were not the first officials to be faced with the allegation of treasonable conduct against a Roman emperor. Earlier, leading Jews brought to the attention of Pontius Pilate on his annual assize in Jerusalem the accusation that Jesus had made himself 'king', the implication being that 'everyone one who makes himself king opposes the Caesar' (ἀντιλέγαι τῷ Καίσαρι) (John 19:12). As the governor of Judaea, great pressure was put on him. If he did not pursue legal action he was not 'Caesar's friend'[20] but by inference a traitor. Therefore the charges brought against Paul and Silas were the most serious in the Roman Empire.

Normally such allegations would have come within the remit of the criminal jurisdiction of the provincial governor. While 'Thessalonica was the residence of the imperial procurator of the province',[21] in A.D. 44 Claudius had introduced changes in both Achaea and Macedonia in the jurisdiction of the magistrates, who were now 'entrusted [with] various judicial cases that the consuls had previously tried'.[22] It is important to note that Thessalonica under the Romans had been awarded the status of 'a free city' *(civitas libera),* as was Athens, and as a result was not under the jurisdiction of the Roman governor of the province in the way that others cities were.[23]

19. J. R. Harrison, *Paul and the Imperial Authorities at Thessalonica and Rome,* WUNT 273 (Tübingen: Mohr Siebeck, 2011), p. 86.

20. See pp. 30, 43 for discussion of the special status of being made a friend of Caesar.

21. P. M. Nigdelis, "A New *Procurator Augusti* in the Province of Macedonia," *Greek, Roman, and Byzantine Studies* 52 (2012): 207.

22. Dio, *Roman History* 60.24.3.

23. A. Lintott, *Imperium Romanum: Politics and Administration* (London: Routledge, 1993), pp. 36-41, for a discussion of a 'free city' under the Romans. See also p. 129 for ev-

Therefore it was within the remit of its most senior officials to act in a legal capacity. This may well explain the immediate move by the politarchs to hear and deal with these charges made within their jurisdiction.

Acts records that the officials responded to the crowd as they shouted allegations against Jason and 'some of the brothers'. Luke further notes that 'having taken the surety' (καὶ λαβόντες τὸ ἱκανὸν) they released them (καὶ τῶν λοιπος ἀπέλυσαν αὐτούς) (17:9). The term 'to release' is used elsewhere in Acts in legal contexts where there was no criminal case to answer or to proceed with.[24]

Although some have concluded it was a bribe,[25] the legal term τὸ ἱκανόν indicates that they were required to give 'the security', i.e., 'the surety' — a known legal transaction involving money.[26] Non-literary sources confirm its legal meaning.

In Alexandria a letter written to a brother in A.D. 22 indicates that 'a marshal and the official sword bearer are in prison on the instructions of the Prefect and will remain so unless they can persuade the chief usher "to give surety" (δο[ῦν]αι ἱκακόν) for them until the session'.[27] Both the Alexandrian papyrus and Acts 17:9 are, in effect, referring to the same legal action; the only difference is that the former was the 'giving' of and the latter the 'taking' of security. The action was a legal one, and based on the Alexandrian evidence and *The Digest*, it meant that no Christians were incarcerated while awaiting trial. An earlier inscription from Messene uses the phrase 'taking the security' (λαβόντα τὸ ἱκανόν).[28] Like Acts 19:9 it also used the article, indicating that 'the surety' was a recognized term.

---

idence of the same status for Athens. Of the concern regarding the possible loss of status or some other penalty imposed by the governor of the province for riotous behaviour, see Acts 19:35-41, esp. v. 40.

24. In the legal sematic domain, the term ἀπολύω means 'to release' as used elsewhere in Acts where Agrippa told Festus that Paul could have been released if he had not already appealed to Caesar (Acts 26:32). See also 3:13; 4:21, 23; 5:40; 16:35-36; 28:18.

25. For a discussion of different views, see C. S. Keener, *Acts: An Exegetical Commentary 15:1–23:35* (Grand Rapids: Baker Academic, 2014), III, pp. 2557-58.

26. Liddell and Scott cite Acts 17:9 as an example of the legal meaning 'to take the security'. See also Polybius, *Historicus* 32.3.13, with reference to conduct being to the satisfaction of the Senate. Cf. Diogenes Laertius *Bion*. 4.50, 'I will satisfy your demand' (τὸ ἱκανόν σοι ποιήσω); he then states 'if you only get others to plead your cause and stay away yourself'.

27. *P.Oxy.* 294, *ll.* 19-23, citation *l.* 23. On the giving of surety for such situations in Roman law see *The Digest* 48.3.4.

28. *SEG* 41, 332, *l.* 19.

These legal implications point to the fact that it certainly was not some illegal payoff. Under Roman law a 'surety' was not a bribe, but an integral part of the court processes.[29]

Sherwin-White stated, 'The term is the Latin equivalent to the Latin *satis accipere,* correlate of *satis dare,* in connection with the offering and giving of security in civil and criminal procedures'.[30] It means 'to receive surety'. Hardin disagreed with him, arguing, 'In fact, the term *satis accipere* can refer to a creditor who is satisfied with the security of a debtor, i.e., the politarchs were satisfied with the security paid by Jason and the rest',[31] citing in support Campbell's definition of the term 'to take surety for' with respect to commercial transactions.[32]

However, the context in Acts 17:9 indicates it was a criminal rather than a civil process, given the serious nature of the charges and the evidence gathered in the penultimate paragraph. Under the section "Criminal Proceedings" in *The Digest,* surety was given if the reputation of the persons was such that they would not be expected to break their word as a matter of honour.[33] It was also the case that 'a person prepared to give sureties should not be put in chains'.[34] It could be that if the person failed to produce the alleged offender at the official hearing, he would suffer a financial penalty.[35]

Were Jason and 'the rest' under a legal obligation to see the two outsiders leave Thessalonica immediately (Acts 17:9) in order to maintain peace, or did they agree not to attend further meetings of the Thessalo-

---

29. I am grateful to Dr. S. Butler, Director of Studies in Roman Law, St Edmund's College, Cambridge, for providing references in Roman law on 'surety' and his opinion that the reference in Acts 17:9 was not to a bribe but was part of the due process in criminal actions. On "Criminal Proceedings," see A. Watson, *The Digest of Justinian* (Philadelphia: University of Pennsylvania Press, 1998), II, book 48.

30. A. R. N. Sherwin-White, *Roman Society and Roman Law in the New Testament: The Sarum Lectures 1960-61* (Oxford: Clarendon Press, 1963), p. 95, citing Ulpian, *Digest* 48.3.1, noting that 'Men of substance give sureties for appearance but the most exalted are not required to do this', p. 82, n. 2.

31. Hardin, "Decrees and Drachmas at Thessalonica," p. 46, citing in support A. Berger, *Encyclopedic Dictionary of Roman Law* (Philadelphia: American Philosophical Society, 1953), p. 690.

32. G. Campbell, *A Compendium of Roman Law: Founded on the Institutes of Justinian* (Clark, NJ: The Lawbook Exchange, 2008), p. 218.

33. *The Digest* 48.3.1.

34. *The Digest* 48.3.3.

35. *The Digest* 48.3.4.

nian synagogue? Acts 17:10 records that the former happened — 'and the brothers immediately sent away by night both Paul and Silas to Berea' (οἱ δὲ ἀδελφοὶ εὐθέως διὰ νυκτὸς ἐξέπεψαν τόν τε Παῦλον καὶ τὸν Σιλᾶν). This indicates that they got away as soon as possible and under the cover of darkness even though that was a dangerous time to travel outside the protection of a city in the Roman world.[36] Paul recounts the personal pain he felt at having to leave as he did from Thessalonica when he wrote of the feeling of being 'torn away from you' (ἀπορφανίζω), i.e., 'be bereaved of you' (1 Thess. 2:17).[37]

Acts 17:9 notes that the Thessalonian crowd and the politarchs were troubled when they heard of the allegations against Paul and Silas. It seems the politarchs were more concerned about getting rid of Paul and Silas from the city than they were about actually exploring the nature of the allegations (17:7). This can be paralleled with a potential riot in Ephesus that was also ignited over the coming of the Christian message to the city (Acts 19:21-40). When Timothy and Erastus were hauled into its enormous theatre and when Alexander wanted to make a defence, it prompted a prolonged noisy demonstration. It was the 'town clerk' (γραμματεύς) who quieted the crowd, drawing attention to the fact that it was not a legal assembly (ἐννόμῳ ἐκκλησίᾳ). He was concerned that if this illegal gathering came to the ears of the governor there would be punitive consequences for the city as a whole. It may help to explain the quashing of a hearing that followed the due process of Roman law as witnessed in official proceedings before the governors in Caesarea Maritima in Acts 24:1-23 and 26:1-23.[38]

However, there is a difference between the two public disturbances. In Ephesus they were told and indeed exhorted to go through the due legal process before the appointed 'officials' (ἀγοραῖοι) (Acts 19:38). This was actually done in Thessalonica but, given the officials' decision, with what must have been a much less satisfying result than that expected by their accusers.

---

36. The adverb εὐθέως indicates this was done as soon as possible. The sentence parallels the verb ὑπεκπεμπω, 'sending out secretly'; cf. Euripides, *Andromache* l.47 'but him, my only son, I sent out secretly'.

37. Liddell and Scott cite 1 Thess. 2:17 as to how Paul described what had happened in Acts 17:10 (εὐθέως δὲ τότε Παῦλον ἐξαπεστειλαν).

38. For a discussion on this see my "Official Proceedings and Forensic Speeches in Acts 24–26," in *The Book of Acts in Its Ancient Literary Setting*, ed. A. D. Clarke and B. W. Winter (Grand Rapids: Eerdmans, 1993), ch. 11.

IV. 'Exalts Himself over Every So-Called God',
2 Thessalonians 2:4

Given that a characteristic of their faith was that they were those who 'wait for His Son from heaven' (1 Thess. 1:10), Paul in his second letter to the Christians in Thessalonica explains further aspects of 'the day of the Lord', dealing with 'the times and the seasons', its total unexpectedness and important ethical implications. He emphasizes that it is not necessary for him to repeat certain aspects of his teaching on this issue because they had readily embraced his eschatological perspective (2 Thess. 5:1-11) in spite of the Roman claims of the *pax romana* of 'peace and security' that Rome boasted it had brought to all those in the empire.

It emerges in 2 Thessalonians that subsequently a radical change had come about in their eschatological understanding because of recent teaching from a source that was mischievously attributed to Paul.[39] As a result, the Thessalonians had become alarmed and unsettled. The circumstances that gave rise to this came from what others were saying, i.e., what they prophesized. Paul told them to ignore these sources including the misleading letter, as it definitely was not from him — 'neither a letter seeming to be from us that the day of the Lord had arrived' (μήτε δι' ἐπιστολῆς ὡς δι' ἡμῶν ὡς ὅτι ἐνέστηκεν ἡ ἡμέρα τοῦ κυρίου) (2 Thess. 2:1-2). This declared that the day they had been waiting for in 1 Thessalonians 1:10 had actually occurred — hence the use of the perfect tense, ἐνέστηκεν of the verb 'to arrive'.[40]

Paul exhorts them not to be beguiled in any way, explaining that some Christians would commit apostasy as a prelude to that eschatological event, presumably including some from Thessalonica. They would also rebel, and after that 'the man of lawlessness' would appear. Paul describes further what would happen when 'the son of destruction' appeared —

who opposes (ὁ ἀντικείμενος) and exalts over every so-called god (καὶ ὑπεραιρόμενος ἐπὶ πάντα λεγόμενον θεὸν) or object of worship (ἢ σέβασμα), so that he takes his seat in the temple of the God (ὥστε

39. Hence Paul's placing of his actual 'signature', 'in my own hand' (τῇ ἐμῇ χερί), for them to compare with the counterfeit in the false letter (2 Thess. 3:17).

40. Liddell and Scott distinguish between the use of the tenses of this verb ἐνίστημι, 'that the state of completion expressed by the perfect tense' over against the aorist 'when the moment has arrived', hence the ESV rendering 'the day of the Lord has come'.

αὐτὸν εἰς τὸν ναὸν του θεου καθίσαι), proclaiming himself that he is God (ἀποδεικνύςτα ἑαυτὸν ὅτι ἔστιν θεός). (2:3-4)[41]

Here Paul exposes the motivation of the man of lawlessness, whose claims and actions are reminiscent of those in Daniel 11:36-7, where similar terminology is used to describe the divinity of the emperors. Cited here from the Septuagint, it also records a similar eschatological perspective and motivation. The terms chosen by the translators of the LXX as appropriate renderings of the Hebrew were similar at times with that used in 2 Thessalonians 2:1-5.

> [A]nd the king shall do as he wills. He shall exalt himself and magnify himself above every god (καὶ παροργισυήσεται καὶ ὑψωθήσεται ἐπὶ πάντα θεὸν) and shall speak astonishing things against the God of gods (καὶ ἐπὶ τὸν θεὸν τῶν θεῶν ἐξαλλα λαλήσει). He shall prosper till the indignation is accomplished; for what is decreed shall be done. He shall pay no attention to the gods of his fathers. . . . He shall pay no attention to any other god for he shall magnify himself above all (καὶ ὑποταγήσεται αὐτῳ ἔθνη ἰσχυρά). (Dan. 11:36-37)

Some of this language also resonates with that found in official inscriptions in the East relating to the Julio-Claudian emperors. The use of the superlative 'the greatest' succinctly echoes Paul's reference to the one who exalts himself over every so-called god or object of worship. Others use another superlative, 'most divine', when referring to the Caesars.

For example, on 5 April, A.D. 54, Claudius, just six months before his death, was declared to be 'the most divine Caesar and truly our saviour' (τοῦ θειοτάτου Καίσαρος καὶ ὡς ἀληθῶς σωτῆρος ἡμῶν).[42] The first extant recording of this term used of emperors was by Paulus Fabius Maximus, the proconsul of Asia from 10 to 8 B.C., who wrote to the League of Asia. He chose the superlative θειοτάτος when referring to Augustus in his lifetime as the 'most divine Caesar' (τοῦ θειοτάτου Καίσαρος).[43] (See p. 134.)

A somewhat synonymous concept, 'the greatest', was later used of Nero. He was referred to as the 'emperor greatest Caesar Nero Claudius

41. Liddell and Scott also cite this actual passage indicating that the verb means to 'appoint, proclaim, create'.

42. *IGRR* 1, 1118, *ll.* 34-35 (5 April, A.D. 54).

43. *OGIS* 458. A search of the *TLG* database shows how prevalent this term became with emperors in the Flavian era.

Sebastos Germanicus, son of a god' (αὐτοκράτορα μέγιστον Νέρωνα Καίσαρα Κλαύδιον Σεβαστὸν Γερμανικὸν θεοῦ υἱόν).[44] He was also declared to be 'the son of the greatest of gods (τὸν υἱὸν τοῦ μεγίστου θεῶν), Tiberius Claudius'.[45] In the East an inscription dated 28 November, A.D. 67, records, 'Nero, Zeus the Liberator, the one and only, the greatest imperator of our times' (εἷς καὶ μόνος τῶν ἀπ' αὐῶος αὐτοκράτωρ μέγιστος).[46]

The only appropriate response of those who were the recipients of his 'incredible gift' was to address him as 'the Lord of the entire world' (ὁ τοῦ παντὸς κόσμου κύριος) and 'the new sun that has shone on the Greeks' because he bestowed benefactions on Greece and has shown piety towards 'our gods who have stood by him everywhere for his care and safety'.[47]

This inscription also adds that Nero would be 'worshipped ever hereafter as Nero Zeus Liberator' (Νέρωνος Διὸς Ἐλευθερίου).[48] Calling Nero 'Zeus Liberator' was a very great honour. Pausanias recorded the significance of this designation, 'Zeus is king of heaven', and then added 'this is a common saying of all men' (οὗτος μὲν λόγος κοινὸς πάντων ἐστὶν ἀνθρώπων); 'this same god rules in all the three "allotments" of the Universe, as they are called'. This was the highest accolade and the most divine title the Achaeans could confer upon him.[49]

This decree was promulgated for all to see, being inscribed 'on a column set beside Zeus the Saviour in the agora and in the temple of Ptoian Apollo'.[50] Nero's speech in Corinth in which he aggrandizes himself by implication in relation to his predecessors and the response in terms of the greatest honours bestowed on him parallels the divine self-promotion recorded in 2 Thessalonians 2:1-5. The terminology found in the epigraphic evidence concerning Claudius and Nero helps in seeking to identify the god being referred to by Paul.

Paul also adds the phrase 'every so-called god' (πάντα λεγόμενον θεὸν) in 2:4, which is exactly the same term he used in 1 Corinthians 8:5,

---

44. *IG* 2/3, 2, 3, 3277, 2

45. *Die Inschriften von Magnesia am Mäander*, no. 156b, cited in G. A. Deissmann, *Light from the Ancient East: The New Testament Illustrated by Recently Discovered Texts of the Graeco-Roman World*, ET (London: Hodder & Stoughton, 1927), p. 347.

46. *SIG*³ 814, *ll.* 40-45.

47. *SIG*³ 814, *ll.* 31-32.

48. *SIG*³ 814, *l.* 41.

49. Pausanias, "Corinth," *The Description of Greece* 2.24.4.

50. *SIG*³ 814, *ll.* 56-57.

'so-called' (λεγόμενοί). It is argued that there the reference was to imperial gods and that Paul chose the term 'so-called' to indicate that they were popularly but erroneously regarded as such. (See pp. 212-13.)

How have scholars sought to identify the *Sitz im Leben* of the passage in 2 Thessalonians 2:1-5? With respect to imperial self-promotion in the East, Sartre concludes of the other Julio-Claudians who promoted themselves — 'As for Caligula and Nero they contrastingly became its keen propagators, to the point that Caligula sought to have his statue introduced into the temple in Jerusalem.'[51] Harrison suggests it may be as a result of Caligula attempting to place his statue in the Jerusalem Temple that Paul believes the emperors have exceeded their mandate and hence 2 Thessalonians 2:4.[52] However, Caligula reigned from 37 to 41 A.D., prior to Paul's first visit to Thessalonica. By contrast van Kooten defends the dating to the era of Nero (A.D. 54-68), relating it to A.D. 68-69 after his suicide.[53]

> Astrologers had predicted of Nero that he would one day be repudiated. . . . Some of them, however, had promised him the rule of the East, when he was cast off, a few expressly naming the sovereignty of Jerusalem and several the restitution of all his former fortunes.[54]

One of the challenges in seeking to locate the *Sitz im Leben* of the references in 2 Thessalonians 2:1ff. is to bear in mind that it is important to note that they point to the future. Paul had already given them this prophetic eschatological teaching presumably on what seems to have been his one and only visit, i.e., the evangelistic one recorded in Acts 17:1-10. If this

---

51. M. Sartre, "Co-opting the Conqueror: The East from Augustus to Trajan," in *A Companion to Roman Imperialism,* ed. D. Hoyos, History of Warfare (Leiden and Boston: E. J. Brill, 2013), LXXXI, p. 282.

52. J. R. Harrison, " 'The Ultimate Sinner': Paul and the Anti-Christ in Political Context," asks 'Does Paul Speak of Caligula in 2 Thessalonians 2:3-4, 8?' in *Paul and the Imperial Authorities at Thessalonica and Rome,* ch. 3 and esp. pp. 85-95.

53. G. H. van Kooten, "The Jewish War and the Roman Civil War of 68-69 C.E.: Jewish, Pagan, and Christian Perspectives," in *The Jewish Revolt against Rome: Interdisciplinary Perspectives,* ed. M. Popovic, Supplements to the Journal for the Study of Judaism 154 (Leiden and Boston: Brill, 2011), pp. 427-31. For his previous discussion, see " 'Wrath Will Drip in the Plains of Macedonia': Expectations of Nero's Return in the Egyptian Sibylline Oracles (Book 5), 2 Thessalonians, and Ancient Historical Writings," in *The Wisdom of Egypt: Jewish, Early Christian, and Gnostic Essays in Honour of Gerard P. Luttikhuizen,* ed. A. Hillhorst and G. H. van Kooten (Leiden: E. J. Brill, 2005), pp. 177-215.

54. Suetonius, *Nero* 40.2.

is the case, then it occurred *c.* A.D. 50-51 if note is taken of the dates that Gallio was proconsul of the province of Achaea. Both epigraphic evidence and events mentioned in Acts 18:12-17 occurred after Paul left Thessalonica and settled in Corinth.[55] He therefore asked, 'Do you not remember that when I was still with you I told you these things?' (2 Thess. 2:5). He had previously written to them about this in 1 Thessalonians 5:1-11. So the teaching in 2 Thessalonians was not a new topic.

The language used to describe this man of lawlessness who sought to exalt himself over all other gods resonates not only prophetically with Daniel 11 but also with that in some official inscriptions where the terms 'the most divine' and 'the greatest' are used of the last two Roman emperors of the Julio-Claudians, i.e., Claudius and Nero. (See pp. 66, 69.) Furthermore, numismatic evidence reveals that provincial coins did not portray emperors as gods with the divine radiate crown in imperial provincial coinage in the Julio-Claudian era 'with the exception of Caligula and, especially, Nero'.[56]

It is important how the Thessalonian Christians coped with the fact that they could no longer participate in giving divine imperial honours. They had been confronted with this both in the past and again in their present situation. Paul writes that he had boasted to other Christians 'in the churches of God' about the believers located in Thessalonica because of 'your steadfastness and faith (ὑπμονῆς ὑμῶν καὶ πίστεως) in all your persecutions and afflictions (διωγμοῖς καὶ θλιψεσιν)' that they 'are enduring' (ἀνέχεσθε) (2 Thess. 1:4). He asserted, 'this is an indication that you may be counted worthy of the kingdom of God for which you are also suffering' (ὑπὲρ καὶ πάσχετε) (1:5), and assures them that God will act to 'afflict those who are afflicting you' (καὶ πάσχετε τοῖς θλίβουσιν ὑμᾶς θλῖψιν) while judgement will occur when the Lord Jesus is revealed from heaven with his mighty angels in flaming fire (1:6-7).

Within the parameters of the extant evidence of Thessalonian Chris-

---

55. For a discussion of the dating see my "Rehabilitating Gallio and His Judgement in Acts 18:14-15," *TynB* 57, no. 2 (2006): 296.

56. A. Burnett, M. Amandry and P. P. Ripollès, *Roman Provincial Coinage: From the Death of Caesar to the Death of Vitellius (44 B.C.-A.D. 69)* (London and Paris: British Museum Press and Bibliothèque nationale de France, 1998), p. 47. Also C. Howgego, "Chronological Development of Roman Provincial Coin Iconography," in *Coinage and Identity in the Roman Provinces*, ed. C. Howgego, V. Heuchert and A. Burnett (Oxford: Oxford University Press, 2005), p. 45, notes that it had been used in the time of Tiberius of the deceased *Divus Augustus*.

tianity, these events relate to the theme of this monograph. These Christians in Thessalonica were confronted from 'day one' with a conflict of loyalty over whether they could render divine honours to the Caesars now that they were followers of Jesus. They were also warned to expect on-going confrontation over the 'so-called' imperial gods as confirmed by their present sufferings. Subsequent chapters will reveal that they were not alone in turning away from idols of the imperial gods, to worship and wait for the return of the Son of God from heaven (1 Thess. 1:9-10).

CHAPTER 11

Impending Exile for Christians in Hebrews

A first-century person in the Roman Empire reading the opening paragraph of the Letter to the Hebrews would have been struck by the way it commenced with the bold declaratory statement of the perpetual divinity of Jesus (1:2-3). Would he not be seen as a rival of some of the departed Roman emperors in the Julio-Claudian era who were officially awarded the status of perpetual divinity by the Roman Senate?[1]

Even more significant is the fact that all new Caesars were automatically designated the *pontifex maximus* of the Roman Empire as a given function of their rule. This Latin term was officially rendered in the Greek East as ἀρχιερεύς, i.e., 'high priest'. His ritual tasks and imperial intercessions to the gods in the eternal city of Rome were seen as the means of securing divine blessings so that all who dwelt in this vast empire would be safe and prosper materially. Rome had its own great high priest as the essential mediator between the gods and the empire. As well as Jews having their own high priests, the high priests of provincial imperial cults in

---

1. J. A. Whitlark, *Resisting Empire: Rethinking the Purpose of the Letter to 'the Hebrews'*, Library of New Testament Studies 484 (London: Bloomsbury T & T Clark, 2014), in chapters 5-8, headed "Resisting Imperial Claims," explores these aspects of Roman rule as the context of Hebrews. He also posits the view that there is 'possibly the threat of exile or death', p. 97, but cites no evidence from Roman legal stipulations and its due process to support this or the grounds for persecution up to the time of the writing of this letter. This forensic evidence and the reason for suffering were originally discussed in my "Suffering with the Saviour: The Reality, the Reasons and the Reward," in *The Perfect Saviour: Key Themes in Hebrews*, ed. J. Griffith (Leicester: Apollos/Wheaton, IL: Crossway, 2012), ch. 8, which is the basis of this chapter but with an expansion of the argument and its *Sitz im Leben* relevant to the theme of this book.

the East were officially appointed by Rome to fulfill important liturgical functions in overseeing divine honours for the Caesars.

This letter reveals a challenge to these cultic positions, as a major portion is devoted to discussing the rôle of Jesus as the great high priest (4:1–8:1) whose appointment was by God and whose office was held in perpetuity (5:5-6). The letter later states that the Christians no longer had any need for sacrifices, given the efficacy of Christ's sacrifice (10:21, 23). They had to be encouraged to remain loyal to Jesus, whose great high-priestly office was a central feature of their faith (10:21). Their compatriots would have seen this as a direct challenge to Caesar's critical high-priestly office that was essential to maintaining the blessedness of the *pax romana*.

The letter also records that its recipients had already undergone severe legal penalties on account of their faith, having 'endured a great conflict of sufferings' (10:32). They had been subject to humiliating punishments along with others in the public arena — 'having been publicly exposed to both reproaches and afflictions and sometimes partners with those being so treated' (10:33). In addition they had experienced a period of imprisonment during which it is recorded that they had acted with compassion towards their fellow prisoners (10:34). Although they had also faced the plundering of their own possessions, their response had been that of 'joy' as they remembered the permanence and superiority of their ultimate heavenly inheritance (10:34). These were severe punishments that could only have been administered under Roman law.

Up to this point in their Christian lives they had coped with all these adversities and still kept their faith. Only towards the end of this letter is it disclosed that a further official form of punishment under Roman law was pending — one that in their day was greatly dreaded. This was exile, the suffering of which the writer described as comparable to that which Jesus suffered 'outside the gate' (13:12). Under Roman law, exile to an isolated place was regarded as a dire penalty only surpassed by the death sentence. An ancient historian has aptly described the experience as 'The Curse of Exile'.[2] Another, 'The Horror of Isolation', recorded the experiences of leading Romans and officials who had been banished into exile from Rome, and some of whose dire experiences have been vividly preserved.[3]

---

2. G. D. Williams, *The Curse of Exile: A Study of Ovid's Ibis* (Cambridge: Cambridge University Press, 1996).

3. J.-M. Claassen, "The Horror of Isolation," in *Displaced Persons: The Literature of Exile from Cicero to Boethius* (London: Duckworth, 1999), ch. 7, discusses Cicero and Ovid's depiction of horror of their experiences of exile along with Dio Chrysostom. While they may

The writer of the Letter to the Hebrews exhorted the Christians — 'Therefore now let us go forth to him outside the camp bearing his reproach' (τοίνυν ἐξερχώμεθα πρὸς αὐτὸν ἔξω τῆς παρεμβολῆς τὸν ὀνειδισμὸν αὐτοῦ φέροντες) (13:13). Does the prospect of exclusion go to the heart of the matter? Why do its recipients have to be argued out of yielding to the strong temptation to flee to Judaism as the only safe haven from persecution, and in so doing commit apostasy?

In order to examine whether this is a credible reconstruction of the *Sitz im Leben* of the Letter to the Hebrews, it is intended (I) to explore the catalogue of officially imposed punishments that the Christians to whom the letter was written had already endured; (II) to seek to understand the change in Nero's era of the imposition of multiple punishments under Roman law as a legal development that helps explain what had happened to these Christians and what was threatening them at the time of writing; and (III) to unpack the nature of the feared punishment of exile and the arguments mounted against yielding to the temptation to commit apostasy by shrinking back from confessing the sole perpetual divinity of Jesus, the Son of God and his permanent, effective great high-priestly rôle.

I. The Nature of Multiple Past Sufferings

The author of Hebrews acknowledges that his readers 'had endured much conflict of sufferings' (πολλὴν ἄθλησιν ὑπεμείνατε παθημάτων) (10:32), but had not capitulated because of them. The term 'conflict' (ἄθλησις) was aptly chosen because it evokes a combative image appropriately borrowed from contemporary sporting contests and also linked to warfare in Greek thinking.[4] The punishments after they were first 'enlightened' by the gospel are catalogued in 10:32-34. The writer repeats them as a reminder of how intense these had been and just how remarkably they had kept the faith to this point in their spiritual journey.

---

use exile as a 'literary' device, one cannot be dismissive of the severity of the punishment in Roman law for exiling individuals recorded in extant material.

    4. Z. Newby, *Athletics in the Ancient World* (London: Bristol Classical Press, 2006), p. 93. Their trainers sometimes beat them with whips; see the vase painting, p. 72, plate 14. Liddell and Scott, *Classical Greek-English Lexicon,* record that the term means 'contest', 'combat', especially of athletes; see Polybius, *Histories* 5.64.6, SIG 1073, 24 (Olympia), IG 14, 1102 'in the athletic competitions'. They also cite the metaphorical use of this word in Hebrews 10:32 to refer generally to a 'struggle' or 'trial'.

(i) Verbal Public Abuse in the Theatre

It was noted that 'on the one hand' (τοῦτο μέν) there had been 'public exposure' in the one place where this sort of thing happened in the ancient world, i.e., the theatre. The term θεατρίζω used here means 'to put on stage', i.e., 'to publicly expose' (10:33). The verb is in the passive, indicating that what happened was not of their own volition but was forced on them. In Liddell and Scott's *Greek-English Lexicon,* this verb is rendered as 'to be made a show of', 'held up to shame', and it actually cites Hebrews 10:33 in the literary sources as an appropriate example.[5] A hostile audience had assembled in the theatre, hurling 'insulting abuses' at these Christians and other criminals at the commencement of their imprisonment.

Acts 19:21-41 records an occasion when Christians and Paul's fellow workers, Gaius and Aristarchus, were dragged into the theatre in Ephesus which seated over 20,000 people. The purpose was to humiliate and punish them in such a way that it would discredit their faith before a vast number of Ephesian citizens. When Alexander, who was 'Jewish', 'motioned with his hand, wishing to make a defense to the people', the crowd was further incited and shouted for about two hours 'Great is Artemis of the Ephesians' (Acts 19:23-28). Some Christians along with the Asiarchs, the leading civic authorities and friends of Paul, convinced him not to venture into the theatre because it was far too dangerous (19:30-31). The intention of that public spectacle was to subject Gaius and Aristarchus to public shame and physical harm, possibly death if things got out of hand. The civic official declared the gathering was not lawful as it was the offence of 'rioting' under Roman law. He further indicated that if there were charges to be brought against the Christians, they should go through the due legal process involving the proconsuls (Acts 19:38-40).

In another instance involving the temple of Artemis in Ephesus, due

---

5. For the use of this term, 'expose to public shame', see Polybius, *Histories* 11.8.7. For a cognate θεατρίζω, 'make a public show of', see Polybius, *Histories* 3.91.10. *Contra* N. Clayton Croy, *Endurance in Suffering: Hebrews 12.1-13 in Its Rhetorical, Religious and Philosophical Context,* SNTS 98 (Cambridge: Cambridge University Press, 1998), p. 163, who argues that the rarity of this word thwarts a more precise definition. Paul also uses the cognate θέατρον, as he invites them to 'follow' him and other apostles where traditionally convicted criminals were humiliated before their public execution as entertainment of the citizens in the theatre, cf. 1 Corinthians 4:9. See V. H. Nguyen, "The Identification of Paul's Spectacle of Death Metaphor in 1 Corinthians 4:9," *NTS* 53 (2007): 489-501, for a helpful discussion of this text.

legal processes were observed and the death penalty was administered to forty-three named offenders.

> [T]he advocates on behalf of the goddess [Artemis] brought in a sentence of death, as defined in this publication of the judgement: when ambassadors had been sent to our city to present robes to Artemis in accordance with ancestral custom and when the priests and the ambassadors arrived at Sardis and at the temple of Artemis which was founded by the Ephesians, the accused violated the sanctity of the ceremonies and insulted the envoys.[6]

It is well documented that to subject anyone to this sort of public spectacle in the given location in the Roman world was also a recognized form of 'entertainment' for the crowd. The theatre was not restricted simply to cultural performances and holding gladiatorial and other events but also served as a public place of torture and official execution of convicted criminals.

(ii) Public Scourging

Unlike Paul's two fellow workers in Ephesus who escaped any severe punishment, the converts addressed in this letter had early in their faith experienced publicly both 'verbal abuses (ὀθνειδιμοῖς) and also physical punishments (τε καί θλίψεσιν)', i.e., public floggings (10:33). Philo of Alexandria records a similar process overseen by the prefect of Egypt in his day.

> [He] arranged a splendid procession to send through the middle of the market-place of a body of old men prisoners, with their hands bound, some with thongs and others with iron chains, whom he led in this plight into the theatre, a most miserable spectacle, and incongruous with the occasion. And then he commanded them all to stand in front of their enemies, who were sitting down, to make their disgrace the more conspicuous, and ordered them all to be stripped of their clothes and scourged with stripes, in a way that only the most wicked of malefactors are usually treated, and they were flogged with such severity that some of them the moment they were carried out died of their wounds,

6. See *I. Eph.* 572, *ll.* 1-12.

while others were rendered so ill for a long time that their recovery was despaired of.[7]

Philo gave this account of how Aulus Avillus Flaccus, the prefect from A.D. 32 to 38, humiliated Alexandrian Jews in a public 'spectacle' in the city's theatre and later records how this 'show' (θέα) had been carefully staged as part of the wider day's entertainment for the citizens. '[T]he first of the public spectacles' (θεα, μάτων) were the physical punishments of naked Jews 'in the middle of the orchestra [pit]' (ὀρχήστρας). These lasted 'from the morning to the third or fourth hour' and then they were dragged off from the theatre to their execution. He then recounts derisively, 'and after this beautiful "exhibition" came the dancers, and the buffoons, and the flute-players, and all the other diversions of the theatrical contests'.[8]

It is also important to note that Philo recorded this to be 'the way that only the most wicked of malefactors are usually treated' (αἷς ἔθος τούς κακούγων πονηροτάτους προπηλακίζεσθαι).[9] These early Christian converts were similarly ill-treated as were the Alexandrian Jews — 'on the one hand' (τοῦτο μέν) there was public abuse 'and also physical beatings' (τε καί θλίψεσιν). This was a standard form of punishment 'just as (οὕτως) others were who were so treated' (10:33). These were officially administered punishments inflicted on Christians who had been convicted of indictable offences under the law, although they are not specified in this letter.

(iii) Previous Imprisonment of Christians

Their humiliation in the theatre was followed by incarceration, as it is recorded they had been 'fellow' (κοινωνοί) prisoners (10:33). Time in prison in the first century involved not only the loss of freedom but also harsh conditions, for prisoners who had no sustenance from outsiders

---

7. Philo, *Flaccus* 74-75. For recent discussions of *Against Flaccus* see P. Bilde, "Philo as a Polemist and a Political Apologist: An Investigation of His Two Historical Treatises Against Flaccus and The Embassy to Gaius," in *Alexandria: A Cultural and Religious Melting Pot,* ed. G. Hinge and J. A Krasilinikoff, Aarhus Studies in Mediterranean Antiquity 9 (Aarhus: Aarhus University Press, 2010), pp. 97-114, and D. R. Schwartz, "Philo and Josephus on the Violence in Alexandria in 38 C.E.," *Studia Philonica Annual* 24 (2012): 149-66.

8. Philo, *Flaccus* 84-85; Josephus, *Against Apion* 1.43, also succinctly records how these same Jews were physically punished in the theatre and then put to death.

9. Philo, *Flaccus* 75.

faced a dire situation.[10] These Christians 'also became partners with those treated thus' (τοῦτο δὲ κοινωνοὶ τῶν οὕτως ἀναστρεφομένοι γενηθέντες) (10:33b),[11] 'and for those in bonds you had compassion' (καὶ γὰρ τοῖς δεσμίοις συνεπαθήσατε) (10:34). Later the writer tells them they had to remember those in bonds (μιμνῄσκεσθε τῶν δεσμίων) 'as bound with them' (συνδεδεμένοι) who are ill-treated (τῶν κακουχουμένων) (13:3), i.e., suffered 'abuse and afflictions'.

In Rome, as elsewhere, officials were in control of prisons. The famous poet Ovid was one of an official board of three, appointed for supervising capital crimes in Rome, *triumvir capitalis*.[12] Official court proceedings could involve lengthy periods of incarceration as in the case of the Jews *versus* Paul, where he himself underwent a long detention as his case was adjourned for two years. Luke reports that he was 'kept in custody but had some liberty, and none of his friends should be prevented from attending his needs' (Acts 24:23). Felix granted this concession, for he expected a bribe.[13] 'At the same time he hoped that money would be given him by Paul. So he sent for him often and conversed with him' (24:26).

Croy suggests of the situation in Hebrews that '[t]he source of this hostility cannot be determined with precision but the occurrence of imprisonments over a period of time suggests persons with some degree of official sanction'.[14] However, the evidence in Hebrews reflects the Roman judicial procedures being followed with respect to these Christians. Roman governors appointed by the emperor exercised criminal jurisdiction in the provinces, or a *iuridicus* was appointed to relieve him if other responsibilities were overwhelming.[15]

At the time of writing, these Christians had already served their first

10. B. Rapske, *Paul in Roman Custody,* The Book of Acts in Its First Century Setting (Grand Rapids: Eerdmans, 1994), III, pp. 20-28.

11. F. Blass and A. Debrunner, *A Greek Grammar of the New Testament and Other Early Christian Literature,* English Translation by R. W. Funk (Cambridge and Chicago: Cambridge University Press and University of Chicago Press, 1961), # 290 (5), p. 151, '"τοῦτο δὲ . . . but also" is also adverbial, actually citing Hebrews 10:33.'

12. See Rapske, *Paul in Roman Custody,* pp. 246-47, for this in Rome and elsewhere.

13. See R. Syme, "C. Vibius Maximus, Prefect of Egypt," *Historia* 6 (1957): 484, for discussion of an example of a comparable situation where there was the expectation of a bribe.

14. Clayton Croy, *Endurance in Suffering: Hebrews 12.1-13 in Its Rhetorical, Religious and Philosophical Context,* p. 164.

15. J. Rogan, *Roman Provincial Administration* (Stroud, UK: Amberley Publishing, 2011), pp. 61-63.

jail sentence because of the reference to imprisonment having occurred 'in former days'. Their incarceration had a positive result in that 'they had sympathy' (σύμεπαθήσατε) with others also imprisoned with them. Today that would be described as 'empathetic', hence the command 'you must call to remembrance (ἀναμιμνήσκεσθε) how you endured such a great conflict of sufferings' (10:32).

(iv) Confiscation of Their Possessions

Another blow had occurred during their incarceration, i.e., 'the seizure of your possessions' (τὴν ἁρπαγὴν τῶν ὑπαρχόντων ὑμῶν) (10:34b). Liddell and Scott parallel this term ὕπραξις, 'like', and τὰ ὑπάρχοντα, actually citing Hebrews 10:34 as an example of 'substance, property', i.e., 'possessions'. The concept of 'seizure' is also reflected in the cognate 'to seize' (ἁρπάζω) used of the sequestration of property through the due process of the law.[16] The context is clear that it was an official confiscation of the Christians' property.

Yet in spite of this substantial loss they had accepted all this 'with joy'. This response was determined by their awareness 'of a better possession and an abiding one' (10:34), where a distinction is drawn between what was theirs then and what they would ultimately have — 'a great reward' (μεγάλη μισθαπαδοσία) (10:35).

However, given this catalogue of sufferings and losses — penalties for their crime — it is readily understandable that some would be tempted to abandon their faith if there was the threat of more to come.

II. Multiple Legal Punishments for Infringements of the Law

Why were multiple punishments, with the possibility of more, being meted out to these Christians? Literary sources reflect that this was a recent trend in Roman criminal proceedings. This section seeks to unlock the legal reasons why Christians at that time were under enormous pressure to renounce their faith rather than face further punishment.

---

16. Liddell and Scott note that the use of the verb ὑπαρχω is 'frequently in neuter plural participle [form], ἡ ὑπάρχουσα οὐσί [refers to] possessions, resources'. They cite as an example Isocrates, *Speeches* 1.28, τὴν ὑπάρχουσαν οὐσίαν.

(i) Harsher Penalties and Mandatory Exile Under Roman Law

Aubert draws attention to harsher punishments in Roman criminal law in the time of Nero.[17] He also notes that 'Roman magistrates had acquired some leeway in the interpretation of the law' and they also blurred the punishments of different penalties for different social classes. This trend, he concludes, was a 'discrepancy or congruence, between theory and practice in Roman criminal law and practice'.[18]

Under the subheading of 'Harsher Punishments', Aubert also notes, 'Legislators devised new and harsher penalties, such as hard labour, mandatory exile and deportation to an island.'[19] This legal paradigm shift helps to explain the multiple punishments these Christians experienced as well as the pending exile specifically addressed at the conclusion of the letter (13:13).

Roman governors did not always follow the letter of the law, even though its administration was their primary remit. 'Governors often condemn people to be held in prison or kept in chains, but they are not supposed to do so, for such penalties are forbidden; prisons ought to be for detaining men [i.e., for trial], not for punishing them' and 'people may have had to languish in jail awaiting the infrequent assizes, in the provinces in particular' as Crook noted.[20]

For indictable offences, Roman law prescribed that 'the property of those who ought to be accused, or have been caught committing a crime, or who have killed themselves should be confiscated [by the Treasury]'. It also stipulated that 'the property of anyone who kills himself after he has been accused should be confiscated by the Treasury only where he was accused of a crime for which, if he were convicted, he should be punished with death or deportation', i.e., exile.[21]

Had these Christians committed a criminal offence? Rapske in dis-

17. J.-J. Aubert, "A Double Standard in Roman Criminal Law? The Death Penalty and Social Structure in Late Republic and Early Roman Empire," in *Speculum Ivris: Roman Law as a Reflection of Social and Economic Life in Antiquity,* ed. J.-J. Aubert and B. Sirks (Ann Arbor: University of Michigan Press, 2002), p. 103.

18. Aubert, "A Double Standard in Roman Criminal Law?" p. 106.

19. Aubert, "A Double Standard in Roman Criminal Law?" p. 103.

20. J. A. Crook, *Law and Life in Rome, 90 B.C.–A.D. 212* (Ithaca, NY: Cornell University Press, 1967), p. 274, citing *The Digest* 48.19 fragments 8.9 and 35. See also Paul's delay, Acts 24:26-27.

21. *The Digest* 21.3.1.

cussing 'prison and coercion' notes, 'Since legal provisions kept magistrates from using the most severe forms of *coercitio* upon citizens, imprisonment was used instead.' This applied not only to the earlier Roman Republic but to the empire as well. He further comments, 'It [imprisonment] was also a recourse of magistrates to compel the obedience of individuals of lesser stature in Roman eyes — namely, foreigners, slaves and women'. Had the former imprisonment of these Christians been intended 'to compel [their] obedience'?[22]

(ii) Christian Infringement of Roman Law

Was there a legal charge for which Christians could be indicted? In an early constitution, *Lex coloniae Genetiae Juliae* (45 B.C.), Section CVI records, 'No colonist of the colony [Roman] Genetiva, established by order of G. Caesar the dictator, shall (get together) any assemblage or meeting or conspiracy'. According to Hardy who was its editor, 'These would come under the category of *majestas*', i.e., 'treason'.[23] All the Julio-Claudian emperors saw associations as hotbeds for fomenting political dissents and therefore a thorn in their side.[24]

Robinson in *The Criminal Law of Ancient Rome* discusses 'Offenses against the State', i.e., 'treason', 'sedition' and the official repressing of *collegia* (associations). Augustus' legislation on associations meant that Christians could not legally meet weekly, although Jews had been specifically exempted in the same legislation and could do so. For all others, 'regular meetings were to be no more than monthly'. Robinson also notes the consequences — 'This is one reason why Christians could hardly have formed legal *collegia*, since they need to meet weekly for worship.'[25]

In the eyes of the emperors of the first century, and sometimes governors and ruling authorities in cities of the empire, *collegia* 'represented

---

22. Rapske, *Paul in Roman Custody*, p. 15.

23. E. G. Hardy, *Three Spanish Charters and Other Documents* (Oxford: Clarendon Press, 1912), p. 50, n. 121, citing *The Digest* 48.4.1.2.

24. For evidence of this with Augustus, Tiberius, Claudius and Nero, see my discussion of the Julio-Claudian emperors' suspicion of associations as hotbeds of treason, "Roman Law and Society in Romans 12–15," in *Rome in the Bible and the Early Church*, ed. P. Oakes (Carlisle and Grand Rapids: Paternoster and Baker, 2002), pp. 72-75.

25. O. F. Robinson, *The Criminal Law of Ancient Rome* (London: Duckworth, 1995), p. 80.

a threat to Roman order rather than a standing offence, but they could be repressed severely; accusations were made before the Prefect of the City'.[26] In *Lex Irnitana* there was a specific provision 'concerning illegal gatherings, societies and colleges *(collegia)*'.

> No one is to take part in an illegal gathering *(coetum facito)* in that *municipium* (self-governing town) or to hold a meeting of a society or college for that purpose or to conspire that it be held or to act in such a way that any of these things occur. Anyone who acts contrary to these rules is to be condemned to pay 10,000 secterces to the *municipes* of the *Municipium Flavium Irnitanum* and the right of action, suit and claim of that money and concerning that money is to belong to any *municipes* of that *municipium*.[27]

González, the editor of this bronze inscription, draws this significant conclusion — 'It is important to observe that the only thing actually banned is a *coetus*', i.e., an 'assembly'.[28]

One legal prohibition in Roman law applied to Christian gatherings for weekly worship.[29] This may well explain the significant exhortation 'not neglecting the meeting together (ἐπισυναγωγή) as is the habit of some (καθὼς ἔθος τισίν)' (10:25). Hedged around this exhortation is the prelude 'to hold fast the confession of our hope that it does not waver' (v. 23), also the call to 'love and good works' (v. 24) along with the subsequent warning not to sin willfully because there were no more sacrifices for sin, and there was an alarming fate for disloyal Christians (vv. 26-30). The reason for absenting oneself was not specified but, given the evidence in Hebrews, a good case can be made for some realizing that attendance on a weekly basis was in breach of Roman law, for only the Jews were permitted to do this.[30]

Pliny the Younger later noted that all associations in Pontus were prohibited because of their suspected anti-Roman stance. 'When people gather together for a common purpose, whatever name we may give them

---

26. Robinson, *The Criminal Law of Ancient Rome*, p. 80.

27. The *Lex Irnitana*, ch. 74. For the text see González, "The *Lex Irnitana:* A New Copy of the Flavian Municipal Law," *JRS* 76 (1986): 193.

28. González, "The *Lex Irnitana*," p. 223.

29. Robinson, *The Criminal Law of Ancient Rome*, p. 80.

30. W. Cotter, "The *Collegia* and Roman Law: State Restrictions on Voluntary Associations 64 BCE-200 CE," in *Voluntary Associations in the Graeco-Roman World,* ed. J. S. Kloppenborg and S. G. Wilson (London: Routledge, 1996), pp. 77-78.

and whatever function we may assign them, they soon become political.' In the same letter he reported to the emperor, Trajan, following the interrogation of Christians — 'They affirmed, however, the whole of their guilt or their error was that they were in the habit of meeting on a certain fixed day before it was light, when they sang a hymn to Christ, as to a god.' They were in breach of Roman law by meeting as they did on 'a certain fixed day.'[31]

(iii) Conventional Expressions of Loyalty to Rome's Imperial Gods

How did the Christians in this letter cope with 'the overwhelming pressure to conform'? All citizens were required to express loyalty to emperors who in the first century were addressed with the same titles that the Christians used of Jesus. (See pp. 62-74.) Loyalty to Rome had obligatory, reciprocal demands for all subjects of the empire to perform cultic honours to the emperor in their temples, the Jews being exempted. This had to create a problem for Christians. It was not dissimilar to that faced by a subsequent generation brought before the governor Pliny the Younger (*c.* A.D. 61–*c.* 112). His successful interrogation of some Christians resulted in their apostasy.

> They [Christians] repeated after me an invocation to the gods, and offered religious rites with wine and incense before your statue which for that purpose I had ordered to be brought, together with those of the gods, and even reviled the name of Christ: whereas there is no forcing, it is said, those who are really Christians into any of these compliances: I thought it proper, therefore, to discharge them. Some among those who were accused by a witness in person at first confessed themselves Christians, but immediately after denied it.[32]

Thus in the early second century, Christians who refused and remained steadfast in their faith faced summary execution if provincials, or if they were Roman citizens, they were officially confined as a prisoner to be sent to Rome for trial. Capital punishment was threatened elsewhere for Christians who refused to give divine honours before imperial statues in imperial cult temples. (See chapter 12.)

31. Pliny the Younger, *To the Emperor Trajan* 10.96.
32. Pliny the Younger, *To the Emperor Trajan* 10.96.

The examination of Roman law concerning associations can also help to understand the enormous pressure that tempted Christians to move into the safe haven of Judaism. This must have seemed a good way forward to avoid giving divine honours to the Caesars and not suffer a much more dreaded punishment.

III. Fearing and Fleeing or Fortified and Facing Exile

Even though they had already suffered punishments, the immediate threat that hung over the heads of the Christians was 'exile'. The metaphorical phrases for exile used in the Letter to the Hebrews were 'outside the camp' and 'outside the gate' (13:11-14). Just as under the Jewish law sacrifices for sin were burnt outside the camp (κατακαίεται ἔξω τῆς παρεμβολῆς), so also Jesus 'suffered outside the gate' (ἔξω τῆς πύλης ἔπαθεν) [of the city] in order to sanctify the people through his own blood' (13:12).

(i) The Penalty of Exile

As already noted, the very title of Williams' monograph *The Curse of Exile* epitomizes the ignominy, loneliness, harshness and other losses experienced by Ovid (43 B.C.–A.D. 17), who in his *Ibis* and *Ex Ponto* bears eloquent witness to his own experiences.[33] Claassen likewise records the emotional feelings and terrible deprivation felt by a wider group of people in Roman society in "The Horror of Isolation." He shows that it was abhorred because of the places of desolation that were chosen for punishment as well as the deprivation suffered from adverse climatic conditions, and access to fertile land for producing good food and clean water.[34] It carried with it the possibility of not being able to return, as banishment could be permanent.

Crook has shown that going into exile was 'an accepted way of avoid-

---

33. G. D. Williams, *The Curse of Exile: A Study of Ovid's Ibis.* Some of his chapter headings succinctly reflect the emotional feelings and the psychological effects on those banished: "Needing to Scream: Restraint and Self-abandon in the *Ibis,*" "The *Ibis* in Context: Melancholy, Mania and Exile" and "Cruel Pleasure: Mystery and Meaning in the *Ibis*-Catalogue," chs. 2, 4, 5.

34. J.-M. Claassen, "The Horror of Isolation," in *Displaced Persons: The Literature of Exile from Cicero to Boethius* (London: Duckworth, 1999), ch. 7.

ing the [death] penalty'.[35] Exile under Roman law was to a distant place, an island or 'to the most desert part' of a province, to cite the Roman legal code.[36] The verb 'to be cast out' (ἐκβάλλω) was used to describe being banished, while φυγάς was the legal term for 'exile'.[37] Ovid is a good example of this experience. He managed to offend Augustus in one of his poems and, for another reason not disclosed, Augustus exiled him *c.* A.D. 1 to Tomis, an isolated city on the Black Sea coast, where he remained until his death in A.D. 12.[38]

Exile also involved the loss of citizenship and all property.[39] On the latter penalty Augustus sent a decree to Ancyra in the East stipulating the legal confiscation of property because of theft from a Jewish synagogue — 'And if anyone is caught stealing their sacred books or their sacred monies from a synagogue or an ark [of the law], he shall be regarded as sacrilegious, and his property shall be confiscated to the public treasury of the Romans.'[40]

When Cicero was faced with the confiscation of his property through a due legal process[41] he asked, 'What is more sacred, what is more protected by all religion than the house of each and every citizen?' 'Within its circle are his altars, his household gods, his religion, his observances, his ritual; it is a sanctuary so holy in the eyes of all, that it were sacrilege to tear an owner from it.'[42] In this era the household in many ways defined the family and one's identity.[43]

In Roman law the loss of property was not a consequence of being sentenced to 'relegation' *(relegatio),* but it was prescribed for more serious offenders who were sentenced to 'exile' *(exsul).*[44] Under relegation the per-

---

35. Crook, *Law and Life in Rome,* p. 272.

36. *The Digest* 48.21.7.9.

37. P. Garnsey, *Social Status and Legal Privilege in the Roman Empire* (Oxford: Clarendon Press, 1970), pp. 111-21.

38. Ovid, *Trist.* 2.131-32.

39. P. Garnsey, *Social Status and Legal Privilege in the Roman Empire,* pp. 111-21.

40. Josephus, *Jewish Antiquities* 16.163, *l.* 11–165 *l.* 19.

41. A term used for the confiscation of property was δήμευσις with the cognate δημεύω, 'to seize as public property'. See Thucydides, *Hist.* 5.59.3.l.3.

42. Cicero, *De Domo Sua* 109.

43. R. P. Saller, "*Familia* and *domus:* Defining and Representing the Roman Family and Household," in *Patriarch, Property and Death in the Roman Family* (Cambridge: Cambridge University Press, 1994), ch. 4.

44. H. F. Jolowicz, *Historical Introduction to the Study of Roman Law* (Cambridge: Cambridge University Press, 1932), pp. 408-9.

son was usually banished for a limited time, but exile was long term and incurred not only loss of citizenship but also all of one's material possessions.

The writer of the letter prescribes the following remedy to help the Christians mentioned here face the future, rather than to turn their backs on the dire prospect of exile and thus experience even greater 'penalty' i.e., apostasy. 'So then (τοίνυν) let us go forth to him outside the camp and bear the abuse he [Jesus] endured' (13:13). The term τοίνυν indicates the logical consequence, while 'abuse' (ὀνειδισνός) is the same word already used of public verbal abuse endured in their first imprisonment (10:33).

(ii) On-Going Endurance — the Athletic Metaphor

The first reason given for endurance is that Christ himself suffered 'outside the gate' to secure the sanctification of God's people through the cost of shedding his own blood 'outside the gate' of the city of Jerusalem (13:12). They are also reminded of another reason for enduring — 'for we have here no abiding city but (ἀλλά) we are seeking the one that is to come' (13:14). Both reasons are intended to provide help in ameliorating the thought of impending suffering of exile. This explains further the statement already made in 10:34 that they have 'a better possession and abiding one'. It contradicted the propaganda that the everlasting city was the 'eternal Rome' (Roma Aeterna) that boasted of its permanence and the blessings of the pax romana to city life. Other empires and cities had come and gone, but the power and permanence of heaven could never be superseded.

The exhortation to these Christians is that they should not make the worst decision ever by 'throwing away our confidence, which had a great reward' (10:35). They should weigh up the guaranteed eternal security awaiting them in heaven with the temporary nature of their present residence (10:34).

The writer does not minimize the fact that the time immediately ahead would be very difficult; hence he uses the present tense, 'For you have need of endurance' (ὑπομονῆς γὰρ ἔχετε χρείαν) (10:36). The term ὑπομονή referred to the capacity to hold on in adverse circumstances, to survive and even thrive.[45] They were reminded that there was a 'great re-

---

45. For example, it was used to describe a tree surviving in very adverse conditions such as growing on a rocky cliff face; see Theophrastus 5.16.3.

ward' awaiting them in the future, and the incentive for continuing to endure was 'so that you may do the will of God and receive what is promised' (10:36). Tenacity was needed to persist in doing God's will and thereby receive his reward.

The remedy was not only the anticipation of the 'great reward' but also the eschatological promise that there was an end in sight. The author cites from the Old Testament prophets — 'For yet a little while, and the coming one shall come and not delay' (10:37).[46] The view of the imminent Messianic return was in direct opposition to the first-century philosophical view of the eternity of the world and the propaganda concerning the eternal city of Rome.[47]

These Christians faced a choice to live in the light of the promised return of Christ, 'and my righteous one shall live by faith' (10:38a), or to cut and run because they could not bear to face any more adversity. If they retreated from the faith, God's blessing would not be with them — 'if he shrinks back, my soul will have no pleasure in him' (10:38b), is the grave warning cited from Habakkuk 2:3-4. The writer hastens to add with emphasis, 'and we ourselves (ἡμεῖς) are not those who shrink back for destruction'. His use of 'destruction' (ἀπώλεια) as a synonymous concept for apostasy indicates how dire the consequences would be. Because of this he affirms, 'but (ἀλλά) we are those who have faith and preserve their souls' (10:39).

A definition of real 'faith' is provided — 'the assurance of things hoped for, the certainty of things not seen' (11:1). Then follows a long 'homily' on what perseverance meant for some of God's people from the past who lived by faith, listing many examples of trust and endurance in times of comparable and sometimes fatal outcomes (11:4-40).

The writer uses the image of an athlete who runs a challenging race in a stadium while being watched by a huge crowd — 'so great a cloud of witnesses' (12:1). Like competing athletes, Christians have metaphorically to strip down, laying aside 'every weight' (ὄγκον). This term can refer literally to 'weight' or can be used of 'trouble' that weighs a person down.[48] In this case it is a burden they can rightly abandon. They must also 'shed

---

46. For a helpful treatment of the texts gathered from Isaiah 26:10 and Habakkuk 2:3b see P. T. O'Brien, *The Letter to the Hebrews* (Grand Rapids and Nottingham: Eerdmans and Apollos, 2010), pp. 389-92.

47. Philo of Alexandria, *The Eternity of the World,* argues the ancient Greek philosophical view.

48. See the entry of ὄγκος, Liddell and Scott II for this metaphorical use.

the sin that clings so closely'. Just as athletes traditionally discarded all their clothes to run their race unencumbered,[49] so too must Christians cast aside these hindrances. The analogy continues. Greek marathon runners had to stay the arduous course; Christians 'must run with endurance' in order to finish the race (12:1). The term 'endurance' was previously used in 10:36, where comparable sufferings had to be 'endured', difficult as that was (10:32). Total focus on the finishing line was essential for athletes to complete the course. Christians, then, must 'look to Jesus' to do so. This verb ἀφοραω means 'to look away from all others at one'.[50] The use of this powerful athletic imagery illustrated how the Christians were to run their life's race without being distracted by their present circumstances, as their concentration was to be on reaching the finishing line (12:1).

Another focus of their attention was the sacrifice of Jesus on the cross, which also provided a paradigm for them in their present situation. Knowing the ultimate 'joy' awaiting him, Jesus poured scorn on the humiliating shame experienced at his crucifixion. He did this as 'the founder and perfector (τελειωτής) of our faith'. The word 'perfector' was rightly chosen, as it refers to one who brings something to a successful conclusion. Jesus looked beyond his humiliating death knowing he would secure his inheritance, i.e., the place of permanent honour and power at the right hand of God (12:2).

When these Christians had been in prison their focus on the future resulted in their joyful response even when they had had their possessions confiscated. They knew their long-term inheritance was all-important (10:34-5). It paralleled the 'joy' Jesus anticipated as the result of his sacrifice and enabled him to endure suffering (12:2). However, the writer, aware of their fragility, admonishes them not to grow weary or faint-hearted in running this spiritual race with its lasting prize.[51] Their present struggles

---

49. The abandoning of the loincloth in athletics enabled runners to participate unencumbered. Pausanias, *Description of Greece* 1.44.1, attributes this originally to Orsippos at the Olympic Games in 720 B.C., who 'intentionally let the loincloth slip off him, realizing that a naked man can run more easily than one with it on'. For a discussion of other ancient sources that attribute this convention to others, see Newby, *Athletics in the Ancient World*, pp. 71-72, 93.

50. Herodotus, *Histories* 8.35 *l.* 9.

51. Prizes for races won at the games at Olympia and Delphi were 'simple crowns of vegetation', crowns of celery in Isthmia, and monetary rewards in the Capitoline Games instituted in A.D. 86, where winners were given 'a simple wreath, apparently of oak leaves'; see Newby, *Athletics in the Ancient World*, pp. 37, 41.

were in no way comparable to those suffered by Jesus because they 'have not yet resisted to the point of shedding your blood' (12:3-4).

(iii) Fortified to Face Exile

The prelude in Hebrews 12:3-6 to the quotation of Proverbs 3:11-12 is the requirement to consider the endurance of Christ that led to the shedding of his blood — it was not leading to capital punishment in their case, but rather exile. Furthermore their suffering was not a sign of divine disapproval but the assurance of their divine filial relationship. Suffering or adversity was certainly not seen in this way in the first century, as Liebeschuetz notes — 'there is abundant evidence that the Romans were even obsessively convinced of the need to placate the gods' when faced with either.[52] These Christians must take care to heed the exhortation to endure this 'discipline'. Although painful, they are exhorted to see it as beneficial because it is part of their sanctification that will produce 'the peaceful fruits of righteousness by those who are trained by it' (12:7-11).

The theme of the shared suffering in identical circumstances is again raised. Lest these Christians forget their past plight in prison, their attention is drawn to the value of the empathy that grew out of their previous adversity with an exhortation to continue 'to remember those who are in prison, as though in prison with them; and those who are ill-treated, since you are in the body' (13:3). 'This unusual expression is intended to convey the notion of intense identification with those who are suffering.'[53] It links up with previous comments on their empathy with fellow prisoners in their first internment (10:34). The letter ends with the encouraging news of Timothy's release from prison, so the recipients who had shared the same experience would undoubtedly have rejoiced on learning of this (13:23). It would also have given them hope in their present situation.

The extended discussion of suffering in Hebrews 10:32–12:13 concludes with a final exhortation to the Christians to take responsibility, pull themselves together and run on the straight path — 'therefore lifting up your drooping hands and strengthening your knees you must make straight paths for your feet in order that what is lame may not be put out of joint but

---

52. J. H. W. G. Liebeschuetz, *Continuity and Change in Roman Religion* (Oxford: Clarendon Press, 1979), p. 3.

53. O'Brien, *The Letter to the Hebrews,* p. 508.

rather be healed' (12:12-13). Those who felt downhearted and disoriented because of impending suffering are called upon to get themselves back on track and continue to endure to the completion of their earthly race. As Attridge notes of this whole section on suffering, 'The exhortation to faithful endurance built on athletic imagery and the proverbial understanding of suffering as educative discipline thus closes on a positive note.'[54]

The writer ends his letter with an appeal by way of an imperative. 'I exhort you, brothers, you must listen (ἀνέχεσθε) patiently with my word of exhortation', which is his description of the overall intention of his letter (13:22). Its bottom line is to persevere in the face of impending suffering as the response to what Mitchell describes as 'the overwhelming pressure to conform [to imperial cultic activities] imposed by the institutions of his city and the activities of his neighbors'.[55] This included exile.

After using the evocative image of 'suffering outside the camp', the instruction for the difficult and lonely path of exile, they are exhorted to 'go to him' (13:12-13). The thought of Christ's presence with them would ameliorate the sense of being alone suffering in an isolated place that was so greatly dreaded in the Roman world. Their high priest was empathetic, given what and where he suffered, and he could therefore give sufficient grace to help them cope adequately in desperate circumstances with his timely assistance (4:16).[56]

The recipients of this letter must not retreat into what seemed the safe haven of Judaism to escape ignominy and suffering, for the compelling reasons outlined at length in this letter. For them the crucial rôle of the Jewish high priest appointed by Rome had now been superseded by the one who alone possessed perpetual divinity, the eternal Son of God, and was a powerful, personal and empathetic high priest, superior to all others.

Unlike the divine Caesars in their high-priestly office held only while reigning, Jesus' divinity and high-priestly office was held in perpetuity. Jesus' everlasting kingdom would never be disestablished. Having outlined all this, the only credible option for the Christians addressed here was to take a long-term view and go 'to him outside the camp and bear the abuse

54. H. W. Attridge, *A Commentary on the Epistle to the Hebrews* (Philadelphia: Fortress Press, 1989), p. 365.

55. S. Mitchell, *Anatolia: Land, Men, and Gods in Asia Minor* (Oxford: Clarendon Press, 1993), II, p. 10.

56. Attridge, *A Commentary on the Epistle to the Hebrews,* p. 142, links this back to 2:18, 'For because he himself has suffered when tempted he is able to help those who are being tempted.'

he endured' (13:13). He suffered, he held fast, and he can give them grace to endure a similar alienation.

The intensity of opposition and suffering, the pressure to capitulate and the impending threat addressed in this letter would not be unique to its recipients, as the final chapter will show.

CHAPTER 12

Conformity and Commerce or Capital Punishment: New Honours for Caesar

A major innovation in the imperial cult proved to be a decisive and direct challenge for the first Christians in the seven churches mentioned in the Book of Revelation. As a prerequisite to engaging in any commercial transaction they had to give specific divine honours to the Caesar. Without doing so they would not have been able to secure provisions for their daily needs, as all goods could only be bought or sold through the authorised markets in a first-century city. Officials controlled these markets and were also responsible for the collection of taxes levied on the sale of every commodity. All were required to have 'the name' of 'the beast' inked on their right hand or forehead, after which they were to worship the statue of the emperor in the imperial cult temple also located in the city centre. Then, and only then, could they sell or purchase essential commodities. The implications for those who did not comply were extremely serious. While those addressed in Hebrews 13:13 were threatened with exile, here refusal to participate would result in summary execution (13:15-17). This final chapter explores this innovation connecting imperial cultic veneration with trade and commerce.

It is proposed to examine (I) the official control of all commercial activities in cities in the East; (II) the numbers given to identify the reign and the name of the emperor; (III) the identity and cultic innovations of the 'second beast' and the unprecedented provincial innovation requiring all citizens to have his 'mark' and give divine honours in the imperial cult temple before trading; and (IV) the dire consequences for Christians who did not comply.

I. Official Control of All Local, Commercial Trading

Revelation 13:16-17 states that 'both small and great, both rich and poor, both free and slave [are] to be marked on the right hand or forehead so that no one can buy or sell unless he has the mark'. De Ligt's observation in *Fairs and Markets in the Roman Empire* throws light on the significance of this statement. '[T]he imperial and (urban) authorities retained a firm grip on all indirect taxes that were levied at markets, including those levied at periodic markets established by private individuals on their [imperial] estates.'[1]

A poignant example from a later period epitomises the absolute control the city authorities exercised over all commerce. A humble egg-seller was caught trading outside the official market. He promised never again to trade either in his home or secretly, acknowledging that if he did so, he would be penalised.

> To Flavius Thennyras, local magistrate of the district of Oxyrhynchus, from Aurelius Nilus, son of Didysus, of the most illustrious city of Oxyrhynchus, an egg seller by trade. I hereby agree on the august, the divine oath by our lord, the Emperor and the Caesars to offer for sale in public my eggs in the market place, and to supply to the said city, every day without break. I acknowledge that it is illegal for me in the future to sell secretly or in my house. If I am found out doing so, I shall be liable to be punished.[2]

There is also evidence from Sardis, another city in the province of Asia, confirming that officials had been elected or appointed by the Council to control the markets in cities in the province. Josephus reproduced an official decree to Sardis issued in 47 B.C. It restored the rights of Jews to live in this city and included the obligation of the superintendent of the market to provide for kosher food to be brought into the market for them to purchase —

> it has therefore been decreed by the Council and People that permission shall be given to them to assemble on sacred days, to do things

---

1. L. De Ligt, *Fairs and Markets in the Roman Empire: Economic and Social Aspects of Periodic Trade in the Pre-Industrial Society,* Dutch Monographs on Ancient History and Archaeology (Amsterdam: J. C. Gieben, 1993), XI, p. 169.

2. *P.Oxy.* 83 (A.D. 327).

in accordance with their laws, and also that a place be set apart by the magistrates for them to build and inhabit, so that (ὅπως) the market-officials of the city shall be charged with the duty of having suitable food for them [the Jews] brought in.[3]

In addition to approving a location for building a Jewish synagogue, the decree also required officials to establish a market for Jews, enabling them to have access to 'suitable' (kosher) food. They therefore reactivated the Jewish market in the agora. The city, therefore, had a critical rôle in commercial activity. It is important to note that this inscription records the precedent in Rome for this restoration of the Jews' civic rights and privileges in Sardis. It was because 'their laws and freedoms had been restored by the Roman Senate and People'.[4] One of the letters in the Book of Revelation was addressed to the Christian community in the self-same city (Rev. 3:1-5). No such official provision was made for the first Christians.

The officials elected to public office for the day-to-day management of the markets were called the 'superintendents of the market' (ἀγορανόμοι). They 'had general supervision of the sale of merchandise in the city-market, being responsible for establishing prices [as at Pergamum], ensuring adequate supplies and determining the accuracy of weights'.[5] The tax was levied on all commercial transactions and the proceeds went into the city's treasury.

The introduction of this edict applied to all the inhabitants (13:15b), but the effect was especially felt by Christians because non-participation resulted in summary execution.

There was already a precedent for imperial innovations by Roman provincial governors in the province of Asia. In 9 B.C. Paullus Fabius Maximus, the governor, 'Caesar's friend' and connected to Augustus by marriage, had played the leading rôle in promoting new honours for 'the most divine Caesar' (τοῦ θηοτάτου Καίσαρος).[6] Because Augustus' birthday was seen, in effect, as 'the beginning of all things' for the empire, New Year's Day had been changed to commemorate his auspicious birth. (See pp.

---

3. Josephus, *Jewish Antiquities* 14.259-60.

4. Josephus, *Jewish Antiquities* 14.260.

5. A. D. Macro, "The Cities of Asia Minor under the Roman Imperium," in *Principat: Politische Geschichte,* ANRW (Berlin and New York: De Gruyter, 1980), XI.7,2, p. 679.

6. *OGIS* 458. R. K. Sherk, *Roman Documents from the East: Senatus Consulta and Epistulae to the Age of Augustus* (Baltimore: Johns Hopkins University Press, 1969), LXIV.l, p. 22.

28-36.) Evidence from the same era had seen Publius Cornelius Scipio, a senior Roman official and later governor of the same province, also vigorously promoting divine honours subsequent to his next appointment in the province of Achaea soon after 3 B.C. (See pp. 168-72.)

Was history repeating itself with another Roman provincial governor of Asia undertaking an unprecedented, indeed a highly innovative step aimed at promoting still further specific divine honours for the reigning Caesar? He prescribed that each person in the province was to give such honours before a statue of the reigning emperor in the temple. While the Jews had secured exemption from worshipping idols, all other residents would 'voluntarily' have had placed on their right hand or their forehead a special mark as an act of loyalty. They then had to give divine honours before a statue of the emperor in his temple (13:16).

II. Playing the Numbers Game to Identify the Beast

The original readers of the Book of Revelation were challenged to undertake two sets of calculations to identify this imperial person referred to as 'the beast'. One, it asserted, was within the competence of all to make (17:10), but only those who possessed 'wisdom' would be able to undertake the second (13:18).

(i) The Number of Roman Emperors

The clue for the Christians was 'there are also seven kings' (βασιλεῖς ἑπτά), five of whom are fallen, 'the one is' (ὁ εἷς ἔστιν), the other has not yet come, and 'when he does come he must remain only a little while' (17:10). How were emperors numbered in this era? The dating of this official innovation hinges primarily on how the numbers of emperors were calculated, including the present holder of the office.

The following evidence records the Roman emperors that were referred to as 'kings' in Revelation. Although Augustus (27 B.C.–A.D. 14) was not an immediate blood relative of Julius Caesar, his mother, Atia, was Caesar's sister; hence he was his nephew and in fact his closest living relative. In an official letter to Mylasa, Augustus declares himself 'Imperator Caesar, son of the divine Julius', and in others 'Imperator Caesar Augustus, son of a god, the ruler of land and all sea, her own saviour and benefactor' and 'Imperator Caesar Augustus son of a god', the latter being Julius Caesar.[7]

His successor, Tiberius (A.D. 14-37), was cited in an inscription from Lepcis as 'Tiberius Caesar Augustus, son of divine Augustus, grandson of divine Julius'.[8] He was formally addressed as 'Tiberius Caesar, son of the divine Augustus, grandson of the divine Julius, and Drusus Caesar, son of Tiberius Augustus, grandson of the divine Augustus, great-grandson of divine Julius' in an inscription from Philippi *c.* A.D. 37.[9]

On a milestone on the *Via Augusta,* Cordoba, Gaius (A.D. 37-41), the successor of Tiberius, was declared to be 'Gaius Caesar Germanicus Augustus, son of Germanicus Caesar, grandson of Tiberius Augustus, great-grandson of the divine Augustus, great-great-grandson of the divine Julius'.[10]

An official document from Alexandria that Lucius Aemilius, the Roman prefect of Egypt, put on public display on 10 November, A.D. 41, for all the inhabitants to read, commences with the accolade he used of Claudius — 'the greatness of our god Caesar' (τὴν τε μεγαλιότητα τοῦ θεοῦ Καίσαρος). It contains a copy of the letter of Claudius in which he addressed the Alexandrians using his own official name and title — 'Tiberius Claudius Caesar Augustus Germanicus, *pontifex maximus.*'[11] Claudius is also cited on official Alexandrian coins as 'Tiberius Claudius Caesar Augustus Germanicus Imperator. Year 1' (ΤΙ. ΚΛΑΥΔΙ. ΚΑΙΣ. ΣΕΒΑ. ΓΕΡΜΑΝΙ. ΑΥΤΟΚΡ. ΛΑ).[12] A search of official inscriptions published to date, including the major database, has failed to find any references to his predecessors, not least of all Gaius, who had been 'dispatched', thus resulting in Claudius' succession. This may go some way to explaining the different convention he adopted with respect to official imperial titles.[13]

---

7. *Syll.*[3] 768; *IGRR* 1, 901; V. Ehrenberg and A. H. M. Jones, *Documents Illustrating the Reigns of Augustus & Tiberius* (Oxford: Clarendon Press, 1976[2]), nos. 303, 268.

8. *ILS* 113.

9. Ehrenberg and Jones, *Documents Illustrating the Reigns of Augustus & Tiberius,* no. 148.

10. *CIL* 2, 6208.

11. *P. Lond.* 1912, *ll.* 9-12.

12. *RPC* no. 5113 (A.D. 41). On the obverse side of the coin is 'Messalina, wife of Caesar Augustus'.

13. See also *IGRR* 4, 584; *Tituli Asiae Mororis* 2.760; and *SEG* 12, 153. For a discussion specifically focusing on Claudius in the province of Egypt see E. G. Huzar, "Emperor Worship in Julio-Claudian Egypt," in *Heidentum: Die Religiösen Verhäktnisse in den Provinzen,* ed. W. Haase, ANRW 18, no. 5 (Berlin and New York: De Gruyter, 1995), pp. 3134-38.

By contrast, Nero gave great emphasis to the divine origin of all his predecessors. This confirmed his own legitimacy as Claudius' successor, hence his imperial divinity. It could be, given the poisoning of his younger step-brother, Britannicus, the natural-born son of Claudius, soon after Nero was declared the successor of his adopted father, that he needed all the more to assert the legitimacy of his rule in terms of descent. (See p. 67.) There are a number of official extant inscriptions in which he traces such imperial and divine origins back to Augustus. 'Nero Claudius Caesar Augustus Germanicus, son of the divine Claudius (*divi Claudi f.,* θεοῦ Κλαυδίου υἱός), grandson of Germanicus Caesar, great-grandson of Tiberius Caesar Augustus, great-great-grandson of the divine Augustus (*divi Augusti,* θεοῦ Σεβαστοῦ)'.[14]

The Neronean inscription was not the sole arbiter in identifying the number of kings. Revelation 17:10 records seven kings, five of whom have died; 'the one is' (ὁ εἷς ἔστιν) Nero, 'the other is not yet come and when he comes he must continue a little while' — Galba would reign for only three months.[15] Also, slightly later and important literary sources, *Jewish Antiquities* and *Jewish War,* written by Josephus (*c.* A.D. 37-110), actually list the Julio-Claudian and earlier Flavian names of emperors, even recording the years, months and days they held office.

Josephus writes that Augustus refers to 'my father, Caesar the emperor',[16] though he was by birth his uncle. Importantly, unlike Nero's list of his predecessors in the epigraphic evidence, Josephus thus understood that Augustus was not the first but the second. He ruled for '57 years, 6 months and 2 days,' and the third emperor, Tiberius, ruled '22 years, 5 months and 3 days'.[17] Gaius succeeded him as 'the fourth emperor. . . . he had reigned four years within four months', and his nephew, Claudius Caesar Augustus Germanicus, ruled 'thirteen years, eight months and twenty-four days' and

14. For this bilingual inscription of Nero, see M. P. Charlesworth, "Nero," in *Documents Illustrating the Reigns of Claudius & Nero* (Cambridge: Cambridge University Press, 1939), no. 4. See also other identical ones: S. Dusanic, "A Military Diploma of A.D. 65," *Germania* 56 (1979): 461-75, "Pannonia Near the Danube Relating to Three Cohorts of Upper Germany," *L'Anné épigraphique* 44 (1969/70); Lower Germany and the Cyrenaica bilingual inscription, L. Bacchielli and J. M. Reynolds, "The Public Land of the Roman People in Syrenaica," *Libya Antiqua* 8 (1971): 47-49.

15. On 9 June, A.D. 68, at age thirty, assisted by one of his servants, Nero committed suicide just before the guards came to assassinate him. E. Champlin, *Nero* (Cambridge, MA: Harvard University Press, 2003), p. 49.

16. Josephus, *Jewish Antiquities* 16.162.

17. Josephus, *Jewish War* 2.168, *Jewish Antiquities* 18.224.

therefore was the fifth.[18] Hence the sixth is Nero, who succeeded him at the age of sixteen years and nine months on 13 October, A.D. 54, and reigned until 11 June, A.D. 68. 'Nero was dead, after he had reigned thirteen years and eight months'.[19] The latter's successor, Galba, 'was slain . . . after he reigned seven months and as many days', and his successor, Otho, 'slew himself . . . after he had managed the public affairs three months and two days', while Vitellius subsequently 'retained the government eight months and five days'.[20]

Josephus specifically named Gaius as 'the fourth emperor'; therefore on this reckoning Nero had to be the sixth 'king', and the one described as 'the one who is' (17:10), i.e., now ruling.[21] Nero's successor is described as 'and when he comes he must remain a little while' (καὶ ὅταν ἔλθῃ ὀλίγον αὐτὸν δεῖ μεῖναι) (17:10). This refers to Galba.[22] Josephus' evidence agrees with the epigraphic evidence cited earlier and confirms that Nero is the one referred to, as does the number of his name as the subsequent discussion shows.

(ii) The Number of the Emperor's Name

A greater challenge was issued that would test the skills of his readership to undertake a more complicated form of numerical calculation — 'this calls for wisdom', literally 'here is the wisdom' (ὧδε ἡ σοφία), a term used in Greek for 'skill' in various disciplines of learning including music, poetry, medicine and divination, and here the author of the letter uses it of *gematria*.[23] He further defines the person possessing this skill as 'the one

18. Josephus, *Jewish Antiquities* 18.224, 19.201 and 20.148.

19. Josephus, *Jewish War* 4.491, and also Dio Cassius, *Roman History* 62.3.

20. Josephus, *Jewish War* 4.499, 548, 652.

21. Josephus' comments show that he may not have agreed with the number in the titles of two recent books where Augustus is the 'first'. See M. D. H. Clark, *Augustus, First Roman Emperor: Power, Propaganda and the Politics of Survival* (Liverpool: Liverpool University Press, 2010), and A. Goldsworthy, *Augustus: First Emperor of Rome* (New Haven and London: Yale University Press, 2014).

22. Vespasian subsequently held this office from 1 July, A.D. 69, until he died of natural causes on 24 June, A.D. 79. Titus, his son, succeeded him, and then his grandson Domitian ruled from A.D. 81 until 96. Dating the book to the era of Domitian does not coincide with the internal evidence in Revelation 17:10, as he was the tenth emperor.

23. See the entry on σοφία in Liddell and Scott for references to this use in different spheres.

having knowledge' (ὁ ἔχων νοῦς). The clue is in the use of an imperative when he writes that 'he must calculate the number of the beast' (ψηφισάτω τὸν ἀριθμὸν τοῦ φηρίου)', and then explains, 'for the number of the beast is a man and his number is 666' (13:18). The actual text does not have the Greek letter for six (Σ) repeated three times but ΧΞΣ, i.e., 600, 60 and 6. This followed the Greek convention of spelling each of the letters that were represented numerically — 'six hundred' (ἑξακόσιοι), 'sixty' (ἑξήκοντα) and 'six' (ἕξ) (13:18).[24]

What is the numerical value of the Greek letters for 'beast' (φηρίον)? It totals 247 (θ = 9, η = 8, ρ = 100, ι = 10, ο = 70, ν = 50). So he is not referring to a calculation in Greek of letters of this term. However, 'the same numerical technique was used in the Hebrew alphabet, and "beast" in the Hebrew alphabet is 666 (ת = 400, ר = 200, י = 10, ו = 6, נ = 50)'.[25]

The number of the beast is explicitly said to coincide with another number. The writer explains, '[F]or it is the number of a man' (ἀριθμὸς γὰρ ἀνθρώπου ἐστίν) and then discloses that number is '666' (Rev. 13:18). So the total number for 'beast' and that for 'man' are the same. There is official external evidence of the numerical value of the name of Nero in a Hebrew-Aramaic script on an official deed of debt in A.D. 55 declared to be the second year of 'Nero'. The numerical value of the letters of his name is recorded in Hebrew (נ n = 50, ר r = 200, ו w = 6, נ n = 50, ק q = 100, ס s = 60, ר r = 200) and totals 666.[26]

An alternative proposal with respect to 'the name of a man' in Revelation 13:18 has been to opt for a textual variant of '616' as the possible reading. Nero's name and title 'Nero Caesar' in Greek is Νέρων Καῖσαρ; N = 50, E = 5, P = 100, Ω = 800, N = 50, K = 20, A = 1, I = 10, Σ = 200, A = 1, P = 100 totals 1337. However, the Greek numerical value of the word 'beast' (θηρίον), Θ = 9, H = 8, P = 100, I = 10, O = 70, N = 50 is 247 and not 616, but in Hebrew, the final 'n' in his name was omitted, the numerical value being '616'. The words in the title 'Caesar God' (καῖσαρ θεός) when

---

24. Greek used the letters of their respective alphabets as numbers, e.g., α (alpha)=1, β (beta)=2, γ (gamma)=3 as did Hebrew, but unlike Latin whose *gematria* differed, with a numerical system of I, II, III and IV. See S. R. Llewelyn, "The Christian Symbol XMΓ, an Acrostic or an Isopsephism?" *New Documents Illustrating Early Christianity* (Grand Rapids: Eerdmans, 1998), pp. 165-66.

25. R. Bauckham, "Nero the Beast," in *The Climax of Prophecy: Studies in the Book of the Revelation* (Edinburgh: T & T Clark, 1993), p. 389.

26. P. Benoit, J. T. Milik and R. de Vaux, *Les Grottes de Murabba'ât,* Discoveries in the Judaean Desert 2 (Oxford: Clarendon Press, 1962), no. 18.

rendered alphabetically in Greek (K = 20, A = 1, I = 10, Σ = 200, A = 1, P = 100, Θ = 9, E = 5, O = 70, Σ = 200) total 616.

Was this use of what was known as *gematria* widespread in the East in Nero's time? At the beginning of his reign he issued an imperial decree citing the official use of *gematria* for a long-recognized group of Greeks within a particular city. He twice used their name, 'six thousand, four hundred and seventy-five'. They were descendants of early Greek settlers comprising part of the city of Ptolemais Euergetis in Egypt. This was Nero's official response to imperial divine honours that the delegation indicated they intended for him as the new emperor.

> But of the two remaining offers, I decline that of a temple because this honour is rightly assigned by men to the gods alone; and as for the gold crown that you sent, I shall gratefully remit it, for at the beginning of my Principate I do not wish to burden you . . . of all that together with the 6475 (ἑξακισχιλίοις τετ[ρακοσίιο]ς ἑβδομήκοντα [πέντε]), you received from the emperor before me . . . of all of you in common and of each individually, and to preserve you from injury and molestation, as also my deified father desired. Since you bear witness to all that he provided both for the city and the 6475 (τῇ τε πόλι καὶ ἑξακισχιλίοις τετρακοσίιος ἑβδομήκοντα πέντε), I praise and command you. The ambassadors [were] Aeacides, son of Ptolemaeus, Antenor, son of - - -, Nibytas, son of Nibytas, Polycrates, son of Didymus, - - - - -, Themison - -.[27]

In the first occurrence of the numerals in this imperial document, Nero identified the city as 'of all that, together with the 6475' and later to 'both for the city and the 6475'. He noted that Claudius granted them former privileges by way of an imperial favour. This city and the group named within it were early Greek settlers of the Arsinoite nome in Egypt who were Hellenes possessing special privileges and officially known by the number 6475, as Montevecchi noted.[28] In the delegation that came to Rome there are clearly Greek names.[29]

In Rome and Italy *gematria* was not only used in official circles, but

27. See also J. H. Oliver, *Greek Constitutions of Early Roman Emperors from Inscriptions and Papyri,* Memoirs of the American Philosophical Society (Philadelphia: American Philosophical Society, 1989), no. 39.

28. O. Montevecchi, "Nerone a una polis e ai 6475," *Aegyptus* 50 (1970): 5-33.

29. Oliver, *Greek Constitutions of Early Roman Emperors,* no. 39, col. 2, *ll.* 10-13.

we have examples of its popular use for romantic purposes and sometimes in a derogatory way politically. In Pompeii it was used as a means of communicating love for another. 'I love her whose name *is phi mu epsilon*' (545) (φιλῶ ἧς ἀρισθμὸς πμέ)' Π = 500, M = 40 and E = 5. Although this was a Roman colony in Italy, the initials of her name were rendered in Greek 'numerals' ΠΜΕ.[30]

In the same city another piece of romantic graffiti was found on a wall written in Greek. 'Amerimnus thought upon his lady Harmonia for good. The number 45 (or) 1035 is her honourable name (τοῦ καλοῦ ὀνόματος). In both instances the number of the name is encrypted, as in the latter case the number of her name was 541.[31]

Suetonius in his *Nero,* written in Latin, recorded its use politically for derogatory purposes. He notes Nero's unpopularity before his suicide.

> [H]e [Nero] bore nothing with more patience than the curses and abuses of the people and was patiently lenient towards those who assailed him with gibes and lampoons. Of these many were posted or circulated both in Greek and Latin *(Multa Graece Latineque proscripta aut vulgata sunt)* . . . Nero his own mother slew (Νεοπσηφον Νερων ἰδιαν μητερα απεκτεινε).[32]

What was 'a calculation new'? This reference is to Nero's instigation of the murder of his mother, Agrippina II (popularly referred to as '1005') in A.D. 59. The Loeb edition of Suetonius notes, 'The numerical value of the Greek letters of Nero's name (1005) [N = 50, ε = 5. ρ = 100 ω = 800, ν = 50] is the same as that of the rest of the sentence; hence we have the equation, 'Nero' = 'the slayer of his mother'.[33]

This example of the use of *gematria* in one language cited in another is helpful in resolving the enigma in Revelation 13:18, as only in Hebrew are

30. G. A. Deissmann, *Light from the Ancient East: The New Testament Illustrated by Recently Discovered Texts of the Graeco-Roman World,* ET (London: Hodder & Stoughton, 1927), p. 277. See K. Milnor, *Graffiti and the Literary Landscape in Roman Pompeii* (Oxford: Oxford University Press, 2014) with respect to Pompeii.

31. Deissmann comments, 'The name is probably only bestowed playfully by the writer on his mistress; her real name is hidden in the number', in *Light from the Ancient East*, p. 277, n. 3.

32. Suetonius, *Nero* 39.

33. For comment on Suetonius, *Nero* 293, see J. C. Rolfe, *The Lives of the Caesars* (Cambridge, MA, and London: Harvard University Press, 1998), II, p. 158.

'the number of the beast' and 'the number of a name' a way of identifying the usurping of the throne of God, alluded to prophetically in Daniel 7, with Nero. Furthermore, the issues are somewhat comparable in that both were evaluating and passing negative judgements on him.

If it required a bilingual person to interpret the 'new calculation' to cite Suetonius' note, so too the task set by the writer of Revelation was for someone skilled in *gematria* to break the encoded message using Hebrew and not Greek numerals but without giving him the key. It is recorded that Jewish converts from Paul's mission in Asia also lived in this province (Acts 19:17).

Later in Revelation 17:10 there is a reference to the sixth king as the present emperor, 'the one is' (ὁ εἷς ἔστιν). This would have provided a clue for any person, not necessarily a 'wise' one. It would, however, have required someone with a working knowledge of Hebrew to decode the numerals as the solution for 'the number of the beast' and 'the number of a man', both of which added up to 666. The sixth king is Nero both by reason of the number of kings and *gematria*.

III. The Second Beast and Imperial Cultic Innovations

It is important to seek to identify this 'second beast and the possible reason for his unprecedented provincial innovation in imperial honours as a further clue in seeking to establish more securely this *Sitz im Leben*, i.e., the promotion of the further divine honours for and to the Caesars.

(i) Identifying the 'Second Beast'

It is said of the second beast that he 'exercises all the authority of the first beast' (Rev. 13:12). While it has been suggested that this refers to the rôle of Caesar as the high priest of the empire,[34] there was another person who fulfilled this office with respect to the imperial cult in the province. His remit was certainly not to exercise 'all the authority' of the emperor. The appointment of the provincial high priest was confirmed by the Roman Senate and was not seen as comparable to the emperor's rôle as *pontifex*

---

34. R. Bauckham, "Nero the Beast," in *The Climax of Prophecy: Studies in the Book of the Revelation*, p. 446, is not persuaded that this was the case.

maximus. The provincial imperial high priest's rôle was a liturgical one, to be exercised on special days so designated for presiding over major cultic events in the imperial calendar.[35]

Rather, it was the function of governors to exercise the *imperium* of the reigning Caesar especially in relation to Roman criminal cases.[36] The New Testament itself bears witness to this. Pontius Pilate presided at the trial of Jesus, and Gallio the proconsul, Felix the governor and Festus ruled in the criminal proceedings instituted against Paul in Corinth and Caesarea Maritima (Luke 23:1-25; Acts 18:12-17; 24:1-22; 25:13–26:32). The second beast caused those who did not worship the statue in the temple to be given the death sentence. As this penalty was alone within the jurisdiction of provincial governors (13:15), this beast has to be the governor.

Is it possible to identify the actual holder of this office in the province of Asia? An extant record reveals that C. Fonteius Agrippa, who earlier had been the suffect consul of Rome in May to June A.D. 58, succeeded Aponius Saturninus as commander of the Roman province of Asia with proconsular power in A.D. 68-69. Tacitus recorded —

> Fonteius Agrippa was transferred from Asia, where as proconsul, he had governed for a year, and put in charge of Moesia [a Roman province on the south bank of the River Danube] where he was given additional troops from the army of Vitellius, which it was wise from the point of view of both policy and peace to distribute in the provinces and to involve in war with a foreign foe.[37]

His political inclination and imperial loyalty may also be reflected subsequently in a prosecution that he initiated with three others against Libo Drusus 'accused of revolutionary schemes. . . . Besides Trio and Catus, Fonteius Agrippa and Gaius Vibius had associated themselves with the prosecution, and it was disputed which of the four should have the right of

---

35. For this role see D. Fishwick, *The Provincial Cult: The Imperial Cult in the Latin West* (Leiden: E. J. Brill, 2002), III.2, pp. 301-2. *Pace* S. R. F. Price, who sees the second beast as the provincial high priest and the attribution of penal power to the imperial statues, *Rituals and Power: The Imperial Cult and Asia Minor* (Cambridge: Cambridge University Press, 1984), pp. 196-97.

36. A. Erskine, *Roman Imperialism: Debates and Documents in Ancient History* (Edinburgh: Edinburgh University Press, 2010), p. 76, 99-100 citing Cicero, *Letters to his brother Quintus* 1.1.20-25.

37. Tacitus, *Histories* 2.46.

stating the case against the defendant'.[38] Clearly Fonteius Agrippa wanted to be to the fore as the accuser in the treason trial of Libo Drusus. The description of the second beast would best fit the proconsul.

(ii) New Divine Honours for Caesar in the East

Three-quarters of a century before the reign of Nero, the province of Asia had seen the innovation of divine honours with the official date marking the commencement of each new year to coincide with the birthday of 'the most divine Caesar' (τοῦ θειοτάτου Καίσαρος) Augustus. This was the result of a competition instituted by a Roman governor of the province, Lucius Volcacius Tullus, but not awarded in his time. Paullus Fabius Maximus, a subsequent governor from 10 to 8 B.C., revived it some twenty years later, and surprisingly he himself won it and thus was awarded a golden crown. (See p. 29.)

It has been demonstrated that provinces and individual cities traditionally sent embassies to new emperors on their accession. They also hoped to return with reciprocal imperial favours or concessions for the giving of innovative divine honours to Caesar. It was an established custom. (See pp. 55-60.) This is important, as it goes some way in understanding the motivation and intention of the proconsul named 'the second beast' in the same province governed by Paullus Fabius Maximus at the end of the previous century. The latest unique honour bestowed on Nero by those bearing on their person the mark of his name was something never recorded up to this point in the history of the empire.

What was behind this proconsul's edict is somewhat enigmatic. It could have been that a recent event may have motivated this Roman proconsul of Asia to take these extraordinary steps that were to have such consequences for all under his jurisdiction. It went beyond the conventional remit of governors of provinces of seeing that temples did not fall into disrepair, but it did not extend to the death penalty for those refusing to worship imperial cult statues (13:15-17).

Three pieces of extant evidence record the importance of Nero's visit to Greece during Paul's era. Here he actually competed in the famous traditional games, i.e., the Isthmian, Olympic, Nemea, Argive, Delphi and Actia, where he won all his events. He was also lauded when he returned

---

38. Tacitus, *Annals* 2.27.30.

to Rome in his third official triumphal entry to the city in late A.D. 67 at the age of thirty. The reason for this entry was unprecedented because it celebrated not a victory in battle but his victories in the games.[39]

At the same time Alexandria, the capital of Egypt, issued coins in A.D. 66-67 likewise celebrating Nero's success in Greece. On the reverse the presiding deities of the five great festivals, Poseidon, Olympian Zeus, Nemean Zeus, Hera Argeia, Pythian Apollo and Actian Apollo were portrayed.[40] Earlier, in A.D. 62-63, the words on an Alexandrian coin declared Nero to be 'the saviour of the world' (ὁ σωτὴρ τῆς οἰκουμένης).[41] In close proximity to Isthmia, where one of the games was traditionally held, the Roman colony of Corinth, the capital of Achaea also celebrated his successful participation in its events by issuing a coin.[42]

Corinth and all other cities in the province of Achaea had far more reason to respond because Nero exempted all those living there from the Roman provincial taxes. On 28 November, A.D. 67, at a specially called assembly in Corinth, Nero had announced this exemption, especially stressing, not so indirectly, the incredible generosity of his imperial benefaction.

> It is an unexpected gift, Hellenes — though there is nothing that may not be hoped for from my magnanimity — which I grant you, one so great that you were incapable of requesting it. All Hellenes who inhabit Achaea and the land until now called the Peloponnesus receive liberty and exemption from tribute ... to bestow so great a benefaction; for to cities other rulers too have granted freedom, but Nero alone to an entire province.[43]

His dramatic conclusion intentionally drew attention to this unprecedented imperial gift — 'Nero only to the entire province' (Νέρων δὲ μόνος καὶ ἐπαρχείαν), thus stressing its parameter.[44]

---

39. See Champlin, "Triumph," in *Nero*, pp. 229-32, for a detailed discussion of the processions and the carrying of the crowns he won in the competitions. He also draws attention to aspects of it that differed from military triumphs.

40. See A. Burnett, M. Amandry and P. P. Ripollès, *Roman Provincial Coinage: From the Death of Caesar to the Death of Vitellius (44 B.C.–A.D. 69)* (London and Paris: British Museum Press and Bibliothèque nationale de France, 1998), p. 706, nos. 5307-12.

41. *RPC* no. 5271 E.

42. *RPC* nos. 1207-9 issued by the magistrates with Nero portrayed with a laureate head celebrating his success at the Isthmian Games.

43. *SIG*³ 814, *ll.* 10-26.

44. *SIG*³ 814, *l.* 26. The term καί was used to express assent, Liddell and Scott.

In response to this incredible gift, Epaminondas, the successor of Spartiaticus (p. 200) made this official proclamation in his capacity as 'the high priest for life of Nero Claudius Caesar Augustus' of the provincial imperial cult of Achaia. It followed the traditional genre of official proclamations, laying out the reason — in this case two major reasons — for the resolution and more importantly the appropriate honours bestowed on Nero as a token of their enormous appreciation of his reciprocal benefits to them.

The first accolade was addressing Nero as 'the Lord of all the world' (ὁ τοῦ παντὸς κόσμου κύριος), 'the new sun that has shone on the Greeks' who had bestowed benefactions on Greece and shown piety towards 'our gods who have stood by him everywhere for his care and safety'.[45]

The second cause for their gratitude 'to the one and only, greatest imperator' was the unparalleled honour he had bestowed —

> the one and only greatest imperator of our times, lover of Greeks (εἷς καὶ μόνος τῶν ἀπ' αὐῶος αὐτοκράτωρ μέγιστος φιλέλλην γενόμενος) Nero, Zeus the Liberator, bestowed the eternal indigenous native freedom that was formerly taken from the Greeks, he has shown his favour, has brought back the autonomy and freedom from the past and to this great and unexpected gift he has added immunity from taxation, quite complete, which none of the previous Augusti gave us.[46]

Nero's action naturally prompted this reciprocal honour. 'For all these reasons it has been decided by the magistrates and councillors and the people to worship him at the existing altar dedicated to Zeus the Saviour forever (εἰς αἰῶνα)', giving the assurance to Nero that he would be venerated as a perpetual divinity, adding 'Nero Zeus, the Liberator' (Νέρωνος Διὸς' Ελευθερίου), and his wife as 'the goddess, Augusta Messalina'. This occurred 'in the temple of Ptoian Apollo to be shared with our ancestral gods'.[47]

The stated reason for doing this was 'in order that . . . our city may be seen to have poured every honour and piety upon the house of the Lord Augustus Nero' (ἡ ἡνετέρα πόλις φαίνηται πᾶσαν τειμὴν καὶ εὐσέβειαν ἐκπεπληρωκυιᾶ εἰς τὸν τοῦ κυρίου Σεβαστοῦ [Νέρωνος οἶκον]).[48] The res-

---

45. *SIG*[3] 814, *ll.* 31-32.
46. *SIG*[3] 814, *ll.* 40-45.
47. *SIG*[3] 814, *ll.* 48-49, 51-52.
48. *SIG*[3] 814, *ll.* 53-54.

olution closes by indicating that Nero's benefactions would be visible and therefore always on display. Thus 'it has also been decided to inscribe the decree on a column set beside Zeus the Saviour in the agora and in the temple of Ptoian Apollo'.[49] The latter was the god to whom Augustus attributed his decisive victory against Mark Anthony when Zeus appeared to him at Actium and therefore always remained his favourite and divine patron.[50]

Such tax exemptions were not unprecedented. Tacitus recorded another in the time of Nero's predecessor, Claudius, in A.D. 53, just a year before his death.

> Next he proposed to exempt [the island of] Cos from taxation. In a lengthy discourse about its ancient history, he said that its first inhabitants had been Argives — or perhaps Coeus, the father of the goddess Latona; then Aesclepius had brought the art of healing, which had achieved remarkable distinction among his descendants. The emperor indicated their names and the periods at which each had lived. Then he added that a member of the same family was his own doctor, Gaius Stertinius Xenophon: in response to whose petition the people of Cos would in future be exempted from all taxation, holding their island as a sacred place, and serving the god alone. Claudius might, of course, have recalled their frequent assistance to Rome, and the victories they had shared with us. But he preferred not to disguise behind external arguments the favour that, with his usual indulgence, he had conceded to an individual.[51]

Even earlier in the time of Augustus, the city of Aphrodisias had been granted tax exemption and was declared a Roman colony as a reward for fighting for Augustus against Mark Anthony and for the substantial suffering the city had thus endured.

> [I]t is agreed by the Senate that the people of Plarasa and Aphrodisias, their children and descendants should themselves have and possess freedom and immunity from taxation in all matters on the legal basis which is that of a community with the fullest right and law, having free-

---

49. *SIG*³ 814, *ll.* 56-57.

50. Propertius, *The Poems* 4.6.36. R. M. Ogilvie, *The Romans and Their Gods* (London: Random House/Pimlico, 2000), p. 108.

51. Tacitus, *Annals* 12.61.61.

dom and immunity from taxation granted by the Senate and people of Rome, and being a friend and ally of the Roman people.[52]

The loyalty of their citizens was described as 'the Caesar-loving (φιλό-καισαρ) demos of the Aphrodisians, free and autonomous from the beginning by the grace of Augustus'.[53] By comparison the reason for Nero's exemption seems trivial.

Augustus had been aware that, as a result, the inhabitants of Samos also sought tax exemptions because it had been granted to Aphrodisias, a city not that far from them. They actually succeeded in recruiting his wife as their advocate for this request.

> It is possible for you yourselves to see that I have granted the favour of freedom to no demos except to that of the Aphrodisians, who having taken my side in the war, suffered capture on account of loyalty to us. It is not just for the greatest favour of all to be accorded at random and without cause. I for my part am well disposed to you and would like to humour my wife who is zealous on your behalf, but not so as to destroy my customary policy. . . . But I do not wish to have given my most valuable favours without a good reason.[54]

Nero acknowledged that another delegation was suggesting innovative imperial honours in an official response. 'I heartily commend the firmness of your goodwill towards me and your constant concern to add some new invention [to my honour]. If [only] your ambition for us might be without expense to you who have already made it clear in so many cases.'[55]

If Greece awarded honours, accolades and citations as official sources and imperial correspondence confirmed, Nero could publicly boast about these on his return to Rome in his official triumphal entry. These imperial honours implemented across the Aegean Sea by the governor of the

52. J. Reynolds, *Aphrodisias and Rome,* The Society for the Promotion of Roman Studies (Hertford: Stephen Austin, 1982), no. 8, *ll.* 51-55.

53. M. McCrum and A. G. Woodhead, *Select Documents of the Flavian Emperors* (Cambridge: Cambridge University Press, 1966), no. 495, *ll.* 2-3.

54. Oliver, *Greek Constitutions of Early Roman Emperors from Inscriptions and Papyri,* no. 1.

55. Oliver, *Greek Constitutions of Early Roman Emperors from Inscriptions and Papyri,* no. 35, *ll.* 6-7.

province of Asia would not be without precedence. He added 'some new invention' of imperial honours.

What effect did this have on the Eastern provinces outside of Achaea? It is possible that the divine honours outlined in Revelation 13:15-17 were yet another provincial innovation aimed at securing an imperial benefit for the province. Certainly possible tax exemption for the province of Asia could have been the motivation behind the unique innovation of the mark of the beast as a sign of loyalty to the emperor. However, there is no extant evidence that actually discloses the governor's motivation.

IV. Capital Punishment for Non-Compliance

Expressions of divine honours in this province were taken seriously, and failure to worship statues of the emperor in imperial cult temples incurred the death penalty. This was not without precedence, as the death penalty was given to those 'violating the sanctity of the ceremonies' connected with the temple of Artemis in Ephesus in the province of Asia as seen in this inscription.

> Advocates on behalf of the goddess [Artemis] brought in a sentence of death as defined in this publication of the judgement: When ambassadors had been sent to our city to present robes to Artemis in accordance with ancestral customs (κατὰ τὸμ πάτριον), and when the priests and the ambassadors arrived at Sardis and at the temple of Artemis which was founded by the Ephesians, the accused violated the sanctity of the ceremonies and insulted the envoys. The verdict was death. And sentence was pronounced upon the following. . . .[56]

It consists of fifty-seven lines, only the first twelve of which are reproduced here. The remainder actually record the full names of forty-three who were summarily sentenced to death, because they 'violated' cultic veneration and insulted official envoys from Ephesus. All this was meant as a deterrent to others who read it, reminding them that this was a capital offence.

---

56. *I. Ephesos* 572, *ll.* 1-12 and *ll.* 13-57 lists the names of those who were put to death. The harshness of this sentence is explicable because '[a]ll the cities worship Artemis of Ephesus and individuals hold her in honour above all the gods', according to Pausanias in his *Description of Greece* 4.31.8.

The Neronian era was known for more severe punishments than those given under all other Julio-Claudian emperors. In the previous chapter, it was shown that '[l]egislators devised new and harsher penalties, such as hard labour, mandatory exile and deportation to an island.'[57] Aubert calls this trend a 'discrepancy or congruence, between theory and practice in Roman criminal law and practice'.[58] This legal paradigm shift may go some way to explaining why the provincial governor invoked the death penalty for all who refused to follow his edict.

In a subsequent era of the emperor Trajan, Pliny the Younger, who was the governor of Bithynia, summarily executed Christians who were not Roman citizens if they did not worship the emperor by burning incense to his imperial statue. Those who possessed Roman citizenship and who refused to do this were transported to the capital for judgement through the due legal process. (See p. 4.)

Nero himself had Christians put to death in Rome in A.D. 64, assigning to them blame for the great fire of Rome or anti-social behaviour. He did so in such a draconian way that it evoked pity, as Tacitus later recorded.

> But neither human resources, nor imperial magnificence, nor appeasement of the gods eliminated the sinister suspicion that the fire had been instigated. To suppress this rumour, Nero fabricated scapegoats — and punished with every refinement the notoriously depraved Christians (as they were popularly called). The originator, Christ, had been executed in Tiberius' reign by the governor of Judaea, Pontius Pilate. But in spite of this temporary setback the deadly superstition had broken out afresh, not only in Judaea (where the mischief had started) but even in Rome. All degraded and shameful practices collect and flourish in the capital. First, Nero had self-acknowledged Christians arrested. Then, on their information, large numbers were condemned — not so much for incendiarism as for their anti-social tendencies. Their deaths were farcical. Dressed in wild animals' skins, they were torn to pieces by dogs, or crucified, or made into torches to be ignited after dark as substitutes for daylight. Nero provided his Gardens for the spectacle, and exhibited displays in the Circus, at which he mingled with

---

57. J.-J. Aubert, "A Double Standard in Roman Criminal Law? The Death Penalty and Social Structure in Late Republic and Early Roman Empire," in *Speculum Ivris: Roman Law as a Reflection of Social and Economic Life in Antiquity,* ed. J.-J. Aubert and B. Sirks (Ann Arbor: University of Michigan Press, 2002), p. 103.

58. Aubert, "A Double Standard in Roman Criminal Law?" pp. 102, 106.

the crowd — or stood in a chariot, dressed as a charioteer. Hence, in spite of the guilt that had earned the most ruthless punishment, there arose a sentiment of pity, due to the impression that they were being sacrificed not for the welfare of the state but for the ferocity of one man's brutality.[59]

A categorical statement was formulated as a legal penalty — 'if any would not fall down and worship the image of the beast, they shall be put to death' (ἵνα ἐαν μὴ προσκυνήσωσιν τῇ εἰκόνι τοῦ θηρίου ἀποκτανθῶσιν) (13:15). The verb προσκυνέω connotes 'to prostrate oneself before kings', 'to fall down and worship' or 'to throw a kiss to a god' as a cultic gesture. The term 'image' (εἰκών) can be used of either a picture or a statue. As the god being worshipped was the emperor, it was an apposite term to have used for his veneration.

Thus loyalty to the emperor was to be expressed by venerating his statue and actually bearing his name on their persons as the prerequisite to buying or selling in the market. Both Revelation 14:9 and 16:2 linked these two activities, while 20:4 records a vision reflecting the inevitable outcome of those who refused to worship the emperor — 'Also I saw the souls of those who had been beheaded for the testimony of Jesus and for the Word of God, and who had not worshipped the beast or its image [in the temple] and had not received its mark on their foreheads or hands.'[60] Later it is recorded that 'they will see his [the Lamb's] face and his name will be on their foreheads' (22:4).

The recent execution of fellow Christians in Rome in A.D. 64 had created a legal precedent for the Caesar's vice-gerent in the province of Asia, hence the urgent exhortation not to commit apostasy by capitulating to imperial cultic stipulations. 'Here is a call for the endurance and faith of the saints' (13:10). What was the outcome for those who refused to participate in the outpouring of divine honours for the emperor? Revelation 20:6 gives the eternal result — 'they were resurrected and reigned with Christ for a thousand years'.

The writer gives two reasons for the first Christians never to participate in giving divine honours to the Caesar, enormous though the cost

59. Tacitus, *Annals* 15.44.

60. E. A. Judge, "The Mark of the Beast, Revelation 13:16," in *The First Christians in the Roman World* (Tübingen: Mohr Siebeck, 2008), p. 426, suggests it was a mark of ink on wrist or forehead.

would be. The first occurs immediately after disclosing the number. 'Then I looked, and behold on Mount Zion, stood the Lamb and with him 144,000 who had his name and his Father's name written on their foreheads' (14:1), the implication being that both names could not be written on the same person's forehead and more specifically a Christian could not have divided loyalties and venerate both. A warning was also given of the dire consequences for those who capitulated — 'If anyone worships the beast and his image and receives a mark on his forehead or on his hand, he also will drink the wine of God's wrath, poured full strength into the cup of his anger, and will be tormented with fire and sulphur in the presence of the Lamb' (14:9-10).

If the governor of Asia's intention was an attempt to secure a comparable provincial taxation concession from Nero, then there was only a short period of time between Nero delivering his speech in Corinth on 28 November, A.D. 67, recording this generous concession, and his death by assisted suicide the following year on 11 June, A.D. 68. The city of Alexandria certainly acted promptly in issuing coins celebrating Nero's achievements at the Greek Games before he died. So it is possible that across the Aegean Sea in the province of Asia its governor sought to implement a unique outpouring of an expression of loyalty to Nero in order to secure a similar generous imperial concession that the provinces of Achaea and Macedonia had been granted although it would be subsequently withdrawn. The province of Asia had a long history of imperial cult innovations stretching back to the time of Augustus.

Garnsey and Saller concluded that 'Christians invited persecution by their denial of the gods of Rome'.[61] This study has shown it was an inevitable confrontation that they faced with the imperial powers because of the demand to render divine honours to the Caesars, something they could never do in all good conscience given their allegiance to their new king.

---

61. P. Garnsey and R. Saller, "Religion," in *The Roman Empire: Economy, Society and Culture* (London: Duckworth, 1987; and Oakland: University of California Press, 2015²), p. 197.

Bibliography

Alcock, S. E. *Graecia Captia: The Landscapes of Roman Greece.* Cambridge: Cambridge University Press, 1993.

———. "The Peculiar Book IV and the Problem of the Messenian Past." In *Pausanias: Travel and Memory in Roman Greece,* edited by S. E. Alcock, J. F. Cherry and J. Elsner. Oxford: Oxford University Press, 2001.

———. "The Problem of Romanization, the Power of Athens." In *The Romanization of Athens: Proceedings of an International Conference,* edited by M. C. Hoff and S. I. Rotroff. Oxbow Monographs 94. Oxford: Oxbow Books, 1997.

Alves, F. *Portugal from Its Origins through the Roman Era.* Lisbon: Mosaico, 1989.

Ando, C. *Imperial Ideology and Provincial Loyalty in the Roman Empire.* Berkeley: University of California Press, 2000.

Arafat, K. W. *Pausanias' Greece: Ancient Artists and Roman Rulers.* Cambridge: Cambridge University Press, 1997.

Atkinson, K. M. T. "Governors of the Province of Asia in the Reign of Augustus." *Historia* 7 (1958): 300-330.

Attridge, H. W. *A Commentary on the Epistle to the Hebrews.* Philadelphia: Fortress Press, 1989.

———. "The Philosophical Critique of Religion under the Early Empire." *ANRW* II 16.1 (1978): 45-78.

Aubert, J.-J. "A Double Standard in Roman Criminal Law? The Death Penalty and Social Structure in Late Republic and Early Roman Empire." In *Speculum Ivris: Roman Law as a Reflection of Social and Economic Life in Antiquity,* edited by J.-J. Aubert and B. Sirks, pp. 94-133. Ann Arbor: University of Michigan Press, 2002.

Bacchielli, L., and J. M. Reynolds. "The Public Land of the Roman People in Syrenaica." *Libya Antiqua* 8 (1971): 47-49.

Balch, D. L. "The Areopagus Speech: An Appeal to the Stoic *Historica Posidonius* against Later Stoics and Epicureans." In *Greeks, Romans and Christians: Es-*

says in Honor of Abraham J. Malherbe, edited by D. L. Balch, E. Ferguson and W. Meeks, pp. 52-79. Minneapolis: Fortress Press, 1990.

Barclay, J. M. G. *Obeying the Truth: A Study of Paul's Ethics in Galatians.* Edinburgh: T&T Clark, 1988.

Bardill, J. *Constantine, Divine Emperor of the Christian Golden Age.* Cambridge: Cambridge University Press, 2011.

Barnes, T. D. "An Apostle on Trial." *JTS* 20 (1969): 407-19.

Barrett, A. A. *Agrippina: Sex, Power and Politics in the Early Empire.* New Haven: Yale University Press, 1996.

————. *Caligula: The Corruption of Power.* London: Batsford, 1989.

Bauckham, R. "Nero the Beast." In *The Climax of Prophecy: Studies in the Book of the Revelation.* Edinburgh: T&T Clark, 1993.

Beard, M., J. North, and S. Price. *Religions of Rome.* Vol. 1: *A History.* Cambridge: Cambridge University Press, 1996.

Beard, M., J. North, and S. Price. *Religions of Rome.* Vol. 2: *A Sourcebook.* Cambridge: Cambridge University Press, 1998.

Benjamin, A., and A. E. Raubitschek. "Arae Augusti." *Hesperia* 28 (1959): 68-87.

Benoit, P., J. T. Milik and R. de Vaux. *Les Grottes de Murabba'ât.* Discoveries in the Judaean Desert 2. Oxford: Clarendon Press, 1962.

Berger, A. *Encyclopedic Dictionary of Roman Law.* Philadelphia: American Philosophical Society, 1953.

Bilde, P. "Philo as a Polemist and a Political Apologist: An Investigation of His Two Historical Treatises Against Flaccus and The Embassy to Gaius." In *Alexandria: A Cultural and Religious Melting Pot,* edited by G. Hinge and J. A. Krasilinikoff, pp. 97-114. Aarhus Studies in Mediterranean Antiquity 9. Aarhus: Aarhus University Press, 2010.

Bitner, B. "Augustan *Iurisdictio Praesidis:* Procedure and Legal Documents in CIG 2222." Paper read at the American Philological Association Annual Meeting, January 2011.

Blass, F., and A. R. W. Debrunner. *A Greek Grammar of the New Testament and Other Early Christian Literature.* English translation by R. W. Funk. Cambridge and Chicago: Cambridge University Press and University of Chicago Press, 1961.

Bookidis, N., and R. S. Stroud. "Apollo and the Archaic Temple." *Hesperia* 73 (2004): 410-42.

Borgen, P. *Philo of Alexandria: An Exegete for His Time.* Leiden: E. J. Brill, 1997.

Bowersock, G. W. *Augustus and the Greek World.* Oxford: Clarendon Press, 1965.

————. "Eurycles of Sparta." *JRS* 51 (1961): 112-18.

Braund, D. C. *Augustus to Nero: A Sourcebook on Roman History, 31 B.C.–A.D. 68.* London and Sydney: Croom Helm, 1985.

Breytenbach, C. *Paulus und Barnabas in der Provinz Galatien: Studien zu Apos-*

telgeschichte 13f: 16,6: 18,23 und der Adressaten des Galaterbriefs. Leiden: E. J. Brill, 1996.

Bruce, F. F. *The Acts of the Apostles: Greek Text with Introduction and Commentary.* Leicester and Grand Rapids: IVP and Eerdmans, 1990[3].

Brunt, P. A., and J. M. Moore, eds. *Res Gestae Divi Augusti: The Achievement of the Divine Augustus.* Oxford: Oxford University Press, 1967.

Buck, C. D. *Introduction to the Study of the Greek Dialects.* Chicago: University of Chicago Press, 1955[2].

Burnett, A., M. Amandry and P. P. Ripollès. *Roman Provincial Coinage: From the Death of Caesar to the Death of Vitellius (44 B.C.–A.D. 69).* London and Paris: British Museum Press and Bibliothèque nationale de France, 1998.

Burton, G. W. *Galatians.* ICC. Edinburgh: T&T Clark, 1921.

Campbell, G. *A Compendium of Roman Law: Founded on the Institutes of Justinian.* Clark, NJ: Lawbook Exchange, 2008.

Carbon, J.-M. "ΔAPPΩN ΔAIMΩN: A New Inscription from Mylasa." *Epigraphica Anatolica* 37 (2005): 1-6.

Cartledge, P., and A. J. S. Spawforth. *Hellenistic and Roman Sparta: A Tale of Two Cities.* London and New York: Routledge, 1989.

Champlin, E. *Nero.* Cambridge, MA: Harvard University Press, 2003.

Charlesworth, M. P. "Nero." In *Documents Illustrating the Reigns of Claudius and Nero.* Cambridge: Cambridge University Press, 1939.

———. "The Refusal of Divine Honours: An Augustan Formula." *BSR* 15 (1939): 1-10.

Claassen, J.-M. *Displaced Persons: The Literature of Exile from Cicero to Boethius.* London: Duckworth, 1999.

Clark, M. D. H. *Augustus, First Roman Emperor: Power, Propaganda and the Politics of Survival.* Liverpool: Liverpool University Press, 2010.

Clayton Croy, N. *Endurance in Suffering: Hebrews 12.1-13 in Its Rhetorical, Religious and Philosophical Context.* SNTS 98. Cambridge: Cambridge University Press, 1998.

Comedeca, G. "I consoli del 55=56 e un nuovo collega di Seneca nel consolato: P. Cornelius Dolabella." *ZPE* 63 (1986): 208-10.

Cotter, W. "The *Collegia* and Roman Law: State Restrictions on Voluntary Associations, 64 BCE–200 CE." In *Voluntary Associations in the Graeco-Roman World,* edited by J. S. Kloppenborg and S. G. Wilson. London: Routledge, 1996.

Crook, J. A. *Consilium Principis: Imperial Councils and Counsellors from Augustus to Diocletian.* Cambridge: Cambridge University Press, 1955.

———. *Law and Life in Rome, 90 B.C.–A.D. 212.* Ithaca, NY: Cornell University Press, 1967.

Crosby, M. "Greek Inscriptions." *Hesperia* 6, no. 3 (1937): 442-68.

Crossan, J. D., and J. L. Reed. "The Golden Age or as Golden as It Gets." In *In*

Search of Paul: How Jesus' Apostle Opposed Rome's Empire with God's Kingdom. London: SPCK, 2005.

Curran, J. *"Philorhomaioi:* The Herods between Rome and Jerusalem." *Journal for the Study of Judaism* 45 (2014): 493-522.

Cuss, D. *Imperial Cult and Honorary Terms in the New Testament.* Fribourg: Fribourg University Press, 1974.

Deissman, G. A. *Light from the Ancient East: The New Testament Illustrated by Recently Discovered Texts of the Graeco-Roman World.* English trans. London: Hodder and Stoughton, 1927.

De Ligt, L. *Fairs and Markets in the Roman Empire: Economic and Social Aspects of Periodic Trade in the Pre-industrial Society.* Dutch Monographs on Ancient History and Archaeology 11. Amsterdam: J. C. Gieben, 1993.

DeMaris, R. "Cults and the Imperial Cult in Early Roman Corinth: Literary *Versus* Material Record." In *Zwischen den Reichen: Neues Testament und römische Herrschaft: Vorträge auf der ersten Konferenz der European Association for Biblical Studies,* edited by M. Labahn and J. Zangenberg, pp. 73-91. Texte und Arbeiten zum neutestamentlichen Zeitalter 36. Basel: A. Francke Verlag, 2002.

Dinsmoor, W. B. *Archons of Athens in the Hellenistic Age.* Amsterdam: Hakkert, 1966.

Dobbin, R. *Epictetus, Discourses Book 1.* Oxford: Clarendon Press, 1998.

Dobbins, J. J. "The Imperial Cult in the Forum at Pompeii." In *Subject and Ruler: The Cult of the Ruling Power in Classical Antiquity,* edited by A. Small, pp. 99-114. JRA Supplement 17. Ann Arbor: University of Michigan Press, 1996.

Dun, C., and J. Pouilloux. *Recherches sur l'Histoire et les Cultes de Thasos.* Vol. 2. 1958.

Dusanic, S. "A Military Diploma of A.D. 65." *Germania* 56 (1978): 461-75.

Dutch, R. S. *The Educated Elite in 1 Corinthians: Education and Community Conflict in Graeco-Roman Context.* London: T&T Clark, 2007.

Edmondson, J. "Introduction: Flavius Josephus and Flavian Rome." In *Flavius Josephus and Flavian Rome,* edited by J. Edmondson, S. Mason and J. Rives, ch. 1. Oxford: Oxford University Press, 2005.

Edwards, C. M. "Tyche at Corinth." *Hesperia* 59, no. 3 (1990): 529-42.

Ehrenberg, V., and A. H. M. Jones. *Documents Illustrating the Reigns of Augustus and Tiberius.* Oxford: Clarendon Press, 1976².

Eilers, C. "The Date of Augustus' Edict on the Jews (Josephus, *Jewish Antiquities,* 16.162-165) and the Career of C. Marcius Censorinus." *Phoenix* 58, no. 1 (2004): 86-95.

Elkins, N. T. "Placement of Imperial Images in the Colosseum." *Papers of the British School at Rome* 82 (2014): 73-107.

Engles, D. *Roman Corinth: An Alternative Model for the Classical City.* Chicago: University of Chicago Press, 1990.

Epstein, D. *Personal Enmity in Roman Politics, 218-43 B.C.* London and New York: Routledge, 1987.

Erskine, A. *Roman Imperialism.* Debates and Documents in Ancient History. Edinburgh: Edinburgh University Press, 2010.

Evans, H. B. *Water Distribution in Ancient Rome: The Evidence of Frontinus.* Ann Arbor: University of Michigan Press, 1994.

Evans, N. "Embedding Rome in Athens." In *Rome and Religion: A Cross-Disciplinary Dialogue on the Imperial Cult,* edited by J. Brood and J. L. Reed, pp. 83-98. Atlanta: Society of Biblical Literature, 2011.

Fairweather, J. "The History of Declamation." In *Seneca the Elder.* Cambridge: Cambridge University Press, 1981.

Fantham, E. *Julia Augusti: The Emperor's Daughter.* London and New York: Routledge, 2006.

Fantin, J. D. *Lord of the Entire World: Lord Jesus, a Challenge to Lord Caesar?* New Testament Monograph 31. Sheffield: Sheffield Phoenix Press, 2011.

Ferrary, J.-L. "After the Embassy to Rome." In *Diplomats and Diplomacy in the Roman World,* edited by C. Eilers, pp. 27-42. Leiden: E. J. Brill, 2009.

Festugière, A. J. *Epicurus and His Gods.* Oxford: Blackwell, 1955.

Fishwick, D. "Genus and Numen." *Harvard Theological Review* 62 (1969): 356-67.

———. *Imperial Cult in the Latin West.* Vol. 1. Part 1. Leiden: E. J. Brill, 1993².

———. *Imperial Cult in the Latin West.* Vol. 1. Part 2. Leiden: E. J. Brill, 1993².

———. *Imperial Cult in the Latin West: Studies in the Ruler Cult in the Western Provinces.* Vol. 2. Part 1. Leiden: E. J. Brill, 1991.

———. *Imperial Cult in the Latin West: Provincial Cult.* Vol. 3. Part 1. Leiden: E. J. Brill, 2002.

———. *Imperial Cult in the Latin West: The Provincial Cult.* Vol. 3. Part 2. Leiden: E. J. Brill, 2002.

———. *Imperial Cult in the Latin West: Studies in the Ruler Cult of the Western Provinces of the Roman Empire, Provincial Cult.* Vol. 3. Part 3. Leiden: E. J. Brill, 2004.

———. *Imperial Cult in the Latin West: Provincial Cult.* Vol. 3. Part 4. Leiden: E. J. Brill, 2005.

———. "Our First High Priest: A Gallic Knight at Athens." *Ephigraphia* 60 (1998): 83-112.

Forsythe, G. *Time in Roman Religion: 1,000 Years of Religious History.* New York and London: Routledge, 2012.

Fredricksmeyer, E. A. "On the Background of the Ruler Cult." In *Ancient Macedonian Studies in Honor of Charles F. Edson.* Thessaloniki: Institute for Balkan Studies, 1981.

Freisenbuch, S. *The First Ladies of Rome: Women behind the Caesars.* London: Jonathan Cape, 2010.

Friesen, S. J. *Imperial Cults and the Apocalypse of John: Reading Revelation in the Ruins.* Oxford: Oxford University Press, 2001.

————. *Twice Neokoros: Ephesus, Asia and the Cult of the Flavian Imperial Family.* Leiden: E. J. Brill, 1993.

Fuller, R. H. "First Corinthians 6:1-11 — an Exegetical Paper." *Ex Auditu* 2 (1986): 96-104.

Gardiner, E. N. *Athletics in the Ancient World.* Newton Abbot: Dover Publications, 2002.

Garland, R. *Introducing New Gods: The Politics of Athenian Religion.* London: Duckworth, 1992.

Garnsey, P. *Social Status and Legal Privilege in the Roman Empire.* Oxford: Clarendon Press, 1970.

Garnsey, P., and R. Saller. "Religion." In *The Roman Empire: Economy, Society and Culture,* ch. 11. London: Duckworth, 1987; Oakland: University of California Press, 2015².

Gartner, B. *The Areopagus Speech and Natural Revelation.* Uppsala: C. W. K. Gleerup, 1955.

Geagan, D. J. *The Athenian Constitution after Sulla.* Hesperia Supplement 12. Princeton: American School of Classical Studies at Athens, 1967.

Gerson, L. P. *God and Greek Philosophy: Studies in the Early History of Natural Theology.* London: Routledge, 1990.

Gill, D. "The Importance of Roman Portraiture for Head-Coverings in 1 Corinthians 11:2-16." *TynB* 41, no. 2 (1990): 245-60.

Ginsburg, J. *Representing Agrippina: Constructions of Female Power in the Early Roman Empire.* American Classical Studies 50. Oxford: Oxford University Press, 2006.

Goldsworthy, A. *Augustus: First Emperor of Rome.* New Haven and London: Yale University Press, 2014.

Gonzalez, J. "The *Lex Irnitus:* A New Copy of the Flavian Municipal Law." *JRS* 76 (1986): 147-243.

Gradel, I. *Emperor Worship and Roman Religion.* Oxford Classical Monographs. Oxford: Clarendon Press, 2002.

Grant, M. *From* Imperium *to* Auctoritas: *A Historical Study of* Aes *Coinage in the Roman Empire.* Cambridge: Cambridge University Press, 1946.

Griffin, M. T. *Nero: The End of a Dynasty.* New Haven: Yale University Press, 1984.

Gruen, E. S. "Caligula, the Imperial Cult, and Philo's Legatio." *Studia Philonica Annual* 24 (2012): 135-47.

Habiht, C. "Roman Citizens in Athens (228-31 B.C.)." In *The Romanization of Athens,* edited by Michael C. Hoff and Susan I. Rotroff, pp. 9-17. Oxbow Monographs 94. Oxford: Oxbow Books, 1997.

Hall, J. M. *Ethnic Identity in Greek Antiquity.* Cambridge: Cambridge University Press, 1997.

Bibliography

Hallett, C. H. *Roman Nudity: Heroic Portrait Statuary, 200 BC–AD 300*. Oxford: Oxford University Press, 2005.

Hardin, J. K. "Decrees and Drachmas at Thessalonica: An Illegal Assembly in Jason's House (Acts 17.1-10a)." *NTS* 52, no. 1 (2006): 29-49.

————. *Galatians and the Imperial Cult: A Critical Analysis of the First-Century Social Context of Paul's Letter*. WUNT 237. Tübingen: Mohr Siebeck, 2008.

Hardy, E. G. *Three Spanish Charters and Other Documents*. Oxford: Clarendon Press, 1912.

Harland, P. A. *Associations, Synagogues and Congregations: Claiming a Place in Ancient Mediterranean Society*. Minneapolis: Fortress Press, 2003.

Harrison, J. R. *Paul and the Imperial Authorities at Thessalonica and Rome*. WUNT 273. Tübingen: Mohr Siebeck, 2011.

Henrichs, A. "Vespasian's Visit to Alexandria." *ZPE* 3 (1968): 58-80.

Herz, P. "Die Adoptivsöhne des Augustus und der Festkalender Gedanken zu einer Inscripft aus Messenes." *Klio* 75 (1993): 272-88.

Hillard, T. W. "Vespasian's Death-Bed Attitude to His Impending Deification." In *Religion in the Ancient World: New Themes and Approaches,* edited by M. Dillon, pp. 193-215. Amsterdam: Hakkert, 1996.

Hirschfeld, G. *The Inscriptions of the Greek East in the British Museum*. Vol. 4. Oxford: Clarendon Press, 1893.

Hodges, F. M. "The Ideal *Prepuse* in Ancient Greece and Rome: Male Genital Aesthetics and Their Relation to *Lipodermos,* Circumcision, Foreskin Restoration and the *Kynodesme.*" *Bulletin of the History of Medicine* 75 (2001): 375-405.

————. "Phimosis in Antiquity." *World Journal of Urology* 17, no. 3 (1999): 133-36.

Hoff, M. C. "Civil Disobedience and Unrest in Augustan Athens." *Hesperia* 58 (1989): 267-76.

————. "The Early History of the Roman Agora in Athens." In *The Greek Renaissance in the Roman Empire: Papers from the Tenth British Museum Classical Colloquium,* edited by S. Walker and A. Cameron, pp. 1-8. Bulletin Supplement 55. London: Institute of Classical Studies, 1989.

————. "The Politics and Architecture of the Athenian Imperial Cult." In *Subject and Ruler: The Cult of the Ruling Power in Classical Antiquity,* edited by A. Small, pp. 185-200. JRA Supplement 17. Ann Arbor: University of Michigan Press, 1996.

————. "The So-Called Agoranomion and the Imperial Cult in Julio-Claudian Athens." *AA* 109 (1994): 93-117.

Horsley, G. H. R. "Appendix: The Politarchs." In *The Book of Acts in Its Graeco-Roman Setting,* edited by D. W. J. Gill and C. Gempf, pp. 419-31. Book of Acts in Its First Century Setting, vol. 2. Grand Rapids and Carlisle: Eerdmans and Paternoster, 1994.

————. *The Greek and Latin Inscriptions in the Burdur Archaeological Museum.*

British Institute at Ankara Monograph 34. London: British Institute at Ankara, 2007.

———. "Invitations to the *Kline* of Sarapis." In *New Documents illustrating Early Christianity: A Review of Greek Inscriptions and Papyri Published in 1971*, pp. 5-9. Sydney: Ancient History Documentary Research Centre, Macquarie University, 1981.

Horster, M. "Coinage and Images of the Imperial Family, Local Identity and Roman Rule." *Journal of Roman Archaeology* 26 (2013): 243-61.

Howgego, C. "Chronological Development of Roman Provincial Coin Iconography." In *Coinage and Identity in the Roman Provinces*, edited by C. Howgego, V. Heuchert and A. Burnett, ch. 3. Oxford: Oxford University Press, 2005.

Hurd, J. C. *The Origins of 1 Corinthians*. London: SPCK, 1965.

Hurley, D. H., ed. Suetonius, *Divus Claudius*. Cambridge: Cambridge University Press, 2001.

Huzar, E. G. "Emperor Worship in Julio-Claudian Egypt." In *Heidentum: Die Religiösen Verhältnisse in den Provinzen*, edited by W. Haase, pp. 3092-143. ANRW 18.5. Berlin and New York: De Gruyter, 1995.

Ilgim, M. *Aphrodisias Sebastion Sevgi Gönul Hall*. Istanbul: Kayis, 2008.

Isaac, B. H. *The Limits of Empire: The Roman Army in the East*. Oxford: Clarendon Press, 1990.

Jewett, R. "The Agitators and the Galatian Congregation." *NTS* 17 (1971): 198-212.

Johnston, D. *Roman Law in Context*. Cambridge: Cambridge University Press, 1999.

Jolowicz, H. F. *Historical Introduction to the Study of Roman Law*. Cambridge: Cambridge University Press, 1932.

Jones, A. H. M. *The Roman World of Dio Chrysostom*. Cambridge, MA: Harvard University Press, 1978.

Jones, B. W., and R. D. Mills. *The Use of Documentary Evidence in the Study of Roman Imperial History*. Sydney: Sydney University Press, 1984.

Judge, E. A. "The Decrees of Caesar in Thessalonica." In *The First Christians in the Roman World: Augustan and New Testament Essays*, edited by J. R. Harrison, ch. 11. WUNT 229. Tübingen: Mohr Siebeck, 2008.

———. "Did the Churches Compete with Cult Groups?" In *Early Christianity and Classical Culture: Comparative Studies in Honor of Abraham J. Malherbe*, edited by J. T. Fitzgerald, T. H. Olbricht and L. M. White, pp. 501-24. Leiden and Boston: E. J. Brill, 2003.

———. "The Mark of the Beast, Revelation 13:16." In *The First Christians in the Roman World: Augustan and New Testament Essays*, edited by J. R. Harrison, ch. 28. WUNT 229. Tübingen: Mohr Siebeck, 2008.

———. "The Roman Base of Paul's Mission." In *The First Christians in the Roman World: Augustan and New Testament Essays*, edited by J. R. Harrison, ch. 35. WUNT 229. Tübingen: Mohr Siebeck, 2008.

Bibliography

─────. *The Social Pattern of Christian Groups in the First Century.* London: Tyndale Press, 1960. Republished as *Social Distinctives of the Christians in the First Century: Pivotal Essays by E. A. Judge,* edited by D. M. Scholer, ch. 1. Peabody, MA: Hendrickson, 2008.

Kearsley, R. A. "Greeks and Romans in Imperial Asia." In *Mixed Language Inscriptions and Linguistic Evidence for Cultural Interaction until the End of AD III.* Inschriften Griechischer Städte aus Kleinasien, vol. 57, no. 165, 2001.

Keener, C. S. *Acts: An Exegetical Commentary: 15:1–23:35,* pp. 2557-58. Grand Rapids: Baker Academic, 2014.

Kent, J. H. *Corinth: Inscriptions, 1926-1950.* Vol. 8. Part 3. Princeton: American School of Classical Studies at Athens, 1966.

Knöppler, T. "Paulus als Verkünder fremder δαιμόνια. Religionsgeschichtlicher Hintergrund und theologische Aussage von Act 17,18." In *The Demonology of Israelite-Jewish and Early Christian Literature in Context of Their Environment,* edited by A. Lange, H. Lichtenberger and K. F. Diethard, pp. 577-83. Leiden: E. J. Brill, 2005.

Kokkinos, N. *Antonia Augusta: Portrait of a Great Roman Lady.* London: Routledge, 1992.

─────. *The Herodian Dynasty: Origins, Role in Society and Eclipse.* Journal for the Study of Pseudographic Supplement Series 30. Sheffield: Sheffield Academic Press, 1998.

Koukouli-Chrysanthaki, C. "Philippi." In *Brill's Companion to Ancient Macedonia: Studies in Archaeology and the History of Macedonia, 650 B.C.–300 A.D.,* edited by R. J. Lane Fox, ch. 19. Leiden and Boston: E. J. Brill, 2011.

Kovulmaz, B. *Aphrodisias Sebasteion Sevgi Gönöl Hall.* Istanbul: Yapi Kredi Publications, 2008.

Lampe, P. "Die dämonologischen Implikationeen von 1 Korinther 8a und 10 vor dem Hintergrund paganer Zeugnisee." In *The Demonology of Israelite-Jewish and Early Christian Literature in Context of Their Environment,* edited by H. Lichtenberger, A. Lange and K. F. D. Römheld, pp. 584-99. Tübingen: Mohr Siebeck, 2003.

Laurence, R. *Roman Pompeii: Space and Society.* London and New York: Routledge, 1994.

Lehmann, C. M., and K. G. Halum. *The Joint Expedition to Caesarea Maritima: Excavation Reports, the Greek and Latin Inscriptions of Caesarea Maritima.* Boston: American School of Oriental Research, 2000.

Lendon, J. E. *Empire of Honour: The Art of Government in the Roman World.* Oxford: Clarendon Press, 1997.

Levick, B. *Claudius.* London: Batsford, 1990.

─────. *Tiberius the Politician.* London: Thames and Hudson, 1976.

Liddell, H., and R. Scott. *Greek English Lexicon.* 9th ed. with revised supplement. Oxford: Oxford University Press, 1996.

Liebeschuetz, J. H. W. G. *Continuity and Change in Roman Religion.* Oxford: Clarendon Press, 1979.

Linder, A., ed. *The Jews in Roman Imperial Legislation.* Detroit: Wayne State University Press, 1987.

Lintott, A. *Imperium Romanum: Politics and Administration.* London and New York: Routledge, 1993.

Litwa, David M. *Iesus Deus: The Early Christian Depiction of Jesus as a Mediterranean God.* Minneapolis: Fortress Press, 2014.

Livesey, N. E. *Circumcision as a Malleable Symbol.* WUNT 2.295. Tübingen: Mohr Siebeck, 2010.

Llewelyn, S. R. "The Christian Symbol CMG, an Acrostic or an Isopsephism?" In *New Documents Illustrating Early Christianity,* pp. 156-68. Grand Rapids: Eerdmans, 1998.

MacMullen, R. *Romanization in the Time of Augustus.* New Haven: Yale University Press, 2000.

Macro, A. D. "The Cities of Asia Minor under the Roman Imperium." In *ANRW* II 7.2, pp. 658-97. Berlin and New York: De Gruyter, 1980.

McCrum, M., and A. G. Woodhead. *Select Documents of the Flavian Emperors.* Cambridge: Cambridge University Press, 2011.

McKay, K. L. "Foreign Gods Identified in Acts 17:18?" *TynB* 45, no. 2 (1994): 411-12.

Méndez Dosuna, J. "The Doric Dialects." In *A History of Ancient Greek,* edited by A.-F. Christidis, vol. 3, ch. 7. Cambridge: Cambridge University Press, 2007.

Meritt, B. D. *Corinth: Greek Inscriptions, 1896-1927.* Vol. 8. Part 1. Cambridge, MA: American School of Classical Studies at Athens, 1931.

Mikalson, J. D. *Religion in Hellenistic Athens.* Berkeley, Los Angeles and London: University of California Press, 1998.

Millar, C. "The Imperial Cult in the Pauline Cities of Asia Minor and Greece." *CBQ* 72 (2010): 314-22, 329-31.

Millar, F. "Epictetus and the Imperial Court." *JRS* 55 (1965): 141-48.

———— "The Imperial Cult and the Persecutions." In *Le Culte des Souverains dans l'empire romain,* edited by W. den Boer, pp. 145-66. Geneva: Vandoeuvres, 1972.

————. "Two Augustan Notes." *CR* 18 (1968): 263-66.

Milnor, K. *Graffiti and the Literary Landscape in Roman Pompeii.* Oxford: Oxford University Press, 2014.

Mitchell, L. G. *Greeks Bearing Gifts: The Public Use of Private Relationships in the Greek World, 435-323 B.C.* Cambridge: Cambridge University Press, 1997.

Mitchell, S. *Anatolia: Land, Men and Gods in Asia Minor: The Celts and the Impact of Roman Rule.* Vol. 1. Oxford: Clarendon Press, 1993².

————. *Anatolia: Land, Men and Gods in Asia Minor: The Rise of the Church.* Vol. 2. Oxford: Clarendon Press, 1993.

Mitford, T. B. "A Cypriot Oath of Allegiance to Tiberius." *JRS* 50 (1960): 75-79.

Moles, J. L. "The Career and Conversion of Dio Chrysostom." *JHS* 68 (1978): 79-100.

Montevecchi, O. "Nerone a una polis e ai 6475." *Aegyptus* 50 (1970): 5-33.

Mueller, H.-F. *Roman Religion in Valerius Maximus.* London and New York: Routledge, 2002.

Nédoncelle, M. "Prosopon et persona dans l'antiquité classique." *Revue des Sciences Religieuses* 22 (1948): 277-99.

Neyrey, J. H. "Acts 17, Epicureans and Theodicy: A Study of Stereotypes." In *Greeks, Romans and Christians: Essays in Honor of Abraham J. Malherbe,* edited by D. L. Balch, E. Ferguson and W. Meeks, pp. 118-34. Minneapolis: Fortress Press, 1990.

Newby, Z. *Athletics in the Ancient World.* London: Bristol Classical Press, 2006.

Nguyen, V. H. T. "The Identification of Paul's Spectacle of Death Metaphor in 1 Corinthians 4:9." *NTS* 53 (2007): 489-501.

———. *Social Identity and Persona, Christian Identity in Corinth: A Comparative Study of 2 Corinthians, Epictetus and Valerius Maximus.* WUNT 2.243. Tübingen: Mohr Siebeck, 2008.

Nigdelis, P. M. "A New *Procurator Augusti* in the Province of Macedonia." *Greek, Roman, and Byzantine Studies* 52 (2012): 198-207.

Norena, C. F. "Values and Virtues: The Ethical Profile of the Emperor." In *Imperial Ideals in the Roman West: Representation, Circulation, Power.* Cambridge: Cambridge University Press, 2011.

O'Brien, P. T. *The Letter to the Hebrews.* Grand Rapids and Nottingham: Eerdmans and Apollos, 2010.

Ogilvie, R. M. *The Romans and Their Gods.* London: Random House, 2000.

Oliver, J. H. *The Athenian Expounders of the Sacred and Ancestral Law.* Baltimore: Johns Hopkins University Press, 1950.

———. *Greek Constitutions of Early Roman Emperors from Inscriptions and Papyri.* Philadelphia: American Philosophical Society, 1989.

Orr, D. G. "Roman Domestic Religion: The Evidence of the Household Shrines." In *ANRW* 16.2 (1978): 1557-91.

Osgood, J. *Claudius Caesar: Image and Power in the Early Roman Empire.* Cambridge: Cambridge University Press, 2011.

Owen, E. "Δαίμων and Cognate Words." *JTS* 32 (1931): 133-53.

Patrich, J. *Studies in the Archaeology and History of Caesarea Maritima: Caput Judaeae, Metropolis Palaestinae.* Leiden and Boston: E. J. Brill, 2011.

Porton, G. G. *The Stranger within Your Gates.* Chicago Studies in the History of Judaism. Chicago and London: University of Chicago Press, 1994.

Potopoulos, J. *Food Offered to Idols in Roman Corinth.* Tübingen: J. C. B. Mohr, 2003.

Price, S. R. F. *Rituals and Power: The Roman Imperial Cult and Asia Minor.* Cambridge: Cambridge University Press, 1984.

Prokhorov, A. V. "Taking the Jews out of the Equation: Galatians 6:12-17 as a Summons to Cease Evading Persecution." *JNTS* 36, no. 2 (2013): 172-88.

Pucci ben Zeev, M. "Greek and Roman Documents from Republican Times in the Antiquities: What Was Josephus' Source?" *Scripta Classica Israelica* 13 (1994): 47-59.

——. *Jewish Rights in the Roman World: The Greek and Roman Documents Quoted by Josephus Flavius.* Texts and Studies in Ancient Judaism 74. Tübingen: Mohr Siebeck, 1998.

Rabello, A. B. "The Legal Condition of the Jews in the Roman Empire." *ANRW* II 13 (1980), 662-762.

Rainbow, P. A. "Monotheism and Christology in 1 Corinthians 8:4-6." D.Phil. diss., Oxford University, 1987.

Rajak, T. "Was There a Roman Charter for the Jews?" In *The Jewish Dialogue with Greece and Rome: Studies in Cultural and Social Interaction,* ch. 16. Leiden: E. J. Brill, 2002.

Rajak, T., and D. Noy. "*Archisynogogoi:* Office, Social Status in the Graeco-Roman World." *JRS* 83 (1993): 75-93.

Rapske, B. *Paul in Roman Custody.* Book of Acts in Its First Century Setting, vol. 3. Grand Rapids: Eerdmans, 1994.

Raubitschek, A. E. "Octavia's Deification at Athens." *TAPA* 77 (1946): 146-50.

Reynolds, J. M. *Aphrodisias and Rome.* JRS Monograph 1. London: Society for the Promotion of Roman Studies, 1982.

——. "The Origins and Beginnings of Imperial Cult in Aphrodisias." *PCPS* 26 (1980): 70-82.

——. "The Public Land of the Roman People in Syrenaica." *Libya Antiqua* 8 (1971): 47-49.

Reynolds, J. M., and J. B. Ward Perkins. *The Inscriptions of Roman Tripolitania.* Rome: British School of Archaeology, 1952.

Richardson, P. *Herod: King of the Jews and Friend of the Romans.* Columbia: University of South Carolina Press, 1996.

Riley, G. J. "Demon." In *The Dictionary of Deities and Demons in the Bible,* edited by K. van der Toorn, B. Becking and P. W. van der Horst, pp. 235-40. Leiden: E. J. Brill, 1999[2].

Rives, J. B. "Diplomacy and Identity among Jews and Christians." In *Diplomats and Diplomacy in the Roman World,* edited by C. Eilers, pp. 99-126. Leiden and Boston: E. J. Brill, 2009.

——. *Religion and Authority in Roman Carthage from Augustus to Constantine.* Oxford: Clarendon Press, 1995.

Robinson, O. F. *The Criminal Law of Rome.* London: Duckworth, 1995.

Rogan, J. *Roman Provincial Administration.* Stroud, UK: Amberley Publishing, 2011.

Bibliography

Rolfe, J. C. *The Lives of the Caesars.* Vol. 2. Cambridge, MA, and London: Harvard University Press, 1998.

Roller, D. W. *The Building Program of Herod the Great.* Berkeley: University of California Press, 1998.

Romano, D. G. "A Roman Circus in Corinth." *Hesperia* 74, no. 4 (2005): 585-611.

Roskam, G. *"'Live Unnoticed' λαθες βιώσα": On the Vicissitudes of an Epicurean Doctrine.* Philosophia Antiqua, vol. 111. Leiden: E. J. Brill, 2007.

Rudd, N. *Horace Odes and Epodes.* Loeb Classical Library. Cambridge, MA: Harvard University Press, 2004.

Rüpke, J., and A. Glock. *Fasti Sacerdotum: A Prosopography of Pagan, Jewish and Christian Religious Officials in the City of Rome, 300 BC to AD 499,* pp. 123-96. Oxford: Oxford University Press, 2008.

Rutgers, L. V. *The Hidden Heritage of Diaspora Judaism.* Leuven: Peeters, 1998².

Saller, R. P. *Patriarch, Property and Death in the Roman Family.* Cambridge, Cambridge University Press, 1994.

Sandback, F. H. *The Stoics.* London: Chatto and Windus, 1975.

Sandelin, K.-G. "Philo's Ambivalence towards Statues." In *Attraction and Danger of Alien Religion,* pp. 60-76. Studies in Early Judaism and Christianity. Tübingen: Mohr Siebeck, 2012.

Sartre, M. "Co-opting the Conqueror: The East from Augustus to Trajan." In *A Companion to Roman Imperialism,* edited by D. Hoyos, pp. 277-90. History of Warfare, vol. 81. Leiden and Boston: E. J. Brill, 2013.

Scheid, J. "Epigraphy and Roman Religion." In *Epigraphy and the Historical Sciences,* edited by J. Davies and J. Wilkers, ch. 3. Proceedings of the British Academy no. 177. Oxford and New York: Oxford University Press, 2012.

Scherrer, P., ed. *Ephesus: The New Guide.* Turkey: Graphics Ltd., 2000.

Schlossmann, S. *Persona und πρόσωπον im Recht und im christlichen Dogma.* Kiel, 1906.

Schwartz, D. R. "Philo and Josephus on Violence in 38 C.E." *Studia Philonica Annual* 24 (2012): 149-66.

Scotton, P. D. "A New Fragment of an Inscription from the Julian Basilica at Roman Corinth." *Hesperia* 74, no. 1 (2005): 95-100.

Seager, R. *Tiberius.* London: Methuen, 1972.

———. Afterword to *Tiberius,* by R. Seager, pp. 213-22. Oxford: Blackwell, 2005².

Sevenster, J. N. *Paul and Seneca.* Leiden: E. J. Brill, 1961.

Sherk, R. K. *Roman Documents from the Greek East: Senatus Consulta and Epistulae to the Age of Augustus.* Baltimore: Johns Hopkins University Press, 1969.

———. *The Roman Empire: Augustus to Hadrian; Translated Documents of Greece and Rome.* Vol. 6. Cambridge: Cambridge University Press, 1988.

———. *Rome and the Greek East to the Death of Augustus.* Cambridge: Cambridge University Press, 1984.

Sherwin-White, A. R. N. *Roman Society and Roman Law in the New Testament: The Sarum Lectures, 1960-61.* Oxford: Clarendon Press, 1963.

Small, A., ed. *Subject and Ruler: The Cult of the Ruling Power in Classical Antiquity, Papers Honouring D. Fishwick.* JRA Supplement 17. Ann Arbor: University of Michigan Press, 1996.

Smallwood, E. Mary. *Documents Illustrating the Principates Gaius, Claudius and Nero.* Cambridge: Cambridge University Press, 1967.

―――. *The Jews under Roman Rule from Pompey to Diocletian: A Study of Political Relations.* Leiden: E. J. Brill, 1981.

―――. "The Legislation of Hadrian and Antonius Pius against Circumcision." *Latomus* 18 (1959): 334-47.

―――. *Philonis Alexandrini Legatio ad Gaium.* Leiden: E. J. Brill, 1961.

Smith, R. R. R. "The Imperial Relief from the Sebastion at Aphrodisias." *JRS* 77 (1987): 88-138.

Sordi, M. *The Christians and the Roman Empire.* London: Routledge, 1994.

Southern, P. *Augustus.* London and New York: Routledge, 1998.

Spaeth, Barbara S. "Pausanias and the Cults of Roman Corinth." Paper delivered at the SBL conference in San Francisco, 19-21 November 2011.

Spawforth, A. J. S. "The Achaean Federal Imperial Cult I: Pseudo-Julian Letters 198." *TynB* 46, no. 1 (1995): 151-68.

―――. "Corinth, Argos, and the Imperial Cult: A Reconsideration of Pseudo-Julian, Letters 198." *Hesperia* 63, no. 2 (1994): 211-32.

―――. "The Early Reception of the Imperial Cult in Athens: Problems and Ambiguities." In *The Romanization of Athens,* edited by Michael C. Hoff and Susan I. Rotroff, pp. 183-201. Oxbow Monographs 94. Oxford: Oxbow Books, 1997.

―――. *Greece and the Augustan Cultural Revolution.* Cambridge: Cambridge University Press, 2012.

―――. "Roman Corinth: The Formation of a Colonial Élite." In *Roman Onomastics in the Greek East: Social and Political Aspects,* edited by A. D. Rizakēs, pp. 167-82. Meletemata 21. Athens: De Boccard, 1996.

Steward, P. *Statues in Roman Society, Representation and Response.* Oxford: Oxford University Press, 2003.

Swartz, D. R. "Philo and Josephus on the Violence in Alexandria in 38 C.E." *Studia Philonica Annual* 24 (2012): 149-66.

Swift, E. H. "Imperial Portraits at Corinth." *AJA* 25, no. 4 (1921): 337-63.

Syme, R. *The Augustine Aristocracy.* Oxford: Clarendon Press, 1986.

―――. "C. Vibius Maximus, Prefect of Egypt." *Historia* 6 (1957): 480-87.

―――. *The Roman Revolution.* Oxford: Clarendon Press, 1939.

Taylor, L. R. "Tiberius' Refusal of Divine Honors." *TAPA* 60 (1929): 87-101.

Taylor, L. R., and A. B. West. "The Euryclids in Latin Inscriptions from Corinth." *AJA* 30 (1926): 393-400.

Thompson, H. A. "The Annex to the Stoa of Zeus in the Athenian Agora." *Hesperia* 36 (1966): 171-87.

Trebilco, P. *The Early Christians in Ephesus from Paul to Ignatius.* Grand Rapids and Cambridge: Eerdmans, 2004.

van der Horst, P. W. "The Altar to the 'Unknown God' in Athens (Acts 17:23) and the Cults of 'Unknown Gods' in the Graeco-Roman World." In *Hellenism-Judaism-Christianity,* pp. 165-202. Kampen: Kok Pharos, 1994.

van Kooten, G. H. "The Jewish War and the Roman Civil War of 68-69 C.E.: Jewish, Pagan, and Christian Perspectives." In *The Jewish Revolt against Rome: Interdisciplinary Perspectives,* edited by M. Popovic, pp. 419-50. Supplements to the Journal for the Study of Judaism 154. Leiden and Boston: E. J. Brill, 2011.

————. " 'Wrath Will Drip in the Plains of Macedonia': Expectations of Nero's Return in the Egyptian Sibylline *Oracles* (Book 5), 2 Thessalonians, and Ancient Historical Writings." In *The Wisdom of Egypt: Jewish, Early Christian and Gnostic Essays in Honour of Gerard P. Luttikhuizen,* edited by A. Hillhorst and G. H. van Kooten, pp. 177-215. Leiden: E. J. Brill, 2005.

van Nijf, O. M. *The Civic World of Professional Associations in the Roman East.* Amsterdam: J. C. Gieben, 1997.

van Nuffelen, P. *Rethinking the Gods: Philosophical Reading of Religion in the Post-Hellenistic Period.* Greek Culture in the Roman World. Cambridge: Cambridge University Press, 2011.

Varneda, P. V. I. *The Historical Method of Flavius Josephus.* Leiden: E. J. Brill, 1986.

Versnel, H. S. *Ter Unus: Isis, Dionysos, Hermes; Three Studies in Henotheism, Inconsistencies in Greek and Roman Religion.* Vol. 1. Leiden: E. J. Brill, 1990.

Walbank, M. E. H. "Aspects of Corinthian Coinage in the Late 1st and Early 2nd Centuries A.C." In *Corinth: The Centenary, 1896-1996,* edited by C. K. Williams and N. Bookidis, ch. 20. Athens: American School of Classical Studies at Athens, 2003.

————. "Evidence for the Imperial Cult in Julio-Claudian Corinth." In *Subject and Ruler: The Cult of the Ruling Power in Classical Antiquity, Papers Honouring D. Fishwick,* edited by A. Small, pp. 201-13. JRA Supplement 17. Ann Arbor: University of Michigan Press, 1996.

————. "Pausanias, Octavia, Temple E." *Annual of the British School at Athens* 84 (1989): 361-94.

Walker, S., and A. Cameron, eds. *The Greek Renaissance in the Roman Empire.* BICS Supplement 55. London: University of London, Institute of Classical Studies, 1989.

Wardle, D. "*Deus* or *Divus:* The Genesis of Roman Terminology for Deified Emperors and a Philosopher's Contribution." In *Philosophy and Power in the Graeco-Roman World: Essays in Honour of Miriam Griffin,* edited by G. Clark and T. Rajak, pp. 181-209. Oxford: Oxford University Press, 2002.

———. "The Preface to Valerius Maximus." *Athenaeum* 87 (1999): 523-25.

———. "Valerius Maximus on the *Domus Augusta,* Augustus, and Tiberius." *CQ* 50, no. 2 (2000): 479-93.

Watson A. *The Digest of Justinian.* Vol. 2. Philadelphia: University of Pennsylvania Press, 1998.

West, A. B. *Corinth: Latin Inscriptions, 1896-1926.* Vol. 8. Part 2. Cambridge, MA: American School of Classical Studies at Athens, 1931.

Whitlark, J. A. *Resisting Empire: Rethinking the Purpose of the Letter to "the Hebrews."* Library of New Testament Studies 484. London: Bloomsbury T&T Clark, 2014.

Williams, C. K., II. "The Refounding of Corinth: Some Roman Religious Attitudes." In *Roman Architecture in the Greek World,* edited by S. Macready and F. S. Thompson, pp. 26-37. Society of Antiquities, Occasional Papers 10. London: Society of Antiquaries of London, 1987.

———. "Roman Corinth as a Commercial Center." In *The Corinthia in the Roman Period,* edited by T. E. Gregory, pp. 31-46. Journal of Roman Architecture Supplementary Series 6. Ann Arbor: University of Michigan Press, 1993.

Williams, C. K., II, and P. Russell. "Corinth: Excavations of 1980." *Hesperia* 50 (1981): 1-44.

Williams, G. D. *The Curse of Exile: A Study of Ovid's Ibis.* Cambridge: Cambridge University Press, 1996.

Wilson, S. G. *Voluntary Associations in the Graeco-Roman World.* London: Routledge, 1996.

Winter, B. W. *After Paul Left Corinth: The Influence of Secular Ethics and Social Change.* Grand Rapids and Cambridge: Eerdmans, 2001.

———. "A Cambridge Lexical Handbook of New Testament Greek: Social Settings, Semantic Domains and First-Century Synonyms." In *Actas do Coloquio Lexicography and Lexical Semantics: Questions at Issue in the Making of a Greek Lexicon,* pp. 93-105. Lisbon: Centro de Estudos Classicos, 2008.

———. "*Christentum und Antike:* Acts and the Pauline Corpus as Ancient History." In *Ancient History in a Modern University,* edited by T. W. Hillard, R. A. Kersley, C. E. V. Nixon and A. Nobbs, vol. 2, pp. 121-30. Grand Rapids: Eerdmans, 1998.

———. "Gallio's Ruling on the Legal Status of Early Christianity (Acts 18:14-15)." *TynB* 50, no. 2 (November 1999): 213-24.

———. "The Imperial Cult and the Early Christians in Pisidian Antioch (Acts 13 and Galatians 6)." In *Acts du 1st Congres International sur Antioche de Pisidie,* edited by T. Drew-Bear, M. Tashalan and C. M. Thomas, pp. 67-75. Lyon: Université Lumière-Lion, 2002.

———. "Official Proceedings and Forensic Speeches in Acts 24-26." In *The Book of Acts in Its Ancient Literary Setting,* edited by A. D. Clarke and B. W. Winter, ch. 11. Grand Rapids: Eerdmans, 1993.

———. *Philo and Paul among the Sophists: Alexandrian and Corinthian Responses to a Julio-Claudian Movement.* Grand Rapids and Cambridge: Eerdmans, 2002².

———. "The Public Honouring of Christian Benefactors: Romans 13.3 and 1 Peter 2.14-15." *JSNT* 33 (1988): 87-103.

———. "Rehabilitating Gallio and His Judgement in Acts 18:14-15." *TynB* 57, no. 2 (2006): 291-308.

———. "The Rôle of the *Captatio Benevolentia* in the Speeches of Tertullus and Paul in Acts 24." *JTS,* n.s., 42, no. 2 (November 1991): 505-31.

———. "Roman Law and Society in Romans 12–15." In *Rome in the Bible and the Early Church,* edited by P. Oakes, pp. 72-75. Carlisle and Grand Rapids: Paternoster and Baker, 2002.

———. *Roman Wives, Roman Widows: The Appearance of "New" Roman Women and the Pauline Communities.* Grand Rapids: Eerdmans, 2003.

———. *Seek the Welfare of the City: Early Christians as Benefactors and Citizens.* Grand Rapids and Carlisle: Eerdmans and Paternoster, 1994.

———. "St. Paul as a Critic of Roman Slavery in 1 Corinthians 7:21-23." *Proceedings of the International Conference on St. Paul and European Civilization,* Παύλεια 3 (Varia, 1998): 339-54.

———. "Suffering with the Saviour: The Reality, the Reasons and the Reward." In *The Perfect Saviour: Key Themes in Hebrews,* edited by J. Griffith, ch. 8. Leicester: Apollos Press; Wheaton: Crossway, 2012.

———. "Theological and Ethical Responses to Religious Pluralism: 1 Corinthians 8–10." *TynB* 41 (1990): 209-26.

———. "The 'Underlays' of Conflict and Compromise in 1 Corinthians." In *Paul and the Corinthians: Studies on a Community in Conflict, Essays in Honour of Margaret Thrall,* edited by T. J. Burke and J. Keith Elliott, pp. 139-55. Leiden: E. J. Brill, 2003.

Wiseman, T. P. *Myths of Rome.* Exeter: University of Exeter, 2004.

Wistrand, E. *Felicitias Imperatoria.* Studia Graeca et Latina Gothoburgensia 48. Arlölv: Berlings, 1987.

———. "The Stoic Opposition to the Principate." *Studii Clasice* 15 (1979): 93-101.

Wood, S. E. *Imperial Women: A Study of Public Images, 40 B.C.–A.D. 68.* Leiden: E. J. Brill, 1999.

Wright, J. R. G. "Form and Content in the Moral Essay." In *Seneca Medea,* edited by C. D. N. Costa, pp. 39-69. Oxford: Oxford University Press, 1973.

Zanker, P. *The Power of Images in the Age of Augustus.* Ann Arbor: University of Michigan Press, 1987.

Zetzel, J. E. C. "New Light on Gaius Caesar's Eastern Campaign." *GRBS* 11 (1970): 259-66.

Index of Modern Authors

Index of Subjects

Index of Scripture References
and Other Ancient Sources